GLOBE FEARON

ENGLISH
at School and on the Job

Globe
Fearon

Upper Saddle River, New Jersey
www.globefearon.com

TEACHER REVIEWERS

Essie Flennoy
Education to Careers Coordinator
DuSable High School
Chicago, IL

Dennis W. Giger
Tech Prep/English Teacher
Raybrooks School
Cleveland, MS

Carol Holtz
Principal
Yuba County Career Preparatory
  Charter School
Marysville, CA

Patricia Horgan
Senior High School Language Arts
  Teacher of Technical Composition
Rice High School
Sauk Rapids, MN

Stefni Kueht
Business Instructor
Barbara Jordan High School for Careers
Houston, TX

Lisa McPherson
High School English Teacher
Oswego High School
Oswego, NY

Sarah Williams
High School English Teacher
Oswego High School
Oswego, NY

Mary Alice Wisowaty
English Teacher/Applied Communications
  Consultant
Spaulding High School
Rochester, NH

INDUSTRY REVIEWERS

Kathy H. Cruse
Quality Assurance Analyst
Vision Software, Inc.
Castle Hayne, NC

Laurene O'Donnell
Telcordia Technologies
Morris Township, NJ

Cindi Meredith
Director of Health Careers/Minority
  Workforce Development
Coastal Area Health Education Center
Wilmington, NC

Supervising Editor: Lynn W. Kloss
Senior Editor: Lewis Parker
Editors: Monica Glina, Kevin Iwano
Editorial Assistant: Dara Eisenstein
Production Editor: Marcela Maslanczuk
Senior Designer: Janice Noto-Helmers
Designer: Sharon Scannell
Illustrator: John Bleck
Art Supervisors: Tracey Gerber, Cindy A. Talocci
Artists: Robin Hoffmann, Cheryl Train, Jeff Zoda
Composition and Layout: Jeffrey Engel, Leslie Greenberg, Susan Levine, Lissette Quiñones
Manufacturing Supervisor: Mark Cirillo

Printed in the United States of America   1 2 3 4 5 6 7 8 9 10   05 04 03 02 01 00

ISBN: 0-130-23262-9

GLOBE FEARON EDUCATIONAL PUBLISHER
Upper Saddle River, New Jersey
www.globefearon.com

Contents

UNIT 2 ■ THE PATH TO WRITING SUCCESS

UNIT 4 ■ WRITING REPORTS TO DESCRIBE AND PERSUADE 145

Chapter 9: Writing to Persuade 174

Handbook

FEATURED SKILLS

TECH CONNECTION

CAREER FILE

HOW TO USE THIS BOOK

Writing skills are critical to your success in school. You need to be able to write to answer questions on tests and to draft reports. You may not know, however, that writing is also critical on the job. Workers must be able to communicate with clients, with supervisors, and with co-workers. They must write memos, letters, and reports.

Whatever career you choose, writing will be important to your success. The principles of good writing and good usage are the same whether you are writing a report on World War I or a business proposal. If you can write well, you will have a good chance for success both at school and on the job.

This book offers you practical lessons and everyday examples of writing, grammar, and mechanics topics that you will see throughout your working life. By learning skills that you will use on the job, you will take a first step on the path to career success.

Before you begin using this book, preview it. Look at the lesson titles, and at the photographs, tables, and charts. You will notice that the book has special features. Here is what they are and how they can help you.

UNIT OPENER

This page will give you a quick overview of what you will find in each unit. As you read this page, think about what you might know about the topics. You can also use this page to help you locate a topic that you need to review.

CHAPTER OPENER

As you begin each chapter, you will read about a student or a worker who is facing a problem that is common to newer workers. These people may remind you of yourself. By thinking about how you might react in a similar situation, you can prepare to solve problems at work. In addition, you can prepare yourself to learn about the chapter topic.

PORTFOLIO PROJECT

The Portfolio Project, which also appears on the Chapter Opener page, grows out of the worker
profile. It will give you a chance to create a real-world writing assignment that will be helpful to you both as you look for a job and when you are working. For example, you will create a résumé to use as you search for employment and a business letter that you can use as a reference when you write a letter on the job.

WHAT DO YOU ALREADY KNOW? AND THINK ABOUT IT

As you read these features, think about the topic of the lesson. You have probably had some experience with the subject matter either in school or outside of school. If you think about your experiences with the topic, you prepare yourself to learn new information.

WRITING IN THE REAL WORLD

These pages show writing that you will see in your working life. Each model has labels to help you identify the parts of the memo or letter so that you can apply what you learn to your own writing.

GRAMMAR WORKSHOP

On these pages, you will focus on grammar and mechanics topics that you will often use at school and on the job. For example, there are words that many writers confuse, such as *affect* and *effect*. One Grammar Workshop gives you hints on how to untangle these words. In another Grammar Workshop, you will learn how to make sure the subjects and verbs in your sentences agree.

TECH CONNECTION

Technology is used frequently to help people communicate in business. Workers send messages through e-mail, keep track of projects with spreadsheets, and share documents quickly with fax machines. The Tech Connection shows you how to use technology to succeed in writing tasks you will see frequently in the workplace.

CAREER FILES

On these pages, you will learn about careers that use writing skills. You will find information about what people do who work in these jobs, the kinds of skills and training needed, and an address to write for more information.

HANDBOOK

You can use this section, which is located at the back of the book, to learn strategies for reading, writing, grammar, and mechanics. Think of the Handbook as your personal tutor. When you have a question about grammar, or editing, or style, this is the place to look.

This book will help you learn to communicate both at school and on the job. Use it to develop your spoken and written communication skills. Remember that these skills are practical and relevant; you will apply them now and throughout your life.

" ... with words I have the power to

make people listen, to make them think

in a new way, to make them cry, to

make them laugh. It's a powerful thing

to make people listen to you. "

Sandra Cisneros (1954–)
Author

"I've always believed that if you put in the work, the results will come."

Michael Jordan (1963–)
former professional basketball player

UNIT 1

YOU AND YOUR CAREER

How important is it to set goals? In this unit, you will learn to set goals that will help you to succeed in school and at work. You will explore your skills and habits. Next, you will learn about writing résumés and application letters. You will also learn how to present yourself at a job interview. Last, you will find out what it is like to be on the job. You will learn how to develop successful job skills that help you make decisions, organize your work, and resolve conflicts. You also will see if you have a future as an entrepreneur.

YOUR CAREER GOALS

Charles held after-school and summer jobs all through high school. He liked some jobs, but there were others he did not like. Then, he got a part-time job in a landscaping business during his junior year. Charles's supervisor often allowed him to come along on jobs to learn from experienced landscapers. The more Charles learned about the landscaping business, the more he wondered whether he wanted to make it a career. However, Charles did not know how to set career goals.

Key Words

career

economy

assess

entry-level

self-esteem

career plan

mentor

attitude

trade-offs

networking

Goals for Success

In this chapter, you will learn these skills:

Assessing your work-related skills

SCANS SELF-MANAGEMENT

Developing confidence in yourself as a decision maker and a worker

SCANS SELF-ESTEEM

Recognizing effective work habits and striving to achieve them

SCANS RESPONSIBILITY

Creating and assessing the stages of a job search

SCANS TIME MANAGEMENT

Researching a specific occupation using the Internet

SCANS APPLYING TECHNOLOGY TO TASKS

PORTFOLIO PROJECT

CAREER PLAN

By the time you complete this chapter, you will know what Charles has to do to write a career plan. You also will be able to write a career plan of your own to add to your portfolio.

Assessing Your Skills

What Do You Already Know?

Think about people you know who do their jobs well. List five of those people. Describe five skills that make these people outstanding workers.

Think About It Why is it important to assess your workplace skills? What effect might this assessment have on your career plans?

Maybe you have always wanted to be an electrician, a jewelry designer, or a sculptor. These kinds of hobbies and interests often turn into jobs. Like many people your age, you might not be sure what you want to do with your life. Perhaps you have not picked your career goals. In fact, you may not be sure what career goals are. When people ask, "What kind of work do you want to do?" you answer, "I don't know."

PLAN FOR A CAREER

Now is the time to begin thinking about career goals. You should also think about the difference between a job and a career. A job brings in money and gives you independence. A **career** is the general course of your working life. For example, you may hold a series of jobs, such as clothing salesperson, jewelry counter salesperson, women's clothing buyer, women's clothing marketing assistant, store manager, and fashion consultant. You would say your career over time has been in the fashion industry.

Jobs and the Economy

You should keep in mind the impact that the economy will have on your career goals. The **economy** means how a nation produces and uses its goods and services. When the demand for goods and services is high, the economy is growing and strong and jobs are plentiful. When demand decreases, production falls, the economy is weak, and there are not many jobs. You have to be ready for changes in the economy.

Job Trends

Understanding that the economy changes can help you look at the big employment picture. As you plan a career and look for a job, you have to think about employment trends. Predictions about job trends are best guesses about what jobs will be most available in the future.

You can use information from sources such as the U.S. government to figure out which fields will offer the most opportunities. Being aware of job trends helps you to be realistic about preparing yourself for fields that are most likely to have jobs.

MAKE A SELF-ASSESSMENT LOG

Career planning begins with *you*. Your interests, your personality, and especially your skills are the key elements in helping you set career goals. Before you set your career goals, you should create a self-assessment log to **assess**, or evaluate, your abilities. FIGURE 1-1 on page 5 shows a student's self-assessment log.

List Your Accomplishments

Begin by listing your accomplishments—things you have done well. This list can include a lot of different things—winning a tennis match, taking a role in the school play or working part time with the city recreation department. Just write down as many accomplishments as you can think of.

FIGURE 1-1 shows a student's self-assessment log. **What kinds of careers do you think this person might be interested in finding out about?**

List Your Interests

Listing your accomplishments will help you think about your interests. The two may be closely linked. An interest is something that you are curious about or like to do. Your interests might include such things as sports, music, computers, clothes, or food.

List your interests, and think carefully about them. Which ones do you feel strongly about? If you had to make choices, which ones would you choose? Ranking your interests can help you decide which you would like to spend the most time on.

Later, you can link these interests to possible careers. For example, suppose you have an interest in both animals and computers. Dogs and cats are pleasant as pets, you think, but you wouldn't want a career as a veterinary assistant. Your interest in computers may far outweigh your interest in animals. You would take this difference into account when choosing a career.

List Your Personality Traits

Your personality traits, or characteristics, may also be your strengths. Examples of personality traits might include loyalty, calmness, and curiosity. Some personality traits show up at birth. For example, some babies are fussy while others are quiet; some smile a lot while others cry easily. Personality traits are also shaped by experience. For example, people who are rewarded for outgoing behavior will tend to repeat that behavior. If they are punished for being outgoing, they may become withdrawn. Your personality is something that does not change easily, yet it may change over time.

You can also link your personality traits to your accomplishments. For example, if you won a tennis tournament, you showed that you were competitive and persistent. Those personality traits could benefit you if you worked as a salesperson.

In your self-assessment log, list personality traits that describe you. You might consider listing such traits as being adventurous, analytical, dependable, direct, loyal, sensitive, supportive, and well-disciplined. You also might be a risk taker or a team player.

WORKPLACE SKILLS AND JOBS

Employers want to know about your workplace skills. Some kinds of workplace skills are specific and differ from job to job. For example, being able to type and use a cash register are specific skills, as is being able to operate an X-ray machine. Employers look for people who demonstrate specific skills to perform particular jobs.

KEY WORKPLACE SKILLS

KEY WORKPLACE SKILL	SITUATION
1. Being trustworthy and honest	A customer pays with a large bill, then complains that you didn't return the correct change.
2. Behaving appropriately with clients and customers	You're deep in conversation with another employee. A customer comes over and stands next to your cash register.
3. Respecting people from different cultures	A new co-worker doesn't speak English very well. She doesn't understand how the job is done.
4. Reporting emergencies	While most people are out to lunch, you smell smoke. Then, you see wisps of smoke coming out of the air ducts.
5. Responding to spoken directions	Your job is to stack boxes of supplies. Your boss gives you detailed directions. You're not sure where two items should be stacked.
6. Asking questions at the right time	Your manager explains how a particular machine works. You don't quite understand, but tomorrow you're going to be working alone with the machine.
7. Understanding written instructions and directions	Important information is posted on the company bulletin board. Today, a reminder notice explained that first-year employees earn no vacation time until the end of their first year. You started eight months ago.
8. Managing work time effectively	You have trouble getting your work done on time. There seems to be too much to do and too little time.
9. Understanding company manuals and policies	The company manual defines sick days, personal days, vacation time, and emergency leave. You're getting a new couch delivered to your home.
10. Interacting with co-workers to get the job done	You and two co-workers are assigned to decorate the store window. You know what you would like to do, but your co-workers have their own ideas.
11. Checking your own work	You have the job of updating and printing the company price list. However, you forgot to look at a printout that listed all the products the company no longer sells. The list is due to go to the printer at the end of the day.
12. Considering risks and safety	You work on the tenth floor. You hear an alarm go off. A person wearing a suit and carrying a briefcase is standing at the fire door. He tells you that he has lost his way. He is looking for the Human Resources office. You know that this office is on the first floor.

FIGURE 1-2 shows key workplace skills and how they could be used on the job. **How could these skills be useful in a job that interests you? How would they help you in each situation?**

Entry-Level Skills

All jobs, however, require **entry-level**, or basic, workplace skills. Workers need entry-level skills to start a job. Other skills can be acquired on the job.

A few years ago, the Texas Department of Commerce asked employers what entry-level skills they expected workers to have. FIGURE 1-2 on page 6 is a chart that shows what skills they expect. The first column of the chart lists workplace skills; the second column gives situations that workers may find themselves in.

DOT Skills

The *Dictionary of Occupational Titles* (DOT), a book published by the U.S. Department of Labor, includes descriptions of many different jobs and the skills required for each one. The DOT divides all skills into three categories—data, people, and things. Data skills involve working with information, such as statistics. People skills can be used with anyone in the world of work, such as co-workers, managers, and customers. Things skills relate to working with machines and materials.

Here are examples of some skills in each of these categories:

Data	People	Things
analyzing	instructing	driving
computing	serving	handling
comparing	speaking	operating
coordinating	persuading	setting up

DEVELOP YOUR STRENGTHS

By now, you should be developing an idea of what your strengths are. If you haven't already done so, begin listing them in a self-assessment log, like the one shown in FIGURE 1-1 on page 5. Add to the list as you become more aware of your strengths and as you think about which skills you want to continue using.

This man is using his photography skills. **What skills do you have that could help you find a job?**

Get into the habit of thinking about your daily accomplishments and writing them in your log. Some accomplishments will be small, such as learning to use a copy machine. Others, such as graduating from high school, will be the result of long, hard work. With each new accomplishment, think about the interests, skills, and personality traits that are related to it. Knowing yourself and your strengths is an important step in your career search.

Lesson Review

CHECK YOUR UNDERSTANDING

1. ANALYZING Why would employers expect an employee to have the entry-level skills shown in FIGURE 1-2 on page 6? Choose one skill, and explain why it would be important.

2. SYNTHESIZING Choose two key workplace skills from FIGURE 1-2. Write a few sentences that describe how that skill could be used in each situation.

APPLY WHAT YOU LEARN

Make a list of the entry-level skills in FIGURE 1-2. Then, rate yourself as to whether you have average or superior abilities in each entry-level skill. If you need improvement in any particular skill, note that, too.

Grammar Workshop

Writing Complete Sentences

A sentence expresses a complete thought and has a subject and a predicate. The subject is what or whom the sentence is about. The predicate (verb or verb phrase) tells what the subject is doing. When you write at school or on the job, use complete sentences so that your ideas will be understood.

Here is an example of a complete sentence:

SUBJECT	PREDICATE
↓	↓

Example The clerk in the mailroom sorted the packages.

A sentence fragment is missing either a subject or a predicate.

Example The cook in the kitchen [**MISSING PREDICATE**: What did the cook do?]

Example Chopped the onions [**MISSING SUBJECT**: Who chopped the onions?]

You can change a sentence fragment to a complete sentence in two ways:

- Add a missing subject or a missing predicate.

  Example The cook in the kitchen prepared dinner. Anika chopped all the vegetables.

- Join a sentence fragment to another sentence.

  Example The computer crashed, and documents were lost.

Application

Read each of the following statements. On a separate sheet of paper, write **S** for each complete sentence. Write **SF** for each sentence fragment. Then rewrite each sentence fragment so that it is a complete sentence.

1. The bus driver with the tickets
2. A new piece of machinery
3. Took our orders and smiled at us
4. Sharon considered becoming a doctor
5. Came into John's office yesterday
6. Talked all during lunch hour
7. He left early in the morning for work
8. Finished without any problems
9. Said the park was closed until summer
10. Joining the new company

For more information, **SEE PAGE 346.**

Building Self-Confidence

What Do You Already Know?

Think about a situation in which you needed self-confidence. How did having self-confidence help you handle the situation?

Think About It Why do you think an employer would want workers who have self-confidence?

Suppose you overheard the following conversation: "Man, I really messed up! How could I let that happen?" "Here, let me fix it. I can figure it out—watch me." You might think the second speaker is more self-confident. This person gives the impression that he or she can get the job done. Would you be more likely to have confidence in the second person? You probably would. Acting self-confident can give other people confidence in you.

THE SOURCE OF SELF-CONFIDENCE

Self-confidence comes from believing in yourself. It means that you trust that you have the skills and the abilities to get a job done right.

The source of self-confidence is **self-esteem**, the amount of respect you have for yourself and your abilities. Having a high level of self-esteem means you can overcome setbacks and problems. You may fail, but failure does not defeat you. When your self-esteem is high, you know that it is okay to make mistakes. You learn from your mistakes, and you apply your learning to new tasks.

Give Yourself Positive Inner Messages

You affect your self-esteem through what you say to yourself. Most of us "talk" to ourselves during the day. Sometimes, we give ourselves positive messages: "You look good today." "What you said was really smart." Unfortunately, we can also give ourselves discouraging messages: "You can't do that, no way." "Can't you do anything right?" We can be our own worst critics.

Negative messages affect your self-esteem and your performance. Putting yourself down does not raise your self-esteem or make you a better worker. You can raise your self-esteem by giving yourself positive inner messages and by believing in yourself.

You can build your self-esteem by writing down your personal strengths and how those are evident in your work at school and on the job. Then list an encouraging message to match those strengths. FIGURE 1-4 on page 11 shows one student's list of personal strengths.

Set Reasonable Goals

If you are a student, your work will be evaluated by a teacher. If you are a worker on a job, your performance will be evaluated by a supervisor. Being judged by others can be hard on your self-esteem. You need to ask yourself whether you are setting reasonable goals.

Reasonable goals are goals that you can expect to reach. These goals are part of your **career plan**. A career plan is an outline of where you want to go and of how and when you will get there.

Some career goals are short-term. They are meant to be accomplished in a particular period of time. Short-term goals might include learning how to use a fax machine or getting more education or training. Long-term goals take more time to reach.

WRITING IN THE REAL WORLD: CAREER PLAN

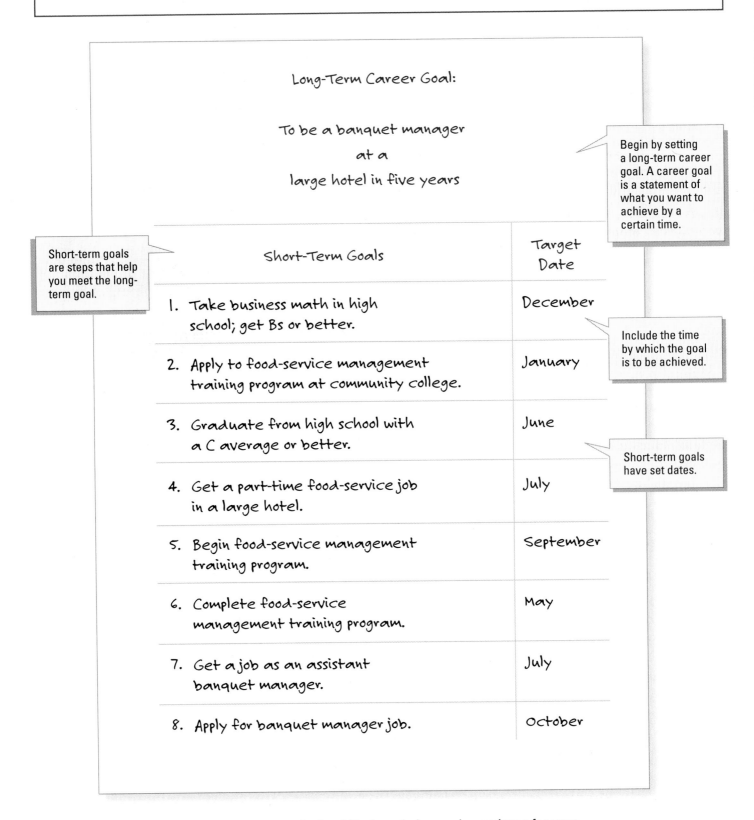

Long-Term Career Goal:

To be a banquet manager
at a
large hotel in five years

> Begin by setting a long-term career goal. A career goal is a statement of what you want to achieve by a certain time.

> Short-term goals are steps that help you meet the long-term goal.

Short-Term Goals	Target Date
1. Take business math in high school; get Bs or better.	December
2. Apply to food-service management training program at community college.	January
3. Graduate from high school with a C average or better.	June
4. Get a part-time food-service job in a large hotel.	July
5. Begin food-service management training program.	September
6. Complete food-service management training program.	May
7. Get a job as an assistant banquet manager.	July
8. Apply for banquet manager job.	October

> Include the time by which the goal is to be achieved.

> Short-term goals have set dates.

FIGURE 1-3 Short-term goals are ways to gain the skills, knowledge, and experience for your chosen career. **Why is it important to create a career plan?**

Personal Strength or Skill	How It Helps at School or on the Job	Positive Message
Good listener	Can remember what people tell me	I listen well and remember information.
Analytical	Can figure out directions	I like to put things together.
Dependable	Never miss a day of work	People know they can depend on me.
Team player	Work well with other people	I am a good partner on a team.

FIGURE 1-4 shows a list that one student made of her personal strengths and how she used them at school and on the job. **How do positive messages reinforce a person's strengths?**

They are usually written as positive statements about the job you want to have and when you want to have it. Accomplishing short-term goals may help you reach your long-term goal. For example, getting a job in an office might be a long-term goal that could be reached if a person learns to use a fax machine and other office equipment. FIGURE 1-3 on page 10 shows a career plan with one person's long-term and short-term career goals.

Ask for Help

Entry-level workers cannot know everything they are supposed to do. More experienced workers, on the other hand, may know a lot. They are usually flattered when a beginner asks them for help. By turning to an experienced co-worker, you may find that he or she becomes your **mentor**. A mentor is a person who takes an interest in your career and helps steer you in the right direction. Take advantage of help from others to become successful. Success increases self-esteem and self-confidence.

Celebrate Your Successes

When you do something well, give yourself a pat on the back. If the work you did was especially challenging, reward yourself with something you like. Don't take for granted that everyone can do what you can. Listen to your supervisor's and co-workers' praise, and accept their compliments. Keep a list of your strengths, and look at it often as a way of keeping your self-esteem strong. Add to it whenever you can.

Lesson Review

CHECK YOUR UNDERSTANDING

1. IDENTIFYING Give yourself two positive messages. Describe how these messages make you feel.

2. EVALUATING Describe why self-confidence is important. Write why it is important at work. Then, explain why it is important at school and in your private life, too.

APPLY WHAT YOU LEARN

Strengths can help us in more than one way. Look at FIGURE 1-4 above. On a sheet of paper, write five of your personal strengths. Then, show how each strength can be useful at school or on the job. Finally, make up a positive message about each strength.

Developing Effective Work Habits

What Do You Already Know?

You have some habits that help you succeed in school. What are these habits? How might they help you succeed on a job?

Think About It Why would an employer want to hire someone with good work habits?

Habits are patterns of behavior that you follow without even thinking about them. When something is a habit, such as brushing your teeth or hanging up your coat, you have done it so often that you do not even think about what you are doing. You just do it. Habits often help you save time or help your day run more smoothly. Effective work habits can help a job run more smoothly, too.

START OUT DOING A GOOD JOB

You don't need to wait until you have a job to practice effective work habits. You can apply good work habits on your way to finding the job you want. There are employment applications to fill out, appointments to keep, and interviews to go on.

At each step, take a practical, businesslike **attitude** toward work. An attitude is a way of acting, feeling, and thinking about something. Your attitude toward work should be, "I'm a good worker. I take my job seriously."

Employers notice workers who show their commitment through good work habits. A worker who is on time, who is prepared to put in a full day, who shows respect to customers, co-workers, and supervisors is a worker who will be valued. Here are six ways to practice effective work habits:

Be Enthusiastic

There are reasons to be enthusiastic about almost any job. Find those reasons—maybe the people you work with are friendly or the location of the work is pleasant. Maybe the work itself is important to other people and what you do is appreciated. Enthusiasm brings energy and a better attitude to your work.

Be a Self-Starter

Don't wait to be told what to do. Look for work that needs to be done, and then do it. Pay attention to tasks your supervisor says are important. It might be that he or she wants the work area to be kept neat or customers to be helped as soon as they come into the store. If so, then those are key parts of your job, too. Knowing that your supervisor wants these things done, do them on your own.

Present a Good Image

There is a saying, "Attitude is everything." How do you want co-workers to think about you? Do they look at you and see someone who is dressed appropriately? Are you wearing the kinds of clothes successful people in the company wear? If so, they will assume you want to succeed, too. A good image says, "I'm responsible." Responsible workers can usually be found at their assigned work station. If an emergency or illness comes up, they notify their supervisor. This kind of behavior contributes to a good image with co-workers.

Make Your Best Effort

When you are hired, you expect to be paid the amount promised. You would not be satisfied if the employer didn't feel like paying you. Similarly, your employer expects you to do your job. Doing your job means making your best effort. Spend your workday working. Stay focused on tasks. Return from breaks on time. This is not only fair, but it also shows your value to the business.

Accept Criticism Thoughtfully

Criticism is not always negative. It can be given in the spirit of being helpful. Learn from the comments that supervisors make about your work. Think about why your work is being evaluated. As a beginner, you might be assigned work that isn't very interesting. Never ignore its importance, though. You have to prove that you can handle bigger tasks by mastering smaller ones first. The criticisms that supervisors give you are actually tips on how to improve your work. Listen to their advice.

Stay Alert

There will always be change in the world of work and in life. Of the 100 largest U.S. companies in 1900, only 16 were left by 2000. You owe it to yourself to stay informed about what is happening in jobs like yours. Keep informed about news in your field. Accept opportunities to learn new skills. Be a worker who looks ahead.

Lesson Review

CHECK YOUR UNDERSTANDING

1. EVALUATING Think of a responsibility you have right now. It could be a new job or a responsibility at home or school. How do you practice the six effective work habits when you carry out that responsibility?

2. IDENTIFYING List three effective work habits good students have. Describe how they could result in better grades.

APPLY WHAT YOU LEARN

Interview someone you respect who has been working for a long time. Ask him or her this question, "If you could start your work life over again, what would you do differently?" Share your interview with the class.

Making Job Choices

What Do You Already Know?
What kinds of jobs are available for people your age? What jobs do you or some of your friends have?

Think About It How can you make choices between different jobs?

One of the exciting things about career planning is that there are so many jobs from which to choose. You might be feeling a little nervous about the choices in the world of work. You are probably wondering what kind of work you really want to do. You may also be wondering how to find out about jobs. Your curiosity will be useful. It will help you look for the right answers.

LOOK TO THE FUTURE

Suppose it is three years from now. What are you doing? Suppose someone were to ask you, "Tell me, what kind of work do you do?" What would you like to say? Go ahead and say to yourself now what you would like to be able to say.

You probably don't yet know all the facts you will need to know about that ideal job in the future. You may not know what it will pay, what kind of training or education is required, or what kinds of **trade-offs** you would be expected to make. Trade-offs are compromises. For example, if you go into sales, you can make your own schedule but you will probably be expected to travel a lot. You will be trading time away from home for your independence. Is that a trade-off you can accept?

RESEARCH JOBS

You need to do research to make a good match between yourself—your interests, abilities, skills, and goals—and opportunities in the world of work. To make the effort worthwhile, you need factual, up-to-date information.

Where can you get current information about jobs? A number of published resources can be used to find job information.

Printed Material

The local library may have books that feature jobs in particular fields, such as *Jobs in Electronics* or *Jobs for Writers*. Other books may focus on one particular city or region, such as *Job Hunting in San Francisco*. In these books, you might be able to find leads for jobs in the area where you live.

One of the best sources of job information is the *Occupational Outlook Handbook*, which is published by the Bureau of Labor Statistics. Practically every public library has a copy, and it is available online, too, at stats.bls.gov/ocohome.htm. The *Handbook* lists 249 occupations, which cover seven out of every eight jobs in the United States. It describes each occupation—what workers do, the kinds of training they need, and the average wage they receive. Best of all, the *Handbook* predicts which occupations will offer the most jobs in the future. FIGURE 1-5 on page 15 shows the home page of the *Handbook*.

Other Print Resources

Libraries usually have directories that list professional groups, trade schools, and employment resources. These books could help you find jobs in particular careers.

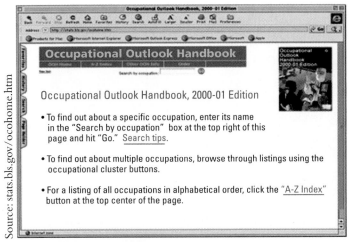

FIGURE 1-5 shows the Web site for the *Occupational Outlook Handbook*. **How might information on the Web site help you?**

Want ads appear in newspapers and trade magazines. These ads provide short summaries of the skills and experience employers want. Want ads tell you how and where to apply for jobs.

SEARCH FOR A JOB

Finding the right job takes time, energy, and willpower. Here are some ways to make your job search effective:

- Always review your career research and career plan before searching for job. Remember why you want a job and which jobs will best match your strengths.

- Be realistic about how long it takes to find a job. Experts say that the average time is between eight and 23 weeks. Sometimes, it takes even longer. If you realize this at the start, you are less likely to become discouraged.

- The more methods you use, the more likely you are to be successful. For example, you might check the want ads in the newspaper and ask friends about job openings.

- Get support from family and friends during your job search. Join a group of job seekers. Supportive people can help keep each other from giving up.

There are several ways to collect information about jobs. Networking with other people, counselors at employment offices, and Internet online sources can provide information.

Networking

There are many ways to search for jobs. One of the most effective ways is **networking**. A network is a system of interconnected lines that transmits information. When you are networking, you are building a system of contacts, people who can receive and pass along job information for you or to you.

In order to network, you should make a list of all the people you want to tell about your job search. Add family members to the list. Next, list the names of friends and acquaintances who might be able to provide you with job information or leads, such as teachers, counselors, and neighborhood store owners.

The next step is to contact the people on your list. When you call, explain who you are and why you are calling. Tell what job you are looking for. If the people you speak to have any leads, write them down. Ask these people to call you if they hear of anything that might help you.

Employment Offices

Many job seekers use employment offices when searching for job prospects. Employment offices have lists of job openings. They usually have employment specialists who help match workers and jobs. Colleges, trade schools, and some high schools also have counselors who place students in jobs.

The United States Employment Service is another resource for jobs. This agency has offices in every state. Your state office might be called the Employment Development Department, the Job Service, or the State Employment Office. These are good places to learn about job openings. To find the office in your area, look in the listings of state offices in your phone book.

There are also private employment agencies, which charge fees to help people find jobs. Sometimes these fees are paid by the employer, sometimes by the employee. Such agencies usually handle certain job areas, such as finding temporary positions for office workers.

Online Sources

If possible, explore the Internet as a resource. First, you can look for jobs posted at new.careerpath.com or www.monster.com. There are many other Web sites, too. Once you get to these sites, type a key-word such as "computers" to search for jobs in the computer field. The jobs will appear on the screen like want ads in a newspaper. Second, the Internet itself is creating new jobs—Web copy writer, Web graphics designer, and many others. Remember, you don't have to own a computer to do research on the Internet. Use of the Internet is free at many public and school libraries.

GET THE TRAINING YOU NEED

As you research the world of work, you may come across some jobs you want that require more education or training than you currently have. Some occupations require professional licenses; others require special coursework. Don't get discouraged. Your short-term goal might be to find out about jobs that interest you. Your long-term goal might be to get the additional training or education you need to work in that field.

You may not have the training or education or experience right now for some jobs you want. But entry-level jobs you enjoy now can lead to careers. As you gain experience, you can get additional training and education. Think of jobs as rungs on a ladder. You progress up the ladder, one rung at a time, toward success.

MAKE A COMMITMENT TO YOURSELF AND TO YOUR FUTURE

People can give you advice. They can offer you assistance. But making a career plan is up to you. The amount of satisfaction you gain from your job also depends on you. You must set reachable job goals for yourself, maintain good work habits, and reward yourself now and then. Building a career is a step-by-step process. Keep giving yourself positive inner messages: "I can do it."

This employment counselor is helping a client find a job. **Where else can people go to find job information?**

"There you go!" "It's going my way now." You'll see that you really can reach your career goals.

Lesson Review

CHECK YOUR UNDERSTANDING

1. DESCRIBING Describe three jobs that interest you. What makes them sound interesting?

2. SYNTHESIZING Do you have a hobby? Is there something you know a lot about? Think about how you might turn your knowledge into a job opportunity. Write a summary of how you could use your hobby in a career.

APPLY WHAT YOU LEARN

Work with a partner. Use the Internet to find the Web site for the *Occupational Outlook Handbook* or another job information Web site. Select an occupation title, and research it. Write down the name of the job, the training needed, and the salary for that job. Share your information with the class.

TECH CONNECTION — THE FAX MACHINE

The word *fax* is short for *facsimile*, which means "an exact copy." A fax machine transmits a copy of a document over phone wires to another fax machine, which prints it. During your job search, businesses may ask you to fax them information.

What are the advantages of faxing information about yourself? If you can get information to an employer almost immediately, you could be rewarded with an interview. You can send a fax from a business that offers a faxing service. Such services usually charge a fee for each page. Sometimes, public libraries offer faxing services. When you send information through a fax machine, always include a cover sheet like the one below. Follow up a fax by sending a hard copy through the mail.

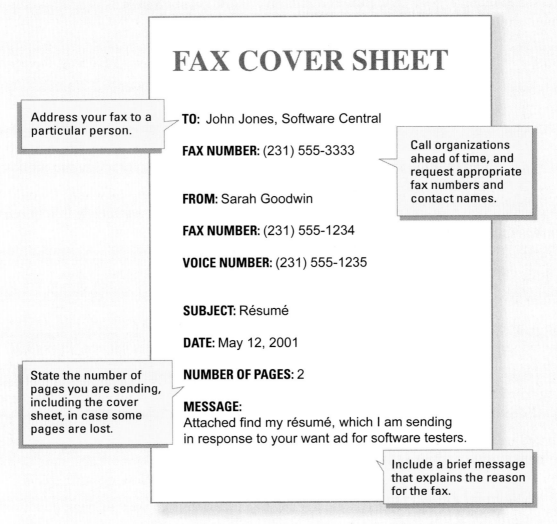

FAX COVER SHEET

Address your fax to a particular person.

TO: John Jones, Software Central

FAX NUMBER: (231) 555-3333

Call organizations ahead of time, and request appropriate fax numbers and contact names.

FROM: Sarah Goodwin

FAX NUMBER: (231) 555-1234

VOICE NUMBER: (231) 555-1235

SUBJECT: Résumé

DATE: May 12, 2001

NUMBER OF PAGES: 2

State the number of pages you are sending, including the cover sheet, in case some pages are lost.

MESSAGE:
Attached find my résumé, which I am sending in response to your want ad for software testers.

Include a brief message that explains the reason for the fax.

Application

Look through the want ads in a newspaper. Select one want ad, and write a fax cover sheet that you might send to the company.

CHAPTER 1

REVIEW

Chapter Summary

Career planning starts with you. Your interests, your abilities, and your skills are the most important considerations in looking ahead to work. But before you begin your job hunt, take a few minutes to assess yourself. Perhaps a hobby or a volunteer activity could become an exciting career. Self-confidence is also an important factor in career success. Your first step should be to set reachable goals and practice effective work habits. These traits will turn any entry-level position into success on the job.

Key Words

career	career plan
economy	mentor
assess	attitude
entry-level	trade-offs
self-esteem	networking

In each sentence below, replace the words in parentheses with a word from the Key Words list. Write your answers on a separate sheet of paper.

1. I try to show that my ____ (level of respect for myself) is high by expressing self-confidence.

2. How the national ____ (production and use of goods and services) affects jobs is something I need to keep in mind.

3. I'm going to find a ____ (more experienced worker) who can help me to learn my job.

4. I'm prepared to make ____ (compromises between myself and the demands) to find a job I will enjoy.

5. Naturally, I'd like a job that pays really well, but ____ (beginner) jobs don't usually do that.

6. I think it's better to ____ (evaluate) my strengths so that I can choose the job that is right for me.

7. A good ____ (way of acting, feeling, and thinking) about your work will help you to succeed.

8. You can start to make your ____ (general course of your working life) plans by doing research and by interviewing workers.

9. My ____ (outline of where I would like to go in my working life) will help me reach my long-term goals.

10. ____ (Building a group of people who can help you) can help you find a job.

Application: Assess Your Work Skills

The *Dictionary of Occupational Titles (DOT)* divides all skills into three categories—people, data, and things. On a separate sheet of paper, write the skills from each category that describe you. Explain your choices.

Category: People

✓ I am good at following instructions.

✓ I communicate well in person and on the phone.

✓ I communicate well in writing.

✓ I am good at showing others how to do things.

✓ I am good at working with people in groups.

Category: Data

☑ I am good at researching.

☑ I am good at observing or studying things.

☑ I am good at managing.

☑ I am good at working with numbers.

☑ I am good at organizing and prioritizing my tasks.

Category: Things

☑ I am skillful with my hands or fingers.

☑ I have good hand-eye coordination.

☑ I am good at cutting, sewing, molding, or sculpting.

☑ I am good at setting up, driving, or operating machines.

☑ I am good at raising or training different kinds of animals.

Application: Recognize Effective Work Habits

Read the following story about Bill's career in food services. Then, work with a small group of students to answer the questions on a separate sheet of paper.

Bill wants to build a career in food services. He likes working with people, and he likes to cook. He is beginning his career by working at a fast-food restaurant. His career plan is to work at larger restaurants as he builds his skills.

Bill has some problems, though. He works at the soda machine, and customers complain that they have to wait too long for their sodas. Bill is always running out of cups, so he has to keep going to the supply room.

Customers also complain that their cups are only half-filled. Bill doesn't know how to fill cups so that they are not full of foam. He is afraid to ask Lisa, the shift manager, because he thinks Lisa does not like him.

1. What has Bill done well in planning his career?

2. What are three things you would tell Bill to help him solve his on-the-job problems?

Grammar Workshop Practice

On a separate sheet of paper, rewrite each of the following sentence fragments. Make each one a complete sentence.

1. Trustworthy and honest

2. Geared up to complete the project

3. Working together to complete a job

4. Linda, John, and Phyllis in the office

5. A special number

6. Sold more than 1 million books

7. Stocked all the shelves in the stockroom

8. Listened to the instructions carefully

9. Just started to work there

10. Lifted the heavy package off the desk

Portfolio Project — Writing a Career Plan

Research a job that interests you, and write a career plan to help you get that job. To do this:

• Write down your long-term goal.

• Assess your work-related skills.

• List the specific skills or training that would help you succeed in the job.

• Think about the work habits you need to succeed in the job.

• List the short-term goals that would help you to accomplish your goal.

Add your career plan to your portfolio.

FINDING THE RIGHT JOB

Beth graduated from high school two years ago. She has been working as a desk clerk in a motel. The pay is low, and there is no chance to advance. Beth likes working in a motel, but she is tired of doing the same tasks all the time. She feels trapped because she does not know how to get a better job. Her goal is to work at one of the big hotels where she could learn new skills and make more money.

Key Words

hospitality

health care

retail sales

position

flexible

diplomatic

references

cover letter

customize

Goals for Success

In this chapter, you will learn these skills:

Writing a résumé and a cover letter

 WRITING

Preparing for a job interview

 SELF-ESTEEM/SPEAKING

Presenting yourself as friendly and polite on a job interview

 SOCIABILITY AND INTEGRITY/HONESTY

Evaluating your interview

 HUMAN RESOURCES

Locating job ads on the Internet and evaluating Web sites

 MONITORING AND CORRECTING PERFORMANCE

PORTFOLIO PROJECT

COVER LETTER

By the time you complete this chapter, you will know what Beth has to do to write a cover letter. You also will be able to create a cover letter of your own to add to your portfolio.

Evaluating Job Opportunities

What Do You Already Know?

What kinds of jobs have you already done? Which of these jobs did you enjoy?

Think About It   Where can you find information about jobs?

Finding the right job can be exciting. Most people call this search the "job hunt." In fact, a better term for it might be "job shopping." You may find plenty of jobs to choose from—just as you find many things to buy. However, there is a limit on the kinds of jobs that are right for you, just as there is a limit on the kinds of things you should buy. A smart job-hunter needs to compare and evaluate choices before making a decision.

WHERE THE JOBS ARE

The job market is a busy place. Employers have to fill openings regularly. Many businesses in your community may be looking for workers. The employment outlook is good, for example, for entry-level workers in the hospitality, health care, and retail sales industries. These are all areas of the economy in which goods and services are in high demand.

Hospitality Industry

The **hospitality** industry employs workers in hotels, motels, convention centers, airports, restaurants, and theme parks—any business in which customers are treated like guests. Hospitality businesses often operate 24 hours a day. They offer jobs that range from desk clerks and ushers to audiovisual technicians, restaurant managers, air-conditioning technicians—even short-order cooks and chefs. Food service is part of the hospitality industry.

Health Care

A second growth area for entry-level jobs is the **health care** industry. These jobs include nurses' aides, home care workers, laboratory technicians, and hospital workers of many kinds. Jobs are plentiful because the people in the United States are living longer. Hospitals, retirement centers, rehabilitation clinics, senior-citizen communities, and nursing homes are expanding. Many jobs in health care require training or education after high school. Such training or education can lead to higher salaries and more responsibility.

Retail Sales

Retail sales is another growing field. In retail sales, goods are sold to customers in stores. You rely on retail salespeople when you shop in department stores and malls. Other workers who help keep the retail sales industry running include maintenance and security people, buyers, sales associates, department managers, and window designers.

FIND THE HIDDEN JOB MARKET

Most entry-level workers rely on newspaper want ads to find jobs. Actually, only a fraction of available jobs are advertised to the public. Many employers do not want to be flooded with applications. To be a smart job-hunter, you should

- contact people you know, and tell them you are looking for employment.

Date	Job Opportunity	Source	Contact Person, Number	To Do
6/17	Sales Clerk at Murphy's	Newspaper ad	Ms. Abreu, 555-3333	Send résumé, call 6/24
6/19	Cashier at Green's Mini-Market	Mr. Adamski, neighbor	Mr. Green, 555-1327	Take résumé to store 6/20
6/19	Sales trainee at Lopez Sports	monster.com	a.lopez@ lopez.com	Send résumé by e-mail 6/20

FIGURE 2-1 This chart shows a student's job log. **How could you use a log like this to help you find a job?**

- use your local telephone book to make a list of businesses in which you would like to work.

- take part-time and volunteer jobs to train for better jobs.

A part-time or summer job in a company can lead to a full-time, permanent job with the company. If you have a part-time job, you can tell your supervisor you want to be considered for full-time work. Volunteer work in a day-care center, hospital, or parks-and-recreation program may also allow you to demonstrate the skills that qualify you for a full-time position.

ORGANIZE WITH A JOB LOG

Information is the most important part of job-hunting. Make yourself a job log like the one shown in FIGURE 2-1 above. One way is to use a notebook to write down every job and every job possibility you hear about or read about. Write down to whom you spoke, the date, and what happened. Check the spelling of the name of every person and company. Make sure that every address and phone number is correct.

Do the same for every classified job ad you answer. Tape a copy of the ad and the letters you sent into your job log. If you promised to contact someone in a week, put the date on a TO DO list. Be sure you make the contact. Write down when

you visit a business, employment agency, or temp agency and fill in an application form. While you are there, write down the name and phone number of the person you spoke with. Try also to get the name and phone number of the person who will make the actual hiring decision. If you promised to send references or other information you did not have, make a note. Keep your promise.

Keep your job log up to date. Check it daily. Follow up on every lead you get.

Lesson Review

CHECK YOUR UNDERSTANDING

1. IDENTIFYING Who are three people you could use to begin your job search?

2. GATHERING INFORMATION How can you stay informed about jobs that are not advertised?

APPLY WHAT YOU LEARN

Find a person who works in the hospitality industry, in health care, or in retail sales. Ask that person what he or she likes and dislikes about the work. What advice can you get? What, for instance, is the best way to get a job in that kind of business? Present your findings to the class.

Writing a Résumé

A résumé is a summary of your work history and job qualifications. It lists all your jobs, your tasks, and your achievements. It introduces you and helps "sell" you to an employer. Many entry-level jobs require only a completed application. However, a résumé gives an employer a much better idea of your abilities.

What Do You Already Know?

How would you describe some of the jobs in which you have already worked? On a separate sheet of paper, list the jobs and the tasks you have done. (Include those done at home, in school, and in the workplace.)

Think About It Why might an employer want to see your résumé?

THE PURPOSE OF A RÉSUMÉ

A résumé is like a billboard, a magazine ad, or a commercial on television. It advertises the qualities that make you a good worker. A résumé lets you **position** yourself as a job hunter. When you position yourself, you direct attention to important things about yourself. Use the following checklist to help you determine what you can offer an employer:

✔ I am reliable.

✔ I can accept responsibility.

✔ I work well with other people.

✔ I accept challenges.

✔ I am a creative problem solver.

✔ I am organized.

Employers use résumés to get a preview of job-hunters, just as you might see a movie preview and think, "Show me more. This looks interesting!" If employers like what they learn from a résumé, they are more likely to offer the person an interview.

JOB SKILLS AND WORK HABITS

FIGURE 2-2 on page 25 shows a model of a student's résumé. Soon, you will be writing a résumé that presents your own work history. When you are starting out, your work habits can be more important than your experience or technical skills. Work habits show the kind of person you are. Employers want to know if you are responsible, reliable, and hard working—and if you are able to learn quickly. They look for answers to other questions: Are you patient? Are you enthusiastic? Are you **flexible**—able to shift between tasks easily? Can you handle stress?

If the job involves contact with people, employers want to know about your people skills. Can you express ideas well? Do you treat others with respect? Are you **diplomatic**—able to resolve conflicts?

Your résumé should be truthful, of course. Just keep in mind that it is important to think like the person who is doing the hiring. Suppose you were an employer who wanted to hire someone. What qualities would you like to see in a worker?

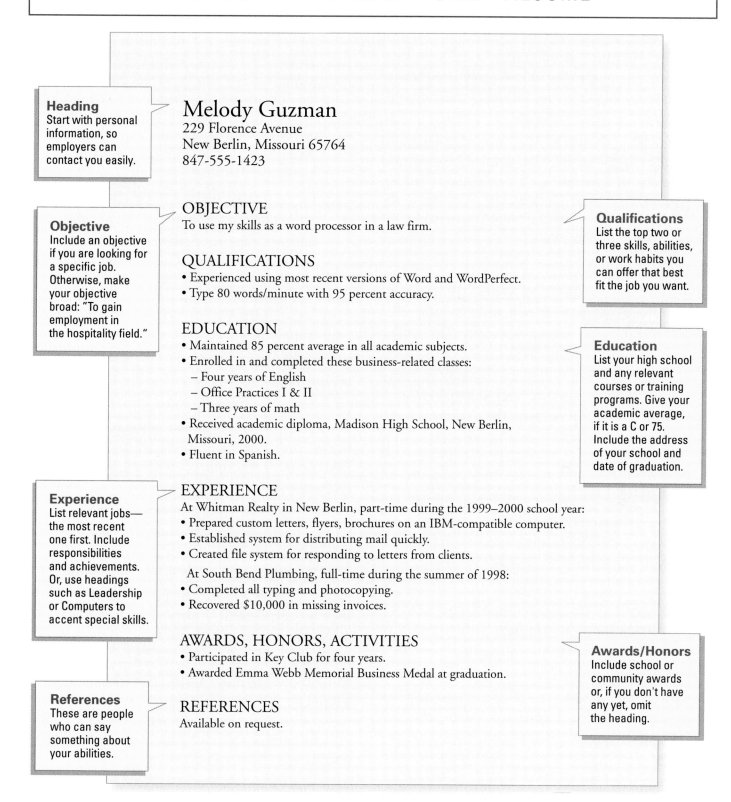

Heading
Start with personal information, so employers can contact you easily.

Objective
Include an objective if you are looking for a specific job. Otherwise, make your objective broad: "To gain employment in the hospitality field."

Experience
List relevant jobs— the most recent one first. Include responsibilities and achievements. Or, use headings such as Leadership or Computers to accent special skills.

References
These are people who can say something about your abilities.

Qualifications
List the top two or three skills, abilities, or work habits you can offer that best fit the job you want.

Education
List your high school and any relevant courses or training programs. Give your academic average, if it is a C or 75. Include the address of your school and date of graduation.

Awards/Honors
Include school or community awards or, if you don't have any yet, omit the heading.

Melody Guzman
229 Florence Avenue
New Berlin, Missouri 65764
847-555-1423

OBJECTIVE
To use my skills as a word processor in a law firm.

QUALIFICATIONS
- Experienced using most recent versions of Word and WordPerfect.
- Type 80 words/minute with 95 percent accuracy.

EDUCATION
- Maintained 85 percent average in all academic subjects.
- Enrolled in and completed these business-related classes:
  - Four years of English
  - Office Practices I & II
  - Three years of math
- Received academic diploma, Madison High School, New Berlin, Missouri, 2000.
- Fluent in Spanish.

EXPERIENCE
At Whitman Realty in New Berlin, part-time during the 1999–2000 school year:
- Prepared custom letters, flyers, brochures on an IBM-compatible computer.
- Established system for distributing mail quickly.
- Created file system for responding to letters from clients.

At South Bend Plumbing, full-time during the summer of 1998:
- Completed all typing and photocopying.
- Recovered $10,000 in missing invoices.

AWARDS, HONORS, ACTIVITIES
- Participated in Key Club for four years.
- Awarded Emma Webb Memorial Business Medal at graduation.

REFERENCES
Available on request.

FIGURE 2-2 A résumé helps you present yourself as a job candidate who deserves to be hired. **How might a résumé help prove that you will be a valuable employee?**

A BASIC RÉSUMÉ

The kind of job you are seeking should influence what you write in your résumé. If you are looking for office work, for instance, then office skills—filing, word processing, organization—should stand out on your résumé. Likewise, if you want to work in the hospitality industry, any experience with serving and getting along with people should stand out.

Do some basic research to find out what qualities and skills employers in your field of interest are looking for. In other words, know your audience. Use the *Occupational Outlook Handbook* to both target the jobs you want and tailor your résumé to fit those kinds of jobs.

Gather Information

Before you begin writing your résumé, gather information about yourself—it will make writing the résumé much easier. You are doing detective work, in a way, to answer this question: How can I present myself as a worker? Use this checklist to help you:

- ✔ *A high school transcript* Select courses that would be useful in doing the job you want. Add the course title, your grade, and a short description of the class to your résumé. Also add the year that you graduated or expect to graduate.

- ✔ *Names of jobs you have held* Give the correct spelling of the place where you worked, its address, your job title, and the exact dates you worked.

- ✔ *Examples of your positive work habits* List examples of how you have demonstrated positive work habits.

- ✔ *Examples of your entry-level skills* Write examples of tasks you did to demonstrate some of the basic entry-level skills that any employer would want to see.

- ✔ *Awards, activities, or honors* They show a desire to succeed and a willingness to work hard. Such honors will attract future employers' interest. Make a list of them.

- ✔ *A job objective* Make a statement about what you want to do. Make this a broad objective such as, "To find a position in health care in which my people skills and dependability can be used." Now you will be able to use the résumé for all kinds of jobs in health care. However, if you are revising your résumé to fit a specific job, make sure that your objective fits that particular job.

- ✔ *References* **References** are people who can speak favorably about your work skills and history. References may be teachers or former supervisors. They should not be relatives. Always ask these people for permission before you use their name. Do not put their name on the résumé. You can supply the names and phone numbers of your references to an interviewer if asked.

Write a First Draft

Look again at FIGURE 2-2 on page 25. Note how the writer put the information she gathered about herself into categories: Objective; Qualifications; Education; Experience; Awards, Honors, and Activities. You can organize your information in the same way to highlight your strengths.

As you begin to write your résumé, keep in mind that the language is similar to what you see in advertisements—short, clear, and energetic. Write in phrases, and start the phrases with active verbs. You can add bullets (•) to draw attention to individual phrases.

Revise the Draft

Keep your résumé brief and well-organized. Eliminate information that is repeated. Check for misspellings and grammar problems, too. It is hard to claim that you are a careful worker if your résumé has errors.

Here are some tips on giving your résumé the right appearance:

This man is preparing his résumé on a computer. **Why do you think an employer might like to see a résumé that is neatly done?**

- Keep the length of your résumé to the size of one business-letter page.

- Use an easy-to-read type style, such as Palatino, Times, or Arial. Use no more than two type styles. In addition, use 10-point to 12-point type. Headings can be two points larger than the body type.

- Print your résumé on white or light-colored paper.

Once you finish a satisfactory draft of your résumé, ask for feedback. Have other people read it. Ask for their reactions. Is your writing clear? Do you sound like a skilled, dependable worker? Is anything important missing? Be open to suggestions. After all, your goal is to create the best profile of yourself that you can.

Lesson Review

CHECK YOUR UNDERSTANDING

1. DEFINING What is the main purpose of a résumé?

2. IDENTIFYING What are three types of information you should include on your résumé?

APPLY WHAT YOU LEARN

Begin working on your résumé. Use the information and tips in this lesson. Write drafts of your résumé until you are satisfied with how it reads and looks. Show it to another student, and ask for suggestions. Continue revising until your résumé presents a clear picture of you.

Writing a Cover Letter

What letters have you written?
What were your purposes
for writing? How does your
purpose for writing a letter
guide what you write?

Think About It   Why should
you send a cover letter with
your résumé?

When you find out about a job opening, you should always write a cover letter. A cover letter explains which job you are applying for and introduces the résumé. Then the résumé gives a more detailed description of you, the worker. Remember that an employer doesn't know anything about you. You must make it easy for an employer to get an idea of who you are and what you can offer.

THE PURPOSE OF A COVER LETTER

Include a **cover letter,** or letter of application, when you have to send information about yourself to an employer. Perhaps the job is far away, or the newspaper ad does not give an address where you can walk in and fill out an application. In cases like these, you are expected to communicate by mail, fax, or e-mail.

Find out information about the job so you can **customize** your cover letter, or make it specific, to fit the job. When you customize a cover letter, you revise it so that it will appeal to a particular person. For example, if the ad says "computer repair experience a plus" or "word processing skills required," use those words in your letter.

Even if the ad is brief, keep in mind that all employers want to know about the skills and work habits you can offer. In addition, they want to hear why you think you should be hired.

Always do what the ad tells you to do. The ad may give a phone number. It may tell you to fax your cover letter and résumé to a particular person. If the ad says "no calls," then do not telephone. The ad tells you the way in which an employer will consider hiring you. Follow the directions.

PLAN YOUR LETTER

Most job ads, like the one in FIGURE 2-3, tell you the skills and background the employer is looking for. Carefully read an ad that interests you, and make a list of the skills needed. Use the list as an outline to write your cover letter.

Customer Service Representatives

Temps to possible perm. We are entering our busy season and need people to provide customer service to our clients. Excellent customer service orientation w/strong sales ability. Excellent telephone skills. Computer literate and sales oriented. Flexible shifts. Paid training. Résumé and cover letter to:

A CLOCK ON EVERY WALL

17513 Springer Avenue
Wildwood, NJ 08260
Previous applicants need not apply.

FIGURE 2-3 is a sample newspaper want ad. **What qualifications does the employer want the job candidate to have?**

PREPARE A FIRST DRAFT

As you write a cover letter, keep the following goals in mind:

- *Clarify your purpose* Every cover letter should focus on a specific job. Avoid sounding as if you have written a form letter that you send with every résumé. Be specific; you want the reader to realize that you are the best person for that job.

- *Know your audience* Who will read the letter? Many times, someone in the personnel office will look over incoming cover letters and select some to send to the manager. You want your letter and résumé to get into the hands of the person who makes the hiring decisions. Get the name of that person, if you can. Ask someone who works at the business for the right name. If the company is large enough, look it up in a directory at the public library or on the Internet.

- *Include the language of the ad in your letter* The ad in **FIGURE 2-3** on page 28 mentions several skills. It isn't cheating or copying to use the same words in your résumé and cover letter. In fact, this effort shows that you notice details and that your skills or training are a perfect fit with the job. If you do not have the skills yet, show how your life experiences have prepared you to succeed in the kind of job described in the ad.

- *Do not repeat your résumé* The cover letter should have about four paragraphs. The first says that you are applying for a specific job. The second summarizes only the highlights of your résumé: the skills that fit the needs stated in the ad. The third briefly describes your work habits. Use such terms as *reliable, cooperative, eager,* and *skilled in taking direction.* The fourth and final paragraph says that your résumé is enclosed and that you hope to hear from the business soon for an interview.

EDIT AND PROOFREAD

Make sure your cover letter looks like a business letter. Check that your letter contains the name of a specific job that interests you. It should also contain the reasons that you are the right person for the job and a request for an interview.

Put the letter aside for a while—maybe an hour or two. Then, read the letter again very slowly. Proofread by paying attention to each sentence. Use a dictionary to find the correct spelling of any words that you think might be misspelled.

If you work on a word processor, use a spell checker. Just remember that a spell checker does not catch words that are spelled correctly but used incorrectly. For example, you might write, "Their are two jobs that have given me experience in this field." You really mean to write, "*There* are two jobs that have given me experience in this field." The spell checker will not catch the difference in how *their* and *there* are used.

As you proofread, make sure all of your sentences are complete. Check for correct punctuation marks. Omit any slang words that you have used. Your cover letter should represent your best writing.

For a final edit, ask a family member or friend to read the letter. Someone else may be able to find errors that you overlooked.

WRITING IN THE REAL WORLD: COVER LETTER

7576 Mission Court
Cape May, NJ 08204

December 2, 2000

Mrs. Emily Mills
A Clock on Every Wall, Inc.
17513 Springer Avenue
Wildwood, NJ 08260

Dear Mrs. Mills:

The First Paragraph
Tell which job you are applying for.

I am writing to apply for the customer-service position that A Clock on Every Wall advertised in the *Shore Express* on November 30.

The Second Paragraph
State that you have the skills needed for the job.

My talents and abilities are well-suited to a growing company such as yours. I use the latest versions of Microsoft Word and several accounting and spreadsheet programs. My courses at Rich East High School prepared me well for this kind of position. As you can see from my résumé, I took several cooperative education classes, including Office Practices II, in which I learned sales and marketing techniques.

The Third Paragraph
Describe your work habits.

As a worker, Mrs. Mills, you will find me to be a good team member. I am punctual and cooperative, and I handle responsibility well. I'm happy to say that one of my references was my supervisor at my first after-school job, who was pleased with my hard work and dependability.

Enclosed is my résumé, which provides more detail about my background as a worker. I hope to hear from you soon about when I may come in for an interview. My phone number is (609) 555-4675.

The Fourth Paragraph
Mention that you are including your résumé and your phone number.

Sincerely,

Eljay Searles

Eljay Searles

FIGURE 2-4 This cover letter was used to apply for the job advertised in FIGURE 2-3 on page 28.
What does this cover letter tell Mrs. Mills about Eljay Searles?

Save the letter. When you save it on the computer, you may be able to reuse paragraphs or parts of paragraphs in future letters.

If the business asks you to fax your résumé, use the cover letter as your fax cover letter. Include your name and phone number, as well as the receiver's phone number and the total numbers of pages sent, just in case the fax has to be sent again.

FIGURE 2-4 on page 30 shows a cover letter that was written in response to the ad on page 28.

Lesson Review

CHECK YOUR UNDERSTANDING

1. CONTRASTING Name three ways that a cover letter is different from a résumé.

2. DRAWING CONCLUSIONS Suppose your cover letter includes skills described in the ad and you follow the ad's instructions for applying. Identify three conclusions an employer can draw about you.

APPLY WHAT YOU LEARN

Work with a group to look through your local newspaper. Each member of the group should find an ad for a job that interests him or her. Copy the ad exactly.

Next, make three columns. Label the first column "Job Skills," the second column "Personal Traits or Work Habits," and the third column "Special Requirements." Read each ad, and fill in the columns for each one.

Grammar Workshop

Using Action Verbs in Cover Letters and Résumés

Your cover letters and résumé should present a positive picture of who you are and what you have done. One way to do this is to use strong action verbs.

Here is a list of verbs you can use:

accomplish	conduct	increase	propose
achieve	contribute	initiate	reorganize
adapt	create	instruct	research
analyze	direct	lead	set up
communicate	establish	organize	supervise
compile	implement	participate	support
complete	improve	perform	train
	invent	present	

You can change the form of any of these verbs. If you are writing about your past work experiences, use verbs in the past tense. In most cases, you add -ed to the verb. To show your present work experience, you may add -ing to the end of a word.

Examples   achieve→achieved→achieving
contribute→contributed→contributing

Application

On a separate sheet of paper, rewrite the following statements. Replace the underlined words with action verbs.

1. In my last job, I <u>was the leader of</u> a team of ten employees.
2. I <u>made</u> company profits bigger.
3. I <u>found</u> ten new uses for products we already sold.
4. I <u>gave training to</u> new sales representatives.
5. I <u>put together</u> a report about our department to the president.
6. I <u>did</u> the opening of a new department.
7. I <u>began</u> a new training program for associates.
8. I <u>was the supervisor of</u> six employees.
9. I <u>told</u> about major changes at a meeting of the whole company.
10. I <u>came up with</u> a new idea that saved my department money.

For more information, **SEE PAGE 351.**

Preparing for the Job Interview

What Do You Already Know?

Have you ever been interviewed for a job? If so, what questions were you asked? If you were to interview someone for a job, what questions might you ask?

Think About It How would you prepare yourself for a job interview?

Your hard work as a job-hunter—completing applications, writing cover letters and résumés—will get you interviews. The purpose of an interview is for an employer to meet you in person. The interviewer will ask you questions to see whether you will meet the company's needs. Preparing for the interview will take some work on your part.

TYPES OF INTERVIEWS

Although the general purpose of interviews is to allow an employer to meet you, there are two different kinds of interviews that you will probably encounter.

Screening interviews reduce the size of a group of job candidates. The interviewer will eliminate unsuitable applicants and decide which applicants should be considered more seriously. Large companies sometimes use professional recruiters to conduct screening interviews.

Employment agencies also screen job-hunters. This helps the agencies to decide whether the job-hunter is qualified for the position. Applicants who are selected after the screening interview are offered a selection interview.

Selection interviews are more personal than screening interviews. In a selection interview, job applicants usually meet the person who does the hiring. If you interview with a supervisor, it is a good sign that you are a finalist in the selection process. If you are called back for a second interview, be flattered—you are high on the list of choices.

PREPARE FOR AN INTERVIEW

Job-seekers use the interview to convince employers to hire them. They also use the interview to decide whether the job is right for them. Some people find job interviews difficult. Others know that interviewing is a skill that can be learned. Preparing for the interview is an important part of learning that skill.

Gather an Interview Packet

The first step in being ready for the interview is to gather some items for an "interview packet" to take with you. You should have

- your high school diploma or General Equivalency Diploma (GED).

- your Social Security card.

- a valid driver's license, if one is required for the job.

- proof of your legal right to work in the United States. Non-citizens must have a valid green card, as it is called. Citizens may need to show proof of birth (a birth certificate or U.S. passport) or naturalization papers.

- the names, addresses, and phone numbers of three people (your references) who can speak favorably about your work skills. References can be teachers or former supervisors. They should not be relatives. Ask references for permission before you supply their names.

- a summary of your work history, which should be described on your résumé.

Find Out More About the Company

A basic mistake many job-hunters make is that they are unfamiliar with the business or industry they are hoping will hire them. Interviewers are not pleased when applicants ask, "What kind of work do you do here?"

Do some research. Find out about the company's products, services, and even its history in the community. Ask for help from your local public librarian in locating current information. Two other sources of information about a company are the Internet, as shown in **FIGURE 2-5**, and the company's ads in the local newspaper. Ask family, friends, and employees, too—they might be able to supply you with interesting background information. Your research will show the interviewer that you are a good candidate for the job.

Source: www.pearson.com

FIGURE 2-5 Shown here is a company's Web page. **What can you learn about a company through the Internet?**

Rehearse Your Answers to Questions

One of the keys to a successful interview is to have answers to routine questions prepared in advance. Most job-seekers should be prepared to answer the following questions:

- ✓ "Tell me a bit about yourself."

- ✓ "Why are you interested in working here?"

- ✓ "Would you be available to work regular hours, and maybe even overtime, if necessary?"

- ✓ "How well do you work under pressure?"

- ✓ "What two or three accomplishments have given you the most satisfaction? Why?"

Here are some tips for giving good responses to interviewer's questions:

- *Give details.* If asked, "How well do you work under pressure?" be prepared with some examples. If you plan to share some important work-related experiences, rehearse how you will describe them so that they are clear.

- *Keep your answers positive.* Express optimism about the future. Employers look for enthusiasm and a positive outlook. Most of all, do not say negative things about former supervisors, teachers, or friends. Emphasize your good points and your good relationships with others.

- *Think how you can turn negative experiences into positive ones.* You might be asked, "Explain a mistake you made at work. What did you do about it?" Focus on how you learned from the experience and how it caused you to become a better employee. For example, you might say, "I was selling tickets at a movie theater. We ran out of tickets before the last show, but I got some pieces of paper and made emergency tickets. That taught me to check the supply of tickets every day." An experience like this shows how you handle mistakes. In this case, it shows how you solved a problem and learned from it.

- *Plan an answer to this question, "Why should we hire you?"* This question is often asked by interviewers, and some applicants are not prepared. They realize that they should sell themselves in a résumé and cover letter, but words fail them when they must talk about themselves in person. Rehearse a short speech. Prepare three or four positive points about yourself such as, "I'm a good team player who will follow through with my share of the work. I ask questions when I don't understand something, so that I do things correctly. Finally, I keep the company's interests in mind while I'm working. I like to think of myself as a representative of my company."

Select Your Interview Wardrobe

First impressions are important. The clothes you wear to an interview should be neat, cared-for, and appropriate. Even if an interview is scheduled to take place in a noisy factory, you want to communicate by your appearance that "I take work seriously, and this is an opportunity for me." A suit or a blazer is appropriate for men and women. Even if the interviewer tells you to dress casually, show that you know the difference between work and relaxation. Jogging suits, baseball caps, sweatshirts, and exercise clothes suggest "play" not "work." They should not be worn on an interview.

PREPARE YOUR OWN QUESTIONS

The interview is also the time to ask questions of your own. Here are some questions you might want to ask:

- What kind of projects or duties will I have?

- What opportunities might the future hold?

- When will you be deciding whom to hire?

- When do you want the person you hire to start?

Quite often, the employer will answer these questions during the interview before you ask them. Be prepared, just in case. It is a good idea to have at least four questions in mind.

Lesson Review

CHECK YOUR UNDERSTANDING

1. IDENTIFYING List three things you should do to prepare for an interview.

2. SYNTHESIZING Summarize your best qualities in response to the question, "Why should we hire you?"

APPLY WHAT YOU LEARN

Role play an interview with a partner. The applicant should be ready to answer the questions in "Rehearse Your Answers to Questions" on page 34. Present your role-play to the class, and ask others to evaluate it.

Evaluating Your Interview Performance

What Do You Already Know?

How have you felt after competing in a sports event or giving a speech in class? How does evaluating your performance help you do better the next time?

Think About It How might you evaluate how well you did in a job interview?

When you are ready to get a job, you should go on as many interviews as you can. Each time you interview, you get more practice. The more interviews you have, the better you will become at evaluating how well you present yourself. Your goal for your first interview might be just to get through it. After several interviews, however, you will be able to evaluate how you appeared and what you can do the next time to improve.

DOING YOUR BEST

Suppose you have gone on the interview. You practiced what to say, and you arrived early. When the interviewer greeted you, you shook the person's hand warmly. During the interview, you let your positive attitude shine through. At the end of the interview, you shook the interviewer's hand again. You said "Thank you," and then you asked when you might hear about the job. Now, you can evaluate our performance.

INTERVIEW CHECKLIST

A simple way to evaluate yourself at the conclusion of an interview is to think in terms of *before, during,* and *after* the interview.

Before the Interview

✔ I researched the company.

✔ I planned the route to the appointment, the distance, and about how much time it would take to arrive.

✔ I arrived on time.

✔ I had the necessary information—my cover letter, résumé, and important documents.

During the Interview

✔ I shook hands firmly and waited to be asked to be seated. Once I was seated, I made steady, friendly eye contact with the interviewer.

✔ I spoke clearly and answered the questions I was asked.

✔ I politely declined to answer questions that were not appropriate or legal: my age, ethnic group, religion, marital status, health, physical appearance, or personal habits.

✔ I prepared questions for when the interviewer asked, "Do you have any questions?"

After the Interview

✔ I sent a follow-up letter, as shown in **FIGURE 2-6** on page 37.

✔ I evaluated my presentation right after the interview.

✔ I made notes in my job log about things I want to improve.

Writing in the Real World: Follow-up Letter

7576 Mission Court
Cape May, NJ 08204

December 20, 2000

Mrs. Emily Mills
A Clock on Every Wall, Inc.
17513 Springer Avenue
Wildwood, NJ 08260

Dear Mrs. Mills:

Thank the interviewer.

Thank you for considering me for the customer-service position in your company. I really enjoyed learning from you what the job requires.

The product line that A Clock on Every Wall sells is a sure winner. Once customers see the clocks, I know they'll buy more than one. The clocks are great holiday gifts. I would be proud to help the company grow.

Remind the interviewer of the skills and talents you bring to the job.

As I told you when we met, I take pride in my ability to straighten out problems and leave people satisfied. I am confident that my conflict-resolution skills, which I learned while serving on the student council at Rich East High School, will make me an excellent customer-service representative.

I am eager to work for A Clock on Every Wall. Let's discuss how we can make this happen. My phone number is (609) 555-4675.

Ask for the job.

Sincerely,

Eljay Searles

Eljay Searles

FIGURE 2-6 A follow-up letter says, "Thank you for giving me an interview." It should also restate your interest in the job and sum up the skills you would bring as a worker. **How might a follow-up letter increase your chance of getting a job?**

NOT GETTING THE JOB

Once the interview is over, you must be prepared to get the job—or to not get it. Being prepared to get the job is easy. You thank the employer. You find out when and where to start working. Then, you hang up the phone and celebrate.

What do you do if you do not get the job? The most important thing is to learn from the experience. Think about what skills you could develop to become a stronger candidate. You might send a note to the employer when you are not feeling sad or angry. Politely ask what you could have done differently to get the job. Again, thank the employer, and ask him or her to keep you in mind for future openings. Use any information you get to prepare yourself for the next interview.

Lesson Review

CHECK YOUR UNDERSTANDING

1. ANALYZING Why should you evaluate your performance at a job interview?

2. IDENTIFYING What is the purpose of a "follow-up letter"?

APPLY WHAT YOU LEARN

With three or four other students, visit an employment agency or the human resources department of a company to find out more information about how job interviews are conducted. Your purpose is to ask the people who do interviews, "How can an interviewee make a good impression?" Take notes that you can share with the class.

TECH CONNECTION   INTERNET JOB SEARCH

You can use the Internet to search for jobs. You can access job banks, research companies, and even submit your résumé through the Internet. On some employer Web sites, you can fill out an application form to apply for a job. Then, you follow directions to send it electronically to the employer. On other Web sites, you send an e-mail message with your résumé attached as a file. Then, employers can access, print, and read your résumé.

RESOURCE	WHAT IT IS
listserv	A discussion group that uses an Internet system to exchange messages. Users subscribe to a listserv by adding their name to a list. Each time someone sends a message to the group, everyone on the list receives the message. Some job-hunters subscribe to a listserv about careers or job-hunting, itself.
Newsgroup	An electronic bulletin board for viewing posted messages about a specific topic. Two popular job newsgroups are misc.jobs.resumes (submit a résumé to a bank where they can be searched) and misc.jobs.offered.entry (entry-level job openings). You use a keyword search to sort through messages.
World Wide Web	A system that helps users browse the Internet by moving them from one site or document to the next with a click of the mouse. Some important career resources on the World Wide Web include Monster.com (www.monster.com) for general job-seeking information; Career Magazine (www.careermag.com); and Hoover's Online (www.hoovers.com) for researching companies.

Application

Access the Internet at home, at school, or in the library. Choose one of the following Web sites, and evaluate it. On a separate sheet of paper, write the name of the Web site, and answer these questions.

1. Is the site easy to use?

2. Is the information useful to entry-level job-hunters? Why or why not?

3. How many current jobs are offered? List three that you found.

CareerMagazine	www.careermag.com
CareerMosaic	www.careermosaic.com
CareerPark Job Categories	www.careerpark.com/jobs/index.html
Employment Guide's Career Web	www.cweb.com
Hoover's Online	www.hoovers.com
JobWeb	www.jobweb.org
Monster.com	www.monster.com

REVIEW

Chapter Summary

To be a successful job-hunter, you need to know where to look for a job. You need the right resources. Want ads, employment agencies, networking, and the Internet will help you find a job. A strong résumé and a well-written cover letter will help you get interviews. Next, you have to prepare for the interviews and present yourself as a capable person who is ready to work. Afterward, you should evaluate the quality of your presentation and improve how you can make yourself look like a strong candidate for the job.

Key Words

hospitality
health care
retail sales
position
flexible

diplomatic
references
cover letter
customize

On a sheet of paper, copy the following statements. Use a word from the list to complete each sentence.

1. My résumé will ____ me as a person with good problem-solving skills.

2. Because I can shift from filing to word processing, I am a ____ worker.

3. I plan to be a physical therapist in the ____ field.

4. I do not send the same résumé to every employer. I ____ it so that it fits the job description in the ad.

5. I wonder if I should consider a job in the ____ field, working in a hotel, for instance.

6. People who work in ____ must be able to deal with customers.

7. I am even-tempered and very ____. I find it easy to resolve conflicts.

8. I listed three people as ____ who will tell how good a worker I am.

9. In my ____, I remind my interviewer that I really want the job.

Application: Prepare for an Interview

Read the following questions and answers that might occur during an interview. For each interviewer's question, write the answer you would give as an interviewee. For each interviewee's response, write the reaction you might have as an interviewer. Write your answers on a separate sheet of paper.

Interviewer Questions

1. Why did you leave your last job?

2. What would you like to know about our company?

Interviewee Answers

3. How have I dealt with an angry customer? Well, I cashed a check for a man. He came back into the bank and complained that I had not given him the right amount of money. I told him that he was probably a thief and that he should go away.

4. What does this job offer me? I'd like to make enough money to buy a new car and a closetful of clothes.

5. How much vacation does this place give the workers? In my last job, we received only two weeks. That was not enough for me.

Job 1

ANIMAL PRO WANTED, F/T
Permanent only. Duties: Bathing,
Feeding, and Cleaning of Dogs
and Cats. Customer Service/
Filing/Answering Phones.
Customer Relations and Sales.
At least one year experience in
similar position required. Great
Salary. Call David 555-1234.

Job 2

BUSINESS DEVELOPMENT
CENTER The Your Town New
Car Showroom seeks qualified
individuals to staff its business
development center. Applicants
must possess excellent telephone skills, customer-service
orientation, basic knowledge
of computers, and have persuasive communications skills.
No previous automotive experience necessary. We offer
one of the best benefits
packages in the industry, a
clean work environment, and
day/evening work schedules.
NO CALLS. FAX résumé and
cover letter to 555-6631.

Job 3

DRIVERS Busy downtown garage.
Position requires solid customer-service
and communications skills, a clean
driving record, the ability to drive a
stick shift and work flexible hours, and
a HS diploma or equivalent. Will train.
If you have these qualities, call toll-free
anytime to arrange an interview: 1-800-
555-5555.

Application: Analyze Job Ads

Read the want ads above. Then, on a separate sheet of paper, copy and answer the following questions about one of the ads.

1. What is the job?

2. What is the training needed for the job?

3. What are four questions you might be asked in an interview?

Grammar Workshop Practice

On a separate sheet of paper, rewrite the qualifications and experience sections from these résumés. When you rewrite, use action verbs.

1. Qualifications

Good on the computer. Know word-processing and spreadsheet programs. Like to troubleshoot software problems. Know MAC and PC. Like organizing things.

2. Experience

Answered telephones. Did general office chores. Handled customer problems and complaints. Kept things going when the boss was out.

3. Experience

Fixed the company's messed up parts-order records. Put all the instruction manuals and parts catalogs back on their proper shelves. Got labels, and put them on the storage shelves. They let me rearrange stuff on the shelves, too.

Portfolio Project — Writing a Cover Letter

Write a cover letter that you could send with a résumé to apply for a job. Your purpose is to get called for an interview. To do this:

- Think about how you want to represent your-self in your cover letter and in your résumé,

- List the important job skills that you offer, your work habits, and special qualifications that would interest an employer.

- Evaluate your draft for tone: Do you sound like you are interested in the job and that you have a cooperative, professional attitude?

- Ask another student or family member to read your cover letter and to suggest changes, if needed.

Add your completed cover letter to your portfolio.

BEING COMPETENT IN THE WORKPLACE

Oversize Copies

Roger was hired at a printing plant right after he graduated from high school. It is now five years later, and he has learned to use the most up-to-date, high-speed machines.

Roger was sure he was doing a good job until Ms. Bendix, his supervisor, warned him that he was costing the company money. Ms. Bendix said that Roger was spending too much time on some jobs and not enough time on others. Roger has learned a lot about the printing business. He wonders whether he should try to keep his job or make a plan to start his own printing business.

Key Words

company culture

alternatives

criteria

proactive

probation

prioritize

productivity

entrepreneurs

franchise

Goals for Success

In this chapter, you will learn these skills:

Becoming a valuable member of a team

 PARTICIPATING AS A MEMBER OF A TEAM/LISTENING

Making effective decisions

 DECISION MAKING

Resolving conflicts between yourself and other employees or customers

 NEGOTIATING/SOCIABILITY

Organizing your work efficiently

 ORGANIZING AND MAINTAINING INFORMATION

Using a spreadsheet to create a business expense report

 USING COMPUTERS TO PROCESS INFORMATION

PORTFOLIO PROJECT

BUSINESS PLAN

By the time you complete this chapter, you will know what Roger has to do to write a business plan. You also will be able to write a business plan of your own to add to your portfolio.

LESSON 3-1

Teamwork

What Do You Already Know?

When have you worked on a team? What was your responsibility?

Think About It   Why do large companies often organize workers into teams?

What does teamwork mean to you? Teamwork is usually identified with sports. On a sports team, the members rely on each other as they work together toward a common goal. Some may plan while others carry out those plans. Workplace teams operate in this way also. Every member of the team has a responsibility to the others.

TEAMS AND TEAMWORK

Teamwork is a cooperative effort by a group of people acting together for a common cause. A team is a group of people who pool their experience, skills, and knowledge to work on a common task.

When you enter the workplace, you become an important member of a team. As a part of the team, you help others and others depend on you. Members of a team are selected because of their skills and abilities, and they are expected to use their talents to help the team reach its goal.

TEAMWORK ON THE JOB

On the job, teamwork plays an important role. It takes teamwork to decorate a department store window or to plan a new sales campaign.

In order for a team to work effectively, the following things must happen:

- Every team member must know what needs to be done.

- Every team member must have a task.

- Team members must have the skills and ability to do the job.

- Team members must solve problems that might make it difficult for them to do their job.

- Team members must be willing to work together to get the job done.

Today, companies rely more and more on teams to get work done. Businesses realize that teamwork is good for the company as well as the employees. Individuals are able to accomplish much more when they work together as a team. The more work a team can complete, the more productive the company can be.

Benefits of Teamwork

As an important part of a company, workers benefit from teamwork, too. First, individuals are given the opportunity to try new things and develop their skills. Second, team members' self-esteem improves. Because they are given a task that they are responsible for, team members realize that they are making an important contribution to the team, the project, and the company. Third, teamwork helps employees improve their communication skills. These skills, in turn, help team members work more efficiently.

Teamwork Skills

In order to achieve their common goal, team members must share important information with one another. Teamwork involves several communication skills—listening, questioning, respecting, helping, sharing, persuading, and participating, as you can see in FIGURE 3-1 below. When you are part of a team, do you listen to instructions? Do you ask questions? Do you defend your ideas? Are you respectful of all your fellow team members? Each one of these skills is an important part of teamwork and helps the team achieve its goal.

Keep in mind that when you are on a team project, none of these skills happens automatically. You have to think about how to use them on each task. It is always tempting to let others do the work. However, if you do, the team will not work well together, and the task will be harder to complete.

Cooperate With Others

Cooperation is a challenge for teams because teams are composed of individual workers, each with his or her own personality and way of working. No one member thinks, acts, or works exactly the same way as another. If everyone did, there would be no disagreements. Although that may sound good, it is important to remember that some of the best solutions to problems are the result of disagreements. When an idea is discussed and questioned, a better idea is often created. That is why teams made up of different personalities are important in the workplace.

You can learn about how to succeed in the workplace by observing the strengths of different personality types. Do not overlook how other workers accomplish tasks, even though their approach is not the same as yours. Instead, learn to recognize the strengths of different personality types, as shown in FIGURE 3-2 on page 46. As a team member, your ability to cooperate with others will increase your team's chances of successfully completing its assigned tasks.

COMPANY CULTURE

Companies tend to reward employees who possess certain personal qualities. Usually, the ones rewarded are those who fit in well with what is known as the **company culture**. Every company, even the smallest one, has a culture; this culture is a mixture of the company's social and work practices. Smart workers watch to see which strengths the company values, and they learn to practice these qualities themselves.

When you start a job, watch for the kind of behavior the company culture rewards. Sometimes, your boss will give you clear-cut directions about it. For example, suppose you are a receptionist. Your supervisor tells you that you should pick up the phone by the second ring. This is the kind of promptness the company expects. It is part of the company culture. A receptionist who answers the phone promptly will be rewarded; one who does not will be criticized.

TEAMWORK SUCCESS

Teamwork is successful when individuals work together to achieve a shared goal. It does not matter

ESSENTIAL TEAMWORK SKILLS

Listening	Paying attention to each other's ideas and building on them
Questioning	Asking about any step of a task that is not clear
Respecting	Being considerate of other people's opinions
Helping	Offering assistance to one another
Sharing	Reporting important information to each team member
Persuading	Defending ideas and rethinking opinions as new information or evidence appears
Participating	Contributing to meet the goals of the project

FIGURE 3-1 Teamwork skills are actually communication skills. **How do you practice each of these skills at school or on the job?**

PERSONALITY TYPES

HOW WE INTERACT WITH OTHERS

Extroverts
Extroverts enjoy interacting with people. They
- enjoy action.
- talk and think out loud.
- need other people around.
- feel restless when they are alone.

Introverts
Introverts enjoy working alone. They
- prefer listening to talking.
- rarely speak up at meetings.
- need time alone.

HOW WE GET INFORMATION ABOUT THE WORLD

Literals
Literals are interested in budgets, numbers, and plans. They
- prefer details and specifics.
- prefer exact information to estimates.
- prefer facts to interpretations.

Intuitives
Intuitives get excited by unusual ideas. They
- dislike considering too many details and specifics.
- think that guessing is creative.
- look at the big picture for ideas.

HOW WE MAKE DECISIONS

Thinkers
Thinkers focus on goals and how to reach them. They
- base their decisions on goals and values.
- are not guided by making people happy.
- decide according to what is right.

Feelers
Feelers place people above goals. They
- base decisions on creating harmony.
- avoid conflict and try to see others' points of view.
- worry about how decisions affect people.

HOW WE MANAGE OURSELVES

Judgers
Judgers prefer to make careful plans. They
- prefer structure and order.

Perceivers
Perceivers think plans get in the way. They
- are creative, spontaneous, and responsive.

FIGURE 3-2 This chart shows how people's personalities can affect their work. **How can understanding differences in personalities help people work on a team?**

if the team is made up of two people or 20 people. Being a team player in any company is a key element in achieving workplace success. As a team player, you should make the team's goal your top priority. Being aware of your common goal and making yourself a valuable resource for the team will be helpful for everyone. Remember to make contributions and to express your ideas. Even though your idea may not be the final answer, it can help the team come to a winning conclusion. When everyone on a team is committed to being a valuable team member, working toward a goal can be fun.

Lesson Review

CHECK YOUR UNDERSTANDING

1. SYNTHESIZING How can a person learn about a company's culture?

2. ANALYZING How can teamwork benefit everyone on the team?

APPLY WHAT YOU LEARN

With a group of three or four students, invent a company that you will run. What product or service will you provide? What kinds of workers will you need to hire? List and explain five rules for teamwork that will help your workers get their jobs done.

Making Decisions

Making decisions is a major part of working. You will make some decisions on your own. Other decisions will be made by someone with authority over you. Sometimes, you will be part of a team that makes a group decision. Workers who regularly make good decisions are respected in the workplace. The process of making decisions is a skill that can be learned. Practice that process and you, too, will be counted among the good decision-makers in the workplace.

What Do You Already Know?

When have you had to make an important decision? How did you finally reach your decision?

Think About It Does having many choices make decisions harder or easier to make? Why?

DECISION-MAKING STYLES

Many people think that everyone makes decisions the way they do. For example, if you prefer to have long discussions before making a decision, you might think other people prefer that style, too. However, there are people who get impatient with long discussions. They complain that these discussions are simply a way of avoiding the hard work of making a decision. In general, there are two kinds of decision makers.

Information-driven Decision Makers

These people want to collect as much information as they can before they decide about something. There is an obvious advantage in this method. By making yourself as informed as possible, you decrease the chance of making a serious mistake. But there also is a disadvantage: You can become more devoted to researching the choices than to actually reaching a decision.

Action-driven Decision Makers

These people trust their instincts and prefer to reach decisions quickly. They believe in the power of action and have faith that things will turn out right. The advantage of this style is that it can provide faster and sometimes more creative decisions.

The disadvantage is that when the decision is wrong, others complain that their ideas were not considered. The decision can be criticized because it was not based on enough research or concrete information.

Is there a foolproof way to reach the right decision? Not really. Yet, there is a link between how you make a decision and the quality of the decision you make. In general, good decision-making combines information and action.

MAKING EFFECTIVE DECISIONS

Suppose you work in a growing company. This company is considering buying new computers. Your boss knows that when you were in high school, you served on a committee that chose new classroom computers. Your supervisor asks you to be a member of the company's committee to help with the same kind of purchase. The following is a list of the steps that you and your fellow committee members could follow to make this important decision:

Step 1: Have a Clear Goal
When you prepare to make a decision, you should be clear on the goal. Having a goal will help you focus on the discussion.

Step 2: Explore Alternatives
Once you have a goal, explore what **alternatives**, or other choices, you have. By doing some research, you will discover that you have additional choices.

Step 3: Narrow Your Choices
If there are too many alternatives, you may want to establish **criteria**, or guidelines, to narrow your choices.

Step 4: Consider the Consequences
One at a time, consider what might happen if you chose each of your alternatives.

Step 5: Make a Proposal and a Plan
The final step in decision making is making a proposal that has a plan of action.

A proposal with a plan has three parts:

- A recommendation of what to do.

- An explanation of why the recommendation is being made.

- A plan of action, so supervisors can act on what you recommend.

USING THE PROCESS

How would you use the decision-making process to select computers for your company?

Step 1: The goal is to buy new computers for the office.

Step 2: You can lease computers or buy new, or you can buy reconditioned computers. Other choices concern monitor sizes, disk drives, memory sizes, and many other hardware and software alternatives.

Step 3: The committee may want to set criteria about price, availability, and service guarantees. This will help you narrow your choices.

Step 4: You might imagine a result such as this one: "If we buy the cheaper, less powerful computers, they might run out of memory sooner."

Step 5: The committee might write this proposal and action plan:

> We recommend buying eight new midrange personal computers and a color printer. This will give us enough computers for all of our current staff as well as for three new hires. These machines will be compatible with the operating system we now use. They also come bundled with newer versions of the software we use most. Computer King in town has given us the best price. Delivery of the new machines can begin next week. We ask for the approval to place the order.

The five-step decision-making process can help you make many decisions on the job, especially when the members of your team make decisions in different ways.

Lesson Review

CHECK YOUR UNDERSTANDING

1. EVALUATING Why is it important to follow a process when making a decision?

2. ANALYZING Remove one of the five steps from the process of making a decision. Explain how the quality of the decision would be affected.

APPLY WHAT YOU LEARN

Find a picture of an item you would like to buy. Find a picture of another item that is very similar to it. Write an explanation of how you would use each of the five steps to make a decision about which one to buy. Post your explanation on a bulletin board.

Grammar Workshop

Writing Compound Sentences

It is good to put your thoughts in writing when working through the decision-making process. If all your writing consists of simple sentences, however, it will sound choppy. You can make your writing smoother by using compound sentences.

A compound sentence has two or more independent clauses. The clauses can be joined in two ways.

- Use a comma and a conjunction (*and*, *but*, *or*, *so*, *yet*) to link the two independent clauses.

    Examples   Ms. James wanted to buy the most expensive computers, **but** the computer team wanted to save money.

    The computer kept crashing, **yet** Maria did her best to finish inputting the letter.

    Kate worked on the plan, **and** John helped her.

- Use a semicolon or a semicolon and another word (*also*, *however*, *therefore*) to link the two independent clauses.

    Examples   Kate worked on the plan; John helped her.

    Imelda liked her new desk; **however**, she did not like its location.

    Ben waits tables at the diner; **also**, he takes computer courses at night.

Application

Copy the following pairs of independent clauses on another sheet of paper. Connect them to make compound sentences.

1. Ray interviewed at a restaurant. He wanted a job as a waiter.
2. We waited outside the employees' entrance. No one unlocked the door.
3. Tony gave a speech. Everyone listened carefully.
4. Claire followed the schedule. Her work was late.
5. We were on a team. The team shared in the profits.
6. The economy is booming. There are many jobs.
7. The company hired temporary workers. Many accepted full-time jobs.
8. He is a skilled machinist. He has had job offers.
9. Raul had two weeks' vacation time. He visited Hawaii.
10. The hammer was defective. The top flew off.

For more information, **SEE PAGE 346.**

Resolving Conflicts on the Job

What Do You Already Know?

When have you had an argument with someone? What caused it? How did the argument end?

Think About It   Should you always try to avoid conflicts?

Conflicts between people are part of everyday life. Even people who are close to each other will disagree from time to time. Conflicts cannot always be avoided. The workplace brings together people with different personalities and styles of work. When you add the pressure of deadlines, the need to make decisions, and a few differences in opinion, the result may be conflict.

CONFLICTS IN THE WORKPLACE

Conflicts happen occasionally in the workplace. Sometimes, they occur because people believe their ideas are best. Conflicts that raise important questions, or help bring about better decisions, are worthwhile.

Conflicts are bad for business if they

- keep people from getting their jobs done.

- cause long-lasting bad feelings between people.

- result in missed deadlines.

- cause people to get sick and have to take time off from work.

On the job or in school, it is important to resolve conflicts and make them work in a positive way.

CONFLICTS WITH CUSTOMERS

A type of conflict that businesses do not encourage is between workers and customers. Conflicts with customers threaten the life of a business. If customers feel mistreated, they can spend their money elsewhere. Thus, a worker who knows how to resolve conflicts with customers is a valuable employee. Having this skill increases a worker's competence in the eyes of co-workers and supervisors.

Representing the Company

As a worker dealing with the public, the first and most important thing to keep in mind is that you represent the company. The way you explain the company's policy about refunds—or how much assistance you offer in finding an item—is evidence of how the company treats the public. Your courtesy and helpfulness makes customers feel welcome; lack of concern, rudeness, or hostility drives them away. If there are no customers, then there is no business—and no jobs, either. As a representative of a company, you have a direct impact on the company's success.

Customers can be difficult to deal with, of course. It is natural to sometimes feel that you want to fight back and have your say. The key to handling conflicts with customers, is to stay in control of the situation.

Resolving Conflicts with Customers

Suppose you work behind the counter at a busy home improvement store. An annoyed customer comes up to the register and loudly demands, "What happened to all the purple plastic buckets that were on sale? Why do you only have orange ones left?"

Respond to the problem while keeping the points in mind on this checklist:

- ✔ Keep the customer's goodwill. Remember that your job is to give correct information, assist the customer, and make a sale, if possible.

- ✔ If you are angry, do not show it. Do not take this problem personally. It is not about you—it is about finding a solution to a problem.

- ✔ Stay in control of the situation. Show that you want to help. Then, agree with the person if you can. "You're right— we should have had more of the purple buckets in stock."

- ✔ Offer to make any reasonable offer the company will allow. "Hang on to the orange bucket," you might say. "Bring it back, and we'll exchange it for a purple one. Keep your receipt, though."

If necessary, refer the person to your supervisor. At least the customer will see that you are taking the problem seriously.

CONFLICTS WITH CO-WORKERS

Conflicts between co-workers are different from conflicts with customers. Co-workers tend to see themselves as equals, whereas customers enjoy special privileges and treatment. However, conflicts between co-workers can create an unpleasant atmosphere. Teamwork suffers when workers do not get along. Usually, the problems of an unhappy staff carry over into how customers are treated, resulting in a loss of business.

Resolving Conflicts with Co-Workers

Imagine that it is closing time at the computer repair department in which you work. Your supervisor wants to know why you did not put the spreadsheet software back into the locked file. Actually, you were not the last person to use the program. You tell your supervisor so, and she agrees with you. Here is what you should do:

- ✔ Find a time to speak to the co-worker in private. People respond better to personal conversations in private. A simple remark such as "Do you have a minute?" is all it takes to get the person's attention.

- ✔ Stick to the facts. Look at the situation, not the personalities of the people involved. Describe a problem without exaggerating it. For example, you could say, "Last night, the boss wanted to know why the software was not in the locked file. I said I wasn't the last person to use it."

- ✔ Make "I" statements. Talk about yourself only. You could say, "I didn't like it when it looked like I wasn't doing my job."

- ✔ End on a friendly note. Try to maintain a good relationship with the co-worker. Try to be constructive. You could say, "OK, thanks for listening. I just wanted you to know."

Using Compromise

One way to help end a conflict is through compromise. A compromise is a way to settle a conflict by having each side agree to give up something so that both people can get what they want. It may be a good idea to find someone who is not part of the conflict to listen to both sides. Let each person suggest a solution to the conflict; talk about the good points and the bad points of each suggestion. Try to put together a solution that uses everyone's suggestions.

CONFLICTS WITH SUPERVISORS

For entry-level employees and new employees, conflict with supervisors often involves job performance issues. If you find yourself in a conflict with a supervisor—not a personal one, but one that is job-related—use this checklist:

✓ Listen carefully to the supervisor's criticism. Try not to be defensive. Your supervisor is telling you that you need to change in order to keep your job. Ask for specifics. It is hard to know what to fix about your performance unless you have details. Ask questions about the right way and the wrong way to do things so you have clear ideas. Say, "Thank you," and promise to show improvement. Keep your promise.

✓ Take the lead. When you take the lead, you are **proactive**. If you know you are having serious problems, do not wait for the boss to call you in. Admit that you have a problem. Make an appointment to speak to your boss, and explain what is happening. Stick to the facts, and ask, "How can I do my job better?"

You might think that admitting to problems on the job is asking for trouble. Keep in mind that as a new worker, you are on **probation**, a trial period to see how you perform. Being proactive about problems actually works in your favor. You are showing you want to keep the job by asking how to do it better.

Discuss your job description during the meeting with your supervisor if you are still unsure about your responsibilities. Most companies have a written list of tasks for each job. Discuss what each task requires, if necessary. Then, ask your supervisor to **prioritize** the tasks for you—put them in order of importance. That way you are less likely to waste time on tasks your supervisor thinks are unimportant.

Work out an action plan with your supervisor. Discuss how you and your supervisor will both know whether you have met your goals. A good way is to set a time for a second meeting—maybe in a week or two—to discuss your progress. Be prepared to give examples during that meeting of how you are improving.

Accept the fact that there will be conflicts in the workplace. Some are minor and annoying; others are necessary; few need to have a negative impact on your job performance. As often as you can, seek to resolve conflicts. Learning to handle conflicts increases your competence in the workplace and your value as a worker.

Try to be proactive about job performance problems. **How might you begin a discussion with a supervisor about a problem?**

Lesson Review

CHECK YOUR UNDERSTANDING

1. IDENTIFYING How would you resolve a conflict with a co-worker? with a customer?

2. DRAWING CONCLUSIONS How might having a job description help you avoid or resolve a conflict?

APPLY WHAT YOU LEARN

Work with group members to role-play a conflict with a customer, a co-worker, or a supervisor. Start by creating a situation in which the worker feels unable to resolve a conflict. Observers should identify what is going wrong and how the conflict could be resolved.

Organizing Your Work

Keeping busy at work is not enough. You can spend too much time on some jobs and not enough time on others. Being busy is not as important as being organized. You cannot just do work as it comes up. You have to figure out which tasks are the most important and make sure those tasks get done first. When you do not manage your time and your tasks, you actually can waste time on the job. Planning and organizing can make your work flow smoothly.

What Do You Already Know?

What tasks at home or school do you need to organize? Explain why organizing them is worthwhile.

Think About It Why is being organized the key to getting things done efficiently?

THE NEED TO BE ORGANIZED

In some jobs, your time is organized for you. If you are a bank teller, you handle customers when they arrive at your window. When the bank closes, you balance your drawer, and you leave. In many other jobs, though, you have the chance to organize all or part of your day's work.

You can benefit from being organized in several ways:

- Organization gives you a sense of being in control of your work—instead of being controlled by it.

- Organization means you do not have to worry that you will not complete your tasks.

- Organization gives you control over your job performance. You can set goals, and you can show results. You do not have to make apologies or excuses because you demonstrate that you are a competent worker who is organized.

- Organization gives you confidence. If you know you are prepared, others will believe in your abilities, too.

BUSINESSES VALUE ORGANIZATION

Businesses value organization because it increases **productivity**, the amount of work that can be accomplished in a given time. In business, workers who are not organized are seen as people who cost the company money.

For example, many delivery services and utilities have standards for their truck drivers and meter readers. Drivers and readers must make an assigned number of stops every day. This is their quota, as it is called. Excuses are not acceptable. Workers are expected to manage their time so that they can meet their quota. Workers who do not meet their quota are first warned—and then fired.

MANAGING YOUR TIME

If you recognize the value of being organized and managing your time, then you can learn to work smarter, not harder. Working smarter means thinking of yourself as the manager of your work. Instead of starting something new before you finish a task, stop and plan. Organize your work so that you can use your time wisely. Many people record their tasks in a daily planner, as you can see in **FIGURE 3-3** on page 54. To manage their time, workers follow the five steps shown on page 55.

WRITING IN THE REAL WORLD: DAILY PLANNER

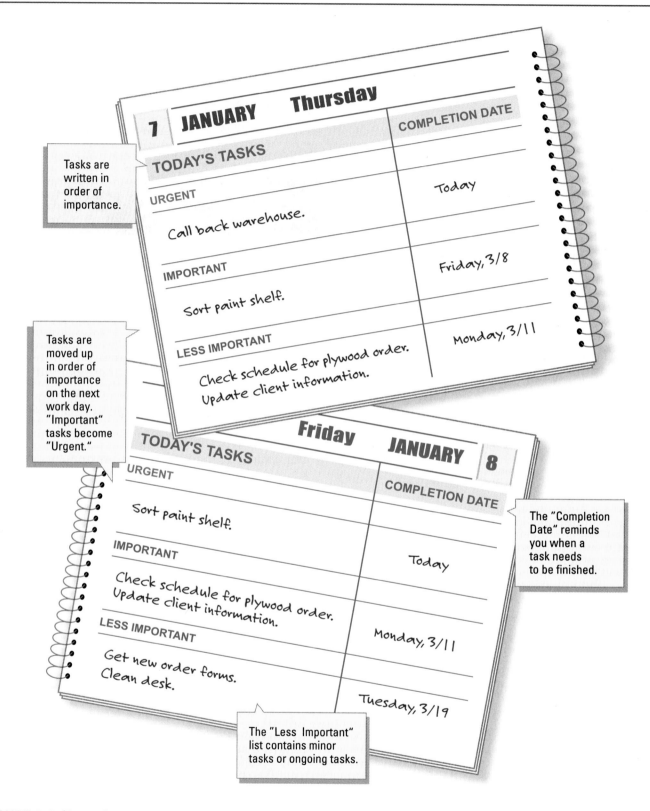

Tasks are written in order of importance.

7 JANUARY Thursday

COMPLETION DATE

TODAY'S TASKS

URGENT — Today

Call back warehouse.

IMPORTANT — Friday, 3/8

Sort paint shelf.

LESS IMPORTANT — Monday, 3/11

Check schedule for plywood order.
Update client information.

Tasks are moved up in order of importance on the next work day. "Important" tasks become "Urgent."

Friday JANUARY 8

TODAY'S TASKS

URGENT

Sort paint shelf.

IMPORTANT — Today

Check schedule for plywood order.
Update client information.

LESS IMPORTANT — Monday, 3/11

Get new order forms.
Clean desk.

Tuesday, 3/19

COMPLETION DATE

The "Completion Date" reminds you when a task needs to be finished.

The "Less Important" list contains minor tasks or ongoing tasks.

FIGURE 3-3 Shown here are two pages from a worker's daily planner. **How can using a daily planner help you organize your work?**

Organizing your tasks and your desk can make your work seem easier. **How do you organize the area in which you study or work?**

Step 1: Put things in their proper place.

At school, you know the confusion that results when you cannot find a piece of homework or a review sheet for a test. Being a worker involves paperwork, too—order forms, receipts, bills, and memos, for instance. Get your workstation straightened up. The immediate benefit is that you will feel more in control. The second benefit is that you will not waste time looking for items you need.

Step 2: Put things in order by importance.

When you put things in order, you prioritize. Each day, group tasks into three categories— "Urgent," "Important," "Less Important"— and do them in that order. The next day, re-evaluate the tasks. Move the "Important" tasks to the "Urgent" category, if needed. This way, you won't create a pile of "Less Important" jobs.

Step 3: Estimate.

Review the work you have to do, and estimate a reasonable amount of time it will take to complete it. Divide the work into parts. Set goals for when you want to finish each part.

Step 4: Do it now.

Often, the hardest part of managing time and tasks is making yourself do work that you do not enjoy. Once you get started, however, the job may not be as bad as you expected.

Step 5: Do minor tasks regularly.

Handle all the incoming bills on Mondays, for example. Order supplies on Tuesdays. Update client information on Wednesdays. Do tasks that are done less frequently on another day and rotate those tasks. Do desk-cleaning every other week, for instance. Following a routine ensures that everything gets attended to on schedule.

CHECK WITH YOUR SUPERVISOR

Once you get organized, make an appointment to see your supervisor and review your job performance. Be prepared with examples of how you are handling your work and meeting goals. If your organization is effective, you will see results right away, and you will be eager to share them with your supervisor.

Lesson Review

CHECK YOUR UNDERSTANDING

1. EXPLAINING Describe three ways to organize information.

2. ANALYZING Why is being organized important on the job?

APPLY WHAT YOU LEARN

List all the things you need to accomplish today and this week. Then, prioritize your list. Rank the tasks as "Urgent," "Important," "Less Important." Add a target date or time when you need to complete each task, too.

Being an Entrepreneur

When you begin to work, you may find your choices are limited to entry-level jobs. After all, you are still acquiring the experiences and skills that will translate into job opportunities that are more challenging and that pay better, too. Some workers decide not to work for other people. They decide to work for themselves instead.

What Do You Already Know?

Have you ever thought about building a business of your own? What product or service could you sell?

Think About It   What skills do you think it would take to start your own business?

WHAT IS AN ENTREPRENEUR?

You probably know of neighbors or relatives who own their own business. They may even have started a business out of their home. They are **entrepreneurs**. An entrepreneur is a person who sets out to create and manage a business. An entrepreneur is willing to take a risk in the hope of great financial and personal rewards.

To be an entrepreneur, you do not have to build a new kind of computer in your garage and sell millions of machines every year, the way Steven Jobs did when he started Apple computers. You can sell housecleaning services, handmade ties, used lawn mowers—anything you think people will buy.

However, entrepreneurs are different from all other workers in this way: Their success depends completely on their own efforts. They do not have the security of an established business behind them, with an accounting department, delivery people, salespeople, and mailroom clerks. Many entrepreneurs do not pay themselves a salary at the beginning, because they use all their money to develop their business.

COULD YOU BE AN ENTREPRENEUR?

Do you have the kind of outlook and personality to be an entrepreneur? Look at FIGURE 3-4.

Which statements best fit you, the ones on the left or the ones on the right? The ones on the right are qualities that are typical of entrepreneurs.

Initiative	I need a big push to get going.	OR	I'm a self-starter.
Working with Other People	People are OK.	OR	People give me energy.
Leadership	I'm a follower.	OR	People listen to me.
Taking Responsibility	Let someone else do it.	OR	I like to be in charge.
Organizational Skills	I'll do it later when I have time.	OR	I get right down to business.
Hard Work	I like my free time.	OR	I'm the hardest worker I know.
Decision Making	You decide for me.	OR	My decisions are usually right.
Perseverance	I get discouraged easily.	OR	I'm not a quitter.
Paperwork	I never seem to get it done.	OR	It's important, so I do it.

FIGURE 3-4 This quiz can help you decide if you could be a successful entrepreneur. **Does creating a business appeal to you? Why?**

HOW TO BECOME AN ENTREPRENEUR

To become an entrepreneur, you need a marketable idea, lots of enthusiasm, and a good plan. If you want to become an entrepreneur, there are some basic steps you will need to follow.

Steps to Success

Step 1: Find a product or service that people will buy.
Proven low-cost entrepreneurial businesses include the following:

- Writing computer software

- Providing a cleaning service

- Washing or walking dogs

- Repairing lawnmowers, motorcycles, or bikes

- Painting houses

- Providing day care for children or elderly adults

Step 2: Think of a descriptive name.
A catchy name that defines the product or service could help your business become a success—"House About a Paint Job?" "Maid Day! Maid Day!" "I Do Windows."

Step 3: Have the necessary equipment.
If the equipment you plan to use belongs to your family, make sure you have permission to use it. Do not assume that a parent or relative can do without a van for a couple of weeks. Buying used equipment or renting it are also possibilities.

Step 4: Do some effective advertising.
Here is an example of the power of getting the word out about your business. A pair of young men who wanted to paint houses printed flyers and put them on car windshields in a supermarket parking lot. They got so much business that they had to hire four helpers to finish 40 houses in three months. They earned $40,000 apiece.

This entrepreneur has made a business of creating dolls. **What skill or hobby do you have that you might turn into a business?**

Step 5: Follow through on commitments to clients.
Keeping the goodwill of customers is as important to entrepreneurs as it is to any business. Referrals from satisfied customers bring more business without any advertising. Once you offer your services to the public, make sure you can fulfill your promises.

Buying a Business

Some people do not start their own business. Instead they buy someone else's business. This still makes them entrepreneurs. They buy the location of the store or business, as well as the services of trained employees. They also buy the company's goodwill—the loyalty of customers and the good name of the business. Another option is to buy an established, brand-name business that is part of a larger chain. This is a **franchise** business.

Running a Franchise

A franchise is a business that is part of a larger network of identical businesses. Many fast-food restaurants are franchises. Being a franchise operator makes you an owner, not an employee. However, you have the advantage of being assisted by the parent company with advertising costs, uniforms, store furnishings—and dozens of other items. When you own a franchise, you cannot create your version of the store. The parent company has a formula for success that it wants you to follow. The advantage is that there is less risk.

Still, buying a franchise requires a considerable amount of money in the beginning. A fast-food sandwich store with a brand name can cost you $90,000 or more. It could take three years to earn a regular salary. Until then, you would have to work hard and believe that your risk is worth it. Franchise owners are entrepreneurs because they would rather work for themselves than for someone else.

TALK TO AN ENTREPRENEUR

Running a business can give you a feeling of independence and a sense of accomplishment. You are the boss. You are proud to offer something people want. The profits from the business are yours to keep. Because you are the boss, you can try new ideas. If they do not work, you can decide to try something else. Flexibility is one of your greatest rewards.

There are disadvantages, however. The main ones are the long hours and the risks that are involved. You have to pay for all the improvements. You need to hire and fire workers. One of the best ways to find out what it is like to be an entrepreneur is to talk to one. If you know of someone who owns a business, ask the person, "Why did you become an entrepreneur? What do you wish you knew before starting a business on your own?" Listen to what the person says. It is the voice of experience speaking.

Lesson Review

CHECK YOUR UNDERSTANDING

1. ANALYZING What special qualities does an entrepreneur need to be successful?

2. COMPARING How does starting your own business compare to buying a franchise?

APPLY WHAT YOU LEARN

You have decided to become an entrepreneur. Make a chart that lists the advantages and disadvantages of your choice. Then, think about what your business will be. What will be your product or service? Will you start your own business or buy a franchise? How will you market your product or service? Make another chart in which you list your product or service, its characteristics, and how you will attract customers or sell the product.

TECH CONNECTION DEVELOP A SPREADSHEET

A spreadsheet is a computer application used to create business plans, budgets, and proposals. Businesspeople use spreadsheets whenever they need an answer based on numbers.

A spreadsheet is divided into rows and columns. Each row and column is made up of cells. You can put words, numbers, or formulas into the cells. The words tell what the information is. The formulas let you add, subtract, multiply, and divide. The formulas also allow you to add up a range of cells, to figure percentage, or to refer to numbers from other parts of the spreadsheet.

Spreadsheet formulas allow you to do complicated math, too. The Help menu on a spreadsheet explains all the mathematical functions the application can perform.

Below is a simple profit-and-loss statement for the first quarter of a year. Remember that profit equals income minus expenses. Each cell has a name (B1, B2, and so on). Notice how the formulas add columns and rows.

	A	B	C	D	E	F
1			JAN	FEB	MARCH	TOTAL
2	Income	Actual Income	$15,000	$27,000	$30,000	$72,000
3	Expenses	Advertising	500	500	1,000	2,000
4		Salaries	14,000	14,000	14,000	42,000
5		Cost of Product	4,000	7,000	9,000	20,000
6		Rent	1,000	1,000	1,000	3,000
7	Profit	Profit (loss)	($4,500)	$4,500	$5,000	$5,000

The formula for cell F2 is Add C2 + D2 + E2
The formula for cell E7 is Add E3 + E4 + E5 + E6, then subtract the sum from E2.

Application

Suppose that you are an entrepreneur who is starting up a new business or selling a service. Make up an expense report for your business. Use a spreadsheet to list all the expenses you will have. Estimate what your profits will be over a particular period of time.

CHAPTER 3

REVIEW

Chapter Summary

Understanding the importance of teamwork and how you can be an effective member of a team are key elements in becoming competent in the workplace. Other important workplace skills include knowing how to make sound decisions, how to resolve conflicts, and how to organize your work. Finally, working for yourself as an entrepreneur is an option, if you have the desire for it.

Key Words

company culture   prioritize
alternatives   productivity
criteria   entrepreneurs
proactive   franchise
probation

Match the key words with their definitions. Write your answers on a separate sheet of paper.

1. additional choices

2. taking the lead

3. people who create and manage their own business

4. guidelines, rules

5. arrange tasks in their order of importance

6. a brand-name store or business that a person can purchase and operate

7. trial period to see how an employee performs on the job

8. the social and work practices of a business

9. the amount of work that is produced in a given time

Application:
Analyze Workplace Conflicts

Read the following two stories about people at work. On a separate sheet of paper, write what you think each worker is doing right or wrong with his or her job.

A. Darren started working for 200 Plus Cheeses right after he graduated from high school. He knows every cheese the store has in stock. Customers like him, too. However, Darren's co-workers do not like him. Why? When it is his turn to clean the display cases, he refuses. He won't take his turn sweeping up, either. He says he makes the company enough money as it is. Darren is also the first one to blame somebody for a mistake or to laugh at the person. Darren's job performance report is coming up soon. What do you think his supervisor will say?

B. Kelly worked with her boss, Kassi, for a year at a shoe store. Then Kassi asked Kelly to help her open the company's new Parkside Mall store. Kelly was a good worker, but she wasn't sure of herself yet. Kassi had a democratic leadership style. She asked Kelly's opinion at every step, as Kassi planned out the new store. Many times, Kelly didn't know what to say. She wanted to learn the business from Kassi, but she wasn't sure what was happening. Studying other shoe stores at the mall could give her ideas, but she hasn't made the time to do that yet.

Application: Prioritize Tasks

Work with a group of four or five other students to complete the following activities.

1. Choose a project about which everyone knows something. It can be school-centered, such as a dance, or it can be hobby-based, such as baking, running a basketball league, or fixing up old cars or motorcycles. You can create a task, too, such as welcoming the President of the United States to your school or establishing a neighborhood holiday for a favorite singer or athlete.

2. Prioritize all the tasks that must be done to complete the project. First, list the tasks. Then, rank them in their order of importance. Explain how your group should share the work, and motivate everyone to do his or her part. Tell how your team can work smarter—not harder—to get the job done.

Grammar Workshop Practice

On a separate sheet of paper, combine the independent clauses to form compound sentences.

1. Sam started to write the weekly schedule. He couldn't finish it until he knew who would be on vacation.

2. He says he has the customers' needs in mind. He won't ask how he can help them.

3. Ling sold the most cars. He received a company award.

4. Rosaly used a computer. She developed a spreadsheet for a budget.

5. Elena was in her office all day. She filled all the orders.

6. She solved a conflict with a customer. She thought that better company guidelines would make her job easier.

7. Donna worked in a factory for ten years. She started a new job last week.

8. JoAnn and Suzanne resolved conflicts in the mailroom. They worked well with other employees.

9. Kurt wanted to work in the landscaping business. He looked at all the job ads in the newspaper.

10. Alan was fired from his job. He came in late to work four days this week.

Portfolio Project Writing a Business Plan

Suppose you are going into business for yourself. You have decided not to buy a franchise. First, think about what your business will be. What will be your product or service? How will you market your product or service?

To make your business plan, follow these steps:

- Title your plan with the name of your new business.

- Write a description of your business, including as much detail as you can.

- Describe your customers.

- Describe how you will attract customers or sell the product.

- Explain how much money it may cost to start this business and how you will get the money. If possible, set up a spreadsheet to display this information.

When you have finished your business plan, add it to your portfolio.

CAREER FILE

Read the following information about two careers in which people use writing skills. Think about the goals and skills the jobs require. Then, answer the questions below.

Landscaper: *Agriculture Services*

If you enjoy planting and gardening and like to work outdoors, you might consider a career as a landscaper. Landscapers are responsible for developing, designing, and maintaining different outside areas such as parks, lawns, and gardens. Landscapers preserve these landscaped areas by mowing lawns; planting trees, shrubs, and flowers; and treating lawns with fertilizers and other chemicals.

A landscaper should

- have an interest in plants and their care.
- understand how to preserve natural areas.

Minimum Education: High-school graduate
Starting Salary: $80 to $220 per week
Related Careers: Botanist, Forest Conservation Worker

For more information, contact the American Nursery and Landscape Association, 1250 I Street, NW, Suite 500, Washington, DC 20005-3922. You can find this organization on the Internet at www.anla.org.

Radiologic Technologist: *Technology Services*

If you are interested in medicine, health, and science and if you want to work in a profession that helps people, you might investigate a career as a radiologic technologist. Radiologic technologists, also known as radiographers, prepare patients before they are X-rayed. They also handle the machinery that is used to create images of the body.

A radiologic technologist should

- have a background in mathematics, physics, chemistry, biology, and photography.
- be licensed in some states.

Minimum Education: Two- or four-year program in radiology
Starting Salary: $23,000 to $37,000 per year
Related Careers: Sonographer, Clinical Laboratory Technologist

For more information, contact the American Society of Radiologic Technologists, 15000 Central Avenue, SE, Albuquerque, NM 87123-3917. You will find this organization on the Internet at www.asrt.org.

EXPLORING CAREERS

1. Suppose that you go on an interview for a job as a landscaper. Explain how you would prepare yourself for the interview. What kinds of questions do you think you might have to answer?

2. If you were applying for a job as a radiologic technologist, what skills and personal qualities would you emphasize in your résumé? Make a list, and then explain how each skill would help you in the job.

> *"You've got to persevere. Stick with it—that's the main thing."*
>
> *Gloria Estefan (1957–)*
> *Singer*

UNIT 2
THE PATH TO WRITING SUCCESS

A process is a well-planned series of steps you follow to achieve a goal or make a product. In this unit, you will learn about the writing process and about how it can help you become a better writer. First, you will learn the value of planning in the prewriting stage. Then, you will learn about drafting and revising your work to make it clear and complete. In the editing and proofreading stages, you will polish your writing. Finally, you will be ready to publish your writing by presenting it to others to read. You will see how being a good writer will help you to achieve success at school and on the job.

BEGINNING THE WRITING PROCESS

Kai has been accepted into a trainee program in the store in which she works. If she does well, she will quickly advance in the company. As a management trainee, Kai is asked to write about herself and her goals. She is unsure of what to write. She does not know which details to include and which ones to leave out. Although Kai knows what her goals are, she does not know how to express them clearly in her writing.

Goals for Success

In this chapter, you will learn these skills:

Deciding how to write for specific purposes and audiences

 PROBLEM-SOLVING

Choosing and narrowing writing topics

 ACQUIRING AND EVALUATING INFORMATION

Collecting information to use in writing

 MATERIALS AND FACILITIES

Using graphic organizers to assemble ideas as preparation for writing

 ORGANIZING AND MAINTAINING INFORMATION

Creating a word-processing document

 USING COMPUTERS TO PROCESS INFORMATION

PORTFOLIO PROJECT

WRITING ABOUT GOALS

By the time you complete this chapter, you will know what Kai has to do to write about her goals. You also will be able to write about your own career goals and add your work to your portfolio.

Understanding the Writing Process

What Do You Already Know?

What steps do you take when you write a paper for school? Do you plan what you will write before you start? On a separate sheet of paper, list the steps you follow when you write.

Think About It Why do you think it might be helpful to have a process for writing?

Everywhere you look, there are things to read. Newspapers, magazines, and books tell about the world and the people in it. Technical manuals and textbooks teach new skills and give information. Stories and novels entertain and enrich people's lives. Writing is the formal way people communicate their ideas to others. The more clear and precise your writing is, the better able you are to communicate exactly what you want to say.

THINKING ABOUT THE WRITING PROCESS

A **process** is a series of steps that help you reach a goal. If you have ever gone on a factory tour and seen baseball bats or car engines being made, for example, you know what a manufacturing process is like. In this kind of process, a task is divided into a series of small steps. When the process is completed, the manufacturer has a product that can be sold to customers.

Writing also follows a process. FIGURE 4-1 describes the stages of the writing process.

THE WRITING PROCESS

Prewriting	The time to plan what you will write, to think about your topic, your audience, and your purpose for writing
Drafting	The writing stage
Editing	The time to take a second look at the ideas you included in your draft and how you organized them. You may decide to revise or rewrite your draft to make a stronger argument.
Proofreading	The time to check grammar, spelling, capitalization, word use, and mechanics to be sure everything is correct
Publishing	The time to share the final product of your work with an audience

FIGURE 4-1 This chart shows you the stages of the writing process. **How do you decide what kinds of revisions you need to make during the editing stage?**

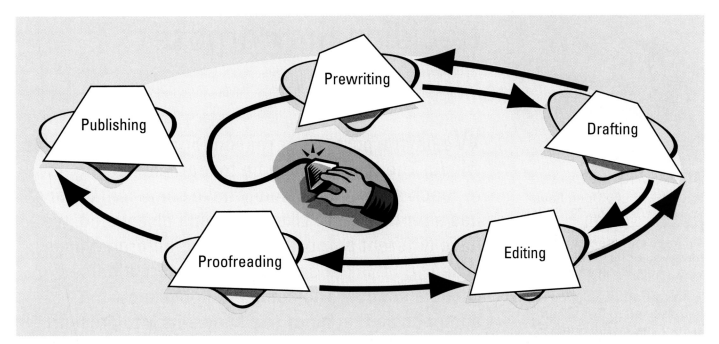

FIGURE 4-2 When you follow the writing process, you can go back and forth between the stages until you are satisfied with your work. **How can the writing process help you improve your writing?**

HOW THE WRITING PROCESS DIFFERS FROM OTHER PROCESSES

Many processes are like an assembly line in a factory. They start at Step A and move one step at a time until they reach Step Z. One step follows the other in the same order each time. As a result, every finished product is the same.

The writing process is different. Writers do not always follow the steps of the process in the same order. They can go back and forth between the steps until they are satisfied with the piece of writing they created, as seen in FIGURE 4-2.

USING THE WRITING PROCESS

The full writing process gives you a structure to help you develop longer pieces of writing. At the end of each stage of the writing process, ask yourself two questions: Do I need to do more? What is my plan for getting it done?

Certain everyday writing tasks do not require the full writing process. If you send co-workers a postcard while you are on vacation, you do not need to send a revised draft of the message.

However, when you are representing your company, you should use the full writing process to make sure your writing is clear and complete. For example, if you are sending a notice to clients to announce a sale or some special offer, you want that notice to be clear, precise, and correct.

Lesson Review

CHECK YOUR UNDERSTANDING

1. SUMMARIZING What are the steps of the writing process?

2. CONTRASTING How does the writing process differ from the manufacturing process?

APPLY WHAT YOU LEARN

Ask a parent or other adult what process or processes he or she follows while working. Ask this person how following these processes makes a job easier and a product better. Share your information with your class.

Deciding the Purpose and Audience

What Do You Already Know?

What kinds of writing have you done for school? What kinds of personal writing, such as notes and greeting cards, have you done? Who was your audience in each case?

Think About It Suppose you had decided to leave your school and attend another school. How would you tell your best friend about your decision? Would you describe the same situation to your guidance counselor in the same way? Why or why not?

We have a purpose or reason for most of the things we do. The purpose may be to learn something new, to reach a goal, or to simply have some fun. Writing has a purpose, too. Like everything else we do, we have different purposes for writing different things. When you think of an audience, picture a person giving a speech. The speaker should know the audience so that he or she knows how to present the topic. The same is true for writing. When you think about who your audience is, you will write in a way these people will understand.

THINKING ABOUT PURPOSE AND AUDIENCE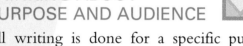

All writing is done for a specific purpose and audience. Your **purpose** in writing is your reason for writing. Some writers may have more than one purpose in mind when they sit down to write. FIGURE 4-3 shows the four main purposes for writing.

Writing for Different Purposes

Informing and persuading are two of the most common purposes for writing. Other purposes are describing and explaining.

In the business world, a writer may use all of these purposes for writing at some time in his or her career. The topic might be a product, the proposed location for a new store, or an item of clothing shown in a catalog. In this last case, the writer's purpose might be both to describe the item and to persuade catalog readers to buy it.

Writing to explain can also have a business purpose. For example, in a brochure, you might tell how a complicated process is used to produce a product in your factory.

Writing for Different Audiences

Your **audience** is the person or people who will read your writing—your readers. In personal

FOUR PURPOSES FOR WRITING	
To **Inform**	Give facts and details
To **Explain**	Tell why or how something takes place
To **Describe**	Show what someone or something looks like
To **Persuade**	Try to convince others to do something or believe in something.

FIGURE 4-3 This chart shows the four purposes for writing. **How might knowing your purpose for writing help you to write more clearly?**

Green Avenue Merchants Association
22 Millbank Street • Mentor, Ohio 44060

GAMA

October 1, 2002
Dear Association Members:

The Association will once again sponsor the Green Avenue Fair on the first weekend in May. Mark your calendar.

All Association members who want to have a special outdoor display in front of their store should notify the Association. The fee for this display space will be $250.00. Please make your checks payable to the Green Avenue Merchants Association. We need your payment by April 15.

Rebecca Cord is once again lining up crafts vendors and food vendors for the fair. With your help, we can make this the biggest and best fair yet.

Sincerely,

Corita Jackson

Corita Jackson

FIGURE 4-4 The purpose of this business letter is to inform. **How might the letter have been written if its purpose had been to persuade?**

writing, your audience is usually a friend or relative, and you choose the topic. In school writing, your audience is your teacher or your classmates. Your purpose is often to give information or to explain something. Your teacher will sometimes choose the topic you will write about. At other times, you may select a topic that interests you.

Effective writers always keep their audience in mind when they plan and write. They adapt their writing to serve their purpose and their audience.

One of the first questions to ask yourself when you write is how familiar is your audience with your topic. If you are describing a new product, you need to describe it completely and exactly if your audience is not familiar with it. On the other hand, if you are describing last year's product, you may have to tell only what has been changed or

improved. Knowing your audience helps you to decide how detailed your writing should be.

Recognizing what your audience needs to know helps you fine-tune your writing in other ways, too. It guides you to choose the main ideas and details that you will use to inform or persuade your readers or explain or describe something to them.

The more you train yourself to consider your audience's needs and views, the clearer your writing will be.

At work, your supervisor will often specify why and to whom you are writing. For instance, what is the purpose and who is the audience for the letter in **FIGURE 4-4**?

Suppose a new store owner moved into the neighborhood. Corita Jackson then might write a letter explaining how the fair started and why it is important to the community. How would her purpose for writing be different in the second letter?

Lesson Review

CHECK YOUR UNDERSTANDING

1. IDENTIFYING What are the four main purposes for writing? How are they different from one another?

2. EVALUATING How do you decide what your purpose for writing should be?

APPLY WHAT YOU LEARN

Assume that you and some friends have designed a toy that you want to sell. First, list your purpose for writing to each of the following people. Then, explain your reasons for choosing each purpose.

1. A toy company owner

2. The president of the company that has agreed to make the toy

3. A person who designs packages for toys

4. Customers who ask when the toy will be ready for delivery to stores

Grammar Workshop

Using Clauses and Phrases

A clause is a group of words that has a subject and a predicate. An independent clause expresses a complete thought; it can stand alone as a sentence. Although a dependent clause has a subject and a verb, it does not express a complete thought. It cannot stand alone. When you add a dependent clause or phrase to an independent clause, you help your audience see how your ideas relate to one another.

> *Examples* The rotor blade fits on this bearing.   (independent clause)
>
> because it drives the motor   (dependent clause)

A phrase does not have a subject and a predicate. Phrases cannot stand alone because they do not express a complete thought.

> *Example*   on this bearing (phrase)

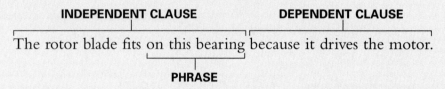

INDEPENDENT CLAUSE   DEPENDENT CLAUSE

The rotor blade fits on this bearing because it drives the motor.

PHRASE

Application

Each of the following sentences is an independent clause. Add a dependent clause (D) or a phrase (P) as directed. Write your new sentences on a separate sheet of paper.

1. Our Web site is new. (D)
2. I waited until the machine cooled. (D)
3. Carol designed a paper cup. (P)
4. We sat outside the employees' entrance. (P)
5. He read the instruction manual. (D)
6. Juanita called the customer service department. (P)
7. Jason fastened the chain to the drill. (D)
8. Dana tightened every bolt. (P)
9. Tina cleaned the display cases. (D)
10. Philip was late for his interview. (P)

For more information, SEE PAGE 347.

Choosing and Narrowing a Topic

What Do You Already Know?
You have probably written about many topics in school. Which topics were given to you by your teacher? Which did you choose?

Think About It When you have been able to choose your own topic, what process did you use to make that choice?

A quick note is usually about a very specific topic. You know what you want to say, and you write your message as quickly and as accurately as you can. When you are writing longer, more involved pieces, you should choose a topic carefully and use the full writing process to develop it. To begin the prewriting stage, choose and narrow your topic with care. A well-chosen topic will make your writing task easier.

CHOOSING A TOPIC

Finding a good topic is one of a writer's most important jobs. At work, your supervisor will probably tell you what to write about, especially if you are new on the job.

As you demonstrate your writing ability, you may be given more freedom of choice. Whatever choice you have, remember that your writing has to be directed toward the company's goals, not your own personal goals.

CONSIDERING A TOPIC LENGTH

One thing to consider when you choose a topic is the length of the piece you will write. The length determines the amount of detail you can include and the amount of information you have to research or gather.

The length of your writing is often determined by your purpose. For example, if you are a management trainee, your manager may ask you to research and make a list of the store's most popular clothing styles. This is a straightforward job.

However, if your manager asks you to write a report describing the most popular styles of clothing and explaining how the store can better serve its customers' needs, you will write a much longer report. You will take the same information, analyze it, and then make recommendations based on your analysis.

Narrowing Your Topic

How does a writer decide how much information to include? Suppose you work for a company that sells office products. Your supervisor asks you to write a one-page report on an area in which you think the company should improve. You need a topic that is both important and narrow enough to fit on one page. FIGURE 4-5 on page 72 shows the process you might use, starting with the broadest topic and narrowing it step by step until you have an appropriate topic.

As you work through the process of narrowing your topic, you find that you can break your business down into five main areas of sales. All of these subtopics are too broad to deal with in your brief

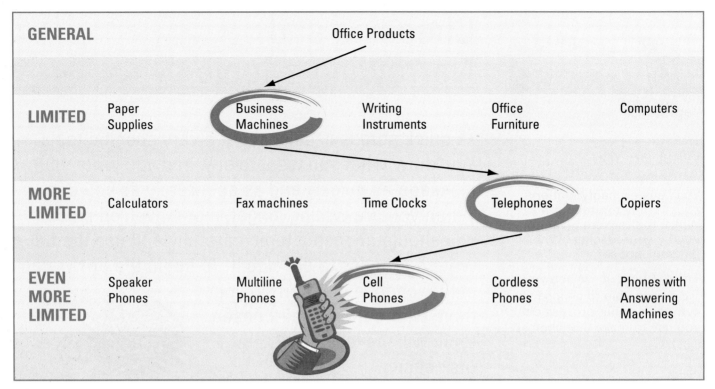

GENERAL		Office Products		
LIMITED	Paper Supplies	Business Machines	Writing Instruments	Office Furniture	Computers
MORE LIMITED	Calculators	Fax machines	Time Clocks	Telephones	Copiers
EVEN MORE LIMITED	Speaker Phones	Multiline Phones	Cell Phones	Cordless Phones	Phones with Answering Machines

FIGURE 4-5 This narrowing process can help you find a good topic. **If your manager asked for a long report on your company's main product areas, on which level of the chart might you focus?**

report. As you continue to narrow your topic, you choose one area in which sales are lagging: business machines.

Then you list all the business machines your company sells. Each of these subtopics is still too broad for your report. Now you choose one kind of business machine—telephones. You think of all the different kinds of phones you sell, but you do not have room to write about all of them. You choose cell phones because this is the fastest-growing part of your market. The focus of your report will be on this topic; you know you can do a thorough job on this topic in one page.

Considering Your Audience

You also need to think about your audience when you narrow your topic. How much information do your readers have? What do they need to know? Answering these questions will help you focus your topic and decide on the kind of details you need to support it.

Lesson Review

CHECK YOUR UNDERSTANDING

1. ANALYZING Why is it important to limit a topic to fit the amount of space you have?

2. COMPARING Suppose you are asked to write two reports: one listing your store's popular clothing styles and one analyzing your customers' interests. How would the two reports be different? How would they be the same?

APPLY WHAT YOU LEARN

Select three of the broad topics below. Then, narrow these topics by listing three limited topics for each one that you chose.

music	sports	computers
buildings	machines	entertainment

Collecting Information

What Do You Already Know?

You have probably had to find information about a topic for a school report. What kinds of sources did you check?

Think About It How do you know when you have found enough information about a topic?

From the police and courtroom dramas you have watched on television and in the movies, you know how important it is for detectives and lawyers to gather good information. They need solid evidence and proof before they can convince a jury—their audience—to convict a person who has been charged with a crime. When you write, you also need to gather information to explain your ideas or prove your point to others.

FOCUS ON CONTENT

Once you have chosen and narrowed your topic and identified your audience, you can start to gather the information you need to develop your topic. Finding this information is an important part of the prewriting, or planning, stage of the writing process.

SOURCES OF INFORMATION

You can find factual information in many places. Three important sources of facts are books and magazines, the Internet, and experienced people.

Books and Magazines

Try to use both books and magazines as you research a topic. Books are longer and usually contain more detailed information than magazine articles do. However, magazines are published regularly and often contain more up-to-date information than books do. When you look for books, be sure to search for the ones with the most recent copyright dates.

Both books and magazines often contain photographs, charts, and maps. You might find useful information in these graphics.

The Internet

The World Wide Web on the Internet gives you access to a wealth of information. However, just because information is on the Internet does not mean it is accurate or up-to-date. Anyone can set up a Web site.

Try to make sure that the information you find comes from a source you can trust, such as a well-known organization, university, or government agency. Web sites set up by individuals or private groups may be inaccurate or biased. Look for the name of the Web site's sponsor to help determine the site's purpose.

People

People also can be an invaluable source of information. Seek out people who are experts on a topic or who are professionals in a given field. For example, a carpenter can help you explain how to hang a door or install a window. A computer expert can point out the differences between two models of computers. As you interview an expert, you might want to tape-record your interview so you can remember the person's exact words. Be sure to ask the person's permission, however, before you record.

Your own knowledge about a topic also could be useful. For example, if you have a garden, you might be the best person to write a brochure about flower care for the garden store you work in. Use your personal experience and knowledge, but look to other experts, too. They may have a different perspective and different experiences from your own. Your employer and the store's customers deserve the best—and most useful—information you can provide.

QUESTION INFORMATION

Get into the habit of questioning the data you find. Every fact and source you discover will not be useful for your purpose and audience. If the information is inaccurate, discard it. If the information seems questionable, verify it with another source. Use only appropriate and accurate information in your writing.

Ask yourself these questions:

- ✔ Is this a reliable source?
- ✔ If the source is a book, does it have a recent copyright date?
- ✔ If the source is a magazine, who publishes it?
- ✔ Is the writer of the book or magazine article someone who is an expert on this topic?
- ✔ If the source is a Web site, does the person or group who created it support the accuracy of the information it presents?
- ✔ Is the Web site selling a product or service?
- ✔ Does the information on the Web site include any obvious bias? Does it leave out important information?

One way to collect information is to interview an expert in the field. **What kind of information can a person provide that a book cannot?**

Lesson Review

CHECK YOUR UNDERSTANDING

1. IDENTIFYING Name three sources of facts for writing. What are the reasons for using each one?

2. EVALUATING In what ways can you judge the accuracy of a source's information?

APPLY WHAT YOU LEARN

What sources might you use to collect information on the following topics? Work with a small group of students to list sources you might use. Then give reasons for your answers.

- New methods in computer graphics
- Soldiers' experiences fighting in World War II
- The history of advertising
- The latest developments in office communications

Grammar Workshop

Making Subjects and Verbs Agree

Subjects and verbs agree when they are both either singular or plural. A singular subject names one person, place, or thing; a plural subject and a compound subject name more than one person, place, or thing.

> *Examples*   **Amy works** in a restaurant.
>
> The **cousins work** in a restaurant.
>
> **Leo and Martin prepare** the main course.

Sometimes, phrases appear between the subject and verb. To check their agreement, think only of the subject and the verb.

> *Examples*   The **cousins**, who live in Denver, **work** in a restaurant.
>
> **Richard**, who works at Brothers' Videos, also **makes** his own films.

A compound subject joined by *or* or *nor* takes a verb that agrees with the closest subject.

> *Examples*   Either Andrea or **my cousins are** working tonight.
>
> Neither Estella nor **José is** coming to the presentation.

Application

Read the following sentences. On a separate sheet of paper, write each sentence, choosing the verb that agrees with the subject.

1. The files in the office (contains, contain) important information.
2. My friends, who took training, (are, is) planning to work for a big company.
3. Sometimes, workers (forget, forgets) what the job is.
4. Orders placed within the last month (has, have) been delayed.
5. Either Ted or Cathy (are, is) writing a résumé.
6. Joseph and the other workers (is, are) required to wear badges.
7. Gloria and Scott will (attend, attends) the conference.
8. Neither Daniel nor Beth (want, wants) to work in the lab.
9. His absences from work (was, were) the reason for his dismissal.
10. The dispatcher, as well as the drivers, (wants, want) a raise.

For more information, **SEE PAGE 347.**

LESSON 4-5

Organizing Your Information

What Do You Already Know?

What kinds of things do you enjoy organizing? How do you put them in an order that makes sense to you?

Think About It Why is it difficult to find something in a disorganized room?

One way to think about information is to see it as the contents of a closet. When you first gather information, you throw it all into the closet without sorting through it. Sometimes you know exactly where something belongs. Most of the time, however, you are not sure what to do with it. To find out how to make the best use of the information you have collected, you have to choose a way to organize it.

THINKING AGAIN ABOUT PURPOSE, AUDIENCE, AND TOPIC

The way you organize your information is linked to your purpose for writing. If your purpose is to inform, you might use chronological, or time, order. If your purpose is to explain, you might find that cause-and-effect order works best. To describe a scene, you may use spatial order. To persuade, you may order your information in comparison-and-contrast form.

In longer pieces of writing, you will have one main purpose, but you will often have a second purpose, as well. For example, if your main purpose is to persuade, you may decide that the best way to persuade is by giving facts and examples as well as reasons.

Ways to Organize Information

Sometimes, the way to organize a piece of writing is obvious from the start. If you are going to tell a story to a friend, you think about the beginning, middle, and end of the story. You think about your main purpose for telling it. When you write, you also organize your ideas in a pattern that your reader can follow.

USING A SINGLE METHOD OF ORGANIZATION

There are five main methods of organizing your writing. Each may be used to organize everything from a single paragraph to a long report. Drawings called graphic organizers can help you plan the way you will organize your writings.

Chronological Order

When you use **chronological order**, you tell events in the order in which they took place. You might use chronological order to relate an incident or explain a **sequence**, or a continuous, connected series of events, as shown in FIGURE 4-6.

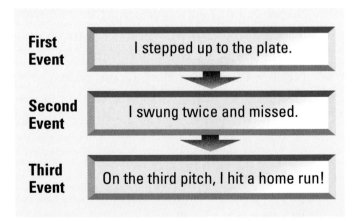

First Event	I stepped up to the plate.
Second Event	I swung twice and missed.
Third Event	On the third pitch, I hit a home run!

FIGURE 4-6 The events are shown here in chronological order, from top to bottom. **Which event occurred last?**

Spatial Order

Spatial order shows where things are located in relation to each other. Writers most often use spatial order when they describe a scene, like the one shown in FIGURE 4-7 below.

FIGURE 4-7 You could describe this scene using spatial order. **What plan would you use to help readers visualize this scene? Would you begin on the left? in the front?**

If you use spatial order, choose a direction to describe your topic: left to right, front to back, or near to far. Use direction words such as *above* and *in front of* to guide your reader.

Order of Importance

When you use order of importance to organize information, you need to decide what is most important and what is least important. FIGURE 4-8 shows how to organize by order of importance.

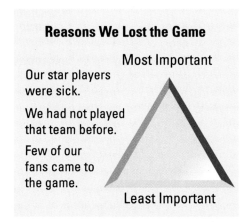

Reasons We Lost the Game

Most Important

Our star players were sick.

We had not played that team before.

Few of our fans came to the game.

Least Important

FIGURE 4-8 This triangle shows how to organize a piece of writing by order of importance. **For what topics might you use this method of organization?**

Order of importance is useful when you are giving reasons or evidence to prove something. The most important information does not have to come first. Writers sometimes save this for last so that they can leave readers with their strongest argument.

Cause-and-Effect Order

On the job, people often have to explain why something happened or did not happen according to plan. One way to do this is to examine a situation for causes and effects. A cause is why something happens. An effect is what happens as a result of some cause. Writers often give the cause first and then tell what happened, as shown in FIGURE 4-9. Sometimes, they describe a series of effects and then guess at a possible cause.

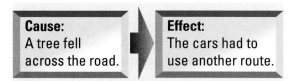

Cause: A tree fell across the road.

Effect: The cars had to use another route.

FIGURE 4-9 Notice the arrow in this figure. **What does it tell you about how the writer is organizing causes and effects?**

Comparison-and-Contrast

A **comparison** describes how people or things are alike. A **contrast** shows how they are different. In work-related writing, you may need to compare or contrast products, advertisements, sales events, or even annual picnics.

A graphic organizer, called a Venn diagram, can help you compare two ideas. It is made up of two overlapping ovals, as shown in FIGURE 4-10.

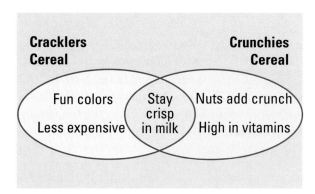

Cracklers Cereal   **Crunchies Cereal**

Fun colors

Less expensive

Stay crisp in milk

Nuts add crunch

High in vitamins

FIGURE 4-10 Venn diagrams help you make comparisons. **What is being compared in this diagram?**

Why Have a Company Picnic?

The information in this paragraph is organized by order of importance. Notice the words *most important*.

It's time for United Data's annual company picnic! Some workers have asked why we have a company picnic. There are lots of reasons. First, it's fun. You can play baseball or talk and relax with your co-workers. Second, all of you have worked so hard all year, and you deserve a break. But most important, a picnic is a great morale builder. It's the manager's chance to show you how much we care about you and how much we appreciate your hard work.

How will this year's picnic be different from last year's? This year, we're going to Gillen Lake. While people liked Grimshaw Park's picnic area and soccer field, we think you'll love Gillen Lake. Gillen Lake has three baseball fields, a swimming pool and a wide deck for sunbathing, a covered picnic area, and lots of shady spots.

This paragraph is organized in comparison-and-contrast order. It shows how the two locations are different.

This paragraph is organized in chronological order. The details are organized in the order in which the events will take place.

Here's the schedule. Workers and their families will arrive at noon. They will be met by a greeting committee that gives them name tags. Scheduled activities will be held from 12:30 P.M. to 3:30 P.M. At 3:30, the catered dinner will be served. The company president will introduce after-dinner speakers at 4:30. At 5, the picnic will officially end.

You probably want to know how Gillen Lake looks. As you enter the gate, you'll see the baseball fields straight ahead. Beyond the fields, you'll see the picnic area. Once you've passed the picnic area, you'll see the swimming pool and the deck.

This paragraph is organized in spatial order. The directions show where things are located, from near to far.

This paragraph is organized in cause-and-effect order. Notice the words *because* and *effect*.

So, what is our plan? We want to spend the day relaxing and having fun together, because we want to show you how much we appreciate your dedication. After all, your hard work equals United's success! We hope this picnic will have a great effect on you, sending you back to your job with a renewed spirit and excitement for the terrific work we all do together at United Data!

FIGURE 4-11 shows a notice that a company executive sent to the staff about a company picnic. **Why do you think the executive chose to use different methods of organization?**

In the outer part of each oval of a Venn diagram, you list how two things are different. In the part that overlaps, you list how they are alike. For example, FIGURE 4-10 on page 77 shows a comparison of two breakfast cereals. It shows how these cereals are unlike by listing differences in the outer part of each circle. It shows how they are alike by listing common characteristics in the overlapping part.

USING MORE THAN ONE METHOD OF ORGANIZATION

In business writing, you can sometimes organize information in more than one way. For example, a brochure on a new type of X-ray machine might use order of importance to give facts about the machine. It might use spatial order to describe the machine's features and performance in detail. FIGURE 4-11 on page 78 shows how you can use different methods of organizing information in one document.

At the same time, the overall purpose of the brochure is to persuade a customer to purchase the X-ray machine. That is the main purpose that determines how the information is presented. Choose every detail with your purpose in mind.

Lesson Review

CHECK YOUR UNDERSTANDING

1. SUMMARIZING Describe the five main methods of organizing information.

2. EVALUATING Look at FIGURE 4-11 on page 78. Why do you think the writer chose to organize each paragraph in a different way?

APPLY WHAT YOU LEARN

For each method of organization below, name a topic for which it would be useful. Explain your choices.

- chronological order
- spatial order
- order of importance
- cause-and-effect order
- comparison-and-contrast order

Grammar Workshop

Writing Complex Sentences

Complex sentences help to show how your writing is organized, because they show how your ideas relate to one another. A complex sentence contains an independent clause and one or more dependent clauses. An independent clause contains a subject and a predicate, and it can stand alone. A dependent clause also contains a subject and a predicate, but it cannot stand alone. Use complete sentences to link your ideas.

INDEPENDENT CLAUSE	**DEPENDENT CLAUSE**

Example   I let the copier cool before I restarted it.

The words listed below can introduce dependent clauses in your sentences.

Some Words That Can Introduce Dependent Clauses

after	before	unless	whenever
although	since	until	when

Examples **When** the mail arrived, my dog barked.

We will not receive bonuses **unless** our sales figures improve.

Application

Write each of the following items as a complex sentence by adding either an independent clause (I) or a dependent clause (D) as directed.

1. Hugh loaded candy into the vending machine (D)
2. The workplace was noisy and dusty (D)
3. Because Janice's mother had been a manager (I)
4. Unless you worry about meeting the supervisor (I)
5. Our team made a list of solutions to the parking problem (D)
6. The job opening was posted in a store (D)
7. Whether Phil preferred landscaping (I)
8. Because Lynn could speak two languages (I)
9. Juan's pay increase was due in May (D)
10. Dena was promoted to director of the accounting department (D)

For more information, **SEE PAGE 346.**

Word processing is one of the most important and useful tasks for which people use computers. You can use a word-processing program for any writing task.

Your company may have special instructions for how it wants written materials to look. However, it is simple to set up a basic document.

Step 1. Open the word-processing program, and click New to begin your document. The page will already be set up with a standard typeface and standard margins, which you can change if you wish.

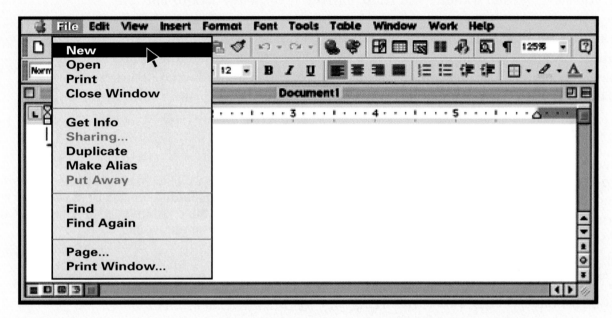

Step 2. As you work on your document, save it on the computer's hard drive frequently. Choose a name that will help you remember the contents of the document. Be as specific as possible. Always save your document when you stop working on it—even if you stop for a short time.

Step 3. To edit your document, move the cursor to the area you want to change. You can use the mouse or the direction arrows on your keyboard to do this.

Step 4. Click Print Preview to see how each page will look before printing. You may change the typeface, do a spell check, or make other changes before printing. Then, click Print to print out your document.

Application

Create a brief word-processing document. It may be a letter, an announcement, or a message. Give it a name that is easy for you to remember. Save it, reopen it, and print it out.

CHAPTER 4

REVIEW

Chapter Summary

The writing process is a series of steps that helps you create a successful piece of writing. Before you can begin the actual writing, you must decide both on the purpose, or reason, for your writing and on who your audience will be. Once you have chosen a topic, you must narrow it to fit the length and the purpose of your assignment; you must also consider your audience. Then, collect information on the topic and evaluate it from different sources. Before you can write, you must organize your information in a logical way. That order might take several forms: chronological, spatial, order of importance, cause and effect, or comparison and contrast. With careful planning, you will now be ready to begin the drafting stage.

Key Words

process	sequence
purpose	spatial order
audience	comparison
chronological order	contrast

Match each word with its definition. Write your answers on a separate sheet of paper

1. comparison
2. purpose
3. audience
4. chronological order
5. spatial order
6. contrast
7. sequence
8. process

a. shows how things are alike

b. a series of steps that helps you reach a goal

c. shows how things are different

d. your reason for writing

e. the people who will read your writing

f. shows where things are located in relation to each other

g. time order

h. a series of connected events

Application: Determining Your Purpose for Writing

What purpose would you have when you write about each of the following topics? On a separate sheet of paper, copy the chart below. Then, fill it in. Explain your choice for each topic.

TOPIC	PURPOSE
Training programs	
An upcoming event	
Voluntary service	
A store interior	

Application: Narrowing Writing Topics

Read the list of broad topics below. Narrow each one from a general topic to a more specific topic. Use at least three steps to create a limited topic. Write your answers on a separate sheet of paper.

1. Repairing bicycles
2. Musical instruments
3. Computers
4. Sports
5. The future

Application:
Organizing Ideas for Writing

Choose one of the following ways to organize your thoughts for each writing task: chronological order, cause-and-effect order, spatial order, order of importance, or comparison-and-contrast order. Explain each choice.

1. As a member of a community group, you want to explain to the mayor and the town council how last week's major rains and flooding have affected the community.

2. In an article for your company's newsletter, you want to show the employees and the stockholders how the new warehouse is a vast improvement over the old warehouse.

3. You want to describe to the owners of a hotel how the new parking attendants' uniforms will look.

4. You believe that it is time to have a casual-dress policy at work. List your reasons in some logical order.

5. Your friend wants to know how your bedroom looks. Describe it for him or her.

Grammar Workshop Practice

On a separate sheet of paper, rewrite the following items to make them correct.

Part I. Write the verb that agrees with the subject in each of the following sentences.

1. Neither Tom nor Laurie (follow, follows) the schedule.

2. The accountants, who were just hired, (want, wants) to attend the budget meeting.

3. The company (pay, pays) benefits to the workers.

4. The manager (allow, allows) talking in the office.

5. Emma and Cheryl (agree, agrees) to work late.

Part II. Rewrite each item below as a complex sentence. Add an independent clause (I) or dependent clause (D) as indicated.

6. Because of hard work and honesty (I)

7. This document has errors (D)

8. When the work is finished (I)

9. After the meeting (I)

10. Lunch was limited to an hour (D)

Portfolio Project Writing About Goals

Think about the career goals you set for yourself in Unit 1. Narrow your list to one particular goal, as was done in FIGURE 4-5 on page 72. Plan a piece of writing about how you could achieve that goal. To do this:

- Choose your purpose for writing.

- Think about the audience who will read your writing. What do these people know about you? What do they know about your choice of career?

- Collect information about your goal and how you might achieve it.

- Use a graphic organizer to arrange your information in a logical order.

Be ready to show and discuss your notes. Add your graphic organizer to your portfolio.

COMPLETING THE WRITING PROCESS

Davenne enjoys working in a small, family-owned restaurant. She likes welcoming customers and showing them to their tables. In addition to these duties, the owner asked Davenne if she would help write a new menu for the restaurant. It would involve writing a descriptive paragraph for each of the restaurant's specialty sandwiches. Davenne enjoys writing, but she has never written anything like this before. She wants to do a good job. If she does, her employer will promote her and might even make her assistant manager of the restaurant.

Key Words

draft

unity

coherence

diction

formal language

informal language

cliché

inflated diction

copy

graphics

format

Goals for Success

In this chapter, you will learn these skills:

Writing a first draft

 SCANS WRITES / THINKS CREATIVELY

Editing a first draft

 SCANS ACQUIRES AND EVALUATES INFORMATION

Proofreading a draft

 SCANS ORGANIZES AND MAINTAINS INFORMATION

Publishing the final document

 SCANS INTERPRETS AND COMMUNICATES INFORMATION

Saving a word-processing document

 SCANS UNDERSTANDS SYSTEMS

PORTFOLIO PROJECT

PRODUCT DESCRIPTION

By the time you complete this chapter, you will know what Davenne has to do to write her product description. You also will be able to write your own product description and add it to your portfolio.

LESSON 5-1

Creating a Draft

What Do You Already Know?

Think of the last time you wrote a paper or a report for school. How did you decide what you would write?

Think About It Why is it important to plan what you will write?

Every magazine article, newspaper editorial, and book started its life as a rough draft. Writers, like all artists and craftspeople, refine their work until it clearly says what they want it to say. But in this first writing stage, writers just get all their ideas down on paper. The work of revising will come later.

DRAFTING AND THE WRITING PROCESS

During the second stage of the writing process, you begin to shape your ideas into words. You write a **draft**. A draft is a piece of writing that is unfinished; it is your first attempt to put what you want to say into words. After you write a draft, you can review your work and change it until the final product says exactly what you want it to say.

MAIN IDEA AND DETAILS

You started by deciding on your topic, purpose, and audience. Based on these decisions, you will now decide on the main idea of your piece of writing. Then, you will gather the details that will help you develop your main idea. In developing your draft, you will state your main idea and support it with specific details.

Decide on Your Main Idea

In most effective pieces of writing, the writer first states a main idea. The main idea should appear in a topic sentence in the first paragraph. What follows are the supporting details that tell more about the main idea.

Choose Supporting Details

Writers use five main kinds of supporting details. The most common kinds of information you will use to support and develop your ideas are shown in FIGURE 5-1.

KIND OF SUPPORTING DETAIL	DEFINITION
Facts	statements that can be proven by experience, observation, or study
Examples	particular cases that show ideas
Incidents	specific events related to your main idea
Sensory Details	words and phrases that appeal to the five senses: sight, hearing, touch, taste, and smell
Reasons	logical arguments that support an opinion

FIGURE 5-1 This chart defines five kinds of supporting details. **Which kind of detail might you use if your purpose is to persuade?**

Writers use facts, examples, incidents, and reasons when they write to inform or explain. Sensory details are important in descriptions. Use the kind of supporting detail that helps you express your ideas clearly and precisely.

Use Facts

A great deal of business writing involves communicating factual information. Factual information can be supported by experience, observation, or research.

FIGURE 5-2 shows some facts that a writer collected about a cordless phone.

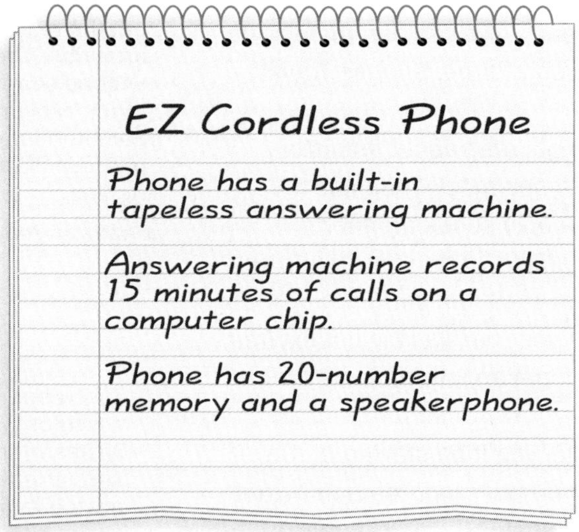

EZ Cordless Phone

Phone has a built-in tapeless answering machine.

Answering machine records 15 minutes of calls on a computer chip.

Phone has 20-number memory and a speakerphone.

FIGURE 5-2 Note how the writer works these facts into the paragraph below. **Which sentence does not contain a fact he collected?**

The writer used these facts to produce the following paragraph:

> The new EZ Cordless Phone has all the features you need for your busy office. It contains a 20-number memory to save you time. Its speakerphone feature allows you to talk from anywhere in your office. The built-in answering machine has no tape to fuss with but contains a computer chip that can record 15 minutes of calls.

Use Examples and Incidents

Examples and incidents help your reader form a mental picture of your ideas. When you use an example, you show how something happened in one particular case. The following paragraph is developed with an example:

> Having a copier in a small office saves time. For example, you will not have to send your assistant out to the copy shop, wait two hours, and then get your print job back. You will have your copies as soon as the document is done.

Here is a paragraph using an incident to illustrate a similar point:

> All copiers are not as easy to set up as the Spectrum 450B. We asked two people to unpack and set up two different office copiers. The person setting up the Spectrum 450B needed five minutes to take it out of the box, plug it in, and load the paper. The person setting up the rival brand was still setting it up 30 minutes later.

Use Sensory Details

Writers use sensory details in novels and short stories to describe settings and characters. Sensory details tell what the thing or scene looks like, sounds like, and feels like. Include smells and tastes if they are important. Use words that appeal to feelings and emotions.

When you write at work, your manager might ask you to write a product description for a catalog. Or, you might have to describe a new business location. Whenever your task is to describe, choose words and images that help your reader to picture what you are describing.

When you gather descriptive details, concentrate on what you most want readers to notice. Then, find words that appeal to the senses to help your audience see what you are describing.

Here are the physical details a writer gathered to describe the Spectrum 450B copier:

Sight: sleek, honey-beige case

Sound: gentle hum of the motor

Touch: rounded edges, slightly rough surface to keep papers from slipping

Smell: clean, no ozone fumes

Use Reasons

Present your strongest, most convincing reasons when your purpose is to persuade readers to change their mind. The best reasons are the ones that address your audience's concerns.

WRITING IN THE REAL WORLD: FIRST DRAFT

The title tells what the writing is about.

Travel Tips
Pre-Travel Planning

The opening asks a question of the reader to get the reader's attention. The second sentence explains the informative purpose of the writing.

Are you planning to travel in the next few months? We've put together a bunch of cool travel tips to make your trip a success.

Call your travel agent early. Remember, the early bird catches the worm. Special offers come up quickly and last only a short time. Sunrise Travel can help you get the most for your money.

If you've already decided where you want to go, read about its history and major attractions. Decide what you want to see most. Then see if there's a tour to take you there maybe. If the people speak another language, learn a few important words. For example, in Spanish, you'd say "hola!" instead of "hello" and "gracias" instead of "thank you."

The writer gives examples of words in Spanish the reader might learn.

If you're going out of the country, make sure your passport is not expired. If you plan to get a motor vehicle or something, get an International Driver's License.

The writer provides a reason to support the advice in this paragraph.

A week before your trip, call the hotel or motel you'll be staying at. Be sure that you're confirmed. Get a confirmation number too. You don't want to land in a strange place and have no place to stay.

Don't run out of important things like medications. Make sure you have enough to last you for the trip. Get sun block, too, if you're sensitive to sun.

Right before you leave, stop the mail. Maybe a neighbor will pick it up for you. Stop newspaper deliveries. Arrange to have someone water your plants.

Call the airline a day in advance if you need special meals in flight—kosher, low salt, low fat, or whatever your doctor recommends.

Have a great trip!

Look to Sunrise Travel for all your travel needs.

The writer ends by reminding the reader of her business, which is providing these helpful tips.

FIGURE 5-3 As you read through the draft, you will note a number of areas that Kendra needs to revise. **What are some of the revisions she must make?**

This paragraph uses reason to convince a customer to buy a copier:

> The Spectrum 450B is the best copier for your small office. It is inexpensive to run. It gives you all the convenience of the local copy shop right in your own office. The Spectrum's crisp, sharp copies make your work look professional. The two-year warranty gives you peace of mind.

PREWRITE TO CREATE A FIRST DRAFT

Kendra Banks works for Sunrise Travel, a small agency. The owner of the company has decided to send monthly travel tips to regular customers. She has asked Kendra to plan and write these tips.

Kendra decided that the purpose of the travel tips is to provide information that is useful to travelers. She pictured the tips being printed as a one-page letter that travelers could refer to when they prepare for their trip and when they are traveling. Kendra and her employer brainstormed topics that might appeal to their clients. FIGURE 5-4 shows the first four topics they listed.

FIGURE 5-4 Kendra and her employer brainstormed some ideas for her first travel letter, "Pre-Travel Planning." **How might this list have helped her create her first draft?**

Narrow the Topic

Because most Sunrise Travel customers fly, Kendra decided to narrow the topic so that it would appeal to people who use airlines. Her employer agreed that this topic is limited enough to write about in a one-page letter.

Gather Information

After she chose her topic, Kendra researched the material. She used travel books and travel-related Web sites to collect information. She also drew on the travel experiences of her family and friends. She wanted the travel tips letter to be a real service to customers.

In FIGURE 5-3, on page 88, you saw Kendra's first draft. Kendra had a feeling of satisfaction when she finished her draft. She knew it was not perfect, but she had written down the important points she wanted to make. She had made a good start.

Lesson Review

CHECK YOUR UNDERSTANDING

1. EXPLAINING What is Kendra's purpose for writing her travel tips?

2. GENERALIZING Look again at FIGURE 5-3 on page 88. How would Kendra's draft be different if her clients traveled by camper instead of by plane?

APPLY WHAT YOU LEARN

Write a draft of tips for a person's first day on a new job or in a new school. Include useful information to help the person get off to a good start.

Grammar Workshop

Using Transition Words

Transition words show the relationship between ideas in sentences and in paragraphs. They show your reader how your ideas relate to one another. As you revise, add transition words to help your reader follow your thoughts.

Here are some transition words that can be useful:

Time: *later, soon, then, next, today, at, before, during*

Add Information: *in addition, besides, also, too, next, moreover, as well as*

Contrast: *but, yet, on the other hand, however, although, otherwise*

Examples: *one, another, for example, for instance, such as*

Show Results: *as a result, consequently, therefore, thus, finally, last*

Application

On a separate sheet of paper, rewrite the sentences below. Add transition words as indicated.

1. Working as a camp counselor can be a great way to spend the summer; ____, you should know what the camp expects. (contrast)

2. We will attend the meeting, ____ we will drive back home. (time)

3. ____ the company will no longer allow vacation days to be carried over to the next year. (add information)

4. ____ the summer, she worked in a hospital. (time)

5. Chuck disliked working with numbers; ____ he took a job as a statistical clerk. (contrast)

6. Some careers require a good education; ____ a computer service technician needs to understand computers. (examples)

7. ____ a marine engineer works in the marine science division of the company. (add information)

8. A toolmaker works in manufacturing; ____ a tool designer works in art. (contrast)

9. She earned a degree in dental hygiene, ____ she took a job with a dentist. (time)

10. There are many kinds of construction jobs, ____, roofer and building inspector. (examples)

For more information,
SEE PAGES 341, 345.

Editing the Draft

What Do You
Already Know?
How have you revised
papers you have written
for school?

Think About It   What kinds
of things should you look for
when you revise your writing?

When you edit your work, you revise so that your writing is clear and accurate. You make sure that your information is up to date. You check that you have said what you wanted to say and that you have said it in a way that your audience will understand.

DECIDING HOW MUCH TO REVISE

Before other people read your writing, you must make it the best that it can be. Some writing does not need to be perfect. For example, you do not need to revise and make a final copy of a quick note to yourself. When you write for others, however, you want to make your writing clear and error-free. Writings such as company-wide notices, customer letters, and product information sheets need careful attention. These kinds of writing may need to be revised several times before the final product is approved by your manager.

What Do You Look for When You Revise?

Each kind of writing requires a different approach to revision. For example, a sales letter should focus on presenting the product favorably so that customers will buy it. However, some issues are common to all types of writing. FIGURE 5-5 on page 92 shows things to remember when you revise any document.

Revise for Purpose and Audience

When you began prewriting, you decided on your purpose and your audience. As projects proceed, these targets can change. You may decide that your letter to an angry customer has to be persuasive instead of informative. You want the customer to accept the solution you propose, not just to have more information about the product. As you revise, keep in mind your purpose and your audience.

Revise for Organization

As you learned in Lesson 4-5, you may organize your information in a number of different ways. Here are a few ways to use those methods of organization:

- Use chronological, or time, order to tell when events happen or should happen.

- Use spatial order to show how items are placed in relation to each other.

- Use order of importance when you have one especially strong reason that you want readers to understand.

- Use a cause-and-effect order to stress what happens as a result of something else.

- Use comparisons and contrasts to show how things are alike and how they are different.

Read your sentences slowly to yourself when you edit your work. Check to be sure that the organization will be clear to your reader.

Revise for Unity

A piece of writing has **unity** when all the sentences develop the main idea. When you edit, reread your writing. Decide if all of your sentences support your main idea. If they do not, revise your writing so that your reader will be sure of what you want to say.

If you find sentences that do not support your topic sentence, you have two choices. You might delete them or decide that they support a different topic sentence. In that case, revise your topic sentence so that it matches your supporting details.

As you reread each paragraph, look for the following elements. They show that your work has unity.

- **A precise topic** Do all of your sentences support the main idea? If not, revise your work until all of your sentences work together.

- **Details that make your points** If your evidence is not convincing, add supporting sentences that give more facts and details about your topic.

- **Smoothly linked sentences** Check for sentences that seem to be out of place. These sentences make your writing sound as if you have changed direction. You may need to move these sentences to another paragraph or delete them.

Revise for Coherence

When your writing has **coherence**, all the ideas are connected in a way that makes sense. A piece of writing is coherent when all the sentences flow clearly and logically into one another. When you edit for coherence, you make sure that your ideas flow from one to another.

When you edit, check to be sure that the movement from one sentence to another is easy to follow. To choose the right transition word, match your topic and your method of organization.

As you revise for coherence, look for these elements:

- **A clear topic** Your reader should know exactly what you are writing about and why you are writing.

- **Clearly presented ideas** When you introduce unfamiliar ideas, make sure that your reader can understand them. To explain your points, for example, you may need to use a technical term. Be sure to explain this term when you first mention it. You may wish to give an example, too, if appropriate.

- **A focused presentation** Do what you promise to do in your topic sentence. If you say that you will discuss why customers should buy a particular computer, do not discuss a different computer.

THINGS TO REMEMBER WHEN YOU REVISE

Purpose and Audience	Have I met my purpose? Am I speaking to the audience I have in mind?
The Quality of Development and Organization	Does my writing develop logically? Is it well organized? Did I choose the right topic, content, and approach?
Unity and Coherence	Do all the sentences relate to one idea or to the topic? Is what I am saying about the topic clear?
Word Choice	Have I used the best, most exact, and appropriate words to convey my meaning?

FIGURE 5-5 If you answer these questions, you will revise your writing more effectively. **How might reviewing your purpose and audience help you edit a draft?**

Travel Tips
Pre-Travel Planning

Are you planning to travel in the next few months? We've put together a bunch of cool travel tips to make your trip a success.

Call your travel agent early. Remember, the early bird catches the worm. Special offers come up quickly and last only a short time. Sunrise Travel can help you get the most for your money.

If you've already decided where you want to go, read about its history and major attractions. Decide what you want to see most. Then see if there's a tour to take you there maybe. If the people speak another language, learn a few important words. For example, in Spanish, you'd say "hola!" instead of "hello" and "gracias" instead of "thank you."

If you're going out of the country, make sure your passport is not expired. If you plan to get a motor vehicle or something, get an International Driver's License.

A week before your trip, call the hotel or motel you'll be staying at. Be sure that you're confirmed. Get a confirmation number too. You don't want to land in a strange place and have no place to stay.

Don't run out of important things like medications. Make sure you have enough to last you for the trip. Get sun block, too, if you're sensitive to sun.

Right before you leave, stop the mail. Maybe a neighbor will pick it up for you. Stop newspaper deliveries. Arrange to have someone water your plants.

Call the airline a day in advance if you need special meals in flight—kosher, low salt, low fat, or whatever your doctor recommends.

Have a great trip!

Look to Sunrise Travel for all your travel needs.

> This is Kendra's first draft.

> This is Kendra's revised draft.

> The writer has deleted the cliché "The early bird catches the worm."

Travel Tips Pre-Travel Planning

Will you be traveling in the next few months?

• Call your travel agent early. Special offers come up quickly and last only a short time. Sunrise Travel can help you get the most for your money.

• Read travel books about your destination. Decide what you want to see most. Learn a few words of the language people speak. For example, visiting Spain, you'd say "hola!" instead of "hello" and "gracias" instead of "thank you."

• Get a passport and visas if you need them. If you're renting a car, get an International Driver's License.

• If you make hotel reservations on your own for side trips, get a confirmation number. You don't want to find on your arrival that you have no place to stay.

• Are you on medication? Bring-along enough for the trip. Are you sensitive to sun? Pack your sun block.

• Stop the mail and newspaper deliveries. Ask a neighbor to water your plants.

• Call the airline a day in advance if you need low-salt or other special meals in flight.

Have a great trip! Look to Sunrise Travel for all your travel needs.

> The formal "motor vehicle" has been changed to the informal "car."

> Unnecessary words and phrases have been taken out to make the paragraph flow more smoothly.

> For better organization, the writer has changed the letter from paragraphs to bulleted items.

FIGURE 5-6 On this page, you can see Kendra's revision of her Travel Tips letter. **Why do you think Kendra has decided to use a bulleted list?**

- **Transition words that smoothly connect your ideas** Transitions help make your writing flow. They act as signposts that show your reader the way from one idea to the next. Appropriate transitions help your reader follow your arguments.

Revise for Word Choice

The words you use in your sentences should be appropriate for your purpose and audience. Once you decide how formal or informal your writing should be, your **diction**, or word choice, needs to be consistent with that decision.

- Use formal and informal language correctly. **Formal language** is the language most often used in serious books and articles. **Informal language** is most often used on television news shows and in general-audience magazines. For example, the word *cosmetics* is an example of formal language; *make-up* is an example of informal language.

- Avoid **clichés**. A cliché is an overworked expression such as "as brave as a lion" and "down in the dumps." When you revise, replace clichés with specific words that show your meaning clearly.

- Avoid **inflated diction.** Inflated diction is language that is used to try to impress people and to make the writer sound important. In most writing, it sounds out of place. For example, "He dispatched his canine companion to procure assistance" is much less clear than "He sent his dog for help."

REVISE FOR ORGANIZATION AND STRUCTURE

To understand the organization and structure of a piece of writing, study the two drafts Kendra wrote in FIGURE 5-6 on page 93. Think about the changes she made. Do you think her revisions made her travel letter easier to understand?

Lesson Review

CHECK YOUR UNDERSTANDING

1. EXPLAINING Describe four things you should think about when you edit your writing.

2. SYNTHESIZING How can you check your writing for unity and coherence?

APPLY WHAT YOU LEARN

Look at Kendra's draft and her revision of her Travel Tips letter in FIGURE 5-6 on page 93. Work with a partner to identify all the changes Kendra made and tell why she made them. Do you see any other changes that she should have made?

Avoiding Dangling Modifiers

A dangling modifier is a phrase that is not connected to the rest of the sentence. It usually appears at the beginning of a sentence. What the phrase should modify is missing. When you revise your writing, look for dangling modifiers. If you find one, rewrite the sentence so that your meaning is clear.

Incorrect Example   On leaving the office, the door slammed.

Who left the office? This sentence seems to say that the door left the office. That is because the phrase **on leaving the office** does not modify anything in the sentence. It is a dangling modifier.

Correct Examples   The door slammed when Ellen left the office.
On leaving the office, Ellen slammed the door.

Application

Each sentence below has a dangling modifier. On a separate sheet of paper, revise the sentences to make their meaning clear.

1. To revise your writing, your software should have a spell checker.
2. Walking down the street, the employment office was straight ahead.
3. Working in the humid factory, her eyes hurt.
4. Filling in the application, the pencil lead broke.
5. Practicing for the interview, his voice became hoarse.
6. Working at three jobs, my résumé was very impressive.
7. Pouring oil into the motor casing, the machine worked quietly.
8. Graduating from college, the company hired three accountants.
9. While attending the meeting, my computer crashed.
10. Listening to the long speech, the air conditioner hummed.

For more information, **SEE PAGE 342.**

Proofreading the Draft

What Do You Already Know?

Did you ever hear a sentence that you immediately knew was incorrect? How do you decide if a sentence is correct or incorrect?

Think About It Why should writers worry about the final form of a piece of writing?

When you wrote your first draft, you were interested mostly in getting your ideas down on paper or on the computer screen. When you edited it, you studied the content of what you wrote. You made sure that it was correct, complete, and well organized. When you proofread, you pay attention to the little things: grammar, usage, spelling, capitalization, and punctuation. These little things can make a big difference in how your writing is received by others.

MOVING TOWARD A FINAL DRAFT

On the job, you might make many revisions to your writing before your manager is satisfied with your work. A store or a Web site that wants to earn money from its fall catalog, for example, must make sure that every product description is appealing and that every price and stock number is correct. Mistakes can cost money and drive away customers.

At some point, however, revisions come to an end. Writers then move on to the proofreading stage of the writing process.

DEVELOPING A PROOFREADING ROUTINE

All writers have a method of proofreading that they prefer. Some writers like to work on a computer screen. Others prefer a pencil or pen on paper.

Some writers proofread a paper backwards, sentence by sentence, so that they can pay attention to the words without being distracted by the content. Some writers even keep a list of personal mistakes to look for, such as spelling errors they repeatedly make. Each time they see a new pattern of mistakes, they add it to their list.

There are other writers who exchange papers with a friend or co-worker and check each other's work. Afterwards, the partners discuss their errors and correct them. Try several of these methods, and stick with the one that works best for you.

PROOFREADING FOR SENTENCE STRUCTURE

When you proofread, check for common problems in sentence structure. Read your words slowly, and question every sentence. FIGURE 5-7 on page 97 shows some things to look for and fix.

Varying Your Sentence Structure

Use sentences of different lengths to create a rhythm and flow. Not every sentence has to be a statement. For variety, you can ask questions or make a request, as in this example:

> Have you ever heard of a store that will give you a gift just for walking in? A. J. Johnson's will. The first 50 people in the store on Monday will receive a free backpack. Come and bring a friend with you.

THINGS TO FIX	WHAT THEY ARE AND HOW TO FIX THEM	EXAMPLES
Sentence Fragments	Parts of sentences expressed as a complete sentence	**Incorrect** Left the building and went home. Because we were tired.
	To fix, add a subject or a verb to both fragments. You can also join the fragments to make one sentence.	**Correct** We left the building and went home because we were tired.
Run-on Sentences	Two or more sentences joined by commas	**Incorrect** The store window was decorated for the holidays, children pressed their noses to the glass.
	To fix, break the run-on sentence into separate sentences.	**Correct** The store window was decorated for the holidays. Children pressed their noses to the glass.
Short, Choppy Sentences	Sentences that do not flow together.	**Incorrect** I made my lunch. I left for work.
	To fix, combine the ideas in short, choppy sentences into one new sentence and use transition words to make the connections clear.	**Correct** I made my lunch before I left for work.

FIGURE 5-7 All these errors relate to sentence form. **Which type of error have you noted in your own writing?**

PROOFREADING FOR WORD CHOICE AND CLARITY

Proofreading is also the time to look at the words you used and how you used them. The purpose here is to make sure your meaning is clear. FIGURE 5-8 on page 98 shows some common mistakes in word choice.

PROOFREADING FOR MECHANICS

When you proofread, you check for mistakes in spelling, capitalization, and punctuation. You may want to use the proofreaders' marks shown in FIGURE 5-9 on page 99.

Checking Punctuation

As you reread your work, use this list to check your punctuation:

- End every sentence with the correct punctuation. *Examples*: Is this right? Yes, it is. Wow!

- Add commas between items in a series and between the independent clauses in compound sentences. *Examples*: I like yogurt, fruit, and granola mixed together. The phone rang, but no one answered it.

COMMON MISTAKES IN WORD CHOICE	RULES	EXAMPLES
Easily Confused Words	Be sure that you have chosen the correct words to express your ideas.	*To/too/two* We sent the dog *to* obedience school. My brother sent his dog, *too.* The family has *two* dogs in that school.
Double Negatives	It is incorrect to use two negatives (*no, never, not,* or *none*) in a sentence.	**Incorrect** I *don't* have *no* carfare. **Correct** I *don't* have *any* carfare.
Comparative Forms	Use the comparative form to compare two things. Use the superlative form to compare more than two things.	**Comparative:** A car is *faster* and *more direct* than the bus. **Superlative:** Mott Street is the *fastest* and *most direct* route to my job.
Forms of Pronouns	Use *I, we,* and *they* as the subjects of sentences. Use *me, us,* and *them* as the objects of sentences and after prepositions.	**Incorrect** *Him* and *me* went to the zoo. **Correct** *He* and *I* went to the zoo.
Double Subjects	A noun that is used as the subject of a sentence does not need a pronoun after it.	**Incorrect** *My friend she* went home. **Correct** *My friend* went home.
Pronoun Referents	Make it clear which word a pronoun refers to in a sentence.	**Unclear** The player told the coach *he* should go home. **Clear** "Coach, *I* should go home," said the player.

FIGURE 5-8 Most of these mistakes are easy to correct once you recognize them. **How do you think correcting these errors could make your writing easier to understand?**

- Write possessives correctly. *Examples*: I did not borrow Anne's hat or her mittens.

- Use capital letters, commas, and quotation marks where they are needed. *Example*: "This town," he said, "is very near the airport."

Capitalizing Words Correctly

- Capitalize all proper nouns—the names of specific people, places, or things. *Examples*: Yes, Lew, Helena is the capital of Montana.

- Capitalize the first word in a sentence that is directly quoted. *Examples*: "The manager will do his part of the project," he said. "You know you can count on him."

- Capitalize specific geographic areas, but do not capitalize general directions. *Examples*: We left the East and headed west.

Spelling Words Correctly

If you are inputting your document, use the spell-check feature of your word-processing program.

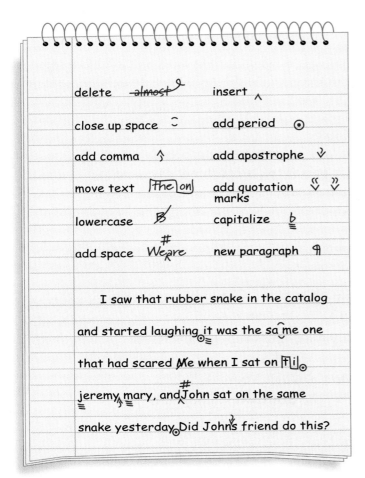

FIGURE 5-9 These are just some of the proofreader's marks that writers use. **Why do you think these marks were created?**

However, do not rely on the spell checker to get every word right. For instance, it cannot tell if you meant to use *all ready* instead of *already*.

Keep a personal spelling list of words you frequently misspell. Look at it as you proofread. When you have misspelled a new word two times, add it to your list.

Here are some tips for spelling troublesome words:

- Watch out for silent letters. Many words have to be memorized. *Examples*: lamb, knife, sword, writing, thought

- Think about homonyms. Homonyms are words that sound alike but are spelled differently. *Examples*: meat/meet, sight/cite/site, peace/piece, real/reel, write/right

- Know the difference between single words and two-word phrases that sound the same. *Examples*: everyday (meaning "ordinary") and every day (meaning "each day")

Lesson Review

CHECK YOUR UNDERSTANDING

1. ELABORATING Explain two important things to check when you proofread your work for word choice and clarity.

2. DRAWING CONCLUSIONS Why is the proofreading stage of the writing process important?

APPLY WHAT YOU LEARN

Copy the following paragraph; then, edit and proofread it to correct the mistakes. *Note*: There are several ways to rewrite this paragraph so that it is correct.

> Are you traveling along the coastline. Plan your itinerary so that you drive on the "view" side, of road. In California, for example, you would drive south from san Francisco You will always see where the good turnoffs are. Even more important, you wont have to keep crossing trafick in order to get to them.

Grammar Workshop

Using Capitalization Correctly

Capital letters work as signals. They tell your reader when a new thought is being introduced. They also show the reader that a particular person, place, or thing is being discussed. Be sure to check for correct capitalization when you proofread.

Here are some of the rules for capitalization:

- Capitalize the first word in a sentence. *Example:* **This** company has good employee benefits.

- Capitalize proper nouns and adjectives. *Example:* **Jacob** met the **Chinese** scientist **May Cheo** at the **Atlantic Building** in **New York**.

- Capitalize the first word of a sentence that is directly quoted. *Example:* The scientist asked, "**Haven't** we met before?"

- Capitalize specific geographic areas. Do not capitalize general directions. *Example:* We started our company in a small town in the **Southwest** just south of Arizona.

- Capitalize the names of monuments and well-known places. *Example:* We will meet the tour guide at the **Washington Monument**.

- Capitalize titles only when they appear in front of names. *Example:* Last week, **Senator** Johnson talked with the president of the company.

- Capitalize the names of ethnic groups, nationalities, languages, and religions. *Example:* Most **Brazilian** people speak **Portuguese**.

- Capitalize the first-person pronoun, *I*. *Example:* May **I** go out?

Application

Rewrite the following sentences on a separate sheet of paper. Make corrections in capitalization.

1. the rigby medical company is in los angeles, california.
2. all the senators will give speeches near the lincoln memorial.
3. in order to complete his degree, larry had to take a course in english.
4. "congratulations," said the director of human resources, doreen peterson.
5. "welcome to our company," said mr. lopez. "our training program will help you succeed."
6. the picnic will be held on mount washington in new hampshire.
7. "i owe this honor to all the people i have worked with."
8. my uncle harry worked part-time in yosemite national park.
9. you have to have a degree to work at burnley chiropractic center.
10. one-third of our employees are african american and one-third are latino.

For more information, **SEE PAGE 364.**

Publishing a Document

Publishing is the final step of the writing process. In this step, your writing reaches its audience. When you publish your work in school, you share your ideas with your teacher, classmates, and perhaps your school community. Publishing in the workplace might mean printing a brochure or sending a letter to customers.

What Do You Already Know?

What are some of the different types of publications you have seen or read?

Think About It How do you think publication would affect the way a writer creates a piece of writing?

PUBLISHING FITS INTO THE PROCESS

After you have made all the corrections in your **copy**, the material to be published, you are ready for the final stage of the writing process. In school and on the job, this is when you achieve your purpose: you communicate your ideas to an audience. Words alone might not be enough. The final product also might contain **graphics**, such as charts, graphs, illustrations, or photographs.

PREPARING THE FINAL DOCUMENT

As you work on any writing project, think about the **format**, or the appearance, of your finished document.

Companies often have standard formats for reports, memos, and letters. Other projects might have more creative formats. Think about all the glossy, full-color brochures you have seen for cars, computers, and other merchandise. The art and the text work together to sell the product.

Kendra wanted her Travel Tips letter to catch people's attention. As a result, she added a bulleted list and graphics. FIGURE 5-10 on page 102 shows the final version of Kendra's letter.

When you publish a document, you present it to your audience. **How does knowing your audience help you to revise your writing?**

Lesson Review

CHECK YOUR UNDERSTANDING

1. EVALUATING Do you think Kendra's audience will find her Travel Tips letter useful? Explain.

2. GENERALIZING Why do you think companies care about the way their printed materials look?

APPLY WHAT YOU LEARN

Work with a classmate to analyze Kendra's published version of her Travel Tips letter in FIGURE 5-10 on page 102. Do you think her work will appeal to her audience? Do you think she achieved her purpose? Present your conclusions to the class.

Travel Tips
Pre-Travel Planning

> The newly designed title grabs the reader's attention.

Will you be traveling in the next few months?

- Call your travel agent early. Special offers come up quickly and last for only a short time. Sunrise Travel can help you get the most for your money.
- Read travel books about your destination. Decide what you want to see the most. Learn a few words of the language people speak. For example, visiting Spain, you'd say "hola!" instead of "hello" and "gracias" instead of "thank you."
- Get a passport and visas if you need them. If you're renting a car, get an International Driver's License.
- If you make hotel reservations on your own for side trips, get a confirmation number. You don't want to find on your arrival that you have no place to stay.
- Do you take medication? Bring along enough for the trip. Are you sensitive to sun? Pack your sun block.
- Stop the mail and newspaper deliveries. Ask a neighbor to water your plants.
- Call the airline a day in advance if you need low-salt or other special meals in flight.

Have a great trip!

Sunrise Travel
For All Your Travel Needs

> The writer has centered the last two lines to make the name of her business and its slogan stand out for the reader.

> The added illustrations gives the letter color and variety.

FIGURE 5-10 Here is Kendra's final draft of her first Travel Tips letter. **How do the graphics change the appearance of her work?**

If you create your documents on a word processor, you need to save them. At school, you save documents on a floppy disk, or diskette. You might also save your documents in a specific folder on a hard drive. If you are using your own computer, you should save your documents both on your hard drive and on a diskette or other storage device. This way, if a document is lost or damaged, you will have a backup copy. You can also share diskettes with other people, including printing companies. Having organized documents and up-to-date backup copies can save you a great deal of work.

Saving Files

To save a file to your hard drive, follow these steps:

- Click Save As on your toolbar or drop-down menu.

- The computer will then ask you to name the file. Choose a name that you will remember, then click Save.

- Close the document.

To copy a file to a diskette or hard drive, do the following:

- Open the document you wish to copy.

- Put a diskette in your floppy drive.

- Click File on your toolbar or drop-down menu.

- Go to Save As on the File menu and click.

- Choose a location for your document; then, click Save.

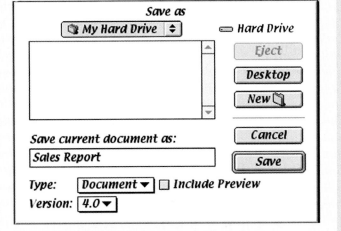

- Close your document, then retrieve it to make sure you have two copies of your file.

Using Subdirectories

Many word-processing programs allow you to store files in a directory called "My Documents." It is useful to create subdirectories, or folders inside folders, to organize your files. Create subdirectories for every major task you have. You might, for example, have separate subdirectories for letters to customers, marketing brochures, sales information, and personnel files.

Application

Create a document and save it. Write a list of steps describing what you did.

REVIEW

Chapter Summary

During the writing process, a document goes from a rough draft to a published product. When you write a draft, you put down your main ideas and the details that support them. Next, you edit the draft for organization, structure, unity, and coherence. This is also the time to check your word choice. In the proofreading stage, you check for errors in grammar, spelling, and punctuation. Finally, you publish the document in the best format for your audience and purpose.

Key Words

draft	cliché
unity	inflated diction
coherence	copy
diction	graphics
formal language	format
informal language	

Copy the following sentences on a separate sheet of paper. Fill in the blank with a word from the list above.

1. "As pale as a ghost" is an example of a ___.

2. Contractions and everyday words can be used in ___.

3. The ___ of a business letter always requires an inside address.

4. The first ___ of the memo was too long and had to be edited.

5. Kendra's tips card has ___ because all of her sentences develop her main idea.

6. There are several types of ___, including photographs and maps.

7. Your work has ___ when all of the sentences flow clearly into one another.

8. "Your presence is requested" is an example of ___.

9. Your ___ is the way you use words and the kind of words you choose when you write.

10. ___ is used to try to make the writer sound important.

11. Check your ___ carefully before you send it to the printer.

Application: Editing a Paragraph

Read the following paragraph. To check that the paragraph will be clear to its audience, answer the questions on a separate sheet of paper.

Everybody travels with luggage of some kind. Put your name, address, and telephone number on a card *inside* every bag you take on your trip, whether you carry it or check it. You can tie a name tag on the handle, too, but it may fall off or get pulled off. Name tags inside bags stay there. Further, if your bag gets lost at the airport, baggage handlers will look inside for identification. Your inside name tag can guarantee the return of your bag.

1. Which phrase best describes the topic of this paragraph? Explain your answer.

   a. How to make name tags for luggage

   b. The importance of putting name tags inside luggage

   c. Ways that luggage gets lost

2. What is the purpose of the paragraph: to inform, describe, explain, or persuade? Explain your answer.

3. Who might be the audience for this paragraph?

Application: Proofreading a Paragraph

On a separate sheet of paper, copy the following paragraph. Use proofreader's marks to make corrections. Then, rewrite the paragraph so that it is correct.

how do you tellapart two look-alike bags on an airport baggage carousle it is easy. you make your bag stand out from everyone elses. wrap brightly collared electrical tape around the Handle of your bag. read yellow or lime really stand out. poisonous Insects use bright colors like these so that Birds won't eat them. the first thing a person grabs orf is the handle. if the Handle is a bright color other people will know that it is not their bag. name Tags are hard to read. Initials in thee side of the bag are not visable when bags are piled next to each other. a brightly colored handle is your best bet.

Grammar Workshop Practice

On a separate sheet of paper, rewrite the following sentences.

Part I. Place transition words where they are indicated.

1. Kendra had a feeling of great satisfaction ____ she finished her project. (time)

2. ____ to those duties, he helped in the kitchen. (additional information)

3. ____, the cafeteria food is inexpensive. (contrast)

4. ____, we recommend purchasing the Delta X-2. (add information)

5. Cooking requires many skills, ____ a good sense of smell and taste (examples).

Part II. Correct the dangling modifiers.

6. Limiting the research time, the computers crashed.

7. Writing three reports, the printer broke down.

8. Driving across town, the company was located on Locust Street.

9. While leaving the table, the plate broke.

10. Starting the car, the key fell to the floor.

Part III. Correct the capitalization.

11. on tuesday we will celebrate the battle of yorktown.

12. senator jenson said that the rugby motor company would receive an award.

13. a branch of our company is located in norway, a country in europe.

14. the passaic river is in new jersey.

15. james and joanna are moving to southern michigan.

Portfolio Project   Writing a Product Description

Think of a sandwich or other food that you particularly enjoy. Write a product description in paragraph form that describes that food. Your audience is readers who are unfamiliar with the food. Your purposes are to describe it and to persuade people to try it. Be sure to complete the following steps:

• Write a first draft of your ideas.

• Edit your draft, revising to be sure you have made your points clearly.

• Proofread your work, checking for errors in spelling, grammar, and mechanics.

• Publish your product description to your audience.

Add your finished description to your portfolio.

Read the following information about two careers in which people use writing skills. Think about the goals and the skills the jobs require. Then, answer the questions below.

Chef: *Food Services*

If you like to work with people and you enjoy preparing food, you might consider a career as a chef. Chefs work in restaurants, hotels, and cafeterias. Chefs must be neat, creative, and have strong senses of taste and smell. They also supervise other workers and write orders and directions for others to follow.

A chef should

- have a background in business and food preparation.
- be able to work quickly and efficiently.
- have the ability to do delicate work with his or her hands.

Minimum Education: post-secondary education or apprenticeship
Starting Salary: $20,000
Related Careers: Bakers, Cooks

For more information, contact the National Restaurant Association, 1200 Seventeenth Street, NW, Washington, DC 20036-3097. You will find this association on the Internet at www.restaurant.org.

Medical Records Technician: *Health Services*

If you want to work in a health-related industry and you enjoy using computers, you might consider a career as a medical records technician. Technicians are responsible for collating and maintaining medical records. They work in hospitals, clinics, HMOs, and other health-care facilities. Medical records technicians may also assist in business or admitting offices.

A medical records technician should

- have experience in a health-care institution.
- display strong verbal and written communication skills.

Minimum Education: a two-year associate degree program accredited by the AHIMA (American Health Information Management Association)
Starting Salary: $20,000 to $25,000
Related Careers: Medical Transcribers, Medical Writers

For more information, contact the American Health Information Management Association, 233 N. Michigan Avenue, Suite 3150, Chicago, IL 60601. You will find this association on the Internet at www.ahima.org.

EXPLORING CAREERS

1. **Suppose you take a job as a chef. How might understanding your audience help you attract customers?**

2. **Why might a medical records technician need editing skills? How do medical technicians publish their documents?**

"Winning the prize wasn't half as exciting as doing the work itself."

Maria Goeppert-Mayer (1906–1972)
Nobel Prize Winner

UNIT 3
WRITING TO EXPLAIN

In school, on the job, and in life, you will need to communicate to explain or inform. You may need to prepare a simple set of directions for a friend or a complicated business plan for a company you hope to start. In each case, you need to understand the reason you are writing or speaking and the audience that you are addressing. This unit focuses on speaking and writing to explain. You will also review the steps of the writing process. Once you complete this unit, you will know how to write and speak to explain your ideas.

READING AND WRITING DIRECTIONS

Monica is a cashier at Super Sun, a supermarket. Yesterday, Mr. Bannigan, the store manager, said to Monica, "We've hired a new employee. His name is Simon, and we would like you to train him to use the cash register."

As Monica started work that day, her mind raced through all the directions she would have to give to Simon. How should she explain the job of being a cashier to him? How can Monica communicate to Simon what he will need to know?

Key Words

directions

time clue words

brainstorming

feedback

memorandum

e-mail

Internet

Goals for Success

In this chapter, you will learn these skills:

Interpreting oral and written directions

 LISTENING / READING

Providing accurate oral and written directions

 SPEAKING

Acquiring and using feedback

 INTERPRETING AND COMMUNICATING INFORMATION

Using writing techniques to compose memos and e-mail

 KNOWING HOW TO LEARN / SELECTING TECHNOLOGY

PORTFOLIO PROJECT

MEMO OR E-MAIL

By the time you complete this chapter, you will know what Monica has to do to give Simon directions for using the cash register. You also will be able to write a set of directions to add to your own portfolio.

Reading and Following Directions

What Do You Already Know?

When have you had to read or ask someone for directions? When have you had to give directions to someone else? How did you make sure the person understood you?

Think About It Why must directions be clear and easy to understand?

You have just bought a new bookcase for your room. How do you put it together? You are working in an office when the Paper Jam light starts to blink on the copier. How do you fix it? In both cases, if you do not know what to do, you look for directions. You read them carefully and do what they tell you to do. If you cannot find directions or cannot understand them, you probably ask someone for help.

WHAT ARE DIRECTIONS?

Directions are instructions that explain a process. They give facts and details that help you learn what you need to know to get a job done. Most of the time, you listen to directions or read them. Sometimes, though, you give directions to other people—on the phone, in person, or in writing. You may be able to give directions for a simple task in only a sentence or two. For something more complicated—using some new computer software, for example—you may need to write much longer, more involved directions.

LISTENING TO DIRECTIONS

In school and on the job, you often do not receive written instructions. Your teacher or your employer might tell you how to do most day-to-day tasks. There are several things you can do to make sure you understand oral directions.

- Listen carefully to what is being said. Do not allow interruptions, such as someone walking into the room, to distract you.

- Concentrate on the directions being given. Do not be distracted by the way the speaker moves or acts.

- Listen to everything. Do not close your mind because you think you know what will be said next. Listen to all the information as if you were hearing it for the first time.

- Use word clues to remember directions. Pick out important words, and repeat them to yourself.

- Ask questions if something is not clear. Have the speaker explain in more detail what he or she is trying to say.

- Visualize, or create a mental picture of, each step of the directions.

- If possible, take notes as you listen. Make sure your notes are clear so that you will be able to understand them later.

READING DIRECTIONS

CD players, cordless phones, VCRs, and many other products you buy or use usually come with instruction booklets or directions. After you install or put together the product, keep the directions in a safe place. You might need to refer to them again to use or to fix the product.

When you read directions, do the following:

- Carefully read *all* of the directions. Do not stop part-way through and decide you know all you need to know. There may be important information that you have missed.

- Look for diagrams that are labeled. They will help you understand the parts of a product or the steps of a process.

- Look for numbers; **time clue words** such as *first*, *next*, and *then*; or phrases such as *in the morning*. These words will tell you in which order to do the steps.

- Look for a key word in each step that tells you exactly what to do. Key words are usually verbs, such as *load*, *turn*, or *press*.

- Follow each step of the directions. Do the steps in the order in which they are presented.

- If the directions do not make sense to you, ask a person with experience for help. If the directions are unclear or if some steps seem to be missing, contact the manufacturer for further information.

FIGURE 6-1 shows an example of the type of directions you see in everyday life. As you read the directions, look for the clues listed in this lesson.

Lesson Review

CHECK YOUR UNDERSTANDING

1. ELABORATING Describe three things you should do when someone is giving you directions.

2. INFERRING Why are time clue words and other key words important in directions?

APPLY WHAT YOU LEARN

Reread the directions for making microwave popcorn in FIGURE 6-1. In your own words, describe how to pop the popcorn. Then exchange papers with a classmate and read one another's explanations. Should any information be added?

FIGURE 6-1 Note that each step of the directions is numbered. **Why do you think that one sentence is written in all capital letters?**

Giving Directions

Think of directions you have used. What about them was helpful? Were any sections unclear?

Think About It Why are directions often written in the form of a list?

Sometimes, you have to give directions for other people to follow. Directions are sometimes written and sometimes spoken. They may not be long, but they should be detailed enough to show how to get the job done. If you are a restaurant manager who is preparing for a banquet, you will probably give very detailed oral instructions to your staff. If you need to tell a delivery person where to stack boxes, you might only need to write a note and tape it to the kitchen door.

IDENTIFY YOUR PURPOSE AND AUDIENCE

When you give directions, always keep in mind that your purpose is to give information. The information in directions is of a specific kind. You divide a task into its important parts. Then, you explain in step-by-step order how to do each part of the job so that other people will be able to do it correctly by themselves.

To identify your purpose and audience, ask yourself these questions:

- Who will read or listen to the directions?

- Is this a new task, or is it a familiar one that someone needs to do better?

- How much does this person already know about what to do?

- How well has he or she carried out directions in the past?

- How can I motivate this person to do a good job?

- How will these directions benefit my group or business?

- What problems or difficulties, if any, are these directions meant to fix?

MAKE A PLAN

Suppose you work in a summer camp. The camp directors have put you in charge of distributing sports equipment, games, and craft supplies. They ask you to post instructions for next year's staff. Your purpose is to make sure that none of the equipment and supplies in the activities locker get lost.

Brainstorm Ideas

After you think about your topic, you decide to write the instructions in the form of a list. You start your planning by **brainstorming**. Brainstorming means thinking about a wide range of ideas; it can be done by two or more people. Some of the ideas might be useful and others might not, but if you keep thinking, you will probably come up with some good ideas.

List Ideas

Consider the entire list of ideas that have come out of a brainstorming session. Eliminate ones that you think could not possibly work. As you narrow your list, you can create categories that cover each area of equipment and supplies. You decide that your directions will be attached to each closet or box containing materials. You will encase the instructions in plastic so that they will be secure and safe until next summer.

SOME DIRECTION TIPS

Here are some tips for giving effective directions:

- Do the task yourself. Record each step as you complete it, and note what is important to know about each one. If you can do the task, then another person can probably do it, too.

- If you are giving oral directions, write notes on an index card. Use the notes to remind yourself to include every important point.

- If you are giving written directions, you might write a list, then reorder the steps so that they are in the best possible sequence. Use time clue words such as *before*, *next*, and *after that*. These words will provide a guide for your audience to follow throughout the directions.

ASK FOR FEEDBACK

Feedback is a response or an answer. You probably do not need to get feedback for simple oral or written directions. You might want to receive feedback, however, for longer, more complex directions.

In such cases, ask for feedback from someone who is directly involved. In a business, customers, co-workers, and supervisors can offer suggestions. In other situations, friends may be helpful. Add their suggestions when you revise your directions.

FIGURE 6-2 shows a list of directions that one student made. The student completed the list after receiving feedback from the camp director and other counselors.

Instructions for the Activities Locker

1. Each morning check the activity schedule and the bins. Bring out the rainy-day board games if necessary.

2. Put up sign-out sheets for the counselors.

3. When counselors return items, check what they return against the sign-out sheet.

4. Collect items promptly. Put them away neatly.

5. Walk around at the end of the day. Look for missing items.

6. Write the camp director a note. List all lost or broken equipment.

7. Leave the locker neat at night.

FIGURE 6-2 shows one student's directions for managing the camp's activities locker. **Would you find it easy to follow these directions? Why or why not?**

Lesson Review

CHECK YOUR UNDERSTANDING

1. PRIORITIZING Why is it important to identify your audience before you give directions?

2. SUMMARIZING What are some ways to make sure your directions are clear?

APPLY WHAT YOU LEARN

Think about an activity you do well. Suppose you have to teach it to someone. First, think about your audience. Then, prepare a set of oral or written directions that will help the person successfully complete that activity. Give the directions to another person to see if he or she can complete the activity using your directions. Add information if necessary.

Grammar Workshop

Correcting Run-on Sentences

A run-on sentence is two or more complete thoughts that are not correctly joined or separated by punctuation. Run-on sentences make it difficult for your readers to understand the information they are reading. Avoid run-on sentences to make your directions clear.

Run-on Sentence   All the copiers broke down we sent for help.
Combined Sentence   All the copiers broke down, **and** we sent for help.

Three Ways to Correct Run-on Sentences:

- Use an end punctuation mark to separate complete thoughts.
     Example   All the copiers broke down. We sent for help.

- Use a comma and a connecting word (*and, but, for, nor, or, so, yet*) to combine sentences.
     Example   All the copiers broke down, **so** we sent for help.

- Use a semicolon to separate complete thoughts.
     Example   All the copiers broke down; we sent for help.

Application

Correct each of the following run-on sentences by using one of the three ways described above. Write your sentences on a separate sheet of paper.

1. Keep directions in a safe place use them when you need to fix a product.
2. Read directions carefully ask for help if you don't understand something.
3. Few people attend the meeting just the president and two board members will attend.
4. Our company sponsors the Special Olympics it is a program of sports for people with disabilities.
5. Sam placed his résumé on the Internet he received 40 job offers.
6. Every employee will learn new skills each person will accept new challenges.
7. None of the jobs is right for me I won't give up.
8. Lifeguards usually work part-time in some states they work full-time.
9. There are jobs in the federal government for fingerprint experts this is stressful work.
10. Other technicians choose to work in air technology they keep planes flying safely.

For more information, **SEE PAGES 342, 346.**

Ways to Communicate

People have more ways to present information today than they did ten years ago. As you decide on the means of communication you will use, remember that first impressions count. Think about your audience and your message. Outsiders often make snap judgments about a company when the first person they meet presents directions poorly. Your work represents not only you, but also your co-workers and your employer.

What Do You Already Know?

On a separate sheet of paper, list all the ways you communicate with others. Consider everything—from hand gestures to the latest technology.

Think About It Why is it important to choose the way in which you will communicate a message?

SELECT A FORMAT

Some instructions only involve writing a few words on a self-sticking note and putting the note on a door or phone. The format is simple. For longer directions, you will have to decide on the best format for your audience. If you are working for a company, ask your supervisor if there is a specific format for you to use when you prepare directions.

Signs and Posters

Signs and posters are effective ways to give directions to groups of people. Make the sign or poster large enough to be seen clearly. Adding a strong graphic or headline will grab people's attention. Be neat and legible. Avoid handwriting if you can. If possible, write your instructions on a word processor. Or ask someone who prints well to help.

FIGURE 6-3 shows a poster that a student created for a school food drive. It is designed to give directions to volunteers.

Accepting and Storing Food

- Do not accept perishable foods like bread, eggs, and milk.

- Put canned goods in separate cartons. Put vegetables with vegetables and fruit with fruit.

- If food products come in boxes, make sure the boxes are factory sealed. Do not accept any open boxes.

- Keep coffee, tea, and beverages together. Sort them at the end of the day.

- Thank people for their contributions!

FIGURE 6-3 Read the list of suggestions in this poster for collecting food for a food drive. **What is the purpose of the last suggestion?**

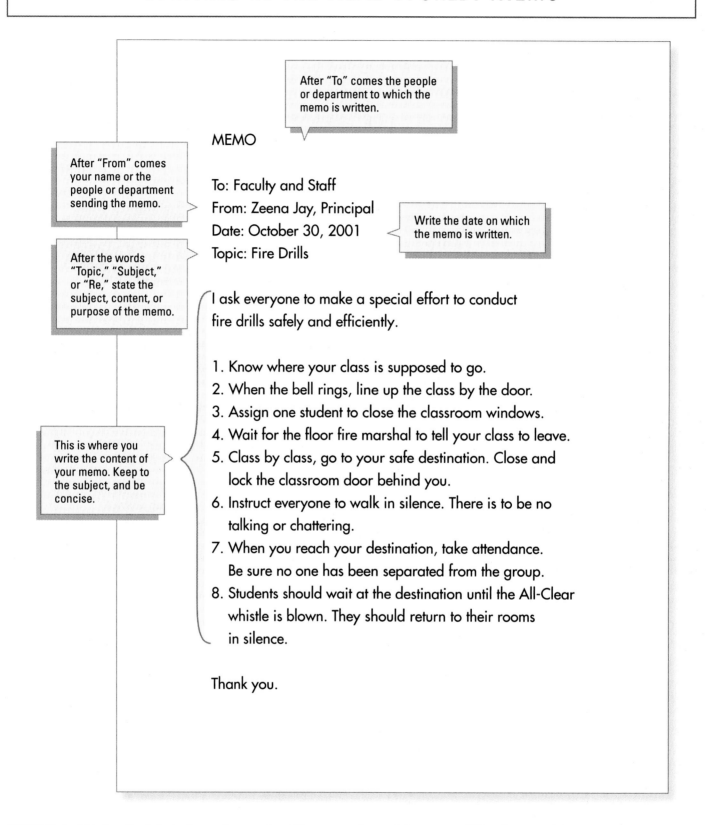

After "To" comes the people or department to which the memo is written.

MEMO

To: Faculty and Staff
From: Zeena Jay, Principal
Date: October 30, 2001
Topic: Fire Drills

After "From" comes your name or the people or department sending the memo.

Write the date on which the memo is written.

After the words "Topic," "Subject," or "Re," state the subject, content, or purpose of the memo.

I ask everyone to make a special effort to conduct fire drills safely and efficiently.

1. Know where your class is supposed to go.
2. When the bell rings, line up the class by the door.
3. Assign one student to close the classroom windows.
4. Wait for the floor fire marshal to tell your class to leave.
5. Class by class, go to your safe destination. Close and lock the classroom door behind you.
6. Instruct everyone to walk in silence. There is to be no talking or chattering.
7. When you reach your destination, take attendance. Be sure no one has been separated from the group.
8. Students should wait at the destination until the All-Clear whistle is blown. They should return to their rooms in silence.

Thank you.

This is where you write the content of your memo. Keep to the subject, and be concise.

FIGURE 6-4 Notice the labels that point out the different sections of the memo. **Why do you think memos have a line labeled *Topic* or *Subject*?**

Memorandums

A **memorandum**—or memo—is a short note written to convey information. A memo may be written from one person or department to another person or department in a company. It follows a particular format, which can change from company to company.

A memo is usually short and discusses only one subject. It also has some basic parts, as you can see in FIGURE 6-4 on page 116.

There are several occasions for which you might use a memo. You might write a memo to announce when and where a meeting will be held, who should attend, and the topics to be discussed. After the meeting, you might write a memo that explains the conclusions that were reached. You also could send a memo to give simple directions, such as to tell others how to order supplies or report absences.

E-Mail

Electronic mail—or **e-mail**—is a communication system that uses a network to send and receive messages electronically. These messages are often sent over the **Internet**, a network that links computer systems around the world.

E-mail has become a popular way to communicate with co-workers and with customers or clients. Many companies expect their employees to know how to send and receive e-mail. Using e-mail to conduct business is becoming as common as using the telephone.

E-mail is much faster than mail sent through the post office. In addition to its speed, e-mail has several other advantages. It is inexpensive. Messages sent to other people in your company usually cost nothing, and e-mail sent to people outside the company may cost as little as 15 cents.

Most e-mail systems also allow you to attach files to messages. Sending files as attachments is easier than printing documents and mailing them. The person who receives the e-mail can open the file, read it, make changes, and send it back to the sender—all in minutes instead of days.

Lesson Review

CHECK YOUR UNDERSTANDING

1. IDENTIFYING What should you consider before selecting a format for writing directions?

2. ANALYZING Why might a company want its employees to use a standard format for memos?

APPLY WHAT YOU LEARN

Suppose you work for a company that is planning a company picnic. Your supervisor has asked you to give directions to the staff about how to dress and what to bring. Select the format that you would like to use to communicate this information. Then, write the message you would send to your co-workers in the format you have selected.

An e-mail message can be sent to an unlimited number of people. **Why is the speed of e-mail important for business?**

Grammar Workshop

Changing Passive Voice to Active Voice

The voice of a verb shows whether the subject performs or receives the action of the verb. When you write or give directions, use the active voice. The active voice makes a direct connection between the person or thing and what is being done.

- In the passive voice, the subject receives the action. The passive voice is usually written with a form of the verb *to be*.

    > *Example*   Doris **was given** an award for her menu design.
    > (It is not clear who gave Doris the award.)

- In the active voice, the subject performs the action.

    > *Example*   The restaurant manager **gave** Doris an award for her new menu design.
    > (It is clear who gave Doris the award.)

To change passive voice to active voice, revise the sentence so that the person or thing that performs the action is the subject of the sentence.

Application

On a separate sheet of paper, revise the following sentences, changing the passive voice to the active voice.

1. The restaurant was owned by Larry, the chef.
2. The vegetables were canned by Julio in the factory.
3. It was thought by Jim that he could have done better in the interview.
4. The project was completed by Akeem.
5. Patricia will be trained by Kurt next week.
6. The schedule will be prepared by Elena.
7. Your bill has not been paid within the last 120 days.
8. The rotor was tightened by Harold.
9. Susan was asked for detailed contracts by the managing editor.
10. The company's new campaign was developed by the advertising department.

For more information, SEE PAGE 352.

TECH CONNECTION E-MAIL

E-mail, or electronic mail, is a convenient and important method of communication. It allows people to send and receive messages electronically. To use e-mail, you need Internet access and the e-mail address of the person who will receive your message. Like a letter, e-mail has specific parts that are included in every message.

When you look at an e-mail message, you see the following parts:

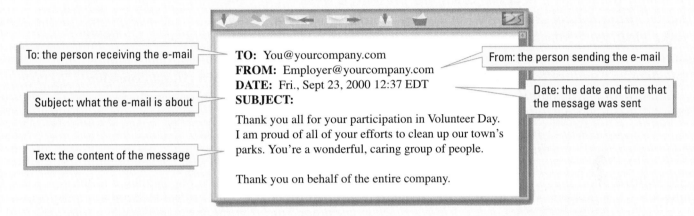

To: the person receiving the e-mail

Subject: what the e-mail is about

Text: the content of the message

TO: You@yourcompany.com
FROM: Employer@yourcompany.com
DATE: Fri., Sept 23, 2000 12:37 EDT
SUBJECT:

Thank you all for your participation in Volunteer Day. I am proud of all of your efforts to clean up our town's parks. You're a wonderful, caring group of people.

Thank you on behalf of the entire company.

From: the person sending the e-mail

Date: the date and time that the message was sent

An e-mail address, like your home address, has several parts. Those parts include the user name or screen name, "@" (at), and the domain locators (the server company + domain).

A typical e-mail address might look like this:

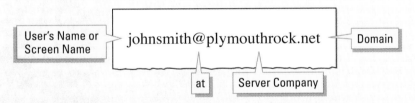

User's Name or Screen Name

johnsmith@plymouthrock.net

Domain

at   Server Company

Here are some tips to follow when you use e-mail:

• E-mail is a communication tool. Be careful and thoughtful about what you say.

• E-mail is public. Your employer could read your e-mail. Do not write anything in business e-mail that you would not want your co-workers to see.

• Remember to check your e-mail messages for spelling errors. Some e-mail programs have spell checkers.

• If the message is important, print a copy and proofread it carefully before sending it.

Application

Compose an e-mail message to a friend. Write it on a separate piece of paper or send it electronically. Be sure to include all the parts of an e-mail message.

REVIEW

Chapter Summary

When you write instructions and directions, your purpose is to explain. This kind of writing gives the important facts and details of a process. Ideas are presented in a logical order, often using time clue words and phrases to make clear the order in which things should be done. When someone gives you directions, be sure you understand all of the information. Identify the important ideas and details; then, follow the directions step by step. When you give directions consider your audience, arrange the steps in the correct order, and be sure that you include all the necessary information.

Key Words

directions	memorandum
time clue words	e-mail
brainstorming	Internet
feedback	

From the list above, choose the word or term that best matches each definition. On a separate piece of paper, write your choice.

1. words, such as *first*, *next*, and *then*, that signal order

2. a short note written to convey information

3. thinking about a wide range of ideas, usually with a group of people

4. an electronic communication system that uses a network or the Internet to send and receive messages

5. instructions that explain a process

6. a response or an answer

7. a network linking computer systems all over the world

Application: Writing Directions

Read these directions for painting a room. Rearrange them so that the steps are in a logical order. Then, rewrite the directions in paragraph form. Use time clue words and phrases to make the directions clearer.

- Move all the furniture into the middle of the room.

- Choose a color.

- Store the clean brushes and rollers.

- Cover the furniture and the floor with plastic drop cloths.

- Use a large brush or roller on large surfaces such as the walls.

- Go to a paint store or a home-improvement store.

- Work carefully, applying the paint in one direction.

- Buy the paint, brushes, and rollers.

- Use a small, narrow brush on smaller surfaces such as window frames.

- Apply a second coat of paint if necessary.

- Wash out your brushes and rollers.

Application: Evaluating Memos and E-mail

Read the following memo and e-mail. On a separate sheet of paper, list the parts that are missing from each one.

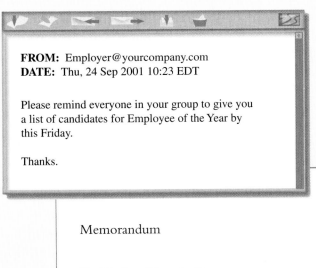

FROM: Employer@yourcompany.com
DATE: Thu, 24 Sep 2001 10:23 EDT

Please remind everyone in your group to give you a list of candidates for Employee of the Year by this Friday.

Thanks.

Memorandum

To: Hadley-Electric Company
From: Jill Hadley

As all of you know, we have updated our "look" to customers with our new logo and packaging.

We at Hadley would like to continue our "make-over" by asking for your ideas about how to update our office building.

Please submit your ideas. A drawing will be held.

Thank you

Grammar Workshop Practice

On a separate sheet of paper, rewrite the following sentences to make them correct.

Part I. Correct the run-on sentences.

1. Cashiers need to know how to make change correctly they will return incorrect amounts of money to customers.

2. Our assistant schedules patients he calls them to remind them of appointments.

3. Place the hot foods on one side of the kitchen fill the patients' food trays.

4. The equipment is new it can be used after we complete the inventory.

5. Brody's restaurant is hiring new workers it needs a cashier and a waiter.

Part II. Change the passive voice to the active voice. You may add or delete words as needed.

6. The meeting was attended by Thomas, Valerie, and Michael.

7. The company bills were paid by Ms. Harrigan.

8. Tamra was influenced by Sarah's management style.

9. Marie was hired by the inventory division.

10. Each employee was given a copy of the manual by the Human Resources Department.

Portfolio Project Writing a Memo or an E-mail

Suppose you have to explain a workplace task to a new employee. You might have to tell someone how to use a cash register, create a window display, or show a person how to do an exercise. Decide which instructions you will give. Then, decide whether to provide the instructions in a memo or an e-mail message. Then do the following activities:

• Write your instructions clearly in one of these formats.

• Ask another student to read them and provide feedback.

• Use the feedback to revise your draft.

Add your completed memo or e-mail to your portfolio.

CHAPTER 7

WRITING TO EXPLAIN A PROCESS

Roberto has been working in the office of a luggage-manufacturing factory for eight months. Recently, the company decided to let visitors tour the factory to watch how luggage is made. Roberto's supervisor, Mr. Sanchez, thinks it would be a good idea to help visitors understand what they are seeing. His plan is to have an explanation of the luggage-making process on display in the lobby. Mr. Sanchez asks Roberto to prepare the explanation. Roberto is not sure what to do next.

Key Words

implement

assumptions

intranet

troubleshoot

sequential order

denotation

connotation

redundant

Goals for Success

In this chapter, you will learn these skills:

Understanding a process

 UNDERSTANDS SYSTEMS

Collecting, sorting, and organizing information about a process

SCANS MATERIALS AND FACILITIES

Identifying and using precise details

 ORGANIZES AND MAINTAINS INFORMATION

Using graphics to explain a process

 CREATIVE THINKING/SPEAKING/WRITING

PORTFOLIO PROJECT

AN EXPLANATION OF A PROCESS

By the time you complete this chapter, you will know what Roberto has to do to write a process explanation. You also will be able to research, organize, and write an explanation of a process to add to your portfolio.

Reading an Explanation of a Process

What Do You Already Know?

To learn to drive a car, you have to follow a process. How might you break this process down into steps?

Think About It Think about a time when you told someone how to do something. How did you decide what to say?

Human beings are inventors, builders, and manufacturers. There is always a new and better way to create a software program, apply paint to a car, or control the movements of an aircraft. When you read about how to do tasks like these, you are reading examples of writing that explains a process.

IDENTIFYING WRITING THAT EXPLAINS A PROCESS

Writing that explains a process is one of the most common forms of writing you will encounter at school, at home, and on the job. This kind of writing is easy to recognize because it usually explains *why* or *how* something works. Its purpose is to allow the reader to visualize the process and to understand it.

The Structure of Writing That Explains a Process

Writing that explains a process usually follows a definite structure. The introduction presents the process that will be analyzed. Then, the piece of writing takes the reader through the process step by step. The first major division is the first step in the process. This is followed by the second and later steps. Sometimes, a step tells the reader what *not* to do.

■ HOW AN ATM WORKS ■

How do the 165,000 automatic teller machines (ATMs) in the United States work? When you slide your ATM card into the reader, the ATM reads the information on the magnetic strip on the card. This information includes the electronic address of your bank, your checking or savings account number, and your personal identification number (PIN).

As soon as you enter your PIN number, the computer inside the ATM connects to the bank's computers. In an instant, the ATM computer checks the PIN with the bank's computers. If the PIN is correct, the ATM computer checks the balance in your account to discover whether you have enough money for the withdrawal you want.

Assuming you have enough money in your account,

the bank's computers tell the ATM that it is okay to give you the money.

The ATM counts the money as rollers inside the machine feed one bill at a time through a conveyer belt. There are some sensors along the sides of the conveyer belt that shine a special light through each bill. The sensors determine whether a $1 bill or a $100 bill will come out of the ATM. If the sensors find a mistake, the bill is sent to a reject box in the ATM.

The process starts again until the correct number of bills is placed at a holding area just inside the ATM. Another set of rollers sends the bills out of the ATM to you. When the correct number of bills has been provided, the ATM closes and sends a message to the bank to update your account.

FIGURE 7-1 explains a different kind of process: using ATMs. **How does this writer use what you already know about ATMs to explain how they work?**

Writing That Explains a Process at Home and in School

At home, you have encountered writing that explains a process if you have looked up a recipe in a cookbook. The recipe listed the ingredients to use, then explained how to combine them and cook them.

In school, you have read about processes when you learned how laws are made or how the digestive system works. You have read about processes if you have read about how a new car engine is designed, how to take a person's temperature, how steel is made, how apples grow, how interest rates are determined, how the President is elected, or how to buy a computer.

Writing That Explains a Process on the Job

On the job, you will find this kind of writing in training manuals and in documents that present a plan. You might find simple versions of a manufacturing process for customers. For example, an ice-cream factory might post signs that explain to visitors the general process of making ice cream. The factory also will have detailed explanations of the process to train new employees to actually make the ice cream.

It is important in the workplace to be able to read explanations of processes. For example, nurses need to be aware of advances in treating burns. Mechanics need to know how to use the newest devices to measure exhaust emissions. All workers

---

BLOOD CIRCULATION

Blood Circulation

Your heart has a left side and a right side. Each side of the heart pumps blood to different places. The right side of your heart pumps blood to your lungs. This is called pulmonary circulation.

Blood from the body enters the right atrium through veins. This blood carries a lot of carbon dioxide and very little oxygen. From the right atrium, blood passes through the pulmonary artery. The pulmonary artery has two branches. One branch goes to each lung. In the lungs, the arteries divide many times to form a network of capillaries. The blood picks up oxygen in the lungs and releases carbon dioxide; then, the oxygen is carried into the left atrium by the pulmonary veins.

Once blood receives a fresh supply of oxygen in the lungs, it is ready to be sent to body cells again. Blood passes from the left atrium into the left ventricle. The left ventricle pumps blood into the aorta, the largest artery in the body. The aorta branches off into arteries, which carry blood to your body cells. The blood returns to the heart and enters through the right atrium.

Making Pita-Bread Pizza

 Wouldn't a slice of pizza taste great right now? Making pita-bread pizzas is easy and fun. This is the way I do it for my friends. This recipe will serve four people.

Before you begin, gather the following ingredients: two pita pockets, one eight-ounce jar of tomato sauce, six ounces of mozzarella cheese, and oregano, garlic, and red pepper flakes. You will also need a cheese grater and a broiling pan.

Shred the cheese by using a cheese grater or by cutting it up into very small pieces. Split each pita pocket in half by cutting it around the rim to make four round pizza crusts. Spread four tablespoons of sauce on each crust; then, sprinkle equal amounts of cheese on top of each pizza. Add oregano, garlic, and red pepper flakes to taste.

Place the pizzas on a broiling pan. Turn the oven to "broil" and place the pan on the broiling rack. Broil until the cheese starts to brown on the top, which should take five to seven minutes.

Serve the pizza piping hot. People can add more seasonings, if they like. Adjust the amounts for different numbers of people.

FIGURE 7-2 shows two different explanations of processes. **How are the audiences different for each explanation? How do you know?**

PREVIEW	Look over the explanation before you read it. Look for sequence words that present the explanation step by step over a period of time. Identify technical words that may be unfamiliar and that you should look up in a dictionary.
READ	Read the explanation carefully and slowly. If there is something you don't understand, go back and read it again. Look for action words such as *connect, assemble, press, pull,* and *make* that tell you what to do. Note any equipment, materials, and skills needed to produce the end result.
WRITE	Writing reinforces learning and helps you remember a process. Do not write the entire explanation, but simplify what happens in each step into a few words. Try to do this without looking at the explanation.
REVIEW	Go back and see if you can figure out the explanation from what you have written. If you cannot, reread the explanation until every detail is clear.

FIGURE 7-3 shows the steps of using a reading strategy to understand a piece of writing that explains a process. **How can previewing help you understand a reading assignment?**

need to understand the process involved in applying for benefits and submitting bills for payment.

A co-worker may be able to explain and demonstrate a process that you will repeat day after day, such as operating a CAT scan machine. Understanding other processes, especially ones a company is about to **implement**, or put into action, will probably involve a combination of reading and practical training. FIGURES 7-1 and 7-2 are examples of process writing you will see at school, at home, and on the job.

READING AN EXPLANATION OF A PROCESS

Because explanations require careful reading, it is important to have a reading plan, or strategy. As you read an explanation of a process, use the strategy shown in FIGURE 7-3. As you can see, the strategy has four basic steps. To learn more about reading strategies, turn to the Student Handbook.

Using a Reading Strategy

Use a reading strategy to analyze the examples of process writing in FIGURES 7-2 and 7-3. Each

example is a little different from the others, and you may have to use a slightly different strategy to understand each one.

Lesson Review

CHECK YOUR UNDERSTANDING

1. IDENTIFYING Name and describe the four steps of a strategy that you can use to read a piece of writing that explains a process.

2. ANALYZING Explain how you used a reading strategy when you read FIGURE 7-1 or 7-2. How did this process differ from the way you usually read?

APPLYING WHAT YOU LEARN

At home or in the library, look in a magazine or book for an explanation of a process that interests you. You might even look in an instruction manual that came with a radio or other electronic device that someone in your family has bought. List the main steps of the process described.

Gathering Information

When you begin working, you will probably have many occasions to read explanations of processes because you will have much to learn. However, as you gain skills and knowledge, your employer may ask you to gather information to write explanations of processes. These might even be processes that you helped to develop. Being able to gather and organize information for these explanations will increase your value to an employer.

THINKING ABOUT YOUR PURPOSE AND YOUR AUDIENCE

Your main purpose when you explain a process is to give complete and accurate information. In business, accuracy is important.

Defining Your Purpose

Your purpose is to explain each step in a process in a way that your audience will understand. If your explanation is too complicated, your audience will be unable to follow the steps. If your explanation is too simple, your audience will not learn enough. As you plan, you need to decide the best way to show how each step works or how it connects with the other steps.

Defining Your Audience

The audience for your explanation depends on the kind of work you do. If you work for a technology company, you will probably be writing for a technically knowledgeable audience. If you work in public relations or in customer service, you will probably be writing for a general audience.

Your knowledge of your audience will guide your **assumptions**, or the things you expect your audience to know. These assumptions will determine the level of detail you will need to build into your explanation. They also will determine the amount of background information you need to present.

Beginning Your Research

The amount of information you need to gather depends on the length of your report. If the topic is new to you, you need to have a strong basic understanding of the facts. You cannot explain to others what you do not understand yourself. When you explain a process, you need to learn enough about your topic to know which details to present and which ones to leave out.

FINDING INFORMATION

Where you look for information depends on what you need to explain. If you work for a large company, you may have many sources of information that are readily available.

Library Sources

A company or school library often has books and technical journals that provide reliable, up-to-date information. Articles written by staff experts and writers will also be on file. Be on the lookout for charts and diagrams that can help you and your readers understand the steps of the process.

Electronic Resources

Many companies also have an **intranet**, an online source of company documents that only employees can use. You can access these documents with a browser and a search program in much the same way as you would access Web documents.

Other Resources

Smaller companies may not have a library or an intranet, but they generally have bookshelves full of product guides, training manuals, and other relevant material. These may contain information about processes that your company already uses.

The World Wide Web on the Internet contains a great deal of information. Some of this information is accurate, and some of it is not. For instance, a company that wants to sell you its new process for recycling cans and bottles is not likely to mention any problems the machinery has. Selling features are not necessarily facts.

Personal Observation

Going out and learning on your own may be another good way to gather information. For instance, if you worked for a furniture store, you could learn how wood and cloth are turned into furniture by observing these operations in a furniture factory. The notes and diagrams you make will be an excellent source of information about the process.

Interviews

Workers who carry out a process can give you valuable information. Before you interview a worker, decide what your goal is. You might want to gather a worker's personal observations and comments about the process. If you are describing cheese making for visitors, for example, you might want to include workers' comments about how the milk, cheese culture, and other ingredients are mixed.

Interviews also can be used to **troubleshoot**, or look for problems, in a process that needs improvement. You might ask supervisors and experienced workers to evaluate the process. Who would know better how the process functions on a daily basis and where the problems are? You will need to combine what they tell you with what you learn from other sources to best explain how the process works.

Lesson Review

CHECK YOUR UNDERSTANDING

1. ANALYZING Why is it important to know your purpose and your audience before you begin to explain a process?

2. EVALUATING What sources of information would you want to use to explain how to make handmade jewelry? Why?

APPLY WHAT YOU LEARN

Work with a partner to find two examples of process explanations. Then, identify the purpose and the audience for which each one was written.

Writing an Explanation

What Do You Already Know?

Think of some activity that you know how to do well. How would you explain that process to an audience of your classmates?

Think About It   What can you do to help your reader understand your explanation?

Writing an explanation is like guiding a friend on a journey. You have to plan your route and work out a step-by-step way to get him or her to the destination. You must give signs that your friend will be able to follow. You need to keep your goal in mind—to get your friend safely to the place he or she is going. When you write an explanation, your goal is to help your reader learn to complete a task.

PLANNING YOUR EXPLANATION

Before you begin writing, think about your purpose and your audience. When you write to explain a process, your purpose is generally to inform. Your audience will probably be one of two groups. Use a different approach for each group.

✓ A general audience may only want an overview of a process.

✓ An expert audience may require a more detailed explanation, one with visual aids and technical terms.

Decide what form your writing will take. Will it be a sign, a brochure, an article, a training manual, a letter to a customer, or a proposal to a manager? Each format helps you decide on the length, the tone, and the complexity of your explanation.

Your research is part of prewriting, too. Before you can explain a process to someone, you must understand it yourself. Master the process in your mind before you write. This is an excellent way to give yourself the facts you need to create a thorough explanation of your topic.

Limiting Your Topic

As you learn more about the process, you may discover that it is more complex than you had first thought. You have two choices. You might extend your explanation to cover the complexity of the process. Or, with your supervisor's approval, you might choose one aspect of the topic to write about. If you narrow your topic, your thinking and your research will have a sharper focus. FIGURE 7-4 is an example of how you could limit a topic.

Organizing Your Information

After you have gathered the information you need, the next step is to decide what to keep and what to discard. You must decide what your readers need to know. You have to ask what will confuse

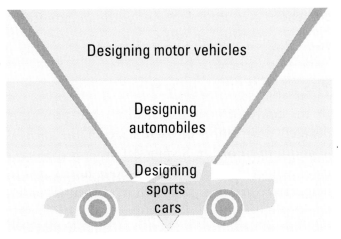

Designing motor vehicles

Designing automobiles

Designing sports cars

FIGURE 7-4 shows how a writer narrowed a broad topic little by little. **What is the broadest topic? What is the narrowest topic?**

them by being too complicated or bore them by being too simple.

Note cards are a good way to organize the information you decide to keep. Use one note card for each step in the process. On each card, list the main points you plan to cover for that step. You should also write definitions of any important technical terms that you will need to use.

Make a final check to be sure all of your steps are in order. Then, store your cards in a safe place. You will use them as an outline to help you organize your draft when you begin writing.

WRITING THE FIRST DRAFT

When you explain a process, you tell what happens, how it happens, and why it happens. To do this clearly, you need to structure your information. Every piece of writing—from a brief letter to a long report—has a beginning, a middle, and an end. These parts are often called the introduction, the body, and the conclusion.

The Introduction

Your opening sentence, or topic sentence, introduces your reader to the process. Your topic sentence identifies the process and gives a brief overview so that your reader will know what you are going to explain.

Your topic sentence also can explain why the process is important or how this step fits into the larger process. If you are writing for a general audience, you might begin with an attention-getting question or story. Your purpose is to motivate your readers to continue reading.

The Body

In the body of your explanation, you provide a detailed description of each stage of the process in **sequential order**. Sequential order is the order in which steps take place. Use your note cards to help you to arrange your ideas in sequential order.

Describe for your readers the steps they need to follow to complete the process. Be sure that the body of the explanation offers sufficient detail.

Keep your attention focused on the questions *what*, *why*, and *how*. Do not worry about writing too much. You can trim your text when you revise.

Consider your audience as you decide which details to present. Define any terms your audience needs to know. Choose words that communicate your meaning clearly.

The Conclusion

The conclusion of your explanation can be one of the following:

- a description of the final action

- a summary of the main steps

- a summary of the results

- an evaluation of the process

Keep your conclusion brief. If the introduction and the body or your explanation are clear, you do not need a lengthy conclusion. FIGURE 7-5, on page 131, shows a detailed example of writing that explains a process.

EDITING THE FIRST DRAFT

When you edit your explanation of a process, check for clarity, completeness, and organization.

Clarity

Be sure that you have explained every step of the process well. If you are not certain about something, reread your notes or go back to the original source of information. Reviewing it might help you think of a better way to explain a point.

Completeness

Reread what you have written, picturing the process as you read. Look for places in which you may have missed part of a step or failed to link one step to another.

Organization

Check to see that every part of the process is presented in sequential order. Number the steps, if needed, to make each part clear. Add transition

The title describes the topic of the explanation.

How a Mouse Works

A mouse is a pointing device used to choose or highlight items on a computer screen. As your hand moves the mouse, the mouse sends an electronic signal to the computer. The signal tells the computer to move the arrow, or cursor, on the screen. In one minute, a mouse sends thousands of separate signals that the computer constantly monitors. Clicking on the mouse button sends another signal to the computer to perform a task.

The introduction gives a simple overview.

Here is how the process works:

The body explains the process step by step.

1. As you move the mouse, a ball on the underside turns in whatever direction you move.
2. As that ball rolls, it turns two connecting rollers inside the mouse. These rollers translate the motion of the ball into forward, backward, and sideward directions.
3. Those rollers are attached to encoders, which are small wheels that turn as the rollers turn.
4. The encoders have tiny electrical contact points. As the rollers turn, they touch separate contact points and "tell" the direction of action through electrical signals.
5. Those signals go to the computer, which translates the many signals into movements of the arrow or cursor on the screen.

Unlike a real mouse, the computer mouse moves on rollers that translate its movement into electrical signals sent to your computer screen. It is a most useful creature!

The conclusion summarizes the explanation for the reader.

FIGURE 7-5 Note how the writer breaks down a complicated process into easy-to-follow steps. **Was there anything in the process explanation you did not understand? What might make the explanation clearer?**

words such as *first, next, last, afterwards, soon, meanwhile, inside,* and *beneath* to help your reader see the connections between the parts of your explanation.

PROOFREADING

Readers will judge your work not only by your ideas but also by how well you express them. Check your writing for run-on sentences, sentence fragments, and grammatical errors. Be sure that you have clearly defined all technical terms for readers. Look for mistakes in spelling, punctuation, and capitalization.

PUBLISHING

When you have finished proofreading your work, make a final copy to share with your audience.

Lesson Review

CHECK YOUR UNDERSTANDING

1. ANALYZING How does knowing your audience help you plan how to write an explanation?

2. EXPLAINING What three things should you look for when you revise a first draft? Explain why they are important.

APPLY WHAT YOU LEARN

Search through magazines and newspapers to find an explanation of a process. First, determine what the writer's purpose and audience were. Then, evaluate the writing for clarity, completeness, and organization. Share your evaluation with the class.

Making Pronouns and Their Antecedents Agree

Pronouns are words that take the place of nouns. A pronoun's antecedent is the person or thing to which the pronoun refers. As you write to explain a process, check each pronoun to be sure the noun it refers to is clear to the reader.

Make sure that pronouns agree with their antecedents in number, gender, and person.

- A singular pronoun must refer to a singular noun, and a plural pronoun must refer to a plural noun or a group of nouns.

    Examples   **Anjuli** cashed **her** paycheck.
    Jack and Phil worked on **their** proposal.

- A noun and pronoun must agree in gender.

    Examples   **Roberto** moved into **his** new office.
    Don't forget to give **Lucy her** briefcase.
    The **factory** lost **its** power supply.

- A noun and pronoun must agree in person (first person—*I*, second person—*you*, or third person—*he, she, it, they*).

    Examples   **I** need **my** passport for the trip to Spain.
    Do **you** need **your** passport?
    Yuko will need **her** passport.

Application

On a separate sheet of paper, rewrite the following sentences, making the pronouns and their antecedents agree. Underline the antecedent to which the pronoun refers.

1. Jane and Rita asked payroll to deposit her paychecks at the bank.
2. The salespeople will present its new product on Tuesday.
3. The man drove her delivery truck to the warehouse.
4. Half the plants at the nursery have lost its flowers.
5. Anna did not want to work with their brothers in the shop.
6. If a woman goes into politics, they need to give good speeches.
7. The manager asked the workers for his attention.
8. Joe's mechanics shop is in their fourth year of business.
9. Your job at the market keeps him pretty busy.
10. I already took the test for our certificate.

For more information, SEE PAGE 348.

Using Precise Details

A basin, a bowl, a tureen, a tub, a pitcher, a barrel, a container, a tank, a carton, a vat, and a kettle are alike because they all hold liquids. Yet there are differences between them. These differences are shown in the details. Details are the individual parts that make up the whole. Details show how each of the objects differ. When you write, details fill in the picture and help explain a process.

STATE THE FACTS

When you write to explain a process, you need to collect the precise details of every aspect of the process. You may not use all these details in the finished piece of writing, but you need to know them to understand the process.

Some writers prefer to write a quick first draft, and then revise it many times. If you are one of these people, then the editing stage of the writing process is the time to check your use of precise details. Other writers take more time with the first draft. If you prefer to write in this way, then drafting is the time you will add precise details.

Present a Complete Picture

When you select details to explain a process, remember to choose those that will provide readers with the important information they will need. These details help readers form a clear picture of the process. Ask yourself questions such as these to find the details you will need:

- ✓ *Material:* What is needed? How much? What kind? What does it cost?

- ✓ *Equipment:* How is it used? How many pieces are needed?

- ✓ *Personnel:* How many people do I need? What must they do? What experience or skills must they have?

- ✓ *Time:* How long does each step take?

EXPRESS IDEAS EXACTLY

Choose your words carefully, and do not write more than is necessary. Be sure to include all of the important details, and make the connections between your ideas clear.

Use a Dictionary to Check Meanings

For help in choosing words, use a dictionary or thesaurus. Choose a word that has the correct **denotation**, or exact meaning. A word's denotation is its dictionary definition. Before you choose a word, though, think about its **connotations**, too. Connotations are the feelings or associations connected to a word. The connotations of a word depend more on the feelings the word brings to mind than on its dictionary definition.

Separate Denotation and Connotation

As you decide on the details you will use, think about both the denotations and connotations of the words you choose. In this way, you will be sure your audience understands the message you want to send.

What do you think of, for example, when you hear the word *snow*? Your first thought might be of a fluffy, white form of precipitation that falls in winter. This would be the denotation of *snow*.

You might have other ideas when you think of *snow*, too. You might think of calm, quiet, freshness, or purity. However, if you have just shoveled a sidewalk, you might think of the ache in your shoulders and how hard it will be to get to work. *Snow* also can mean "to fool, or trick, someone." These examples are all connotations of *snow*. They are ideas that are suggested or implied by the word.

When you explain a process, then, think about your audience. Be sure that the words you choose have both the denotations and the connotations that you intend. In this way, your readers will be sure to understand your ideas.

Use a Thesaurus

A thesaurus is a book of synonyms that you can use to find new and more precise words. Some word-processing programs also have a thesaurus as part of the program. If you use a thesaurus, be sure to use it with a dictionary. The dictionary will help you make sure that you have chosen a word that expresses your meaning exactly.

Use Specific, Concrete Words

To make your writing clear, be sure to choose precise words. A precise word has a specific and concrete meaning. It tells you how something feels, looks, or sounds. Precise words paint a clear picture for your reader.

General	More Precise	Most Precise
food	candy	maple fudge
sound	warning device	buzzer

Precise details can help you explain a process clearly. **How might precise details help an athlete improve his or her performance?**

Use Exact Numbers

When you explain the scientific or technological side of any process, use figures that communicate your meaning exactly.

Not Precise: The unboiled sap has *lots of water in it.*

Precise: The unboiled sap is *97.5 percent water.*

Avoid Wordiness

Look for the simplest, most direct way to express an idea. Eliminate words that are **redundant**, or repeated unnecessarily. In the following examples, you could omit all the words in italics: yellow *in color,* round *in shape,* and small *in size.*

You may need to rewrite some sentences to avoid wordiness. Compare the following sentences.

Wordy: There is a building called a sugar house in which the maple sap is boiled down and made into syrup.

Concise: In the sugar house, the maple sap is boiled down into syrup.

Make Your Comparisons Complete

Do not leave out words that are needed to complete comparisons. This confuses the reader about what two things are being compared.

Confusing: The snow here is as deep as Maine.

Precise: The snow here is as deep as it is in Maine.

Make the Connections Between Ideas Clear

A process may be clear in your mind, but it will not be clear in your reader's mind unless you show how the parts of the process are related. Transition words and phrases can help you show cause and effect as well as sequence.

You can use transition words to make connections. Some of the following transition words may be helpful:

Time or
Sequence: first, later, next, finally, eventually

Example: for example, for instance, such as, like, to illustrate

Enumeration: first, second, next, another

Continuation: also, in addition, and, furthermore, another

Contrast: on the other hand, but, however, in contrast

Comparison: like, likewise, similarly

Cause–Effect: because, therefore, since, as a result

Summation: in short, in summary, to conclude, in brief, in conclusion

Lesson Review

CHECK YOUR UNDERSTANDING

1. EVALUATING Why is it important for writers to use precise details?

2. CONTRASTING What is the difference between the denotation and the connotation of a word? Choose a word from the following list and give examples of its denotations and connotations.

   puppy   star   green   company

APPLY WHAT YOU LEARN

Think about some process that interests you or that you know well. List at least ten precise details about it that you think every writer must include in an explanation of the process.

Using Graphics to Explain a Process

What Do You Already Know?

What types of illustrations have you seen in instruction manuals? How are they different from illustrations in newspapers and magazines?

Think About It   What types of illustrations do you think would work best to explain a process? Why?

The statement "A picture is worth a thousand words" has become a cliché—but it does express a truthful thought. Visuals can be helpful when used in an explanation of a process. Charts, graphs, or other visuals often give readers a clear, accurate, and concise picture of the information they need.

WHAT ARE GRAPHICS?

The word *graphics* is the general term that is used for all types of visuals. Drawings, photographs, charts, graphs, maps, and diagrams are some of the most common types of graphics. Using graphics in an explanation can help the reader better understand a process by showing it. Furthermore, you can use graphics at work to show a supervisor your planning and presentation skills.

THE BEST WAYS TO USE GRAPHICS

Graphics are most effective when they work *with* the text. Remember, though, that using too many graphics may overwhelm your reader. Graphics should be used to supplement, not replace, the text. Use the following checklist when you use a graphic to explain a process:

- ✔ Make the graphic large enough to be read easily.

- ✔ Place the graphic close to the text that deals with the topic.

- ✔ Provide accurate, easy-to-read labels and captions to explain the graphic.

- ✔ Make the graphic simple to understand.

- ✔ Heavily detailed drawings or complex photos can be more confusing than useful.

THE KINDS OF GRAPHICS YOU CAN USE

There are many different kinds of graphics. Four that are particularly useful to explain a process are charts, tables, graphs, and diagrams.

Charts

Charts are graphics that present data and other kinds of information in a clear, visual way. Organizational charts explain the jobs that are held

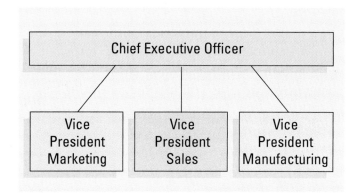

FIGURE 7-6 This chart shows how the jobs in a business are organized. **Which executives are on the same level? How do you know?**

INDUSTRIES WITH PROJECTED FASTEST WAGE AND EMPLOYMENT GROWTH
1998–2008

Source: U.S. Census Bureau, February, 2000

Industry	Employment Change			
	1998	2008	Number	Percent
Computer and data-processing services	1,599	3,472	1,872	117%
Health services	1,209	2,018	809	67%
Residential care	747	1,171	424	57%
Management and public relations	1,034	1,500	466	45%
Personnel supply services	3,230	4,623	1,393	43%
Equipment rental and leasing	258	369	111	43%
Museums, botanical and zoological gardens	93	131	39	42%
Research and testing services	614	861	247	40%
Transportation services	236	329	94	40%
Security and commodity brokers	645	900	255	40%

FIGURE 7-7 This table shows which jobs are projected to have the most growth over a 10-year period. **How does the chart show which jobs are expected to grow?**

in a company and how these jobs relate to one another. FIGURE 7-6 on page 137 is an example of an organizational chart.

Tables

Tables present statistics and other numerical data. A table usually has two or more columns of information and is read from left to right, as you can see in FIGURE 7-7. Tables help you make information concrete and easy to interpret for your readers.

Graphs

Graphs also present numerical information. Line graphs can compare one piece of information with another. They can also show how things change over time, as you can see in FIGURE 7-8.

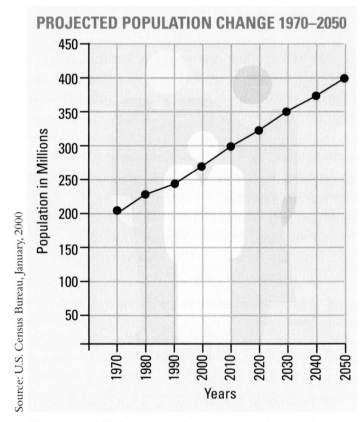

PROJECTED POPULATION CHANGE 1970–2050

Source: U.S. Census Bureau, January, 2000

FIGURE 7-8 This line graph shows how the population of the United States has grown over a 80-year period. **How does the line graph show the relationships among the numbers at a glance?**

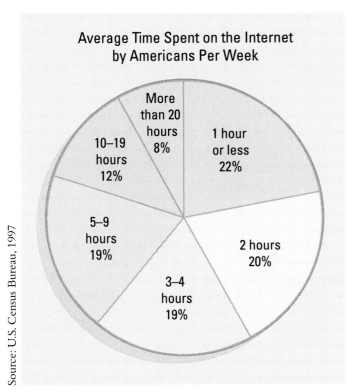

Average Time Spent on the Internet by Americans Per Week

More than 20 hours 8%

10–19 hours 12%

1 hour or less 22%

5–9 hours 19%

2 hours 20%

3–4 hours 19%

Source: U.S. Census Bureau, 1997

FIGURE 7-9 This circle graph is divided into percentages. **Why does a circle graph have to add up to 100 percent?**

A circle graph, also called a pie chart, is used to show how a whole is broken down into parts. FIGURE 7-9 above is a circle graph that shows the average time spent online by Americans with computers.

Diagrams

A diagram is an illustration that shows the parts of something or the steps in a process. It often contains labeled parts. FIGURE 7-10 shows a diagram that can help a writer present an explanation clearly.

A FINAL WORD ON GRAPHICS

To make sure your graphics are effective, ask someone to review them. This feedback will tell you if your visuals communicate the information properly.

Lesson Review

CHECK YOUR UNDERSTANDING

1. SUMMARIZING How can a writer use graphics to explain a process?

2. EVALUATING What is the advantage of using tables or line graphs in presenting information?

APPLY WHAT YOU LEARN

Choose one of the graphics shown in this lesson. Discuss with a group how that graphic could help clarify a writer's points. Present your findings to the class.

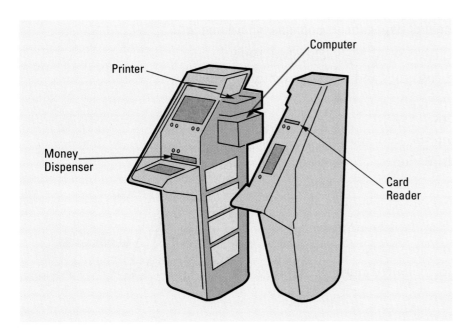

Computer

Printer

Money Dispenser

Card Reader

FIGURE 7-10 This diagram shows the parts of an ATM machine. **How does the illustrator make this diagram easy to read and understand?**

Grammar Workshop

Using Commas to Clarify

The comma's job is to group the parts of a sentence. It helps your reader know when to take a short break while reading. In contrast to periods, commas are used within sentences, not at the end of sentences. Commas are often used to separate a series of steps in a process.

Here are some rules for using commas:

- Separate words, phrases, or clauses in a series with commas.

  Examples   Jill's new dog is brown, white, and black.

  On Monday, Chang cooked dinner, wrote an essay, and worked at the garage.

- Separate a noun of address from the rest of the sentence with a comma.

  Examples   Mr. Parker, did you have an appointment?

  It's too late to send that package by express mail, Lilly.

- Set off a word, phrase, or clause that interrupts the flow of a sentence with a comma.

  Examples   Calvin Manning, my former swim coach, is now teaching at State University.

  The computer, which is on my desk at work, has a great new graphics program.

Application

Rewrite each sentence on a separate sheet of paper. Insert commas where needed.

1. Wendy my business partner graduated from high school in 1993.
2. Dancing in the chorus changing costumes and singing nightly is not as exciting as you might think.
3. Simone it's time to leave for work.
4. Willy George and Lizzie designed the new toaster.
5. Have you finished the billing Ms. Wylie?
6. The job training program which is Harold's idea takes six full weeks.
7. Order staples printer paper and memo pads from Acme Supplies today.
8. Veterinarians treat dogs cats birds and other animals.
9. Please hurry Keisha or we will be late.
10. I'd rather work with Inez the most talented nurse at the hospital.

For more information,
SEE PAGES 358–359.

The Internet has a large number of sites that offer guides, resources, and references for you to use. You can chat with subject-area experts, or e-mail a teacher or another student with a question. Many encyclopedias, dictionaries, almanacs, and thesauruses now have their own Web sites. You can also visit and explore virtual museums to gather information for writing reports or writing to explain.

Here are a few Web sites that will help you with your schoolwork and your writing:

www.ash.udel.edu/ash
This site has tutorials and links about researching and writing techniques. You will find a writing center, a reading center, a homework helper, and a Web workshop.

www.bjpinchbeck.com
This site has more than 570 links to online dictionaries, encyclopedias, and other reference tools. It has homework help sites that allow you to search by subject.

www.homeworkhelp.about.com
Here you can search by subject to get help for your homework and schoolwork. Look for links that will help you use apostrophes, colons, and commas.

www.tekmom.com/students
This site is a tool for learning, writing, and researching. It can also help you with your technology skills. In addition, *TekMom's Search Tools for Students* can help you find other sites on the Internet.

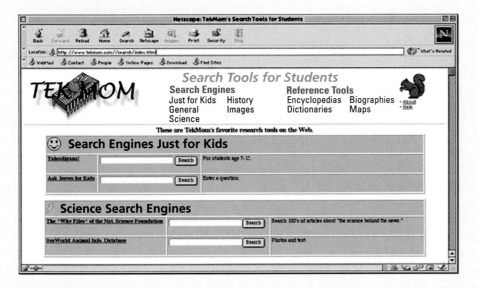

APPLICATION

Go to two of the four Web sites listed above. List three examples of when and how you would use these sites to help you with your schoolwork.

REVIEW

Chapter Summary

An explanation of a process includes a series of steps to be followed. First, you must research and limit your topic. Next, you must gather and organize information about the topic. Then, you must edit and proofread your explanation. Add precise details to sharpen the explanation, and make it clear and understandable. Graphics, in the form of charts, graphs, and diagrams, also can provide strong visual support for the explanation.

Key Words

implement	sequential order
assumptions	denotation
intranet	connotation
troubleshoot	redundant

Match each word with the clue to its meaning. Write your answers on a separate sheet of paper.

1. implement
2. troubleshoot
3. denotation
4. intranet
5. connotation
6. assumptions
7. redundant
8. sequential order

a. the order in which steps take place

b. to put into action

c. things you expect your audience will know

d. the feelings or associations a word brings to mind

e. the dictionary definition of a word

f. an online source of company documents that only employees can use

g. repeated unnecessarily

h. look for problems

Application: Explain a Process to Two Audiences

Work with another student to choose one process from the list below, or choose another process that interests you.

Programming a VCR

Preparing for a vacation

Organizing a birthday party

Now, do the following exercise to explore presenting information to different audiences.

1. Choose two different audiences to whom you could explain your process. You might choose a teacher and a child, a grandparent and another student, or two other audiences who are quite different from one another.

2. Gather the information both audiences will need to understand the process.

3. For each audience, organize the main steps of the process into sequential order.

4. Write each explanation of the process in paragraph form.

5. Edit and proofread your explanations, keeping in mind how much detail each audience needs and the terms you need to define.

6. Present your explanations to a classmate, and ask the classmate to guess which two audiences you have chosen.

Application: Sort and Organize Information

Below are the steps of three different processes. On a separate sheet of paper, organize the steps for each process into sequential order.

A. Making paper

Turn pulp into long sheets of paper.

Prepare pulp from raw wood and cotton.

Cut the new paper into separate sheets.

Remove dirt from the pulp.

B. Grilling a steak

Heat the coals in the barbecue.

Remove the cooked steak from the grill.

Turn the steak over after half the cooking time.

Place the steak on a rack above the coals.

C. Writing a term paper

Take notes.

Research the topic.

Publish the document.

Write the draft.

Choose a topic.

Organize the notes.

Edit the draft.

Grammar Workshop Practice

On a separate sheet of paper, rewrite the following sentences to make them correct.

Part I. Fill in the blank with a pronoun that agrees with its antecedent.

1. Evonne dropped _____ keyboard on the floor.

2. When Janice, Sharon, and Tracey arrive at the building, tell _____ to stop by my office.

3. If you see Wanda, the data clerk, ask _____ to come here.

4. Park rangers do _____ best to answer questions.

5. People at this meeting should not pretend that _____ understand the discussion.

Part II. Add commas where they are needed. If the sentence is correct, write *Correct*.

6. My brother a cat lover got a job at an animal shelter.

7. On the morning of March 1 the company moved to a new building.

8. The fire truck that blocked the street was answering a medical emergency call.

9. Waving her arms the crossing guard stopped the children from crossing.

10. Our goal of running in the Boston marathon would take a lot of training.

Portfolio Project   Writing an Explanation of a Process

Research a process. Use information you find in the library, on the Internet, or through personal observation. Then do the following steps:

- Sort and organize your research, decide what is most important to present, and write your explanation.

- While you research, identify precise details that you can use in your writing.

- As you work, create any graphics you need to make your explanation clear.

- When you finish writing, editing, and proofreading your explanation of a process, present your explanation to the class.

Add your completed explanation of a process to your portfolio.

CAREER FILE

Read the following information about two careers in which people use writing skills. Think about the goals and skills the jobs require. Then, answer the questions below.

Cashier: *Retail Services*

If you want to work with people, can work quickly under pressure, and enjoy working with figures, you might wish to explore a career as a cashier. Cashiers work in supermarkets, restaurants, theaters, business offices, and department stores. They take money, make change, and fill out charge forms.

A cashier should

- possess strong math skills.
- be able to operate a cash register.

Minimum Education: Two to three years of high school
Starting Salary: $6.00 per hour
Related Careers: Bank Teller, Postal Clerk

For more information, contact the Retail, Wholesale, and Department Store Union, 30 East 29th Street, New York, NY 10016. You may find this union on the Internet at www.rwdsu.on.ca.

Restaurant Manager: *Food Services*

If you would like to manage a business and are interested in the food industry, then you might wish to explore a career as a restaurant manager. Restaurant managers purchase food and supplies, select menus, and maintain the cleanliness of their business. They also manage employees who prepare and serve food. Restaurant managers work in hotel dining rooms, banquet halls, fast-food restaurants, and school and hospital cafeterias.

A restaurant manager should

- be organized and able to solve problems quickly.
- enjoy working with people.

Minimum Education: An associate's degree, bachelor's degree, or certification in restaurant and food-service management
Starting Salary: $16,000 to $25,000 per year
Related Careers: Hotel Manager, Food-Service Manager

For more information, contact the Educational Foundation of the National Restaurant Association, 250 South Wacker Drive, Suite 1400, Chicago, IL 60606. You may find this organization on the Internet at www.restaurant.org.

EXPLORING CAREERS

1. **Suppose that you find work as a cashier. What kinds of processes might you need to explain? What are some ways to communicate that cashiers might use?**

2. **Restaurant managers explain different kinds of processes to their employees. How would a restaurant manager gather the information needed to explain a process?**

"One of the best ways to persuade others is with your ears—by listening to them."

Dean Rusk (1909–1994)
U.S. Secretary of State

UNIT 4

WRITING REPORTS TO DESCRIBE AND PERSUADE

Being able to write reports is a skill that will be useful throughout your working life. In this unit, you will learn about the different types of reports. Then, you will learn the steps of writing a report that describes an idea or issue. To do this, you will collect information and organize it, create an outline, and draft and edit a finished report. You will also learn the techniques of persuasive writing.

WRITING REPORTS THAT DESCRIBE

Afhis graduating from a technical school, Yolanda found a job as a data-entry clerk in a mail-order catalog company. Within a year, she had used her computer experience to become the manager of the data-processing department. Now her supervisor has asked Yolanda to write a report that describes ways to make the department more productive. Yolanda has some ideas, but she needs to do more research. She does not know exactly what to put into the report or how to structure it.

Key Words

informal report

formal report

thesis statement

primary source

secondary source

database

search engine

keyword search

synopsis

executive summary

relevant

concise

font

Goals for Success

In this chapter, you will learn these skills:

Recognizing and reading different types of business reports

 READING

Collecting, organizing, and evaluating information for a research report

 ORGANIZING AND MAINTAINING INFORMATION

Outlining a research report

 CREATIVE THINKING

Using relevant supporting details

 KNOWING HOW TO LEARN

Writing a report that includes sources, a bibliography, and footnotes

 WRITING

PORTFOLIO PROJECT

RESEARCH REPORT

By the time you complete this chapter, you will understand Yolanda's task. You will know what she has to do to write her research report. You also will be able to collect information and write a research report of your own to add to your portfolio.

Reading Reports

What Do You Already Know?

What are some reports that you have read or seen? Make a list of all the reports you have read.

Think About It What reports have you read or written in school or on the job?

A report may be a simple description of a business's weekly sales or a complex research paper. Whether a report is simple or complex, however, you need to be able to read this form of writing and understand the particular types of information it contains.

FORMAL AND INFORMAL REPORTS

In school or in the workplace, people often see two kinds of reports. One type is an **informal report**. This type of report usually focuses on a specific problem or subject, often in a single page. Although the writer must think about the kind of information that must be included, an informal report does not take long to prepare. In writing an informal report, the writer must think about its purpose and provide only the details the audience needs to understand the ideas being presented.

The other type of report is a **formal report**. This longer report often requires a great deal of research and takes more planning and organizing.

INFORMAL REPORTS

Two kinds of informal reports you might see in the workplace are sales reports and incident reports.

Sales Reports

Sales reports provide information that keeps a business running smoothly. Such reports are often directed to supervisors. They may briefly describe—generally, in one page—how many items have been sold or the names of customers. FIGURE 8-1 shows you a sample sales report.

The Samuel James Company
14 Frame St., Yonkers, New York 10702

SALES REPORT

Name of Salesperson: _Janice Jordan_

Number of Units Sold: _450_

Sales Made to (person and business):

Erika Poole, Fantastica

Neeva Grant, Your Corner

Names of Others Contacted:

Mae Foshaam, Best Jewelry

Week: _Jan. 7-14, 2002_

Product Selling: _Lacquerware Jewelry_

FIGURE 8-1 This sales report includes detailed information about jewelry sales. **Why might a company want its salespeople to write reports?**

```
FREE RANGE MARKET
3876 COLUMBUS DR.
EDINA, MN 55424
```

INCIDENT REPORT

Name of employee: _Jamaica Wolf_

Date of incident: _May 9, 1999_

Nature of incident: _The shipment of jellies from Makepeace Gardens was damaged. Before I signed the form from the shipper, I looked in the boxes. About half of the jars were broken. I told the shipper I couldn't sign the receipt without a note on the receipt signed by the driver. I said it needed to list the damage. The driver wrote a note, and I signed it._

Further action: _I called Makepeace Gardens and told them about the problem. They will call the shipper to resend the broken jars. The invoice from Makepeace Gardens will be sent again after the new shipment with the rest of the jars of jelly arrives in good order._

FIGURE 8-2 This incident report describes damaged goods received. **Why would the person receiving the report be pleased with this employee?**

Incident Reports

Incident reports describe something that happened in the workplace. They might describe an accident, an error, or another event. Like sales reports, incident reports are usually brief. You might write an incident report if you worked at a rehabilitation center and a piece of equipment broke or if someone was hurt when your group tried to set up a holiday display. FIGURE 8-2 shows an example of an incident report.

FORMAL REPORTS

Research reports for business usually describe particular issues. For example, a report might evaluate whether a company should open a new store or discuss meetings that were held at a conference. These kinds of reports can be long, and they usually include specific parts that you will learn more about later in this chapter.

READING RESEARCH REPORTS

Formal business reports need to be read carefully. It might be helpful to use a reading strategy, such as the Cornell Note-taking Strategy. The Cornell strategy consists of the following four steps:

1. Preview the report. Look at the title, subheadings, and visuals. Quickly read the first and last paragraphs and topic sentences. Write down any questions you have about the report. Begin your questions with such words as *Who, What, When, Where, Why,* and *How.*

2. Read, and then take notes. Divide a piece of paper into two columns. List the key words and main ideas in the left column. List the details that explain each idea or word in the right column.

3. Summarize what you have read. Use your questions from Step 1 to find the main point of the report. When you have answered your questions, write a summary that includes the report's main ideas and the details.

4. Review what you have read. Fold your paper so that only the left side shows. The left side contains the main ideas. Then, see if you can recall the details and evidence that support each point. Reread the report to review the information, if needed.

Lesson Review

CHECK YOUR UNDERSTANDING

1. COMPARING What are the similarities and differences between formal and informal business reports?

2. EXPLAINING When would it be necessary to write an incident report?

APPLY WHAT YOU LEARN

Suppose you work in a health-care center or a restaurant. Something has happened that should be reported to your manager. Work with a classmate to write an incident report that tells what happened and what you did about the situation.

Grammar Workshop

Practicing Word Choice

When you write a report, you should use words that are exact so that your meaning is clear to your readers. To do that, you must know the right words to use and when to use them. Here are some words that are often confused:

accept, except: *Accept* means "to receive"; *except* means "other than."

> *Examples*   Can you **accept** my opinion? Everyone liked the program **except** me.

affect, effect: *Affect* means "to influence"; it is usually used as a verb.
Effect means "the result of a change"; it is usually used as a noun.

> *Examples*   Don't let Harry's attitude **affect** your work.
> The **effect** of a good manager is happier workers.

among, between: *Among* refers to three or more; *between* refers to two people or things.

> *Examples*   Yolanda is **among** the five people to receive a service award.
> On the stage, she will stand **between** Tom and Chris.

fewer, less: *Fewer* refers to a number of separate items and can be counted;
less refers to bulk amounts.

> *Examples*   Ingrid sold **fewer** pies than Sharon.
> The pies required **less** flour than the bread.

good, well: Use *good* after linking verbs such as *is, taste,* and *feel*. Use *well* as an adverb.

> *Examples*   The ravioli tastes **good**. Ben writes very **well**.

Application

Rewrite each sentence on a separate sheet of paper, choosing the correct word from the words in parentheses.

1. I had to decide (between, among) four different desk chairs.
2. When you (accept, except) a job, you must learn the company's business style.
3. There is (fewer, less) space for exercising in the new gym.
4. (Accept, Except) for two days, my attendance at work has been perfect.
5. I hope you score (well, good) on the interview test.
6. The (fewer, less) people who know about the merger, the better.
7. Soap and water cleaned these windows very (good, well).
8. What is the (affect, effect) of rain on the parade?
9. Yuri divided the jobs (between, among) Oscar and Pablo.
10. Does working outside in cold weather (affect, effect) you?

For more information, SEE PAGE 366.

Collecting and Evaluating Information

Before you write a report, you need to choose a topic and a purpose for writing. You also need to think about your audience. Deciding these things in the prewriting stage will help you get a clear picture of how you should write. Your next prewriting task is to collect facts and the ideas of experts that will support what you say. There are many ways to find this information. You can interview people. You can find articles, books, and Web sites about your topic. Once you have the facts, you need to make sure your information is reliable.

PREWRITING STEPS FOR YOUR REPORT

The first step in prewriting is to think about your topic. A topic that is too broad is impossible to cover thoroughly. A topic that is too narrow will not contain enough information to be useful.

After you choose your topic, your next step is to think about your purpose for writing. For example, do you want to report on the success of a new product? Or do you want to describe how employees helped design this new product? Your purpose will help you decide on a way to organize your report.

Your third step is to think about your audience. Knowing who will read your report will help you include the information your audience needs to know to understand your topic.

Then, you are ready to write a **thesis statement**. A thesis statement is a one-sentence summary of your topic. It will help you focus on your report. Your next step is to find sources of information that support your thesis statement.

SOURCES FOR REPORTS

Now that you have a thesis statement, you can begin collecting sources that will give you the main ideas and details you will need to write your report.

There are two types of information sources you will use in reports you write. One is a **primary source**, such as a letter or a speech. Primary sources are original documents that were written by people who participated in the events they report.

You might also use a **secondary source**. Secondary sources, such as books or encyclopedia articles, analyze or discuss primary sources. They were written by people who did not participate in the events they report. A complaint letter by a person telling how poorly he was treated by an airline is a primary source. A book discussing people's opinions about airline service is a secondary source.

Many of the sources people use for reports are printed. These include encyclopedias, magazines, and books. Other ideas come from interviews. Another source of information is the Internet.

PRINTED SOURCES

A good place to start your search for information is in your school or local library. For some business reports, you might need a more specialized library, such as a college business-school library. Many corporations and business groups also maintain libraries. You can call these libraries to find out their policies for visitors.

Books

Most libraries have computers that allow you to search for a book by subject, author, or title. If you are searching by subject, be as specific as you can.

Magazines

You can also look for magazine and newspaper articles on your topic. You can check the library's magazine and newspaper **database**, a large collection of article listings.

Some libraries do not yet have computer-based search services for magazines. These libraries have card catalogs and bound copies of the *Readers' Guide to Periodical Literature*, which can help you find the information you need.

AN INTERNET SEARCH

The World Wide Web (www) is a good resource for information on many topics, especially up-to-date topics. You should be aware, however, that the Internet is unregulated. Anyone can set up a Web site, so not all Web sites are reliable or accurate.

Evaluating Web Sites

To evaluate a Web site, look at the last three letters of the address, called the *domain name extension*. Web sites that end in *.gov* are run by the government; those that end in *.edu* are run by schools or educational organizations. These Web sites are more likely to have reliable information. Web sites that end in *.com* are businesses, which may want to sell you something. Finally, Web sites that end in *.org* are run by organizations, which might be special-interest groups that wish to publicize their opinions. However, look carefully at all of the Web sites you visit and evaluate them for unsupported ideas or wild claims.

Search Engines and the Web

Many Internet services include their own **search engine**, a program that looks for information on any topic. You can access other search engines by typing in their Internet addresses.

These search engines all work in a similar way. You do a **keyword search**, in which you type in words that describe your topic. The search engine scans its database for documents that contain these words. Then, the search engine lists the documents that match the keywords.

Try different search engines to find the ones that work best for you. Also try different search engines for different topics. Here are the addresses of some popular general-subject search engines:

- www.altavista.com
- www.dogpile.com
- www.excite.com
- www.hotbot.com
- www.infoseek.com

Once the search engine has found entries, scan them. If the first ten entries are not helpful, try a new search with different keywords, or add keywords to narrow your search.

Print documents you think might be helpful in your research. Make sure you record the sources of all of the information you find.

This woman is using several sources of information. **Why is it important to use more than one source of information in a report?**

INTERVIEWS

Sometimes, the best way to get information for a research paper is to talk to people. These people may include experts, teachers, and family members.

Getting the Most from an Interview

The better prepared you are for an interview, the more you will learn. Before you set up an interview, find out as much as you can about the person. What is his or her title? What does this person know that can be useful? Having this information will help you ask meaningful questions.

Write your questions in advance. You might want to write them on the first page of a notebook so that you can flip back to your questions as you take notes. Some people like to tape record an interview for accuracy. However, you must ask permission from the person in advance.

Checklist for Writing Interview Questions

✔ Create a list of questions; then, choose the most important ones.

✔ Arrange your questions in the order in which you will ask them. That way, they will flow from one to another.

✔ Ask open-ended questions that require more than a simple "yes" or "no" answer.

✔ Be sure your last question is, "Is there anything important that I forgot to ask?"

Setting up the Interview

Set a time and place for the interview that is convenient for the person being interviewed. Try to meet face to face and not over the telephone. You will likely get more information this way. Confirm the time and place you are to meet.

Conducting the Interview

Dress appropriately and be on time. Shake hands firmly. Look the person in the eye, and thank him or her for meeting with you. Ask all of your important questions, but do not make the interview too long.

When all of your questions are answered, thank your interview subject. Again, shake hands. Ask if you can call back to check the accuracy of a quote or to make sure you understood the information.

EVALUATING SOURCES

Now that you have the information from your sources, you need to evaluate it. If the source is unreliable, your report may contain inaccurate information. Here are some questions to ask yourself:

- *What is the date of publication?* Check the copyright page. Conditions change quickly, especially in business. If a source is out of date, do not use it.

- *Who is the source?* Check to see if the writer is an expert. Do others in the field respect his or her opinions?

- *Does the author quote someone?* If so, you may want to check the original source to see if the quote is accurate.

- *Is the information a fact or an opinion?* If it is an opinion, is it supported by facts?

Now that you have gathered and evaluated your information, you can begin to organize your facts. Look for ideas and opinions that need support; then, do more research, if needed.

Lesson Review

CHECK YOUR UNDERSTANDING

1. SUMMARIZING What is the process for conducting an effective interview? Arrange your tasks in sequential order.

2. DISTINGUISHING When would a primary source be more useful for a report? When would a secondary source be more useful?

APPLY WHAT YOU LEARN

Choose a topic that interests you, and find four sources of information about it. If you have access to the Internet, include an Internet source.

Choosing a Method of Organization

What Do You Already Know?

What are some things you have organized at home, at school, or at work? How did you create your plan for organizing?

Think About It Why is it important to organize information before writing?

There are many ways to organize all of the facts you collect for a report. Each way is suited to a different situation. The better you organize before you begin to write, the easier your writing will be. When you organize well, you rewrite and revise less. Most important, the final report makes sense to the reader because your thoughts are clear to you.

THE PARTS OF A REPORT

All reports are organized in one basic way. There are always three major sections: an introduction, a body, and a conclusion.

The introduction should give a **synopsis**, or brief summary, of the topic. For this reason, the introduction usually includes a thesis statement. In a long, formal report for a business, the introduction might also include an **executive summary**. This is a one- or two-page summary of the main points of the report.

When you write the body of the report, you support and develop the ideas you presented in your thesis statement. The body can be as brief as several paragraphs, or it might be as long as several pages.

The last part of your report is your conclusion. In it, you restate the main points of your report. Some business reports also include recommendations in the conclusion.

WAYS TO ORGANIZE A REPORT

Have you ever tried to read a piece of writing that kept jumping from topic to topic? It probably was difficult to follow the points the writer was trying to make. On the other hand, when a report is well organized, a reader is led along a clear path to a logical conclusion. There are several effective ways to organize a report.

Using Chronological Order

Many reports are organized according to chronological, or time, order. This approach is useful for telling the history of an event or explaining why something happened. A report such as the history of computers for new employees of a computer company is likely to be organized in chronological order.

In 1946, two engineers at the University of Pennsylvania built ENIAC, the first fully electronic digital computer. It was the size of a two-car garage and had 18,000 vacuum tubes that controlled its operations. These tubes were constantly blowing out and causing this monster computer to break down. Three years later, the same team developed the more advanced UNIVAC I, whose letters stood for Universal Automatic Computer. It soon became the first mass-produced computer that the public could buy.

FIGURE 8-3 This paragraph is organized in chronological order. **What clue words tell you this?**

When you use chronological order, write events in the order in which they occurred.

FIGURE 8-3 on page 154 shows a paragraph from a report on early computers that was written in chronological order. Look for the clue words and phrases that show that this paragraph was written in chronological order.

Using Order of Needs

A report may be organized so that a reader learns information when he or she needs it. A report about how to deal with different types of customer concerns is an example. One paragraph might discuss complaints and how to handle them. Another paragraph might deal with rude customers. As the reader needs to know information, the report supplies it. FIGURE 8-4 shows an example of a paragraph organized by order of needs.

When you choose a method of organization, you plan how you will draft your work. **How can having a plan for writing help you write more easily?**

Customers may ask to return items. To do this, they need a receipt. If they do not have one, politely tell them that without a receipt, we can grant neither credit nor a refund. If a customer becomes upset, call the manager on duty.

FIGURE 8-4 This paragraph is organized using order of needs. **How could organizing in this way help an employee find information quickly?**

Using Comparison-and-Contrast Order

One of the most common ways to organize information for a business report is by comparing and contrasting. This method is especially useful when someone needs to make a choice. A report that

When choosing a computer game, one factor to consider in the decision is price. Adult computer games are expensive. They cost more than children's computer games. We can stock three children's games for every adult game. We sell children's games more quickly, too.

FIGURE 8-5 This paragraph is organized in comparison-and-contrast order. **What is the writer comparing in this paragraph?**

describes how two items are alike or different can help someone make a decision.

For example, the owners of a toy store might need to decide what kinds of merchandise to stock. There are two choices: to increase the number of expensive computer games that appeal to adults or to carry more inexpensive toys that appeal to children. For this purpose, it would be best to organize a report in a comparison-and-contrast order. FIGURE 8-5 shows an example of a paragraph organized by comparison-and-contrast order.

There are two ways to organize a report that uses comparison-and-contrast order: to contrast each major point or to present the complete argument for one side followed by the complete argument for the other side.

Using Order of Importance

Another way to organize a report is by placing the items in their order of importance. There are two ways to do this. A writer might organize the points from least important to most important. Putting the most important points at the end of a report leaves your reader with a strong impression.

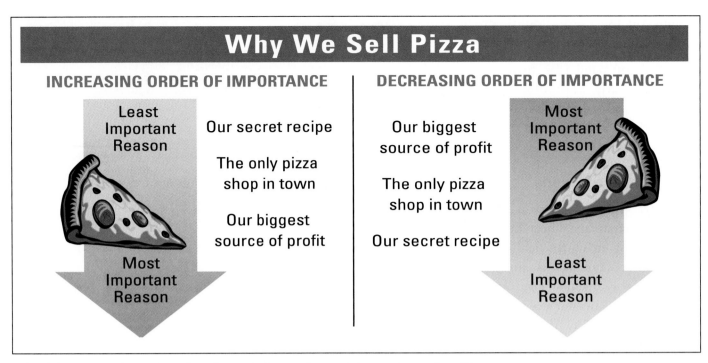

Why We Sell Pizza

INCREASING ORDER OF IMPORTANCE

Least Important Reason

Most Important Reason

Our secret recipe

The only pizza shop in town

Our biggest source of profit

DECREASING ORDER OF IMPORTANCE

Our biggest source of profit

The only pizza shop in town

Our secret recipe

Most Important Reason

Least Important Reason

FIGURE 8-6 contains a chart that shows, in increasing and decreasing order of importance, the reasons a restaurant sells pizza. **Which order do you think would be more effective in a report about business profits? Why?**

You also might present the most important points first and the least important ones last. Organizing in this way can help your reader understand the main idea immediately.

FIGURE 8-6 shows how to use order of importance in a report on why a store sells pizza.

Combining Types of Organization

A good report flows smoothly from one point to the next. It gives readers a sense of where the report is headed and what to expect. Sometimes, the best way to do this is to combine several methods of organization. For example, if you were writing a report about a VCR, you might begin by using comparison-and-contrast order to compare this VCR model with other models. Then, you might use chronological order to describe how it was made.

Lesson Review

CHECK YOUR UNDERSTANDING

1. RECALLING Describe the three sections contained in every report.

2. CONTRASTING What are the main differences between a report organized in comparison-and-contrast order and a report organized according to order of importance?

APPLY WHAT YOU LEARN

List four topics that interest you. Then, exchange papers with a partner and tell which method of organization you would use for each topic. Explain your choices.

Grammar Workshop

Using Parallel Construction

Parallelism is a kind of repetition. One way to achieve parallelism is to repeat grammatical forms, such as verbs, nouns, phrases, or clauses. Using parallel construction will make your sentences stronger and your reports more effective by reinforcing the connections between your ideas.

Here are some examples of parallel construction:

- Parallel Nouns

    Example Lisa studied **shorthand, word processing,** and **databases.**

- Parallel Verbs

    Example Brandon **ran, swam,** and **hiked** while he was on vacation.

- Parallel Phrases

    Example Taylor likes **sorting mail, recording payments,** and **handling complaints.**

- Parallel Clauses

    Example **When he painted the building, when he planted the roses,** and **when he washed the windows,** his back ached.

Application

On a separate sheet of paper, copy these sentences. Correct the errors in parallel construction.

1. Wendell displayed, to sell, and serviced telephone systems.
2. Your job here is to listen, to learn, and asking questions.
3. The reporter wanted to cover football, baseball, and hockey interested him.
4. At the movies, Paul sells popcorn, ushering people to their seats, and runs the projector.
5. The software doesn't work and disappointing everyone.
6. During lunch hour, Teresa is paying her parking fine, ate lunch, and runs other errands.
7. Sales includes calling on customers, to explain products, and gave service.
8. Studying to be a doctor and to practice as an intern requires long hours.
9. When you buy our products, when you use our services, and because you need our company, we put you first.
10. Singing, to dance, and fencing are skills useful for actors.

For more information, SEE PAGE 341.

Creating an Outline

What Do You Already Know?

Think about outlines that you have seen or written. How do outlines look? How are they used?

Think About It   How might outlining ideas for a report be useful for a writer?

An outline is a useful organizing tool. It can help you decide what the main points of a report will be and how the details relate to one another. Outlines can be useful for almost all forms of writing. They can help you think about your topic and about the information you will need. They also can help you organize your information, making the drafting step of the writing process an easier task.

THINKING ABOUT AN OUTLINE

Now that you have gathered information for your report and thought about how you might organize it, you are ready to write an outline. The ideas in a report that is based on an outline flow in a way that makes sense. That is why many writers believe that outlines help them do their best work.

An outline helps you see how your main points and details relate to one another. It also helps you see what information you still need to gather.

The Steps of Writing an Outline

Here are the steps you will need to create a useful outline:

Step 1. Give your outline a title. This will often become the title of your report.

Step 2. Write your main idea in the form of a thesis statement.

Step 3. List the first major section of your report with Roman numeral *I.* This is your first topic heading. All topic headings are designated by Roman numerals.

Step 4. Label your first subtopic with the letter *A.* All subtopics will be designated by capital letters. If you do not have at least two subtopics under a main topic, do not list any subtopics.

Step 5. Label details that support the subtopics with numbers. Begin with *1.* Again, do not list fewer than two details.

Step 6. Label details for the supporting information with lowercase letters. Begin with *a* and do not use fewer than two of these categories. Use Arabic numerals and lowercase letters to show further divisions of a topic.

Step 7. Continue with main point *B* and numbered details, or go on to main section *II.* Follow the same procedure until you have arranged all of your ideas in order.

WRITING THE OUTLINE

FIGURE 8-7 on page 159 shows an outline for a report by a restaurant manager about how her business can grow. She writes her thesis statement and then suggests ways the business can be expanded. She follows these suggestions with her recommendations and conclusions. Notice how she organizes her information in order of needs. In this way, it will be easier for her to write her research report.

TWO KINDS OF OUTLINES

Generally, you can use one of two kinds of outlines. You can also change the way you construct your outline to suit your subject.

Ways Restaurant D'Loggia Can Expand

> The Executive Summary briefly summarizes the main points of the report.

> The thesis statement explains the main point of the research paper.

Thesis: There are several ways Restaurant D'Loggia can expand its business.

I. Executive Summary

II. Ways to Expand the Business

> Each Roman numeral shows a main section in the report.

   A. Enlarge the restaurant

      1. Add tables in patio space

      2. Take over space in buildings next door

         a. Rent space from office building on west side

         b. Buy empty building on east side

   B. Create take-out business

      1. Turn unused coatroom into counter

      2. Offer select group of popular menu items

> The subtopics give more information about the topics.

         a. Lunch specials for local businesses

         b. Dinner specials for commuters

   C. Create delivery business

      1. Deliver to locations within 10-minute drive

      2. Hire students from local high schools and college who have cars or bikes

      3. Minimum orders: $15.00

III. Costs

   A. Tables for patio

   B. New space

      1. Rental of new space

      2. Purchase price of buildings

> List subtopics only if you have two or more items.

   C. Construction of new restaurant area

      1. New table space

      2. Take-out counter

   D. New employees

   E. Advertising

IV. Recommendations and Conclusions

FIGURE 8-7 This is an outline for a report about how a restaurant can expand its business.
What are the four main sections of this report?

A topic outline lists the topics that the writer will develop in the report. It does not provide specific details. The topics are presented in words and phrases, not in complete sentences. If you use a topic outline, write your thesis statement at the top of the page. Then, make sure all the topics in the outline support the thesis statement. FIGURE 8-7 on page 159 is a topic outline.

Another type of outline, the sentence outline, also includes all the major topics to be covered. The writer uses short, complete sentences to describe each point, providing details as well.

REVIEWING YOUR OUTLINE

Before you begin to draft your report, review your outline to make sure it contains the main points you want to make. A clearly organized outline will make the drafting process much easier because all of your ideas will be laid out for you. Your task, then, will be to present your ideas clearly and with the details and language that are appropriate for your audience.

Use the following checklist to review your outline:

✔ My outline title is clear; it describes my topic.

✔ My thesis statement summarizes my report.

✔ All the major sections of my outline are labeled with a Roman numeral.

✔ Each subtopic is labeled with a capital letter.

✔ I have included more than one supporting detail for each subtopic.

✔ All of my details reinforce and explain my ideas.

Lesson Review

CHECK YOUR UNDERSTANDING

1. DEVELOPING Why is an outline a useful tool when writing a research report?

2. SEQUENCING List the steps needed to create an outline for a research report.

APPLY WHAT YOU LEARN

Suppose that an ice-cream shop is considering opening a store in your neighborhood. Work with a classmate to write an outline for a research report that would help the shop owner make this decision.

Making Collective Nouns Agree with Their Verbs and Pronouns

Collective nouns name a group of people, things, or animals that act as a unit. As you write and then revise your report, you might use collective nouns, such as *team, company, group,* or *crew.* Make sure your verbs and pronouns agree in number with the collective nouns you use.

- A collective noun takes a singular verb when it refers to a group as a unit.

  Example   Suzannah's advertising **company produces** ideas worth considering.
  (The company is working as a unit.)

- A collective noun takes a singular pronoun when it refers to a group as a unit.

  Example   The **team** is working together on **its** task.
  (The team is working as a unit.)

- A collective noun takes a plural verb when it refers to each person as an individual.

  Example   The **group** of nurses **are** expected to plan their vacations around the health fair.
  (The nurses are planning separate vacations.)

- A collective noun takes a plural pronoun when it refers to each person as an individual.

  Example   The **team** put on **their** jackets and left the field.
  (The team members are putting on separate jackets.)

Application

On a separate sheet of paper, rewrite each sentence. Choose the correct form of the verb or pronoun in parentheses.

1. What kind of design does the crew want on (its, their) new T-shirts?
2. Emilie's team is training for (its, their) race.
3. The herd is running toward (its, their) pasture.
4. Sharp scissors (cut, cuts) easily through the thick material.
5. The squad (stand, stands) at attention.
6. The audience clapped (its, their) hands.
7. The marketing group liked (its, their) new sales campaign.
8. The team (has, have) chosen to use a new type of packing machine.
9. The United States (is, are) a country with work for those willing to do a good job.
10. The orchestra (practice, practices) from 1:00 to 3:30 every afternoon.

For more information,
SEE PAGE 349.

Using Relevant Details

Details make your writing strong. They support each main idea by giving your readers information to help them develop a clear picture of your main points. Examples, explanations, and other details strengthen your ideas. They help you convince your reader that what you are saying is true.

What Do You Already Know?

How do you explain a movie to a friend that he or she has never seen?

Think About It When you answer the questions *who*, *what*, or *when*, you give details. What other questions lead to important details about a topic?

USING DETAILS

Details that support your main idea or thesis statement are **relevant**, or appropriate, to your report. Your thesis statement is a summary of what you want to say. You develop your thesis statement by providing concrete details that support it. Specific details help your reader understand your ideas.

Although there are many different kinds of details that you can use to support a thesis statement, each detail should answer a question your reader might have. Suppose, for example, you wrote, "The west side of our city is growing rapidly." Your reader might want to know, "How fast is it growing?" or "In what ways is it growing?" Details would help answer these questions.

Relevant Details

There are many ways for writers to add details to a report. In fact, for most writers, finding details is usually not a problem. What can be a problem is

---

Fernando Sanchez is a real immigrant success story. He came to the United States in 1969 with no skills and no money. He joined his brother Enrique, who had arrived a year earlier. During their first few years, the brothers worked as dishwashers, then as cooks, and finally as chef's assistants in New York restaurants. Along the way, they learned both English and business management.

By 1986, Fernando had saved $10,000 and decided it was time to start his own business. He bought a used tortilla press, rented space in an abandoned garage, and went to work, naming his company after his hometown in Mexico.

In his first year, Fernando produced 4,000 tortillas a week. By 1992, his weekly count had reached 400,000, a total that required more than 200 tons of corn flour per month. As he says, "A typical Mexican family, mama and papa and four kids, goes through two or three packages of my tortillas every time they sit down to eat."

Today, Fernando's company has more than $4 million in annual sales; a chain of bakeries in Brooklyn, New York; a grocery store; and a tortilla shop in Rhode Island. Beginning with just two workers in 1986, Fernando now employs as many as 50, most of whom are immigrants like himself.

FIGURE 8-8 This section of a report on successful businesspeople describes the success of Fernando Sanchez. **What is the thesis statement? How do the details in the report support it?**

KINDS OF DETAILS	EXAMPLES
Facts are among the most frequently used supporting details. Unless it is general knowledge, the fact's source should be noted in the text or a footnote.	The city's West Side began to change soon after the new Civic Center was built in 1997. Small boutiques began to open not long after that. The area is now becoming a major shopping area for young people.
Statistics have to do with the analysis of numbers. In a report, you might use statistics to describe a situation or to prove a point.	The percentage of women in the workforce has risen from 18 percent in 1900 to more than 45 percent today, according to the *Information Please Almanac*.
Quotations are statements by an expert that can add valuable supporting information.	"Trends greatly affect what people buy when they shop," said Dr. George Ladrow, economics professor.
Definitions are often included in reports, especially if they support the point of the report.	Point-of-purchase advertising is the advertising that surrounds an item in a store.
Anecdotes are true stories that make a point and can be powerful details in a report.	The customer was so impressed by our product that he bought one for each member of his family.
Examples can be effective supporting details.	The failure of strawberry pudding, blue-colored cheese sticks, and lime-flavored popcorn all show that not every new food idea is a good idea.
Reasons answer the question *Why?* Both facts and well-supported opinions may be reasons.	We need a larger sales force because we are not reaching many potential customers, competition is stiff, and we are not meeting the needs of the customers we currently have.
Comparisons can be useful in proving a point.	Our new container is more effective than the old one. It has bolder lettering and is bigger.

FIGURE 8–9 shows the kind of details that are often included in a report. **How do details help your reader understand your ideas?**

finding *relevant* details. FIGURE 8-8 on page 162 shows how relevant details can be used to show how Fernando Sanchez became successful in business. To determine if your details are relevant, ask yourself this question: Do all of my details support my thesis? If they do, you have built a strong argument. If they do not, look again at your research.

Kinds of Details

Writers who have carefully researched their topic usually find many details to support their points.

Most details can be grouped into a few categories, as shown in FIGURE 8-9 above. These kinds of details will help you support your points in a report.

DIFFERENT TYPES OF DETAILS

Read FIGURES 8-10 and 8-11 on page 164. These figures show sections taken from research reports. As you read, think about the kinds of details each writer used. How do these details support each thesis?

Poor Industrial Working Conditions

About 100 years ago, most industrial jobs were difficult and low-paying. Almost all factories were loud, dirty, and dangerous. In New York City, the largest number of people were employed in the textile industry, which accounted for 47 percent of the city's factories. Workers labored in stuffy, overcrowded rooms with poor lighting and fast-running machines that often caused injuries.

They worked 11- to 12-hour days, six days a week. On top of all this, workers earned only $1 to $2 a day. Women usually performed the least skilled work and earned about half the wages that men earned.

In California and Oregon, workers in the canning industry also worked long hours for low pay. They stood all day in damp, dirty sheds, from 3 A.M. until late afternoon, using razor-sharp knives to shuck oysters and peel shrimp. The odor from the seafood stung their noses and eyes, the lighting was dim, and the liquid in the shrimp was so strong that it caused their fingers to swell and ate holes in their shoes. They worked so quickly that workers frequently cut their fingers with knives.

FIGURE 8-10 This section of a research report shows the difficulty of industrial work in the last century. **What is the thesis statement? How do the kinds of details the writer has chosen help support it?**

How Plants Obtain Food

Most plants obtain what they need to stay alive through photosynthesis. During photosynthesis, green plants make food from carbon dioxide, water, and sunlight. This food provides a plant with the energy it needs to grow and develop. Besides food, plants also need nitrogen, which they usually get from the soil. Plants absorb nitrogen in the soil through their roots.

However, not all plants live in nitrogen-rich soil. The Venus's flytrap grows in moist bogs where nitrogen is scarce. This plant gets nitrogen from insects, which it captures and digests.

These plants wait for their prey to come to them. The hairs on each leaf are sensitive to touch. When an insect lands on the hairs, the trap is sprung, and the leaf closes up, capturing the insect. Once the prey is caught, glands inside the leaf release a fluid that contains chemicals that break down the soft parts of the insect's body. The digested insect flows into the plant, and the plant absorbs the nitrogen it needs to live.

FIGURE 8-11 This section of a research report shows how plants obtain their food. **What kinds of details does the writer use?**

Lesson Review

CHECK YOUR UNDERSTANDING

1. IDENTIFYING Name three types of details and give examples of each one.

2. ANALYZING Why is it important to include relevant supporting details in a report?

APPLY WHAT YOU LEARN

With a classmate, examine FIGURES 8-10 and 8-11, above. List all of the kinds of details you find, and explain how each one is relevant to the writer's thesis statement.

Writing the Formal Report

How is writing a report different from other kinds of writing assignments?

Think About It Why might it be important to think about your audience as you write and revise your work?

You have the topic for your report. You have collected information, organized it, and found relevant details. Because you have already planned how you will organize your report, drafting it should be relatively easy. But you will still need to choose the proper words. You also will need to edit and proofread your work so that your reader will understand your purpose and your ideas.

DRAFTING YOUR REPORT

Now that you have your report organized, you can begin to write a draft. First, review your purpose, your audience, and your outline. Make sure that your main ideas have strong details that support them.

Begin writing with your thesis statement, which should appear at the top of your outline. Then, progress through your outline point by point. Consider starting a new section with every Roman numeral. Be sure to cover all of your important points and to add the description and support your audience will need to understand your topic and purpose.

USING REPORT LANGUAGE

As you write and edit, think about your audience. You might be writing for teachers or employers. For this reason, the language you use should be more formal than the language you use with friends and family members. To be sure that your tone is appropriate, use the following checklist:

- ✔ Do not use slang. It has no place in formal writing.

- ✔ Avoid contractions. Words like *don't* and *can't* are too informal.

- ✔ Stick to the point. Most business people want to read reports that are **concise**, or brief. This is not the place for wordiness.

- ✔ Avoid using exclamation points unless they are part of a quote.

- ✔ Use formal titles when you refer to people. "According to Ms. Barnes" is more formal than "According to Suzy."

SPECIAL PARTS OF A REPORT

While the format of reports may be similar to other kinds of writing you have done, reports have two features you may not have used before: footnotes (or endnotes) and a bibliography. Footnotes and bibliographies can be helpful for readers who want to learn more about your topic. These resource lists tell people where to find more information.

USING FOOTNOTES AND A BIBLIOGRAPHY

Footnotes and endnotes give the source for any facts or quotations you include. Although they contain the same information, footnotes and endnotes appear in different places in a report. Footnotes appear at the bottom, or foot, of the page. Endnotes appear at the end of the report.

Use footnotes or endnotes in these situations:

- when you quote a person's exact words.
- when you use someone's idea.
- when you use facts or statistics that are not commonly known. (You do not have to footnote the fact that Kansas is a state, for example.)

Footnote Form

Footnotes are numbered, beginning with *1*. Each footnote is labeled with a raised number (called a superscript), which appears at the end of the material you are using. The footnote tells a reader to look at the bottom of the page for the same superscript number. There, the reader sees the source of the information. (Endnotes use the same form, but are placed at the end of a report.)

Every footnote includes the author of the information and the place from which it came. Give the source for books, magazine and newspaper articles, and even personal interviews.

Here are some sample footnotes or endnotes:

- from a book: Philip C. McGraw, *Life Strategies*, (New York: Hyperion, 1999), p. 68.
- from a magazine article: Susan Jason, "Tips for Better Marketing," *Marketing Strategies*, March 1998, p. 24.
- from a newspaper article: "Cultural Drifter," by Maureen Dowd, *The New York Times*, Oct. 3, 1999, p. 17.
- from an encyclopedia: "Laser," *The New Webster's International Encyclopedia*, 1991 ed., p. 622.
- from an Internet source: Michael Quinion. "Turns of Phrase." *World Wide Words*, Jan. 29, 2000. www.quinion.com/words/

Bibliography Form

A bibliography is a list of all the works that a writer used to prepare a report. It gives readers sources

they may want to use for further information. It also helps readers check a writer's facts.

Use this checklist when you create a bibliography:

- ✔ Write the entries in alphabetical order by author, last name first. If there is no author, alphabetize the work by the title.
- ✔ Begin each entry at the left margin. The second and following lines of each entry should be indented five spaces.
- ✔ Leave one line between entries.

The bibliography is usually the last page in a report. It appears after the endnotes. Here is a sample bibliography:

Dowd, Maureen. "Cultural Drifter," *The New York Times*, (Oct. 3, 1999) p. 17.

Jason, Susan. "Tips for Better Marketing." *Marketing Strategies*, (March 1998), p. 24.

"Laser," *The New Webster's International Encyclopedia*, 1991 ed., p. 622.

McGraw, Philip C. *Life Strategies*. New York: Hyperion, 1999.

Quinion, Michael. "Turns of Phrase." *World Wide Words*, Jan. 29, 2000. www.quinion.com/words/

The parts of a formal research report shown in FIGURES 8-12 and 8-13 on pages 167–168 contains a sample footnote and a bibliography.

EDITING YOUR REPORT

Now that you have completed a draft of your report, reread your work. Compare your draft with your report to make sure that you have included all of your important ideas and the details that support them. Check that you have used language that is appropriate for your audience. Finally, proofread your work carefully to be sure that you have caught any spelling, grammar, or mechanical errors you might have made. You might wish to have another student or a co-worker read your work and make suggestions for revisions or corrections.

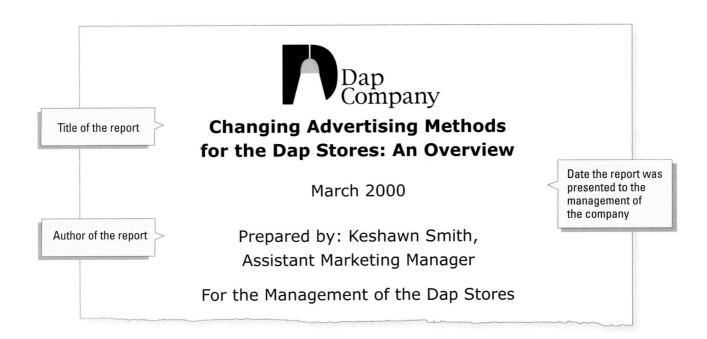

Title of the report

**Changing Advertising Methods
for the Dap Stores: An Overview**

March 2000

Date the report was presented to the management of the company

Author of the report

Prepared by: Keshawn Smith,
Assistant Marketing Manager

For the Management of the Dap Stores

Table of Contents

It is standard to include a table of contents for longer reports so readers who are interested in a specific section can find it immediately.

FIGURE 8–12 These sections are from a report that will help a company decide if it should change its advertising methods. **What do you predict this report will discuss? What clues helped you make your predictions?**

Executive Summary

Dap has been successful because the company sells items customers want: inexpensive and modern furniture and lighting. The company has always used the same advertising methods—magazine and newspaper ads—according to company president Frank Banta[1]. This report will address current advertising methods, survey the advertising trends in the industry, and describe new methods of reaching potential customers.

1. Frank Banta, Personal Interview, Feb. 9, 2000.

> The executive summary gives readers who do not have time to read the entire report a good overview that helps them review and remember the main points.

> The footnote refers to information provided during an interview. It is needed even though the information is not a direct quote from the person.

Recommendations

The Dap Company has been successful using the same advertising techniques for 30 years. It might continue using the same techniques successfully for many years to come. However, industry trends show that an advertising strategy must be updated to fit the changing times.

> The recommendations show the conclusions of the report, which are discussed in greater depth than in the executive summary.

Bibliography

Adamson, Jane. "The New World of Successful Product Advertising," *Advertising Trends*, July, 1998, pp. 35–38.

Banta, Frank. President, Dap, Personal Interview, February 9, 2000.

> Sources are listed in the bibliography in alphabetical order. Note that a person the author interviewed is also included.

FIGURE 8-13 Shown here are the executive summary, recommendations, and bibliography from the report. **What do you think the writer will recommend?**

PUBLISHING YOUR REPORT

The last stage in the writing process is publishing. In this stage, you present your work to your audience. The way you present a report in school or in the business world can be as important as the report itself. If possible, you should type your report on a computer with a clear, readable **font**, or typeface. Use standard margins, and make sure each page is numbered and matches your table of contents.

You also might want to make a cover for your report. Taking this kind of care with your report will show your audience that you are serious about your work.

Formal language, footnotes, a bibliography, and a neat presentation will all help to make your formal report successful.

Lesson Review

CHECK YOUR UNDERSTANDING

1. IDENTIFYING What kinds of information should you include in footnotes for a formal report?

2. EVALUATING List five ways to check that your report has a formal tone.

APPLY WHAT YOU LEARN

Find examples of a book, a magazine article, a newspaper article, an encyclopedia article, and an Internet source. For each resource, write a footnote or endnote. Then, write a bibliography that uses all five of your resources.

Grammar Workshop

Avoiding Redundancies

A redundancy is an idea that is repeated unnecessarily. You would not write *job work* because both words mean the same thing or because they repeat information your audience already knows. As you revise your report, look for redundancies. Here are some redundancies that you should avoid:

actual fact	forever and ever	plan of action
alternative choice	huge in size	reason is because
circled around	I myself	reason why
consensus of opinion	known fact	same identical
could possibly	many in number	sum total
current news	may possibly	verbal discussion
future plan	null and void	

Examples   He brought the project to **final completion** two weeks early.
(*Final* and *completion* have the same meaning.)

An **alternative choice** would be to work four-day weeks.
(*Alternative* and *choice* have the same meaning.)

Application

On a separate sheet of paper, rewrite each sentence, correcting any redundancies you see.

1. Rashondra introduced the company's future plan for new location openings.
2. Juanita and Emma had a verbal discussion about the schedule.
3. The reason why I was late was a traffic jam on Route I-95.
4. Sandy admitted she may possibly handle writing payroll checks.
5. The sales force is many in number, and their training is expensive.
6. The alternative choice for Wilson was the job in Dallas.
7. Alvin asked that the committee's decision be made null and void.
8. Mrs. Pratt has the same identical journal as I do.
9. The sum total of Mario's work experience is a paper route.
10. Have you heard the current news about the merger?

For more information, SEE PAGE 342.

Formal research reports usually have a standard format. This makes them easier for your audience to read.

Today, almost all writing is done on a computer. Once you input your information, there are aids in any word-processing program that can help you create a professional-looking report. The key to formatting is to use the commands in the program.

As you read on page 169, the word *font* means "a style of type." You can probably access many fonts on your computer, as shown in this illustration.

Most reports use a font such as Garamond or Times Roman.

From the Font menu on your computer, you can also choose the size of your type. The larger the point number, the larger the type. Most reports are written in 11- or 12-point type.

This is 13-point Garamond.

This is 9-point Garamond.

Many programs have a Page Setup command under the File command. The toolbar at the top of the screen also can help you set margins for the page. One-inch margins on both sides—as well as top and bottom—are standard.

Application

Use a computer word-processing program to format a title page for a report. The page should look like the title page of the sample report in FIGURE 8-12 on page 167. Then, format a sample first page of a report.

REVIEW

Chapter Summary

Writing clear and effective reports starts with reading and understanding the different kinds of research reports and their main parts. Every good report starts with a plan. Information must be gathered from various sources, including books, magazines, the Internet, and experts in the field. These sources must then be evaluated. Before the report can be written, information must be organized. Relevant details must be included to support the main idea. A good research report follows the five steps of the writing process and also includes footnotes or endnotes and a bibliography.

Key Words

informal report
formal report
thesis statement
primary source
secondary source
database
search engine

keyword search
synopsis
executive summary
relevant
concise
font

From the list above, choose the word that best matches each definition. On a separate piece of paper, write the word and its definition.

_____ 1. a one- or two-page summary of the main points of a report

_____ 2. a style of type

_____ 3. an Internet program that looks for information

_____ 4. a report that usually focuses on a specific problem or subject, often in a single page

_____ 5. a large collection of listings of information

_____ 6. a source that analyzes or discusses original sources

_____ 7. brief, not too wordy

_____ 8. a longer report that often requires a great deal of research

_____ 9. a brief summary of what a report is about

_____ 10. a one-sentence summary of a report

_____ 11. an original document that was written by a person who participated in the events described

_____ 12. a way to look for information on the Internet by using words that describe a topic

_____ 13. something that is appropriate or related

Application: Create an Outline

Speakers at business meetings often introduce themselves with a brief personal history. Using the style you learned in this chapter, write an outline that describes a part of your life that might interest your classmates. Include the main events of that time and two or three details that relate to each event.

Application: Find Sources and Organize a Report

Choose a report topic. It could be the future of space travel, how a lumber company can protect the environment, or any other topic that interests you. Prepare for the report by completing the following tasks. Your audience is your class.

1. Determine your purpose for writing.

2. List the sources you could use to research your report. Check your library to find information.

3. Choose the way you will organize your information.

4. Write an outline for your report. Include relevant details that support your main ideas.

Grammar Workshop Practice

On a separate sheet of paper, rewrite the following sentences so that they are correct.

Part I. Choose the correct word in parentheses.

1. Now that her cough is gone, Dara feels (good, well).

2. The differences (among, between) the three software suppliers was small.

3. The manager requested that her staff do more work and make (fewer, less) excuses.

4. If you open the software package and use the CD, you (accept, except) the manufacturer's terms for use.

5. Working the night shift has a very bad (affect, effect) on Tina.

Part II. Check for parallel construction.

6. Sorting, stamping, and to deliver the mail were daily jobs for Jasmine.

7. Ako cared for patients and gives them medicine.

8. Bring one of each to the meeting: a pencil, a notepad, samples of your writing.

9. Writing a draft, to revise it, and to produce a finished document take time.

10. Wherever you go, whatever you do, who you happen to visit, remember to call the office once daily.

Part III. Choose the correct verb or noun to agree with each collective noun.

11. The army (march, marches) to the camp site.

12. The sales team will call on (its, their) customers.

13. The boat's crew swam to shore after (its, their) boat overturned.

14. The company (produce, produces) record sales figures with each new product.

15. The team (want, wants) to be assigned to different projects.

Part IV. Correct the redundancies.

16. When Apex Rotor moved, it left empty space in our warehouse.

17. I myself wrote the report.

18. It is an actual fact that Wall Street is the money center of the United States.

19. Jan's plan of action was to distribute flyers to every single household.

20. Knowing CPR may possibly save a fellow worker's life.

Portfolio Project — Writing a Research Report

Write a formal report for a community group that describes an issue that interests you. You might write about the new building plan for your community, your town's recycling history, age requirements for voting, or any other issue that requires some research. To create your report:

- Collect and organize your information.

- Make an outline of your points.

- Use relevant details to support your points.

- Edit and proofread your report.

When it is complete, publish your report, and add it to your portfolio.

Writing to Persuade

After volunteering at a local animal shelter, Carla became a dog groomer at Your Beautiful Pets. Carla carries out almost all the services provided by the shop, including brushing, bathing, and clipping dogs.

Yesterday, Ms. Phillips, Carla's supervisor, said that she would like more customers to come to Your Beautiful Pets. She asked Carla to write a newspaper ad and a sales letter to attract new customers. Carla is not sure that she can write the material that Ms. Phillips wants.

Key Words

media

tone

testimonial

bar graph

pictograph

data table

direct mailing

mass mailing

hook

press release

Goals for Success

In this chapter, you will learn these skills:

Recognizing and reading persuasive writing

 READING

Learning the techniques of persuasive writing to write an ad, catalog material, and a press release

 KNOWING HOW TO LEARN

Using graphics to persuade

 PROBLEM SOLVING

Evaluating a sales letter

 WRITING

Editing a document in a word-processing file

SCANS USING COMPUTERS TO PROCESS INFORMATION

PORTFOLIO PROJECT

AD AND SALES LETTER

By the time you finish this chapter, you will understand Carla's task. You will know what she has to do to write a newspaper ad and a sales letter. You also will be able to write an ad and a sales letter to add to your own portfolio.

Reading Persuasive Writing

What Do You Already Know?

You often see examples of persuasive writing at home, at school, and at work. What kinds of things do people try to persuade you to do or buy?

Think About It How do you think businesses use persuasive writing?

On your kitchen table is a catalog. On a counter is a letter from a basketball camp inviting you to join. At work, your supervisor gives you a notice that she wants you to post on the bulletin board at school. The notice announces several job openings and lists new benefits for teenage workers. Catalogs, invitations to join clubs or activities, and job announcements are all examples of persuasive writing.

HOW TO READ PERSUASIVE WRITING

Catalogs try to convince you to buy something. Flyers from political candidates try to convince you to vote for them. The purpose of persuasive writing is to change readers' minds or to get them to act in a particular way.

Kinds of Persuasive Writing

Persuasive writing is all around you. Catalogs and advertisements are among the most familiar forms of persuasive writing. Billboards try to persuade you to buy new products. Writers of newspaper editorials and letters to the editor have opinions that they want others to adopt.

Press releases are another form of persuasive writing. Companies and organizations send press releases to the **media** (newspapers, magazines, and radio and TV stations) to keep the public up-to-date on news, events, and ideas. Press releases give readers the name of the organization or company as well as the name of the person to contact for more information. FIGURE 9-1 shows an example of a press release.

Sales letters, which are another form of persuasive writing, are written for businesspeople as well as for the general public. Sales letters use a standard business-letter format. They try to persuade customers or potential customers to buy the company's products or services.

Jalix Blading, Inc.
398 Mason Ave.
Denver, CO 80202

NEWS For Immediate Release

Contact:
Fitzgerald Gordon 303-555-3876

JALIX HELPS OUT WITH NEW SKATING PARK

June 4, 2000   The new Denver in-line skating park has a new partner—Jalix Blading. Jalix has promised to spend $50,000 on the new park for Denver-area skateboarders and in-line skaters.

FIGURE 9-1 This press release was sent to a local newspaper. **What does the company want people to know?**

Strategies for Reading Persuasive Writing

Being able to recognize the techniques of persuasive writing will help you make up your own mind about products or ideas.

Unfortunately, not all persuasive writing is easy to recognize. Have you ever seen magazine contests that promise riches to those who enter and win? Often, these contests are really trying to sell products, such as magazine subscriptions. To recognize persuasive techniques, you must read carefully.

It is important to have a strategy for reading persuasive writing so that you will be able to identify the writer's claims and make your own decisions. Reading strategies can help you understand and think about what you read.

The strategy you use will depend on the type of persuasive writing you are reading. If you are reading a short piece of writing, such as a billboard, simply think about the writer's purpose. What is the writer trying to convince you to buy or do? Then, analyze the evidence. Do you agree with the writer?

Longer readings use the same idea: thinking about the writer's purpose and evidence. However, a strategy for a longer reading uses several steps to help you understand the greater amount of information.

Here are the steps of a strategy for a longer reading:

Step 1. Preview to predict what you will read.
Get a quick idea of what the writer is trying to persuade you to do by looking at headings, copy, and any visuals. Look for words that try to grab your attention, such as *absolutely free, no charge,* and *you have been selected.* Based on what you see, write down a few predictions about what you will read. Do you think that the product, service, or idea might be worthwhile? Why or why not?

Step 2. Read, and then take notes.
As you read, look for evidence that supports your predictions. Write it down, or write the facts you did find and the evidence that supports them. Then, ask yourself if the writer's evidence supports the ideas presented.

Step 3. Review what you have learned.
After you read, check your understanding of your reading by summarizing it. Note what the writer promised and what he or she actually proved. Should you be persuaded or not? Why?

Lesson Review

CHECK YOUR UNDERSTANDING

1. MAKING CONNECTIONS List three examples of persuasive writing you have seen. What did the writers try to persuade you to think or do?

2. SUMMARIZING What are the three steps of a reading strategy to use for a longer piece of persuasive writing?

APPLY WHAT YOU LEARN

Collect examples of three different kinds of persuasive writing. Use a reading strategy to understand each example. Then, decide what each example is trying to persuade you to do and how you will respond. Share your findings with the class.

Techniques of Persuasive Writing

What Do You Already Know?

Have you ever been convinced to do something after reading a piece of writing? How do you think the writer accomplished this?

Think About It   Have persuasive techniques ever changed your mind about something? How?

When you read reviews of new CDs, the writers want to convince you to accept their opinions about the music. When you read letters to the editor in your local newspaper, the writers want you to agree with them about important issues. Persuasive writers use special tools to help them achieve their purpose.

CONSIDER YOUR PURPOSE

When you write persuasively, first ask yourself, "What am I trying to persuade someone to do?" The answer to this question will determine what and how you write. Each piece of persuasive writing has its own goal. That goal might be to convince readers to help change a law, contribute to a charity, support a candidate in an upcoming election, or buy a new product.

All these goals, however, share one main purpose. They want readers to agree with the writer and then to take an action based on the writer's opinion.

To do this, persuasive writers try to make points in fresh and exciting ways, to convince by using reasons, and to create excitement with language that is often emotional and colorful.

CONSIDER YOUR AUDIENCE

Think about who will read your writing. Is your audience another student? If so, you might want your tone to sound informal. However, if your audience is businesspeople, you will want your tone to sound formal and professional.

Look at the ads in FIGURE 9-2. They both describe the same product. However, one is meant for parents and one is meant for children.

FIGURE 9-2 These ads were written for two different audiences. **How are the ads different?**

Notice how the writing for children uses words like *great* instead of *delicious*. The ads also appeal to the interests of each group. Children are told that the cereal tastes good. Parents are told that it is nutritious.

A writer uses several tools to help support persuasive writing. These tools include tone, self-interest, emotion, and evidence.

Tone

Tone is the feeling writers convey toward their subject or audience. The tone you use in persuasive writing can help convince your reader to accept your ideas. In the example on the left in FIGURE 9-3, the writer makes the mistake of insulting readers by making them sound unintelligent. The example on the right, however, uses the same facts to persuade without offending.

> You may have a telephone. But you probably don't have a clue about how to use it well. Phone Wizard can teach you how to avoid mistakes when you talk on the phone.

> Everyone knows how to use the phone. With Phone Wizard, though, you can learn how to make more effective phone calls.

FIGURE 9-3 These ads have different tones. **Would you buy a Phone Wizard after reading the first ad? the second ad? Why?**

Self-Interest

One of the most effective ways to appeal to people is to show them how a situation affects them. When you appeal to people's self-interest, you make them see how their own lives will be different if they do or think something new.

The notices in FIGURE 9-4 both ask for help. Which one appeals to the readers' self-interest? You can see that the notice on the left focuses on the needs of the writer. The notice on the right focuses on the interests of the reader. Readers may be more persuaded to act if they see how they will benefit from an action.

> To help me out, please wash the coffee cups after you use them.

> *Please wash the coffee cups after you use them. That way, you will have a clean cup whenever you want one.*

FIGURE 9-4 This figure shows different ways to ask for help. **Which of these two sentences is more likely to influence a reader? Why?**

Emotion

Have you ever seen ads for animal rescue groups featuring sad-eyed dogs? The writers of these ads are using emotion to convince readers to send money, adopt pets, or take some other step to help these animals. As FIGURE 9-5 shows, appealing to emotion can be a powerful technique.

Sympathy, however, is not the only emotion to which writers appeal. A writer might say that a sale is for "just our best customers." An ad such as this appeals to the readers' desire to be considered special as well as their interest in saving money. In contrast, a letter encouraging readers to sign up for community volunteer work might appeal to their community pride and concern for other people.

Can you save Ralphy?

He hasn't had a bed to sleep in since his owners dumped him by the side of the road. Call **Animal Rescue**, and give Ralphy and many dogs like him a chance for a better life.

FIGURE 9-5 Shown here is an appeal to emotion. **Do you think this is an effective ad? Why or why not?**

KINDS OF EVIDENCE	EXAMPLES
Facts provide proof. There is a source behind a fact that can be checked. Sources may include first-hand evidence, an expert, a government agency, or a book.	Our price is 30 percent lower than the price of any of our competitors. Just visit your grocery store and compare.
Examples support what you say. They are specific and can appeal to the emotions.	Why should you support the Lowe Fund? Here's why: Because pollution is a constant battle. Many species of fish now swim in the Third River, but some industries are still dumping their waste into it.
Reasons are another way to support what you say. It is important that you justify your ideas and opinions. If readers question your reasons, they probably will not be persuaded by your writing.	Shop at Heroics because we have a great selection, and because we're the friendliest place in town.
Testimonials are stories and comments from people who have had good experiences with a company or a product. They frequently show that real-life consumers believe in a company and its products.	Hi, I'm Mary Weekes. Before I took VitaminPlus, I was always tired. Now, after a month of taking VitaminPlus, I'm full of energy!

FIGURE 9–6 This table shows the kinds of evidence you might use to support persuasive writing. **Why might a reader respond to evidence more readily than to an appeal to emotion?**

A desire to have special things or to be part of a group can be a strong emotion. Appealing to these desires is a technique some advertisers use to urge readers to buy products.

Evidence

Facts, examples, reasons, and **testimonials** are kinds of evidence that win over many people who do not respond to appeals to emotion. Testimonials are statements from people who say that they have had a positive experience with a product. The different kinds of evidence are described in FIGURE 9-6.

ADD A CALL TO ACTION

Every piece of persuasive writing should contain a call to action. A call to action, which usually appears in the conclusion, is a direct appeal to readers. It asks readers to do something that is supported by the writer's facts, arguments, and persuasive

techniques. If the reader is persuaded to act or think in a certain way, the writer has been successful.

Lesson Review

CHECK YOUR UNDERSTANDING

1. EVALUATING Why is it important to consider both your purpose and your audience when you write persuasively?

2. DRAWING CONCLUSIONS Why do you think an animal rescue organization might use emotion as its main persuasive technique?

APPLY WHAT YOU LEARN

Find samples of persuasive writing that use three of the four techniques described in this lesson. Compare the techniques used in each sample and give examples of how the writer uses each one.

Grammar Workshop

Using Conjunctions

Conjunctions join words, phrases, and clauses. They help you combine short phrases and sentences so that your writing flows smoothly and your reader understands how your ideas relate to one another.

Here are examples of several kinds of conjunctions:

- Coordinating conjunctions connect words, clauses, and phrases that have the same grammatical structure. Coordinating conjunctions include *and*, *or*, *but*, *yet*, *so*, and *nor*.

  Example   Creating a new product **and** revising it are the basis of the software business.

- Correlative conjunctions are conjunctions that are used in pairs. Correlative conjunctions include: *either/or*, *neither/nor*, *not only/but also*, *both/and*, *whether/or*, and *just/as*.

  Example   **Not only** did Harry get a promotion, **but** he **also** got a pay raise.

- Subordinating conjunctions join a dependent clause to an independent clause. Subordinating conjunctions include: *after*, *although*, *as*, *as long as*, *because*, *before*, *if*, *in order that*, *since*, *though*, *unless*, *until*, and *when*.

  Example   Brenda will answer all customer complaints **until** Glennie returns from vacation.

Application

Rewrite each sentence on a separate sheet of paper. Use conjunctions to combine sentences, clauses, or phrases.

1. The job was hard. The job paid well.
2. We took a taxi. We were already late.
3. You mop the floor. I'll dust.
4. Kevin won't finish the report. He can't stay late tonight.
5. The manager hired José. He called José's references.
6. Rangers patrolled the park. All visitors had left.
7. You'll learn new skills. The Army will train you.
8. Vets care for small pets. Vets care for large farm animals.
9. Juan got a new job. Adela also got a new job.
10. Donna can't go to the meeting. Terry can't go, either.

For more information, SEE PAGES 355–356.

Using Graphics to Persuade

Some people think visually. You might tell them that the costs of supplies have increased every year for the past five years. Although they hear what you are saying, they will understand your meaning better if they see a chart or graph that shows that increase. Using graphics such as tables and charts can make your writing more persuasive by helping your reader see your ideas.

What Do You Already Know?

Some athletes keep track of how much they exercise. Some salespeople keep track of how much they sell. Think of an activity in your life or work that you could chart. What would you learn from keeping such a record?

Think About It   Could you be persuaded by a chart or graph? How?

USING CHARTS AND GRAPHS

Graphics can be an important part of a persuasive argument. A table could demonstrate that the prices at Tip-Top grocery store are lower than at any other market. A chart could show that the veterinary assistants in Dr. Perkins's office are seeing more animals this year than last year.

Graphics can be important in other ways, too. Table, charts, and graphs can add colors and interesting shapes to a page. They can make a page more visually appealing.

TYPES OF GRAPHS, TABLES, AND CHARTS

There are several different types of graphics, each of which can be used to show a particular kind of information.

Bar Graphs

A **bar graph** uses bars to compare information. A bar graph can be horizontal or vertical. FIGURE 9-7 is a vertical bar graph that shows how the kinds of jobs people do in the United States could change over a 10-year period.

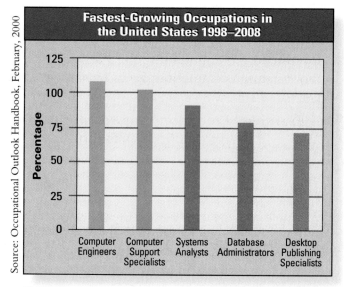

Source: Occupational Outlook Handbook, February, 2000

FIGURE 9-7 A reader can glance at this bar graph and see which occupations are projected to be the fastest-growing. **What might this bar graph persuade you to think or do?**

Pictographs

Pictographs are graphs that use pictures to show information. Pictures of the items being measured are used instead of numbers. For example, in the pictograph in FIGURE 9-8 on page 183, each computer symbol represents 21 million computers.

FIVE NATIONS WITH THE MOST COMPUTERS IN THE YEAR 2000

United States

Japan

France

Germany

United Kingdom

= 21 million

Source: Computer Industry Almanac

FIGURE 9-8 Pictographs like this one are often aimed at a general audience. **About how many computers does France have? How can you tell?**

Data Tables

Tables are another kind of graphic that present information in a way that is easy to interpret quickly.

You may have seen a **data table**, or information table, in an ad. For example, a manufacturer might use a data table to prove that its prices are lower than the prices of other companies. To do this, the manufacturer would create a data table that lists a number of companies and the prices for a variety of items they sell. Data tables can also be used to compare statistics or the features of different products. FIGURE 9-9 shows a data table that compares the expected growth in the need for workers in protective services.

Lesson Review

CHECK YOUR UNDERSTANDING

1. SUMMARIZING How can graphics help persuade a reader to act or think in a certain way?

2. EVALUATING You want to show the rises in the cost of advertising over the last five years. What kind of graphic would you use? Why?

APPLY WHAT YOU LEARN

Work with a classmate to use a newspaper or magazine to find the prices for three identical products from three different stores. Create a data table to display your information. Then, write an explanation of what you discovered.

Purpose of Computer Use at Home							
Age	Total Using Computer at Home	Word Processing	Bookkeeping	E-mail	Games	Graphic Design	Internet
18–24 years	7,562,000	69,700	19,500	42,800	61,400	22,500	44,300
25–49 years	36,691,000	70,300	46,900	45,800	55,000	27,100	45,900
50 years and older	12,163,000	71,400	48,600	41,400	44,700	24,000	39,300

Source: U.S. Census Bureau, October, 1999

FIGURE 9-9 Data tables often contain more complex information than graphs. **Which occupation is expected to show the greatest increase in number of jobs?**

Writing a Sales Letter

Sales letters are one of the many ways that companies use to try to reach customers. Letter writers want to get readers to open the envelope, read what is inside, and buy what they are selling. Writing an effective sales letter will help you get results, whether you have a home business or work for a company.

What Do You Already Know?

Think about the sales letters you have seen. Has a sales letter ever caused you to buy something? If so, why did it work?

Think About It What information might you expect to find in a sales letter?

TYPES OF SALES LETTERS

All sales letters have the same purpose: to make readers take action. One sales letter might try to sell computer software. Another might try to raise money for a charity. A third letter might try to convince a voter to support a candidate for city council. In general, however, sales letters tend to fall into three categories.

The Personal Appeal

A personal appeal is a letter that a writer sends to a particular person. For example, a car dealer might write a letter to a customer because she has a car on her lot that she thinks the customer might like. Her letter describes how beautiful the car is and how well it performs. The dealer might also tell the customer to call soon, because the car will not be available long.

Direct Mailing

A **direct mailing** is a sales letter sent to a specific group of people. The writer might know that these people have a common interest. For example, the owner of a small clothing shop might send a sales letter with news about the arrival of new fall clothes. The letter would be sent only to customers who are on the shop's mailing list.

Mass Mailing

A **mass mailing** is sent to a large audience. These sales letters, often called "junk mail," frequently come from national companies such as banks and magazine publishers. Sometimes, though, mass mailings are local. For example, the owner of a pizza store might try to attract new customers by sending a mass mailing to everyone who lives in the surrounding neighborhood or town.

THE DESIGN OF A SALES LETTER

In general, the more personal a sales letter looks, the more persuasive it will be. A sales letter from a business owner to a good customer might be designed to look like a personal letter. The address on the envelope might be handwritten to lend personal appeal. Usually, there is no return address on the envelope so that the letter seems to be personal.

Other techniques are also used to make the envelopes of sales letters look personal. A stamp might be used instead of a postage meter. A statement to create interest, called a tag line, might be added. For example, a clothing store might print "Check Out Our New Spring Collection!" A magazine company might print "You May Have Won One Million Dollars in Our New Contest!" Mass mailings usually are easy to spot because they feature colorful messages on the envelope and in the letter. In fact, these letters sometimes look more like advertisements than like letters.

HOW TO CREATE A SALES LETTER

FIGURE 9-10 on page 186 shows a sales letter. The writer of the letter followed these seven steps:

Step 1. Research your product or service.
Learn as much as possible about what you are selling. If you have not had direct experience with the product, read about it. Interview experts. Gather testimonials from people who say they have used the product.

Step 2. Think about your customers' needs.
Figure out how your product or service can benefit customers. Learn what is important to your audience—your customers. What will they gain from buying your product or service?

Step 3. Get your readers' attention.
Interest your customers by writing a statement or question in the first paragraph called a **hook**. A hook could be a thought-provoking question, such as "Have you saved the environment today?" It could make a point with which your readers will surely agree,

such as "If you have ever complained about the high cost of designer clothes, you know how important careful shopping is." It might also be a quotation from an expert, such as " 'Dragon's Cough Syrup stops sore throats fast.' —Dr. Winston Winters, noted throat specialist."

Step 4. State your purpose.
After the introduction, immediately tell your readers why you are writing. Your purpose could be to inform them of a sale, to ask for a donation, or to make an appointment. People who have to read an entire letter to find the point may lose interest.

Step 5. Present your evidence.
For readers to realize how your product will improve their lives, the benefits must be obvious. Use facts, examples, and reasons to make your case.

Step 6. Conclude with a strong argument.
To help people remember your message, close your letter by telling them how your product will improve their life. For example, "We are so sure you will love our take-out service that if you don't, lunch is free." That might persuade readers to try your new lunch service.

This photograph shows many examples of sales letters. **What techniques of persuasive writing do you see?**

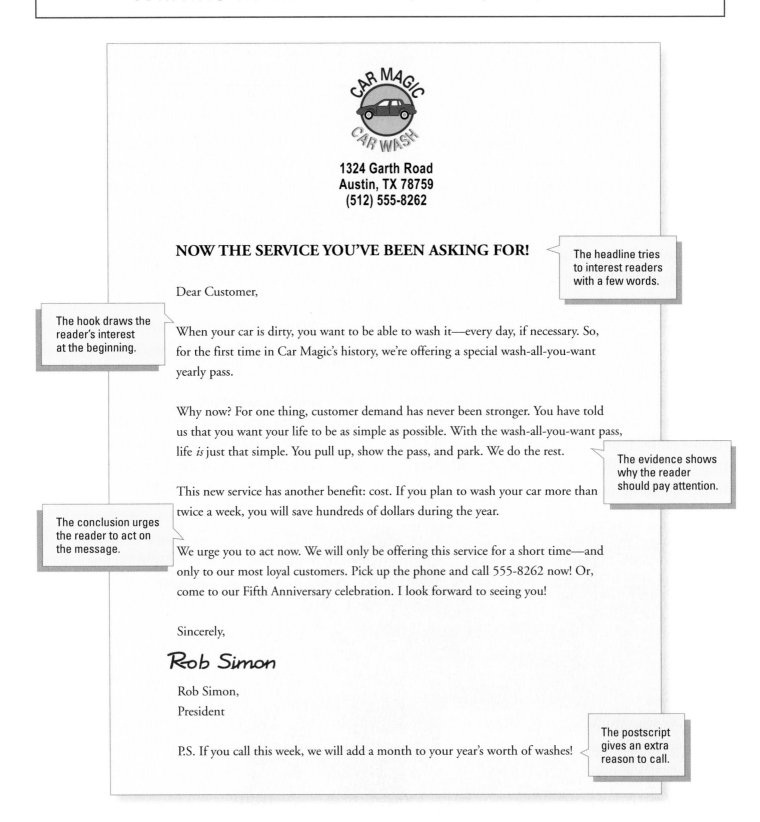

CAR MAGIC CAR WASH

1324 Garth Road
Austin, TX 78759
(512) 555-8262

NOW THE SERVICE YOU'VE BEEN ASKING FOR!

> The headline tries to interest readers with a few words.

Dear Customer,

> The hook draws the reader's interest at the beginning.

When your car is dirty, you want to be able to wash it—every day, if necessary. So, for the first time in Car Magic's history, we're offering a special wash-all-you-want yearly pass.

Why now? For one thing, customer demand has never been stronger. You have told us that you want your life to be as simple as possible. With the wash-all-you-want pass, life *is* just that simple. You pull up, show the pass, and park. We do the rest.

> The evidence shows why the reader should pay attention.

This new service has another benefit: cost. If you plan to wash your car more than twice a week, you will save hundreds of dollars during the year.

> The conclusion urges the reader to act on the message.

We urge you to act now. We will only be offering this service for a short time—and only to our most loyal customers. Pick up the phone and call 555-8262 now! Or, come to our Fifth Anniversary celebration. I look forward to seeing you!

Sincerely,

Rob Simon

Rob Simon,
President

P.S. If you call this week, we will add a month to your year's worth of washes!

> The postscript gives an extra reason to call.

FIGURE 9-10 This sales letter offers a number of reasons to persuade the reader to buy a yearly pass for car washes. **Would this letter persuade you to buy? Why or why not?**

Step 7. End with a call to action.

Now state what you want your readers to do. Should they call? visit your place of business? place an order? Include your business's address and phone number at the end of the letter so your readers will be able to find you easily.

A FEW MORE TIPS

• Keep the letter's language friendly and not too formal. You can do this by using *you* as often as possible to show that you are talking directly to the customer. For example, you might write, "You are receiving this special offer because you like bargains."

• Use a standard business–letter format, like the format in FIGURE 9-10 on page 186.

• Use a greeting that is as personal as possible. If you know the person's name, use it. If not, use a greeting such as "Customer" or "Fellow Music Lover." Avoid "Dear Occupant."

• Close with "Sincerely," "Best wishes," "Keep in touch," or "Warmest greetings," along with your name and title.

• Sign the sales letter yourself. Make sure your signature is neat and clear.

• If possible, add a P.S. that offers a special deal. Research shows this part of a letter is read carefully. A P.S. can restate the main point of the sales letter, repeat the call to action, or provide a new offer. For example, you might write, "And if we hear from you within a week, we will take $2 off your next order." This may encourage customers to buy the product or service.

Lesson Review

CHECK YOUR UNDERSTANDING

1. MAKING CONNECTIONS Review the sales letter in FIGURE 9-10 on page 186. How did the writer try to convince readers to buy the car wash pass? Give examples.

2. COMPARING How are the audiences different for personal appeals, mass mailings, and direct mailings?

APPLY WHAT YOU LEARN

Work with two or three other students to find and bring to class three examples of sales letters. First, identify the parts of each letter. Then, discuss how the writers tried to persuade you to do or buy something.

Grammar Workshop

Using Homophones Correctly

Several sets of words are commonly confused; these words are called *homophones.* Homophones sound the same, but are spelled differently and have different meanings. Review these words to make sure your writing says what you want it to say.

- **its, it's:** *Its* means "belonging to *it.*" *It's* means "it is."

  Examples The office space is popular because of **its** location.
  It's time you came to work.

- **than, then:** *Than* connects two parts of a comparison. *Then* usually refers to time.

  Examples Jeff works harder **than** Greg.
  First, make an outline; **then,** write a first draft.

- **there, their, they're:** *There* shows place or location. *Their* means "belonging to them." *There* is a contraction of *they are.*

  Examples File the copies **there.**
  The mail clerks forgot to sign **their** time cards.
  They're both applying for the same job.

- **to, too, two:** *To* is a preposition that means "in the direction of." *Too* means "also" or "very." *Two* is the number 2.

  Examples Rafael is going **to** lunch.
  There are **too** many paper clips in this drawer.
  Alisa has **two** cats.

Application

Copy these sentences on a separate sheet of paper, choosing the correct word in parentheses.

1. Frank lays bricks faster (than, then) Steve.
2. (Its, It's) mechanical problems never ended, so we sold the old truck.
3. (Their, there, they're) going to be late for dinner.
4. Her supervisor asked her (to, too, two) put the contract over (their, there, they're).
5. Mark will go to the meeting; (than, then), he will go home.
6. The dogs are chasing (their, there, they're) neighbor's cat.
7. Can you come (to, too, two)?
8. Kevin ordered (to, too, two) new office chairs.
9. The dog hated to have (its, it's) coat brushed.
10. (It's, Its) important that Saul and Jaime learn to do (there, their) jobs well.

For more information, **SEE PAGE 366.**

Writing Ad and Catalog Copy

What Do You Already Know?

Think of an ad that you have read in a newspaper or magazine. Did the ad make you want to buy the product? Why or why not?

Think About It What makes an ad appeal to you? What kinds of ads do not appeal to you?

You probably have read thousands of advertisements in your life. Some were in magazines or newspapers. You also might have received catalogs in the mail. All these words and pictures have one purpose: to convince you to buy a product or service. Effective advertisements and catalogs are among the most persuasive selling tools.

ADS AND CATALOG COPY

At some point in your life, you probably will write an ad. It may be an ad for a community activity, a sports program, or a magazine. Regardless of what the ad promotes, however, the principles of writing ads are the same.

WRITING ADVERTISEMENTS

Ads have these basic features:

• They have an attractive design and often a graphic to catch the reader's attention.

• They often are written in phrases and sentences, not in paragraphs.

• They try to persuade the reader to buy or do something.

FIGURE 9-11 shows an ad for a product called a Spaceball.

PARTS OF AN AD

In creating an ad, the writer needs to think first about the ad's main idea. The main idea is the concept used to sell the product. In the ad for the Spaceball, the main idea is that the Spaceball is an

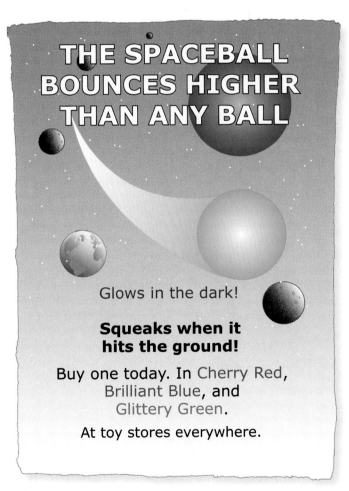

THE SPACEBALL BOUNCES HIGHER THAN ANY BALL

Glows in the dark!

Squeaks when it hits the ground!

Buy one today. In Cherry Red, Brilliant Blue, and Glittery Green.

At toy stores everywhere.

FIGURE 9–11 This ad uses a headline, copy, and a graphic to sell its product. **Which part of the ad caught your attention first? Why?**

exciting toy. This idea focuses on the product's audience: children. The ad is designed to interest children enough so that they will want to own a Spaceball.

The Headline

Look at ads in magazines. Generally, the ads that catch people's eyes have simple, bold headlines. The purpose of a headline is to grab readers' attention so that they read the entire ad. Research has shown that the bigger, bolder, shorter, and simpler the headline is, the better is the chance that the ad will be read. Headlines should stimulate readers' curiosity. When people are curious, they keep reading.

The Graphic

Think about how the graphics used in ads catch your eye. Like headlines, attention-getting graphics are simple and bold. Complex pictures can confuse readers. Headlines printed over graphics are often hard to read. The best rule is to keep graphics simple and memorable. Readers should be able to understand the photo or illustration at a glance.

Copy

Words, of course, are very important in persuasive writing. They are the tools writers use to convince an audience to accept their ideas. The words in an advertisement should make clear

- what benefits readers might get from the product or idea.

- the reasons and facts that show why readers should take action.

- how and where to buy the product or service.

In general, ads use fewer words than sales letters, so it is important to choose your words carefully. Use active, descriptive words. Don't waste words. Keep the tone of your ad personal and friendly. You want to show that the people behind the product or service are friendly and reasonable.

Writers often use charts to help them plan ads. FIGURE 9-12 shows a chart that the writer might have used to create the ad for the Spaceball.

WRITING FOR CATALOGS

Catalog copy also tries to persuade people to buy products or services. FIGURE 9-13 shows a sample product description from a catalog.

There is a reason this ad has so many words. If people are interested in a catalog item, they will read as much information as you provide. The more you write, the more chance you have of

Characteristics of the audience	How to reach audience in ad
• Can't read very well	• Use simple language
• Likes bright colors	• Stress bright colors
• Likes toys	• Show that item is a toy
• Has a fascination with outer space	• Show outer space in graphics
• Likes new and different things	• Explain that toy is brand new

FIGURE 9–12 This chart shows five techniques for reaching one audience. **How might these techniques change if teenagers were the audience for the ad?**

The Shirt You'll Live In

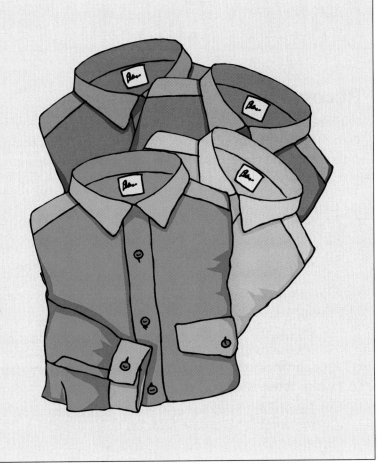

This is the shirt you'll reach for time after time. Made of prewashed 100% cotton, it feels as comfortable as that favorite shirt you've had for years. This shirt, with its jewel colors, sturdy double-stitching, and roomy fit, will last you a long, long time.

#876AR, available in Teal, Goldenrod, Periwinkle, and Ruby.

S, M, L, XL, XXL

FIGURE 9–13 This catalog ad for a shirt has more copy than the ad for the Spaceball. **What descriptive and persuasive words does the writer use to sell this product?**

finding that one detail that will cause your readers to buy the product.

Strong details also are important in catalog copy because readers cannot see the exact color, feel the smoothness of the cloth, or hold the shirt up to see how it might fit them. Persuasive words must substitute for this.

No matter what the catalog sells, the same writing principles apply to all catalogs. To reach catalog shoppers, the writer must

- write for the audience that buys the type of items the company sells.

- include as much relevant information as possible.

- choose words carefully so that the product descriptions are precise and appealing.

Lesson Review

CHECK YOUR UNDERSTANDING

1. COMPARING How is writing different for ads and catalogs? How is it the same?

2. EVALUATING Choose an ad that is popular among people you know. How would you improve it?

APPLY WHAT YOU LEARN

Work with two or three classmates to choose a product you like or to invent a new product. Design and write an ad and catalog copy for your product. Present your work to the class.

Grammar Workshop

Recognizing Verb Tenses

A verb's tense shows the time of an action or a state of being. By using correct verb tenses, you can place the reader of your ad in the past, present, or future. Be careful that the time, or tense, of your verbs is consistent.

There are three basic verb tenses: *past*, *present*, and *future*.

- An action or state of being that has already taken place takes the past tense. Past tense is commonly formed by adding *-d* or *-ed* to the verb.

    Example   Heather **worked** at the DiscoMart last summer.

- An action or state of being that is currently happening takes the present tense. Present tense is commonly formed by adding *-s* or *-es* to the verb.

    Example   Heather **works** at the DiscoMart on Tuesdays.

- An action or state of being that has not yet happened takes the future tense. Future tense is commonly formed by adding *shall* or *will* before the verb.

    Example   Heather **will work** at the DiscoMart until she finishes school.

Application

Rewrite each sentence on a separate sheet of paper. Use the correct verb tense for the verb in parentheses.

1. Last week, Marcus (borrow) my software manual.
2. When the new office is finished, the company (move).
3. Catherine (sell) paper and supplies for a living.
4. Jay (change) jobs because he did not like traveling all the time.
5. Because she (like) to cook, Shantay is training to be a chef.
6. Beginning in June, security (tow) cars that are parked in the visitors' lot.
7. Because the rain (stop), the hikers (walk) to the village.
8. He only (need) to pass the test to become a master electrician.
9. Sid (help) the supervisor interview the new employees last week.
10. Alex (smile) when he received the job offer.

For more information, SEE PAGES 352–353.

Writing a Press Release

What kinds of sources do you think reporters use to find news?

Think About It What kind of information might a company want people to know?

How do reporters learn about the news they write? Sometimes, they go to the scene of a newsworthy event to gather information. At other times, reporters get information from press releases. Companies and organizations use press releases to try to bring information to as many people as possible.

WHAT IS A PRESS RELEASE?

A **press release** is a one- to three-page document that announces a newsworthy event. It is sent to members of the media, such as newspaper editors and radio and TV news program directors. Although it does not try to persuade readers to buy a product or service, a press release is a form of persuasive writing.

The writer of a press release has two purposes. The main purpose is to persuade a reporter that the newsworthy event is important enough to write about in a newspaper or magazine article. The second purpose is to describe the newsworthy event and to show how it concerns a large number of people.

WHEN TO WRITE A PRESS RELEASE

There are several kinds of events that companies want people to know about. Companies send out press releases when they hire a new president, receive an award or honor, or have an employee who is recognized for an achievement. Companies also might want to announce an exciting new product, a spectacular scientific discovery, or a large donation to a charity. Even a grand-opening celebration warrants a press release.

Not everything companies do is newsworthy, however. Newspapers do not run articles about sales because sales are not news. An article about a sale would be free advertising. Information about a sale would only be used in a newspaper article if there were something unusual about it. For example, a local company might be selling extra merchandise to pay for new equipment for the local playground.

The key to deciding when to write a press release is to think about your audience. Ask yourself if the information would interest large numbers of readers who were not connected to your company or organization. If so, your company might ask you to write a press release.

THE PARTS OF A PRESS RELEASE

Over the years, writers have developed a standard format for press releases. This format consists of three main parts: the heading, the body, and the closing.

The most important information goes in the first paragraph so that a newspaper editor can decide quickly if the story is worth covering. The details go in the body. The closing gives contact information.

These parts are shown in the press release in FIGURE 9-14 on page 194.

WRITING IN THE REAL WORLD: PRESS RELEASE

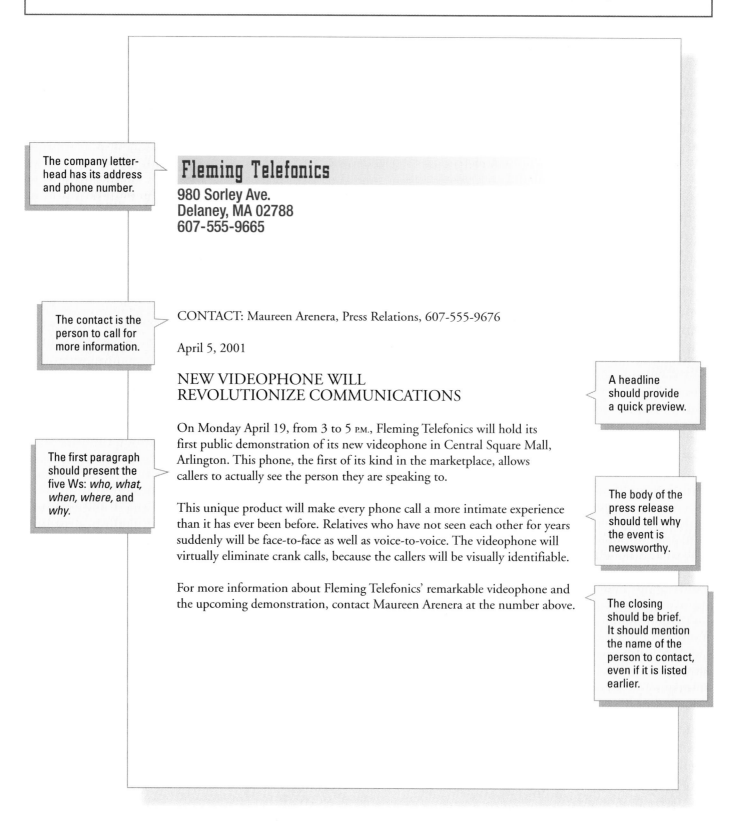

The company letter-head has its address and phone number.

Fleming Telefonics
980 Sorley Ave.
Delaney, MA 02788
607-555-9665

The contact is the person to call for more information.

CONTACT: Maureen Arenera, Press Relations, 607-555-9676

April 5, 2001

NEW VIDEOPHONE WILL
REVOLUTIONIZE COMMUNICATIONS

A headline should provide a quick preview.

The first paragraph should present the five Ws: *who, what, when, where,* and *why.*

On Monday April 19, from 3 to 5 P.M., Fleming Telefonics will hold its first public demonstration of its new videophone in Central Square Mall, Arlington. This phone, the first of its kind in the marketplace, allows callers to actually see the person they are speaking to.

This unique product will make every phone call a more intimate experience than it has ever been before. Relatives who have not seen each other for years suddenly will be face-to-face as well as voice-to-voice. The videophone will virtually eliminate crank calls, because the callers will be visually identifiable.

The body of the press release should tell why the event is newsworthy.

For more information about Fleming Telefonics' remarkable videophone and the upcoming demonstration, contact Maureen Arenera at the number above.

The closing should be brief. It should mention the name of the person to contact, even if it is listed earlier.

FIGURE 9-14 This press release tells about a new and exciting product. **What part of the release immediately caught your attention? Why?**

HOW TO WRITE A PRESS RELEASE

A good way to begin writing a press release is to think about the main idea of the story. Your purpose is to communicate this point.

To find your main idea, make a list of the five Ws. Then, answer each question.

The Five Ws

The five Ws of newspaper and magazine articles are questions that ask *who*, *what*, *when*, *where*, and *why*. You can also use *how*, if it is important.

- *Who?* Tell *who* the press release is about by naming the people involved. For example, if your company is giving $10 million to charity, include the names of people who raised the money.

- *What?* In the *what* section, announce the topic. This might be the discovery of a new medicine or the promotion of an employee.

- *When?* The *when* section tells the date and time of the event. For example, if your company is opening a new store in the mall, provide the month, date, and time of the opening.

- *Where?* Tell the location—the *where*—of the event. This might be where an awards dinner will be held or where the new company headquarters will be located.

- *Why?* In the *why* section, explain the reasons for the announcement. For example, if your company has developed a new vaccine, your press release will tell why the vaccine is important to people.

- *How?* The *how* section provides background information. For example, if a scientist in your company has developed a kind of bacteria that eats oil spills, explain how the discovery was made.

Gather and Organize Your Information

Before you write your press release, construct a five Ws chart like the one shown in FIGURE 9-15. This will help you organize your ideas and be sure you have all of the details you need.

WHO	The Lawson Company
WHAT	Gigashop, an Internet shopping service
WHEN	Sept. 23, 2001
WHERE	On the Internet; address is www.gigashop.com
WHY	This service allows shoppers to have the convenience of browsing the aisles of a store in their own home.

FIGURE 9–15 Each *W* gives important information to be used in the press release. **Why does the writer think readers will be interested in Gigashop?**

Here is a sample first paragraph of a press release based on this information. Look for the five Ws as you read.

The Lawson Company is introducing a new Internet-based shopping service, Gigashop.com, on September 23. This unique service is the first of its kind—a Web superstore that lets shoppers "walk" through more than 300 stores without leaving their home. Shoppers can "browse" the aisles of their favorite shops instead of simply searching for a particular item.

Use Reporter's Style and Tone

Newspaper articles are written in the third person, using the pronouns *he*, *she*, *it*, or *they*. Reporters never use the pronoun *I* because they are observers. To understand newspaper style, read several articles, and notice the tone.

Use Quotations

A quotation can add interest to your press release. Ask a company official or an authority to comment on your event. For example, in the press release about Gigashop, you might include this quotation from the company president: "It's a revolutionary idea. Before long, everyone will be shopping on Gigashop. They will enjoy the shopping experience while saving travel time and money."

Organizations write press releases to get news coverage for an event. **Why might accuracy be important in press releases?**

Be Accurate

Make certain that every fact you state is accurate. Use people's full names, and check that every name is spelled correctly. Do not confuse press release language with advertising language. You may use words such as *unbelievable* and *fantastic* when you are writing ad copy. When you are writing a press release, though, stick to the facts. Use a straightforward, informative tone.

WHERE TO SEND A PRESS RELEASE

Learn the names of the newspaper and magazine editors and the news directors at the TV and radio stations where you plan to send your press release. Send your release directly to these people.

Send press releases two to three weeks before the event will occur. This allows the news director time to assign the article to a reporter.

CHECKLIST FOR WRITING A PRESS RELEASE

Here are some points to check when you write a press release. Does your press release

- ✔ answer the five Ws?
- ✔ have a formal tone?
- ✔ look more like a letter than an advertisement?
- ✔ contain accurate information?
- ✔ provide enough information so that a reporter could write an article about your topic?

Lesson Review

CHECK YOUR UNDERSTANDING

1. SUMMARIZING What are the five Ws? Give an example for each one.

2. COMPARING What are the differences between a press release and an ad?

APPLY WHAT YOU LEARN

Write a press release about an upcoming event in your school, in your community, or on your job. Share it with your classmates.

The editing stage of the writing process is easy to do on a computer. You can add, delete, and move words or sections of text, and then check to see if you have presented your points clearly.

Here are two methods for moving words or sections of text:

- Cut and Paste: Highlight the text you want to move. Click on the Edit section on the toolbar, and then click Cut. The text will disappear from the screen. Move the cursor to the area you want the text to appear. Now, go back to Edit, and click Paste. The text will appear in its new location.

- Drag and Drop: Highlight the text you want to move. Move the mouse to the highlighted area until the cursor becomes an arrow pointing to the left. Then, click the mouse, and hold the button down. Drag the highlighted text to its new location, and release the button. The text will appear in its new location.

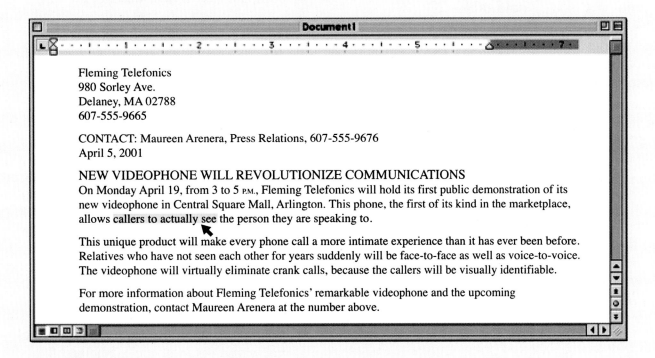

Document1

Fleming Telefonics
980 Sorley Ave.
Delaney, MA 02788
607-555-9665

CONTACT: Maureen Arenera, Press Relations, 607-555-9676
April 5, 2001

NEW VIDEOPHONE WILL REVOLUTIONIZE COMMUNICATIONS
On Monday April 19, from 3 to 5 P.M., Fleming Telefonics will hold its first public demonstration of its new videophone in Central Square Mall, Arlington. This phone, the first of its kind in the marketplace, allows callers to actually see the person they are speaking to.

This unique product will make every phone call a more intimate experience than it has ever been before. Relatives who have not seen each other for years suddenly will be face-to-face as well as voice-to-voice. The videophone will virtually eliminate crank calls, because the callers will be visually identifiable.

For more information about Fleming Telefonics' remarkable videophone and the upcoming demonstration, contact Maureen Arenera at the number above.

Application

Open a word-processing document that you have saved, or create a new document. Edit your document using the two methods discussed on this page. Print out your revised document, and exchange papers with a classmate. Compare the drafts to see how you both used the editing process to improve your work.

REVIEW

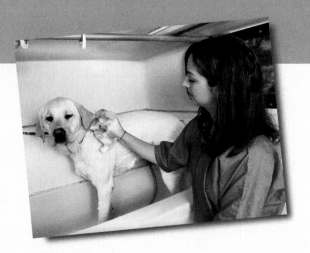

Chapter Summary

Strong persuasive writing can convince your audience to buy a product or take an action. Sales letters, ads, catalog copy, and press releases are all examples of persuasive writing. Writers use persuasive techniques to appeal to their readers' emotions and self-interest, and they use different kinds of evidence to support their points. Graphics, particularly charts, tables, and graphs, are excellent tools that can be used to make a strong persuasive argument.

Key Words

media	data table
tone	direct mailing
testimonial	mass mailing
bar graph	hook
pictograph	press release

Use a word from the list above to complete each sentence. Write your sentences on a separate sheet of paper.

1. A — is a kind of sales letter that is sent to a specific group of people.

2. The — include newspapers, magazines, and radio and TV stations.

3. — are statements from people who say that they have had a positive experience with a product.

4. — is the feeling writers convey toward their subject or audience.

5. A — is a chart of numbers that can be used to compare statistics or products.

6. A — is a kind of sales letter that is sent to a large audience.

7. A — is a one- to three-page document that announces a newsworthy event.

8. A — is a graphic that can be used to compare amounts or numbers.

9. — use pictures to show information.

10. A — is a statement or question in the first paragraph of a sales letter that tries to grab readers' attention.

Application: Techniques of Persuasive Writing

The techniques used in persuasive writing include: self-interest, emotion, fact, reason, and testimonial. Identify the technique used in each of the following statements and explain your choices. Write your answer on a separate sheet of paper.

1. "I have shopped all over the city, and Glad Rags always has the best selection and the best prices."

2. When you wear clothes from Glad Rags, you know you've never looked better.

3. Our prices are guaranteed to be 30 percent lower than those of our competitors.

4. Glad Rags carries the most fashionable clothes in town.

5. You know you want that red silk shirt. Come to Glad Rags, and get it.

Application: Choose a Type of Persuasive Writing

Read each of the following situations. Then decide which type of persuasive writing would be most effective for each one: a sales letter, a direct mailing, an ad, or a press release. Write your answers on a separate sheet of paper. Explain your choices.

1. The company you work for has just created a job-search bank for high-school students and wants to publicize it.

2. You work for a travel agency and recently met the owner of a small business. She said she wanted to learn more about your travel agency because people in her company often travel.

3. The owner of the ice-cream parlor where you work is planning to offer two cones for the price of one on Thursdays. He wants to let people know about the special.

4. You work for an antiques store. The owner has a mailing list of people she wants to contact on a regular basis.

Grammar Workshop Practice

On a separate sheet of paper, rewrite the following items so that they are correct.

Part I. Combine the two sentences in each item with a conjunction.

1. Pat Hill is a veterinarian. She has her own practice.

2. I dislike filing. It's part of my job.

3. Kea will wait for a promotion. Her manager will leave next May.

4. Alan was fired from his job. He was late to work four times this week.

5. Don't expect others to do your work. Don't be afraid to ask for help when you need it.

Part II. Choose the correct word from each pair of homophones in parentheses.

6. (Its, It's) starting to rain.

7. Allyson chose to place her desk (there, their, they're), by the window.

8. Our team is stronger (than, then) Central's.

9. Congratulations (to, too, two) you on a job well done!

10. My dog likes to chase (its, it's) tail.

Part III. Use the correct verb tense in each sentence.

11. The Ramirez Company (finish) construction on the building next Friday.

12. The software (work) as soon as we restarted the computer.

13. The bus (stop) at Second Street every day and (let) off AQC workers.

14. Your community group (explain) its plans to the mayor at last week's meeting.

15. Next, Nicki (describe) what the new policy will be for taking vacations.

Portfolio Project   Writing an Ad and Sales Letter

Think of a product or service that you might like to sell. First, write an ad that will persuade people to buy or use it. Then, write a sales letter to attract potential customers.

To do this:

- Choose the techniques of persuasive writing that will help you make your points.
- Create some graphics.
- Draft your ad and sales letter.
- Edit your document.

Add your ad and sales letter to your portfolio.

Read the following information about two careers in which people use writing skills. Think about the goals and skills the jobs require. Then, answer the questions below.

Data-Entry Clerk: *Business Services*

If you want to work with computers, you may wish to explore a career as a data-entry clerk. Data-entry clerks input information from paper documents into a computer. In small offices, their responsibilities might also include general office work. Data-entry clerks work in financial institutions, research laboratories, department stores, and other types of businesses.

A data-entry clerk should

- complete a data-processing course.
- be able to type quickly and accurately.
- be ready to learn new methods and techniques of inputting.

Minimum Education: High-school graduate
Starting Salary: $15,000 to $18,000 per year
Related Careers: Word Processor, Collection Worker

For more information, contact the Association of Information Technology Professionals, 505 Busse Highway, Park Ridge, IL 60068. You will find this organization on the Internet at www.sinclair.edu/studentlife/aitp/chapters.html.

Paralegal: *Business Services*

If you like to write and are interested in the law, you might wish to explore a career as a paralegal. Paralegals, also known as legal assistants, help lawyers with many tasks. Paralegals research laws and prior cases to help lawyers prepare for trial. Paralegals also draft and write contracts, mortgages, affidavits, pleadings, and other documents.

A paralegal should

- complete a one- to three-year paralegal program.
- be familiar with computers and software.

Minimum Education: High-school graduate
Starting Salary: $24,000 to $30,300 per year
Related Careers: Claims Examiners, Compliance and Enforcement Inspectors

For more information, contact the National Federation of Paralegal Associations, PO Box 33108, Kansas City, MO 64114-0108. You will find this association on the Internet at www.paralegals.org.

EXPLORING CAREERS

1. **As a data-entry clerk, why might you need to know different ways to organize information?**

2. **If you were a paralegal, what kinds of persuasive writing do you think you might need to do?**

> *"Luck is where opportunity meets preparation."*
>
> Denzel Washington (1954–)
> *actor*

UNIT 5

WRITING IN BUSINESS

Being able to write business letters, proposals, and technical materials will help you to succeed at school and on the job. In this unit, you will learn about different types of business writing. You will study different business-letter styles and learn how to write for results. You will find out how to write a proposal to solve problems and how to use charts, tables, and other visuals to increase the success of a proposal. You will focus on reading and writing technical information. Finally, you will learn how to organize and write technical materials such as lab reports, progress reports, and manuals.

WRITING BUSINESS LETTERS

James works as an assistant manager at The Nature Store, a store that sells birdhouses, telescopes, and personal-care products. The manager, Ms. Willis, wants James to run the store when she opens another branch. This morning, she asked James to write a letter to a supplier about some birdhouses that were poorly made. She also asked James to write a letter to find out about some new telescopes.

James knows he is ready to run a store, but he is concerned that he does not know how to write a business letter correctly.

Key Words

marketing

marketing plan

claim letter

adjustment letter

block-style letter

modified-block-style letter

indented-style letter

salutation

return address

empathy

Goals for Success

In this chapter, you will learn these skills:

Reading different kinds of business letters

 SCANS READING

Finding customers and clients

 SCANS SERVING CLIENTS AND CUSTOMERS

Understanding different reasons for writing business letters

 SCANS REASONING

Creating professional-looking business letters

SCANS ACQUIRING AND EVALUATING INFORMATION

Revising business letters for content and organization

SCANS INTERPRETING AND COMMUNICATING INFORMATION

Using mail merge to customize business letters

SCANS IMPROVING OR DESIGNING SYSTEMS

PORTFOLIO PROJECT

BUSINESS LETTER

By the time you complete this chapter, you will understand James's task. You will know what he has to do to write his letters correctly. You also will be able to write a business letter to add to your own portfolio.

Reading Business Letters

What Do You Already Know?

Letters that ask you to apply for a credit card or pay for services are business letters. What kinds of business letters has your family received?

Think About It People write letters for many different purposes. Why might it be important to think about a writer's purpose when you read a business letter?

Although e-mail and voicemail are common forms of communication on the job, business letters are still important. People continue to send letters about payments that are due. They still write to companies about problems or for information. Often, people who write business letters do so because they want a written record of their correspondence. No matter how popular electronic correspondence becomes, people will still need to write effective business letters.

THE PURPOSES OF BUSINESS LETTERS

Most business letters are written for one of three purposes: to request, to inform, or to persuade. FIGURE 10-1 on page 205 shows an example of a typical business letter.

Letters of Request

Businesspeople write many request letters. Here are some reasons for writing a request letter:

- to learn about a product

- to order items

- to ask for samples

- to ask someone to perform a service

- to ask for permission or advice

A person who writes a letter of request follows some simple rules. The writer must

- know the audience.

- be precise when requesting or providing information.

- be brief and to the point.

- clearly describe the kind of information that is needed.

FIGURE 10-2 on page 206 shows an example of a letter of request that a businessperson wrote. Notice that the writer clearly stated what he wanted.

Letters to Inform

A business letter written to inform might

- tell a client about a plan to resolve a problem.

- let a client know about an item that was ordered.

- summarize the decisions or agreements made at a meeting.

- confirm hotel and travel plans.

- remind a client about a scheduled appointment.

Letters to inform are specific. For example, a travel agency might send a letter to inform a

WRITING IN THE REAL WORLD: BUSINESS LETTER

Letterhead
A company's letterhead includes the name of the company, the address, the phone and fax numbers, and the e-mail address. The date the letter is sent is listed under this information.

Green Thumbs
Plant Care Service
708 Morton Avenue, Baltimore, MD 21614
(301) 555–4567 (voice); (301) 555-4568 (fax)
E-mail: JGomez@greenthumbs.com

March 1, 2001

Ms. Marcia Jalon, Office Manager
ABC Travel Agency
653 Washington Street
Bethesda, MD 20814

Recipient's Name, Title, and Address
Business letters include the full name (including the business title) and address of the person or company receiving the letter.

Salutation
This is a greeting to the person to whom the letter is addressed. In a business letter, the salutation always ends with a colon.

Dear Ms. Jalon:

We count the ABC Travel Agency among our most loyal customers, and we deeply appreciate your business. As you know, we have been providing plants and plant service to your business for more than seven years. Now, however, our business is undergoing a major change, and we wanted to let you know about it.

Mary and I have long considered moving to Dallas, where most of our family lives. Because of this, we are selling Green Thumbs to Plantscapes. Plantscapes is a Baltimore-area leader in maintaining plants for businesses, and we believe that Plantscapes will continue to do an excellent job supplying ABC Travel's office plant needs. We looked long and hard for a company we felt had our commitment to quality, and we are confident in Plantscapes. Unless you tell us otherwise, your account will be serviced by Plantscapes beginning April 1.

Body
Most business correspondence is single spaced. There are three sections: an introductory paragraph, the body of the letter, and a closing paragraph.

We have appreciated the chance to serve you during our long association, and we are convinced that Plantscapes will do an excellent job of satisfying your needs. If you have any questions in the meantime, please do not hesitate to call. Thank you again for your business.

Sincerely,

Jorge Gomez

Jorge Gomez
Owner

Complimentary Close
Business letters typically end with one of these closings: *Sincerely, Cordially, Best regards,* or *Yours truly.*

FIGURE 10-1 This business letter follows a standard format. **Why do you think business letters use the same format?**

Dear Mrs. Watkins:

When your firm recently installed a new heat pump for our offices, you gave us a copy of the ten-year warranty, which explains in considerable detail what is covered in the event of product or duct failures. However, we are not clear about the extent of the warranty should we add to the system in the future to increase its capacity.

We plan on doing just that when we add a wing to the north side of our building two years from now. Would the warranty then be extended for two years, covering both the present system and the addition? Or, would we end up with eight years to go on the old equipment and ten on the new installation?

Any information you can provide will be appreciated.

Yours truly,

James Turner

James Turner, Plant Manager

FIGURE 10-2 This is an example of a letter of request. **What is the writer requesting?**

customer about the details of an upcoming trip. The letter might contain information about travel stops and sightseeing tours.

FIGURE 10-3 is an example of a business letter that was written to inform. In this case, the letter provides information to stockholders and investors of a company. It was written to be sent with the company's annual report.

Letters to Persuade

Letters written to persuade might

- ask for a person's support or assistance.

- try to convince a reader to buy a product.

- encourage a client to pay a bill.

- complain about a problem and ask for a solution.

FIGURE 10-4 on page 207 shows an example of a persuasive letter that was written to complain.

READING BUSINESS LETTERS WITH A STRATEGY

Sometimes, business letters, such as sales letters, are not easy to understand. This is why using a reading strategy can both help you better understand what you read and connect your reading to what you already know.

Here some steps for using a reading strategy to read a business letter:

Step 1. Preview to identify the writer's purpose. Read the topic sentence of each paragraph. The topic sentences should give you an outline of what the writer is telling you. Use that information to identify the writer's purpose. Was the letter you are reading a letter written to request, inform, or persuade? Knowing the writer's purpose can help you think about what you will read.

Dear Stockholder:

It is with great pleasure that I enclose United Electric's Annual Report. United has prospered as a result of its steadily increased investment in technology. You will note how favorably this is reflected in the year-end figures when compared with those of a year earlier.

It is our intention to continue our planned program of scientific research so that our company will remain at the forefront of its field.

Sincerely,

Megan Blake

Megan Blake, Assistant Manager, Corporate Communications

FIGURE 10-3 This business letter was written to inform. **What information did the writer want the stockholders to have?**

Dear Ms. Armand,

When you designed the interior of Chase Towers, you did so, I'm sure, with beauty and distinctiveness in mind. There is no doubt that the lobby sparkles with good looks. However, the floor becomes dangerous when it is wet. The other day, when we had an all-day rainfall, the surface became as treacherous as ice. We were fortunate that, despite numerous falls, no serious injuries occurred.

Please see what can be done to coat the surface with a nonskid substance. There must be some way to preserve the beauty yet eliminate the threats to life and limb. Our insurance company insists on this action.

Yours sincerely,

Lauren Green

Lauren Green, Building Manager

FIGURE 10-4 Shown here is a persuasive letter that was written to complain about a situation. **What is the writer trying to convince the reader to do?**

Step 2. Read actively.

Read the letter, and look for the exact details that the writer wants you to know. For example, if you are reading a letter of request, what does the writer want you to do? Write down any ideas that you want to remember or refer to later. Note any points that are unclear.

Step 3. Pay attention to difficult words or terms.

Sometimes, business letters contain new terms or ideas. Look for any clues the writer gives to define these words. The writer might show the word's meaning by using a synonym or an example. Look for such signal phrases as *in other words, for example,* or *for instance.*

Also look for prefixes and suffixes. These word parts might give you clues to the meaning of a word. Prefixes are letters that are added to the beginnings of words to make new words. For example, *pre-* added to *view* makes *preview*, or "to view before or ahead of time." Suffixes are letters that are added to the end of words to make new words. For example, *–less* added to *meaning* makes *meaningless*, or "without meaning."

Step 4. Review what you have learned.

After you read, make sure that you understand and remember what the writer was telling you. Take a few notes or write a summary of the letter to check your understanding.

Lesson Review

CHECK YOUR UNDERSTANDING

1. SUMMARIZING What are the three purposes of business letters?

2. DRAWING CONCLUSIONS What is the purpose of the letter shown in FIGURE 10-1 on page 205? Explain how you know.

APPLY WHAT YOU LEARN

Find a business letter. Work with a small group to label and explain the reason for each part. Use FIGURE 10-1 on page 205 as a guide.

Finding Your Customers and Clients

Customers and clients are people who pay for goods and services. They are critical to every business. Many people work in businesses in which finding and attracting customers and clients is important. If you decide to work in these types of businesses, you will need to think about how your company attracts clients or customers to buy its products or use its services.

What Do You Already Know?

Most schools have bake sales or car washes to raise money. Think of a bake sale or other fundraiser that was held in your school. How did the customers learn about the event?

Think About It   Why is finding customers and clients the key to business success?

WHO ARE YOUR CLIENTS OR CUSTOMERS?

Before you plan how to sell your goods or services, you need to consider who is most likely to use them. Depending on who your customers are, you might choose very different ways of reaching these customers—your audience.

Clients

When you seek clients, you look for people who want or need your company's services. Here are some people who might look for clients:

- gardeners

- lawyers

- dentists

- physical therapists

- designers

- tax preparers

- hair stylists

- engineers

Customers

Customers are people who buy the products a company sells. Businesses that look for customers include the following:

- retail stores (department stores, clothing stores)

- restaurants

- supermarkets

FINDING CUSTOMERS AND CLIENTS

Few business owners open a store and simply wait for people to find them. Instead, they seek customers or clients; then they look for ways to earn and keep their business. This is called **marketing**. Here are some ways that people market their businesses:

Analyzing the Market

Auto-repair shops rarely look for customers in day-care centers. Nor do barbecue restaurants send their menus to vegetarian groups. Every business appeals to a particular group of people. A first step in marketing is to decide who your customers are likely to be and where and how you can reach them.

Checking the Competition

Another important question is: Who are the customers of competing businesses? Smart business-people find out who is buying from similar stores or companies. Then, they think about how to market to those people. When you have a clear idea of who your customers or clients are likely to be, you can begin to design a marketing plan.

CREATING A MARKETING PLAN

Successful businesses create a **marketing plan**, or strategy to attract new customers or clients. Businesses might choose a variety of ways to market their goods or services. A well-known way is to place advertisements in newspapers and magazines or on television or radio. However, advertising in these places can be expensive.

Another way to market is by direct mail—sales letters mailed to people who might be interested in your product or service. As you learned in Chapter 9, businesses find possible customers in several ways. They send sales letters to their regular customers, they buy mailing lists from related businesses, and they create mailing lists of their friends and acquaintances.

Another way to attract customers or clients is to create flyers, which are often single-sheet notices of local sales or services. You might have seen someone distributing flyers in your neighborhood. Flyers work best if they are distributed to possible customers who live in the same neighborhood as the business.

Lesson Review

CHECK YOUR UNDERSTANDING

1. COMPARING What are the similarities and differences between clients and customers?

2. DRAWING CONCLUSIONS Why might it be important to create a marketing plan?

APPLY WHAT YOU LEARN

Suppose you are starting a business at home making clothes, repairing computers, or selling some other product or service that interests you. How would you attract customers or clients to your new business? Work with a group to make a marketing plan.

Grammar Workshop

Using Irregular Verbs

Irregular verbs do not form their past tenses and past participles by adding *-d* or *-ed* to their present-tense forms. They create these forms in different, or irregular, ways. Many common verbs are irregular. Checking for correct verb use is an important step in proof-reading business communications. It shows your clients or customers that you care about your work and about them.

Here is a list of some common irregular verbs and their past and past-participle forms. Be sure to use a helping verb, such as *has* or *have*, with the past participle form.

Present	Past	Past Participle	Present	Past	Past Participle
am	was	been	grow	grew	grown
begin	began	begun	know	knew	known
blow	blew	blown	lead	led	led
break	broke	broken	lie	lay	lain (to take a resting position)
bring	brought	brought	lie	lied	lied (to tell a lie)
catch	caught	caught	ride	rode	ridden
choose	chose	chosen	ring	rang	rung
come	came	come	run	ran	run
do	did	done	see	saw	seen
drive	drove	driven	speak	spoke	spoken
fly	flew	flown	take	took	taken
give	gave	given	throw	threw	thrown
go	went	gone	write	wrote	written

Application

Rewrite the following sentences on a separate sheet of paper. Correct the verb(s) in each sentence.

1. The new librarian choosed the books for the exhibit.
2. The truckers drived across the state each day.
3. We flied to San Diego to have the contract signed.
4. Leo has began writing his press release.
5. The copier was broke when I begun to use it.
6. The article says that soy beans and rice are growed by South Carolina farmers.
7. Bob has rided to work on the train.
8. Thomas brung the new flyers from the printer.
9. Carlos run this company into debt with his big ideas.
10. Have you wrote the ad to send to the newspaper?

For more information, SEE PAGES 352–353.

Types of Business Letters

The way you write a business letter depends on your reason for writing it. For example, you would write a response to an angry client in one way, and you would write a letter of complaint in another way. Your language and tone would be quite different in each letter. To write an effective business letter, think about your purpose before you start to write.

What Do You Already Know?

How would a letter to a friend be different from a letter to an adult? Why would the letters sound different?

Think About It Why would business people need to write different types of letters?

LETTERS IN THE BUSINESS WORLD

As you have learned, letters written for business usually are intended to inform, request, or persuade. Determining your purpose in the prewriting stage will help you focus your letter. It will also help your reader understand what action you want him or her to take.

THE ORDER LETTER

The order letter is a common form of letter of request. Businesses might write an order letter to a manufacturer. An order letter might also be sent to a wholesaler. A wholesaler is a business that sells to retail stores, which resell the item. Finally, a business might write an order letter to a retailer, or a business that sells to consumers.

Even if you write an order letter as an individual, you should use the business–letter style. Include all of the information needed to be sure that you get what you want.

FIGURE 10-5 shows a sample order letter. Notice the elements the letter contains.

FIGURE 10-5 This order letter was written to a sculptor of outdoor statues. **How do you think the sculptor will respond to this letter?**

WILLOW GROVE
768 Bracken St.
San Francisco, CA 94123
415-555-0031

November 3, 2004

Ms. Marcie Means
Garden Decor
345 Spring St.
San Francisco, CA 94126

Dear Ms. Means:

Your latest statues are a great success. In fact, your lovely "Girl with Basket" is sold out.

I realize that our order for six more of these statues is not due to be shipped until next month. However, could we receive those earlier?

Please let me know if you can accommodate our request. As usual, we will pay you by check within thirty days of receiving the merchandise.

Sincerely,

Peter Graham

Peter Graham, Assistant Manager

Here is a list of items that every order letter should contain.

- All of the information about the item you wish to purchase, including quantity, model number, size, material, color, and price.

- The date and number of the catalog, if you are ordering from a catalog.

- An explanation of how you will pay: by check, money order, or credit card.

- The date by which you need the item.

- The word *Enclosure* typed after your signature if you are enclosing an item such as an order sheet from a catalog or a check.

Response to an Order Letter

Most often, a company will simply ship the ordered item. However, if there is a problem with the order or if some additional information is needed, the company may have to ask for more details.

THE REQUEST LETTER

A company might write a request letter to learn more about a product, a client, or another company. For example, a request letter might be written to ask for a brochure. It also might ask for information about a product or service.

The Parts of a Request Letter

As with an order letter, every request letter should include specific information. Remember, however, that a request letter asks someone to do something. Only include information that is crucial to your request. FIGURE 10-6 on page 213 shows a sample request letter.

Responses to a Request Letter

When you respond to a request letter, answer as promptly as possible. If you cannot do what the writer asks or if you do not know the answers to the questions, politely say so. If you have other ideas about where the reader can find answers, include them in your response.

THE CLAIM LETTER

Sometimes, businesses must write letters about problems. These letters of complaint are often called **claim letters**. Tone is particularly important in claim letters. Abusive language and accusations might cause a reader to ignore the complaint rather than resolve the problem. You want to persuade your reader that you have a rightful claim and that you or your company deserves a thoughtful response.

Use this checklist when you write a claim letter:

- ✔ Identify the product or service. Businesses often provide many products or services, so you need to state clearly which item you are complaining about.

- ✔ State the problem clearly and unemotionally.

- ✔ Suggest a solution. You might want the company to exchange the merchandise or give you a refund. You might ask for a service to be redone. Be sure to make the solution you want clear in your letter.

- ✔ Make the reader your ally. Make it clear that you consider the company a partner in resolving the problem.

- ✔ Do not show anger. If you deal professionally and courteously with the company, you will be treated the same way.

THE ADJUSTMENT LETTER

At some time, you might receive a claim letter. In that case, you will have to respond by writing an **adjustment letter**. An adjustment letter is written to try to settle a claim. When you write an adjustment letter, remember these tips:

- Look for a solution that the customer and you can both accept. If your company is wrong, apologize and offer a remedy. If possible, do as the customer suggests.

Greek Islands Restaurant

10 River Lane • Birmingham, AL 35244
205-555-9768

Mr. Mason Fox
The Review
3999 Jackson Ave.
Birmingham, AL 35399

June 4, 2000

Dear Mr. Fox:

> The first paragraph of a request letter states the purpose briefly, clearly, and always politely.

We have recently opened a Mediterranean restaurant, and we would very much like you to consider reviewing our food for your magazine.

> The body of the letter gives reasons the reader should fulfill the request.

Greek Islands Restaurant has been open since March and features entrees in the $9–$11 price range. We know that you have an interest in lower-priced restaurants, and we think you will be impressed by the authenticity, taste, and variety of the items on our menu. We also think your readers will be interested in reading about our fine service. Please call me at the restaurant to schedule a time to enjoy a meal at our expense. My telephone number is 205-555-9768.

> In the closing paragraph, the writer thanks the reader for his or her consideration.

Thank you for your consideration.

Sincerely,

Shaundra Caron

Shaundra Caron, Owner-Chef

FIGURE 10-6 This request letter is intended to persuade Mr. Fox, who is a restaurant critic for a magazine, to take an action. **If you were Mr. Fox, how might you respond to this letter? Why?**

- If your company clearly is not wrong, your job is more difficult. You might want to begin by explaining why your company is not at fault. Always thank a customer for writing. If you are denying a claim, say so clearly, and state why. If possible, try to keep the goodwill of the customer by offering the person something else, such as a discount on a future purchase.

Lesson Review

CHECK YOUR UNDERSTANDING

1. **MAKING CONNECTIONS** Why is it important to consider your audience and your purpose when you write a business letter?

2. **CONTRASTING** How might the tone and contents of an order letter and a request letter be different?

APPLY WHAT YOU LEARN

Suppose you are the manager of a coffeehouse or food shop. In what kinds of situations would you write letters of order, request, and claim? Choose one type, and write a letter to a customer or another business.

This worker is writing a business letter to a customer. **How are business letters and friendly letters different? How are they similar?**

Determining the Letter Style

Just as there are guidelines for the contents of business letters, there are guidelines for the way business letters look. How professional a letter looks can determine the response you receive. Once you learn the styles of business letters, you can compose all kinds of business correspondence.

STYLES OF BUSINESS LETTERS

There are three business–letter formats that you will commonly see. One is a **block-style letter**, in which the paragraphs are separated from each other with spaces and nothing is indented. Another common form is the **modified-block-style letter**, in which paragraphs are separated, but the first line of each paragraph is indented. Finally, there is the **indented–style letter**. In this style, paragraphs are separated only by indented first lines.

Some companies have a preferred style for business letters. These companies want all of their business letters to look alike. If you are writing a letter for a new employer, ask which style the company prefers.

Block-Style Letter

FIGURE 10-7 shows a letter written in block style. This is the most common style of business letter. Here are the features of block style:

- The left margin is set flush, meaning that it aligns on the left side of the paper.

- Every element, including addresses, closings, the date, and the **salutation**, or greeting, starts at the left margin.

- The lines in each paragraph are single spaced.

- There is a blank line between paragraphs.

- The pages are numbered beginning on the second page, not on the first page. Numbers should appear at the top left margin.

The Carpenter Company
155 Brangwen Way
Riverside, CA 92506
919-555-7807

Mr. Norman Wason
879 Gilpin
Denver, CO 80218

December 3, 2000

Dear Mr. Wason:

We at The Carpenter Company wanted to tell you how much we appreciated your talk at our company retreat. Your suggestions on how to manage meetings were particularly appreciated. Since your talk, we have implemented several of your suggestions, and our meetings are now more productive.

Let us know if you ever need a recommendation for your work; we would be very happy to let others know how helpful your talk was.

Sincerely,

Janet Horan

Janet Horan
Assistant Manager

FIGURE 10-7 This thank-you letter is more personal than many business letters. **What other business-letter style could the writer have used?**

Modified-Block-Style Letter

Some companies prefer the modified-block style, which is less formal than block style. Here are the features of modified-block-style business letters:

- The left margin is set flush.

- The first sentence of each paragraph is indented a few spaces.

- As in block style, paragraphs are single spaced, and there is a space between paragraphs.

- The heading is set on the right, unless the letter is written on letterhead paper.

- The date and the closing are set on the right.

FIGURE 10-9 on page 217 shows a business letter that was written in modified-block style. Notice that the paragraphs do not look like even blocks.

Indented-Style-Letter

This style looks the most like a friendly letter. An individual might use indented style when writing to a company to order goods or to make a claim, or when writing to inquire about job possibilities. Indented-style letters may be typed or hand-written. Here are the features of indented-style business letters:

- The left margin is set flush, but the right margin is not.

- Each paragraph is indented.

- There are no extra spaces between paragraphs.

- The letters may be either single- or double-spaced.

- The heading (writer's name and address), the date, the closing, and the signature are set on the right.

BUSINESS ENVELOPES

If your business uses letterhead stationery, it likely has envelopes that contain the company's **return address** as well. The return address is the address of the person who is sending the letter. If your envelope does not have a printed return address, write or type it in the upper left corner.

The name and address of the person or company to which the letter is addressed should be slightly below the center of the envelope. Use the same address you used on the letter itself. Be sure to use postal service abbreviations on envelopes; for example, *Ave.* for *Avenue*.

FIGURE 10-8 shows an example of how the envelope of a business letter should look.

FIGURE 10-8 Note that both Avenue and Street are abbreviated in the mailing address and the return address. **Who is sending this letter to Billi Roman?**

(KH) **Klondike Heating**
Byron Jordon
2998 Jackson Ave.
New York, NY 10003

Ms. Billi Roman
Larope Shade Company
12 Nina St.
New York, NY 10024

Writing in the Real World: Modified-Block Style

Mason Publishing Company
1234 Fifth Avenue
New York, NY 10006
212-555-0990

January 9, 2001

> In modified-block style, the date is set on the right.

Mr. Bill Vincent
Consultant and Flooring Engineer
123 Oak Glen Road
Bedford, MA 01730

Dear Mr. Vincent:

> The paragraphs are single spaced, as in block style.

We are undertaking a major renovation of our offices and will need to install new floors as part of this renovation. Your company has been recommended by Jason Picket of Signal Communications. I understand you recently installed the floor for his company's new offices.

> A space is added between paragraphs.

We would like to talk to you as soon as possible about this project. We would like to install oak floors in about 4500 square feet of our offices. If you are interested in this job, please call me at your earliest convenience. Then, we can arrange a time for you to tour our offices and give us a bid for the work.

I look forward to hearing from you.

Sincerely,
Sophie Marrick
Sophie Marrick
Chief Executive Officer

> The complimentary close and signature are set on the right.

FIGURE 10-9 This business letter is requesting a service from another company. **Why do you think the writer used modified-block style?**

Folding and Inserting the Letter

Business letters are folded in a particular way so that they easily fit into a standard business-size (9 inch by 4 inch) envelope. This method insures that the person who receives the letter opens it and sees the text right side up. The procedure is shown in FIGURE 10-10 below.

Lesson Review

CHECK YOUR UNDERSTANDING

1. DESCRIBING What are the three styles of business letters? Describe each one.

2. APPLYING Look at FIGURE 10-9 on page 217. Identify all of the features of modified-block style that you see.

APPLY WHAT YOU LEARN

Think of a product or service that you enjoy using. Write a thank-you letter to the store or business from which you bought or rented the item. Write it once using the block style and a second time using the modified-block style. Decide which one looks better for this letter, and send it, addressing your envelope properly.

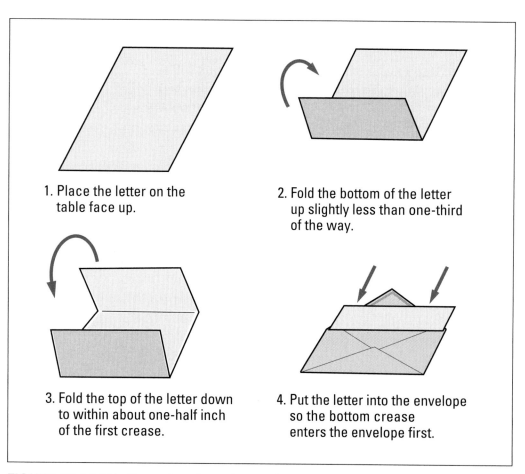

1. Place the letter on the table face up.

2. Fold the bottom of the letter up slightly less than one-third of the way.

3. Fold the top of the letter down to within about one-half inch of the first crease.

4. Put the letter into the envelope so the bottom crease enters the envelope first.

FIGURE 10-10 This illustration shows how to fold a business letter. **Why might it be important to fold a business letter in a standard way?**

Writing for Results

What Do You
Already Know?

Think of a letter you received that asked you to do something. Did you do as the writer asked? Why or why not?

Think About It What results might a person want who is writing a business letter?

If you take the time to write a letter, you want it to be effective. You might want to convince someone to do something, or you might request information on a new product. Whatever your purpose, you can learn to write letters that have the effect you want. In this lesson, you will learn techniques and tips to make sure your letters get results.

LETTER-WRITING LANGUAGE

You may have read a business letter that began like this, "In regard to the aforementioned matter. . . ." The writer made a mistake that letter writers commonly make. He or she thought that larger words make a letter more effective. Such language does not impress readers; it confuses them.

The best business letters have these characteristics:

- They are direct and easy to understand. They contain language that clearly and briefly states the points the writer wants to make. For example, use *now* instead of *at this point in time*.

- They are simple. When a shorter synonym for a word exists, use it. For example, use *thinking* instead of *contemplating*. Unnecessarily long words break the flow of thought and slow readers down.

Remember, your purpose is to communicate a message to an audience. Think of the clearest way to reach the people who need to understand your information.

POINTS TO EMPHASIZE IN BUSINESS LETTERS

The most important thing to remember about business letters is that businesses succeed on the goodwill of their customers and clients. If the tone of your letter angers or annoys your readers, they are less likely to continue reading.

Keep the Letter Positive

People respond more favorably to positive words than to negative ones. If you use positive language when you write a business letter, you are more likely to get the response you seek.

Negative words have the opposite effect. A customer who reads a letter that includes such words as *refuse, cannot, unfortunately,* and *never* will associate negative feelings with your company.

Here are two examples of how a sentence can influence the way a customer thinks about a company. Pay attention to the tone of the sentences.

- *Negative*: You will not get good results with this product unless you use it correctly. If you do not use it at room temperature, it will not work.

- *Positive*: You will get the best results with this product if you use it at room temperature.

Use the Active Voice

When you use the active voice in your writing, the subject performs the action of the sentence. The active voice is direct; it tells readers clearly what is happening. Your reader will understand *who* is doing *what*.

Example: Jaime taught the children to read.

Always use the active voice when you write business letters. It will make your readers feel confident that they can trust you to help them.

Show that You Care

If you write a business letter to solve a problem, put yourself in the place of the person who has the problem. When you do this, you show **empathy**. You tell the customer that you care about him or her and will work to solve the problem.

Use a Respectful Tone

Sometimes, how you say something is just as important as what you say. The clearest way to show that you care is to use a respectful tone.

For example, suppose that an angry customer writes a letter of complaint to a software company about a program that crashed his or her computer. Here are two responses a customer-service representative might make. Think about the tone of each response.

Response 1: We will replace your program immediately. Please send it back.

Response 2: We are sorry for the inconvenience our program has caused you. Such things happen, although problems with our programs are unusual. We will, of course, immediately send you the upgraded version of the program at no charge to you.

Which of these companies would get your business again?

Use this checklist to make sure the tone of your letter satisfies the needs of your customer—and your company.

- ✔ I emphasized the needs of the reader, not those of the company.

- ✔ I showed empathy in answering complaints or criticism.

- ✔ I showed respect and tried to address the concerns of my reader.

Be Persuasive

In every business letter, you have the chance to show people that your company deserves their business.

Keep these points in mind as you write:

- Stress your company's willingness to serve its customers or clients.

- Emphasize the benefits of dealing with your company.

- Address your reader's concerns, and explain how your company can meet them.

Lesson Review

CHECK YOUR UNDERSTANDING

1. EVALUATING How does positive language in a business letter make the letter more effective?

2. ANALYZING In what ways can writers use business letters to sell their company's products or services?

APPLY WHAT YOU LEARN

Suppose you are setting up the complaint department in a department store. List the rules that letter writers will use when they respond to dissatisfied customers.

Tone is important in both writing and speaking. **How can you show that you care about your audience in your writing?**

Using Business Terms Correctly

Some commonly used business terms can be confusing. As you write business letters, check to make sure you are using the following terms correctly.

- **counsel/council:** *Counsel* means "advice" (noun) or "advise" (verb). A *council* is a group of people who give advice.

  > Examples   The director **counseled** me on finding a job.
  > The **council** of volunteers ran the charity.

- **personal/personnel:** *Personal* means "private." *Personnel* are people who work at a job.

  > *Examples*   The letter to Mr. Hicks was marked **"personal."**
  > All **personnel** receive pay raises.

- **principal/principle:** *Principal* means "most important." A *principle* is a basic truth or law.

  > *Examples*   The **principal** reason for our success is our service.
  > Ms. James explained the **principles** of geometry.

- **stationary/stationery:** *Stationary* means "fixed in place." *Stationery* is paper and envelopes.

  > *Examples*   The big desk is **stationary** in the room.
  > Write business letters on company **stationery**.

Application

Rewrite these sentences on a separate sheet of paper, choosing the correct term in parentheses.

1. The director wanted to (counsel, council) the employees about the health insurance plan.
2. Our company says that e-mail is (personal, personnel).
3. Yuko sent out the monthly bills on company (stationary, stationery).
4. Human resources hires all full-time (personal, personnel).
5. Isaac went to the (stationary, stationery) store for office supplies.
6. Knowing the (principals, principles) of letter writing can make a person a valuable employee.
7. The (personal, personnel) office wants to add dental insurance to our medical benefits.
8. The safety (counsel, council) tests hand and ear protection devices.
9. Our company stands by its (principal, principle) that the customer comes first.
10. Because it was so large, Nolan insisted that the bookcase was (stationary, stationery).

For more information, **SEE PAGE 366.**

Revising Business Letters

What steps do you take after you write a draft of a letter? Do you send it right away, or do you reread it and make changes?

Think About It How might revising a business letter differ from revising a personal letter?

A magazine publisher sends you a letter asking you to subscribe. However, the letter has several misspelled words, and parts of it do not make sense. Your reaction is to throw it away. When a business letter is poorly organized and contains mistakes in spelling and mechanics, it may not get the response you want. People may not take you or your company seriously. When you revise business letters, make sure that you have communicated your message clearly.

EDITING YOUR WRITING

In the drafting stage, writers think about what they want to say. When they edit their work, they check to make sure they have expressed their ideas clearly. In the editing stage, writers look for problems in two main areas:

- *Content* Edit every letter to make sure you have expressed your ideas clearly. When you write a draft, concentrate on getting your thoughts down on paper. Do not worry about fixing problems. You can make changes during the editing stage. When you edit, you can check that you have made all your points clearly in a way that your audience will understand.

- *Organization* If your letter is poorly organized, it will confuse your audience. When you edit, make sure that you have structured your letter so that your purpose is clear and your letter is focused.

Editing for Content

When you edit a business letter for content, you try to look at your letter through the eyes of your reader. Ask yourself if you have clearly stated all the points you wanted to make. The chart in FIGURE 10-11 on page 223 shows four areas to check when you edit for content.

Editing for Organization

When you edit for organization, you check that you have communicated your message in a clear and logical way. Pay careful attention to content and style.

To check for content, skim the letter. Be sure you have included the following elements in your letter:

- ✔ An introductory paragraph that states your purpose in writing the letter

- ✔ A body that states your main points and the details that support them

- ✔ A closing paragraph that discusses what action you will take or what action you want the reader to take

As in most writing, each paragraph should have a topic sentence that states the main idea of the paragraph. The rest of the paragraph should include quotes, facts, opinions, and supporting details that relate to the main idea.

EDIT FOR...	ASK YOURSELF...
Message	Does your letter focus on the ideas you intend to convey? Can you read the letter and immediately see what your message is? If you cannot, revise it to state your ideas more clearly.
Purpose	Would a reader be able to tell you the purpose of this letter? Do the style of writing and the tone match the purpose? If they do not, try to see your letter as your audience would see it. What would help them understand your points?
Audience	Is your letter written for the audience you intend to reach? Have you focuse on this audience in your writing, or do you need to revise the letter to better meet this audience's needs and interests?
Tone	Is the tone of your letter in keeping with most business letters—that is, direct, and friendly, but not overly familiar? Have you made sure that the letter does not contain slang? If it does, revise it to include more formal language.

FIGURE 10-11 If you have answered no to any questions in this chart, you probably need to revise your letter. **Which area of editing for content do you think is most important in business-letter writing? Why?**

To check for style, compare your letter to the letter styles shown in this chapter. Your letter should use one of these styles: block, modified-block, or indented. Do not mix styles within one letter.

Check that your letter has included

- ✔ the heading, including the name, address, and, telephone number of your company. Use your company's letterhead, if possible.

- ✔ the date.

- ✔ the salutation, with the name, address, and title of the person who will receive the letter.

- ✔ the body of your letter, containing the message.

- ✔ the closing.

- ✔ your signature and your title, if appropriate.

Peer Editing

An effective way to check your letter is to ask a friend or co-worker to edit it for you. A peer editor may catch problems and errors that you have missed.

A peer editor can tell you if your letter's purpose and audience are clear. If your peer editor cannot tell for whom you are writing, your audience might not get your message. A peer editor can also tell you if your letter has the right tone.

PROOFREADING

Check your letter to be sure you have corrected any errors in mechanics, grammar, and spelling. Remember, the appearance of your letter is important. To make you and your company look professional, be sure your business letter contains no errors.

Mechanics

The mechanics of writing include punctuation marks and other writing details, such as whether numbers are spelled out or written as numerals. Use a reference work, such as the Handbook at the back of this book, to check your work.

Besides looking for errors, look for the overuse of punctuation marks, such as commas or semicolons. These punctuation marks are effective when they are used correctly, but they can be distracting when they are used too often.

Grammar

Checking for grammar is essential. If you use *it's* when you should use *its,* you are telling your audience that you do not care about your work. Some of the most common grammatical mistakes are errors in subject–verb agreement and in sentence structure. Also look for run-on sentences and sentence fragments.

Spelling

Although a spell checker on a computer can help with many spelling errors, it is no substitute for a close read by the writer. If you write *to* instead of *too*, the spell checker will not catch the mistake. However, your reader probably will and might be less likely to consider your ideas.

Lesson Review

CHECK YOUR UNDERSTANDING

1. SUMMARIZING What steps should a writer take before sending out a business letter?

2. EVALUATING How can a peer editor be useful to a writer?

APPLY WHAT YOU LEARN

Work with a small group to create a checklist for peer editors. Include what you most want editors to assess when they read your business letters.

Proofreading carefully ensures that your audience will understand your message. **How can peer editing help you improve your work?**

Mail merge can help you save time by creating mailing labels. You can also use a mail merge to create a form letter. In a form letter, you send the same letter to a list of clients, but you personalize each letter with the individual client's name and address.

Suppose you have written a sales letter. You want to send the letter to 25 people. When you use mail merge, you create two files. One file, called a form file, has the letter. The other file, called a data file, has the names and addresses of the businesses you want to reach.

Find the << and >> symbols in the form file. These symbols show the fields, or the parts of the letter that change. After you create the two files, your computer merges them. Each new letter is addressed to a different person, but the rest of the letter stays the same.

March 15, 2---

<<First>> <<Last>>
<<Street>>
<<City>> <<State>> <<Zip>>

Dear <<First>> <<Last>>:

Thank you for fishing at Summit Lake this year.

We hope you will consider booking an off-season trip with us, when the crowds are fewer, the weather is still lovely, and the fish are biting more than ever.

If you call now, we would be delighted to offer you a 50% discount. We hope to see you!

Sincerely,

Mick Kelly

Mick Kelly, Recreation Manager

Last	First	Street	City	State	Zip
GRIS	ANA	211 MESA	GARY	IN	46401
HALE	JACK	34 MAX RD.	BELL	CA	90201
KULA	J.D.	675 BAY DR.	HONOLULU	HI	96801
MORA	KIM	2 BLYTH CT.	MILO	IA	50166
PAINE	ANN	56 JAG AVE.	ANCHORAGE	AK	71921
ROAS	JOSE	111 EDA LN.	TAOS	NM	87571
TAKA	YOSHI	12 TAN ST.	YUMA	AZ	85364

Application

Write a form letter to encourage people to enter a contest. Then, make a list of five friends or family members who could receive your letter. Create a form file for your letter, and create a data file for your addresses. Finally, do your mail merge.

REVIEW

Chapter Summary

Business letters are an important way to communicate with your customers and clients. Business letters are written to inform, to request, and to persuade. The purpose and audience for your business letter will help you decide what information to include. Style and appearance are also important for business letters, and you should carefully revise and proofread every letter you write. Being able to write effective business letters can greatly increase your company's chances of success. These letters show that the writer and the company care about their customers or clients.

Key Words

marketing	modified-block-style letter
marketing plan	indented-style letter
claim letter	salutation
adjustment letter	return address
block-style letter	empathy

On a separate sheet of paper, use a word from the list above to complete each sentence.

1. The receptionist wrote her company's ___ in the upper-left corner of the envelope.

2. In a(n) ___, each paragraph is indented and there is no extra space between paragraphs.

3. The letter is written in the ___ because the date, subject line, and closing begin on the right side of the paper.

4. The sales representative sent a letter that opened with the ___, "Dear Sir or Madam:"

5. A ___ is a strategy to attract new customers or clients.

6. Our company received a ___ that complained about our new dishwasher.

7. When you feel ___ for customers, you better understand what their problems are.

8. In a(n) ___, the margins align on the left side, and the paragraphs are not indented.

9. The ___ department has done a good job finding new customers.

10. A(n) ___ is a letter that tries to settle a claim.

Application: Reading and Analyzing a Business Letter

Read the body of the business letter below. Then, on a separate sheet of paper, answer the following questions:

Imagine yourself on a safari to film elephants in Africa. Then, see yourself relaxing in a garden in Santa Barbara. You can do all this without leaving your home.

Public TV lets you experience these incredible events: theater, travel, gardening, and children's programming. Look at our program guide to see what we have planned this month.

To offer such great programs, we need your support. Please become a member by sending $45 today to the address at the bottom of this letter.

1. What kind of business letter is this?

2. Which business-letter style does the writer use?

3. What is the letter's purpose?

4. What is the letter's audience?

5. What response does the writer hope to get from the reader?

Application: Revising Business letters

Carla just started a job in the credit department for The Mail Order Catalog. Her boss asked her to write three letters. Read Carla's letters, which are shown below. On a separate sheet of paper, revise each letter. Use clear language and an appropriate tone for each one.

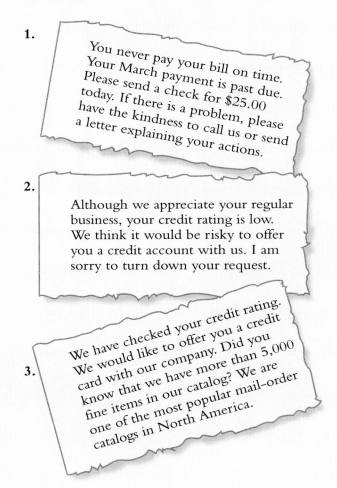

1.
You never pay your bill on time. Your March payment is past due. Please send a check for $25.00 today. If there is a problem, please have the kindness to call us or send a letter explaining your actions.

2.
Although we appreciate your regular business, your credit rating is low. We think it would be risky to offer you a credit account with us. I am sorry to turn down your request.

3.
We have checked your credit rating. We would like to offer you a credit card with our company. Did you know that we have more than 5,000 fine items in our catalog? We are one of the most popular mail-order catalogs in North America.

Grammar Workshop Practice

On a separate sheet of paper, rewrite the sentences, correcting the errors.

Part I. Provide the correct form of each irregular verb.

1. The supervisor finded out that Dave lied on his application.

2. Ahmad catched the late train to Hartford.

3. Wanda done the right thing by keeping track of all her expenses.

4. The report was throwed out with the trash.

5. I seen him painting the Fourth Street Bridge.

Part II. Choose the correct word in parentheses.

6. The (principal, principle) led the Pledge of Allegiance during the assembly.

7. Please ask the (personal, personnel) office for vacation forms.

8. The company (stationary, stationery) shows our new logo.

9. The community (counsel, council) recommended creating a senior center.

10. The (principal, principle) reason for time clocks is to keep track of the hours worked by employees.

Portfolio Project Writing a Business Letter

Think of a product you enjoy using. Suppose you work for a company that manufactures that product. Then, write a business letter.

- Write a business letter that informs customers about a new product.

- Make sure your letter has all of the information your customers need, as well as an appropriate tone.

- Revise your work for content and organization so that your customer will clearly understand your message.

When you have finished your business letter, add it to your portfolio.

Writing a Proposal to Solve Problems

John works in the mailroom of an insurance company. He has noticed that the process of sorting and delivering mail is not very efficient. Much time is lost sorting piles of envelopes. John has an idea about how to make the mailroom more efficient. His idea could also save the company time and money. However, he does not know how to write a proposal that will convince his manager to let him make the changes.

Key Words

proposal

quote

RFP (request for proposal)

appendix

strategy statement

documentation

focus group

vendors

clip-art

Goals for Success

In this chapter, you will learn these skills:

Reading a proposal

SCANS READING

Analyzing a work-related problem

SCANS HUMAN RESOURCES

Developing a strategy to solve a problem

SCANS PROBLEM SOLVING

Collecting supporting information to write a proposal

SCANS ACQUIRES AND EVALUATES INFORMATION

Using charts and tables in a proposal

SCANS APPLIES TECHNOLOGY TO TASKS

PORTFOLIO
PROJECT

WRITTEN PROPOSAL

By the time you finish this chapter, you will understand John's task. You will know what he has to do to write a proposal to solve the problems in his company's mailroom. You also will be able to create a proposal to solve a problem to add to your own portfolio.

Reading Proposals

A tool company has adopted new safety procedures. A bike shop is offering its employees a new health plan. A greeting card company has new rules about overtime. How did these changes happen? Workers in each company suggested them. Then, others in the company recognized that these were good ideas. Many changes in companies happen because workers make proposals for change.

HELPING YOUR COMPANY SUCCEED

Being an employee means more than simply doing a job. As an employee, you may have the opportunity to solve work-related problems. The solutions you create can improve business and working conditions for yourself and for your co-workers. Problem-solving is a valued skill on the job.

Many companies have suggestion boxes. Usually, employees suggest ideas for change on a small scale, such as changes to the dress code. When you have an idea that you feel is more far-reaching, you can write a **proposal**. A proposal is a formal, written plan for an action to improve a situation or to solve a problem. Its purpose is to persuade someone to try something—whether it is a product, a service, or an idea.

Most proposals do not arrive unexpectedly on a manager's desk. They often are the result of many discussions. They are part of a formal decision-making process.

Proposals also can come from outside a company. For example, Sparkle Cleaning Services wants to do business with Bob's Bikes, so Sparkle submits a proposal. The proposal tells about Sparkle's services and explains how an agreement can benefit both companies. It includes all the information Bob's Bikes needs to make a decision.

KINDS OF PROPOSALS

Proposals do not have to be lengthy. Sometimes a short proposal meets a company's needs. The length of the proposal often depends on the difficulty of the problem. It can also depend on the amount of background or supporting information you need to provide.

Quotes

Instead of providing an in-depth proposal, sometimes a company will simply provide a **quote**. A quote is a type of proposal that is evaluated only on price. Quotes do not provide details about the problem and the solution—only the cost of the job or product.

RFPs

Occasionally, you might read an **RFP**, or a **request for proposal**. In an RFP, an organization asks people to submit proposals to solve a problem or to meet a need. For example, a local insurance company might want someone to print its business cards. That company might send all of the local copy centers an RFP.

On the other hand, local and state governments, and even the federal government, publish RFPs for many different services. A way to build your business is to answer an RFP for a specific product or service that you can offer.

When you read an RFP, read the directions carefully. RFPs give instructions about what kinds of information the organization needs, the order in which the information must be presented, the format required, and the deadline for submitting the proposal.

THE PARTS OF A PROPOSAL

Here are the parts of a proposal:

- A cover letter and an executive summary that clearly state the problem that needs to be solved

- A current-situation section that explains the problem in detail

- A recommended solution to the problem

- Details about cost and a timetable for putting the proposal into effect

- An appendix that provides additional information needed to make the proposal clear.

Cover Letter, Title Page, and Table of Contents

Most formal proposals include a cover letter. The cover letter is addressed to the people who make the decisions. It states the problem and briefly tells what the writer proposes to do about it.

Longer proposals begin with a title page. They also have a table of contents that outlines all of the sections of the proposal. Tables of contents help readers find information quickly.

Executive Summary

The executive summary is the first section of a proposal. It gives a one- to two-page summary of the entire proposal. This summary has information about the needs of the organization, the solution to the problem, and the benefits to the organization if the proposal is accepted. Its purpose is to provide busy company executives with a quick overview of the proposal.

Current Situation

The current-situation section explains how the writer sees the organization's current need or problem. In this section, you might find background information about the company and facts about the problem.

Recommended Solution

This section of the proposal suggests a solution to the problem that was explained in the current-situation section.

Cost and Timetable

This section states what the proposed solution will cost. It also contains an estimate of the time it will take to solve the problem.

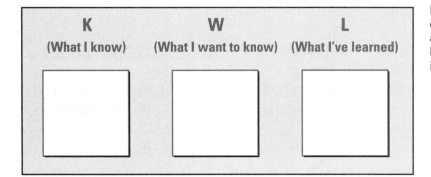

K	W	L
(What I know)	(What I want to know)	(What I've learned)

FIGURE 11-1 shows a KWL chart. **How could thinking about what you already know help you learn new information?**

Appendix

Some proposals have an **appendix**. The appendix appears at the end of the proposal and provides information that supports it. The information might include graphs, charts, brochures, employee résumés, work samples, or a client list.

A STRATEGY FOR READING PROPOSALS

When you read a proposal, you probably are examining it to see if you agree with the suggested solution. To help make this decision, follow these steps as you read:

Step 1. Write what you already know about the problem.
Before you read, write down everything you already know about the problem. This will help you understand if the proposed solution might be effective.

Step 2. Write what you want to know.
Write questions that ask *what, why,* and *how.* They will help you look for the important points of the proposal.

Then, preview the entire proposal. Use the information you find to write more questions about the problem and the proposal. Now, read the proposal again, slowly and carefully.

Step 3. Write what you learned.
See if you can answer the questions you wrote. Note any information that you did not expect to learn.

Step 4. Summarize what you learned.
Writing a summary has two purposes. It will help you remember what you have learned. It also will help you evaluate the proposal and decide whether it is one that your company should pursue.

You might use a KWL chart like the one shown in **FIGURE 11-1** to help you note your ideas as you use this strategy.

Lesson Review

CHECK YOUR UNDERSTANDING

1. IDENTIFYING What is the purpose of a proposal?

2. SUMMARIZING What is an RFP?

APPLY WHAT YOU LEARN

With two or three classmates, discuss a problem that exists in your school or in your community. List some people, products, or services that might help to solve the problem.

Analyzing the Problem

Businesses do not always run smoothly. A key employee gets sick. A new product is so successful that the company cannot make enough to satisfy demand. Suppliers cannot deliver the materials used to make the product. Employees can help solve these problems. To begin creating a solution, you need to identify and understand the problem. Then, a good plan can help you find a solution.

What Do You Already Know?

Think about a problem that you solved at home, at school, or at work. What steps did you take to find a solution to the problem?

Think About It What do you think a business would do to analyze a problem?

DOES THE PROBLEM NEED TO BE SOLVED?

The first step in writing a proposal is to recognize that there is a problem that must be solved. Some problems at work will affect only you, while others will affect the entire company. A valuable employee is one who can recognize which problems must be solved. When you see a problem, you should begin by analyzing it.

If the problem affects many people in the company, costs the company money, and keeps employees from doing their jobs well, then it needs to be solved.

For example, suppose you are a customer-service representative at Roseland Bank. You notice that during slow times—between 8 A.M. and 10 A.M.—there are four customer-service representatives working. At busy times—between 4 P.M. and 6 P.M.—there is only one customer-service representative working. The employees in the morning are bored. The employee in the evening feels overworked, and the bank's customers are unhappy about the long wait for service. After analyzing the problem, you realize that it is serious and that it must be solved.

MAKE A PLAN TO SOLVE THE PROBLEM

Every problem has its own solution. Be realistic when you think about a solution, but also think creatively. In the case of Roseland Bank, the solution is simple and will not cost the bank any money. Simply changing the schedule so that more employees are working during peak hours will solve the problem. Sometimes a solution will be more complicated or costly than this one.

Now, suppose you are an assistant manager at the Bayview Landscaping Company. You receive a request for proposal (RFP) from a large software company. The company asks you to submit a bid to landscape the area surrounding its new office building.

Know Your Customer's Expectations

When you study an RFP or talk with a customer who has a problem, listen carefully to the customer's expectations. For example, a company president wants a certain kind of landscaping for a corporate office. A builder of inexpensive homes wants something else. You need to listen to each person to design your proposals accordingly.

Brainstorm Possible Solutions

After you decide what the problem is, think about what is needed to solve it. One way to do this is to brainstorm a list of possible solutions. For example, to solve the staff scheduling problems at Roseland Bank, you might think of the following ideas:

- Hire additional employees.

- Give a raise to employees who are willing to work at the busier time.

- Provide additional telephone lines for customers.

- Provide a computer service that customers can call.

- Rearrange the work schedule.

For the RFP from the software company, you could brainstorm the information, the materials, or the services you may need. You might think of the following ideas:

- Submit a list of customers who have been satisfied with your services.

- Suggest only the most expensive and the most unusual plants.

- Offer drawings of two possible landscape designs.

- Hire a group of temporary employees to do the job.

Although you may not use every idea that you brainstorm, your list will help you think the problem through and determine the cost of doing the job.

Lesson Review

CHECK YOUR UNDERSTANDING

1. EVALUATING When you are evaluating an RFP, why is it important to understand the customer's expectations?

2. IDENTIFYING Why should you brainstorm a list of possible solutions to a problem?

APPLY WHAT YOU LEARN

Think about a problem you have noticed either in school, at work, or in your community. With a small group, brainstorm a list of possible solutions to solve the problem. After brainstorming, analyze your list and check the items you think will best solve the problem.

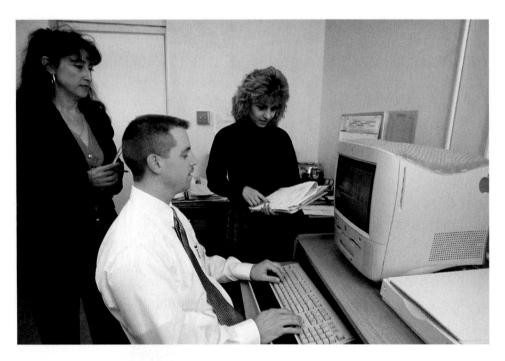

These workers are brainstorming a solution to a problem on the job. **Why is it important to consider all of the ideas listed during a brainstorming session?**

Grammar Workshop

Using Quotation Marks Correctly

You will often use quotations when you write reports, proposals, and business letters. When you use a quotation, name the speaker or writer and enclose the exact words in quotation marks. Make sure you use opening and closing marks so the reader knows where the quotation begins and ends.

- Use quotation marks to set off direct speech—the exact words of the speaker. Note that periods and commas always go inside quotation marks.

   Example   "I wish you all a successful year under your new president," said Mrs. Dorsey.

- When you use quoted words within a quotation, the outside quotation marks are double. The inside quotation marks are single.

   Example   "I told Tom, 'Please make copies of the memo,' and he did it right away," Mr. Valente said.

- Use quotation marks to highlight a slang term or a word that is being used in an unusual way.

   Example   The sales representative insisted that the jacket was "cool."

- Use quotation marks to set off the titles of songs, poems, short stories, lectures, episodes of radio and television programs, chapters of books, magazine and newspaper articles, slogans, and encyclopedia entries.

   Examples   "Business as Usual," a magazine
   "Invest in Your Future," a television episode

Application

Rewrite the following sentences on a separate sheet of paper. Use quotation marks where they are needed.

1. I expect you to put in a full eight hours of work, said Mrs. Gross.
2. My supervisor said, Read this article, called How to Get Ahead.
3. It was hard enough to learn to teach, and even harder to do the daily work, said Ms. Johnson.
4. The slogan for our coffee beans is, Sark's Wakes You Up With a Smile.
5. Tonight's special is pasta with clam sauce, explained the chef.
6. Prices for Tomorrow is the title of our new marketing brochure.
7. Safety First is Parker and Company's slogan.
8. I must agree, said Dr. Standard. The patient is too weak to be moved.
9. The sign read, Beware of Guard Dogs, but there were only three Chihuahuas in the yard.
10. We use this spreadsheet program for accounting, said Chung.

For more information, **SEE PAGE 360.**

Developing a Strategy

When a sports team wins a game, it is likely that the coach had a strategy—a strategy that worked. A strategy is a plan of action to achieve a goal. When you write a proposal in business, your goal is to convince people to accept your ideas. This solution can help you win a contract, solve a problem, or succeed in some other way.

WHAT A STRATEGY DOES

Strategies are used in business to solve problems just as they are in sports. After the proposal writer has identified the need or problem and brainstormed a list of possible ideas, the next step is to develop a strategy. The strategy will focus on how to best solve the problem or meet the need.

Identifying What Needs to Be Done

If your company has a problem to be solved, think about how that problem is making it difficult for your company to reach its goals. This analysis will help you see how a solution will affect your company and its employees. Before you make a definite plan, though, remember that every company has its own goals and needs its own solutions.

For example, suppose that you work in the customer-service department of Notions, a small hobby and crafts company located in Virginia. The company has just started advertising its products nationwide and takes telephone orders during business hours only—from 9 A.M. to 5 P.M. Eastern Standard time.

The problem is that in California, regular business hours end three hours later than they do in Virginia. You risk losing your customers' business if no one is available to answer the telephones during California's business hours.

An overview of the problem shows you that your company is losing important business. It has received 25 calls after 5 P.M. every day this week. This is a serious problem. You may be losing 25 customers every day. You realize that a strategy to solve the problem is needed. You propose adjusting the work schedule to cover the extra hours. Your **strategy statement**, or statement of a proposed solution, would be

> We are losing business, because we are not available to our customers at an important time in their working day. We can solve this problem by adjusting the customer-service representatives' work schedules. We need a shift working from 9 A.M. to 5 P.M. and another shift working from 12 noon to 8 P.M.

Exploring Your Ideas

Now you want to write a proposal that describes your strategy. Use the following checklist to develop your strategy:

✔ What is the problem?

✔ What are my company's goals or the customer's expectations?

✔ What are some possible solutions to the problem?

✔ Which solution will work best? Why?

- ✔ What are the strengths and weaknesses of that solution?

- ✔ Is the company or the customer likely to accept the proposed solution? Why or why not?

- ✔ How will my ideas be implemented, or put into action?

- ✔ What other solutions might others propose?

- ✔ Why will my solution be more effective?

After answering these questions, you can begin to plan your proposal.

Thinking Through Your Strategy

Next, you will gather your thoughts and write out your responses to each of the questions on the checklist.

FIGURE 11-2 shows how the manager at Notions explored the new customer-service strategy for handling telephone calls after regular business hours.

What is the best solution for the problem?	The best solution is to adjust the work schedule so that some representatives are working after east coast business hours. We can afford to have less coverage in the morning in exchange for coverage after 5 P.M.
What are the strengths and weaknesses of the solution you propose?	*Strengths*: 1. We will provide the level of service we want to provide. 2. We will have someone to answer calls that come in after our regular business hours. 3. We will not have to add additional telephone operators.

Weaknesses: 1. None of our regular operators may be able to switch to a noon to 8 P.M. shift. 2. No one from management will be in the building to answer questions. 3. The company will have to pay for heat, air conditioning, and electricity for three more hours each day. |
| **Do you think your solution is something to which your company or the client will agree?** | Yes. Management does not want to lose sales from callers whose regular business hours end after ours just because no one is there to answer phones. The company prides itself on meeting its customers' needs. |
| **How will the proposal be implemented, or put into action?** | I will discuss the needed change with the customer-service repesentatives. I will determine which schedule each representative prefers. Then, I will work with the customer-service manager to create a new schedule. |
| **What other solutions might others propose, and why will my solution work better?** | Others might propose to hire new operators just for a special 5 P.M. to 8 P.M. shift. I do not recommend this solution because the new hires will not know much about the company or the products we carry.

We also could handle after-hours sales through a Web site. However, we need an immediate solution. A Web site would take us months to set up. |

FIGURE 11-2 The proposal writer has explored the strategy by answering these questions. **Do you agree with all of these answers? Why or why not?**

WRITING IN THE REAL WORLD: STRATEGY STATEMENTS

Lazy River Estates Remodeling Project

Strategy 1
Housefitters, Inc., should use its own managers as project supervisors. However, it must add additional skilled and unskilled workers so that it can complete the project on time and within budget.

We propose hiring workers as independent contractors. The company will be able to hire the best people available. However, we will not have to add them to the company's permanent payroll.

Housefitters' regular employees can train the new workers to meet our company's high standards of workmanship and service. At the same time, we will not hurt our regular business, and we will have workers available for other tasks.

Reaction of Housefitters' Owner
This strategy considers both the client's needs and Housefitters' goals. However, I am not sure whether we will be able to find enough skilled workers to join us. We may be overworking our managers by having them work on the Lazy River Estates project and other tasks, too.

> The strategy statement opens by stating the proposed solution simply and clearly.

> The writer gives details about how to implement the solution.

> The writer offers arguments to counter possible negative effects others may see in this solution.

> The writer assesses the strategy.

> The writer opens with a strong, persuasive statement to reinforce the strategy statement.

Lazy River Estates Remodeling Project

Strategy 2
Housefitters, Inc., should put all of its best people on the Lazy River Estates project; it must postpone every other project and work on this one.

To renovate the fifty apartments, the company must require all its employees to work at least 20 hours of overtime each week for the next six months. Working overtime would give employees more pay, and we would have our best people on the job. If we renovate eight apartments a month, we will have just two left to do after the six-month deadline.

To help our workers do their best work, the company should provide food so that people do not have to leave work to eat. The job is a challenge, but we can do it.

Reaction of Housefitters' Owner
This strategy does not fit the company's or the client's needs. The job will not be done on time, and the company will lose income from other projects. This strategy builds in failure.

> The writer gives statistics on what needs to be done.

> The writer tells what the company needs to do in order to make the strategy work.

> The writer assesses the strategy and finds that it will not work for the company.

FIGURE 11-3 These two strategy statements offer different solutions to a problem. **Which strategy do you think will provide the best solution? Why?**

Construction workers must often develop a strategy to solve a problem on the job. **Why might it be important to work with a group to develop a strategy to solve a problem?**

COMPARING TWO STRATEGIES

One way to decide if a strategy will work is to compare it to another strategy that has been proposed to solve the same problem.

The Problem

Imagine that you are the assistant manager of Housefitters, Inc. Housefitters is a small construction company. Its main business is remodeling homes. The company wants to expand the business to include larger projects—and more profitable contracts.

One day, the owner of the company meets with the project managers. The owner announces that Housefitters has received an RFP. It has come from the manager of Lazy River Estates, an older, middle-income apartment complex in town. Lazy River's manager needs to fully remodel 50 apartments.

For Housefitters, the job represents a good opportunity and a good learning experience. The owner invites two project managers to develop strategies to meet Lazy River's needs in a way that best uses Housefitters's resources.

FIGURE 11-3 on page 238 shows the two strategies that were suggested.

Why Is a Good Strategy Important?

A proposal is another form of persuasive writing. You are trying to persuade your company or customer to accept your plan. Many proposals combine the best ideas from different sources. A company must consider its long-term goals, its short-term goals, its project costs, and many other factors. When it has all of this information, the company can choose a strategy. A well-planned strategy may earn you the business you are seeking.

Lesson Review

CHECK YOUR UNDERSTANDING

1. EXPLAINING Why is it helpful to have a strategy to solve a problem?

2. SYNTHESIZING Why would it be important to consider solutions that other people might propose?

APPLY WHAT YOU LEARN

Reread the two strategy statements in FIGURE 11-3 on page 238. Write a third strategy that you think could be more effective. You may borrow elements from Strategy 1 and Strategy 2 to develop a new one. Then explain why your strategy is the one that Housefitters should adopt.

Collecting Supporting Information

Have you ever tried to convince a friend to see a movie? As you tried to persuade your friend to agree with you, you probably used information and reasons to support your position. Supporting information also will help you when you write a proposal. Facts, figures, and other data show that you have done the necessary research. This information shows people that they should listen to your ideas.

THE IMPORTANCE OF RESEARCH

The purpose of your research is to have enough information both to write the proposal and to make the company feel that you know something about its business. Once you have their confidence, people are more likely to accept your ideas.

Supporting information is the facts you use to back up your proposal. You can find supporting information in a variety of sources. These sources include discussions with the customer, surveys, or formal research using written sources. All this information serves as **documentation**, or factual evidence, to help prove that your proposal is the best solution for the problem.

Research for a proposal can be simple, informative, and even fun. If you propose to sell a product or service to a company, gather as much information as you can about that company. Find out about its needs and its type of business. In short, you need to think about your audience.

Identify Company Needs

If you are responding to an RFP, call the person who sent it, and discuss the company's needs. Pay attention to the reasons for the proposal request, the company's concerns, and how the company expects to benefit. Ask about the company's short-term and long-term goals. For example, you might learn that the company is facing a labor shortage. It wants to raise salaries in the next six months in order to keep its best employees. In that case, your proposal might point out ways the company could cut costs so that salaries could be increased.

Whether you are responding to an RFP or solving a problem at your own company, ask yourself what issues need to be considered. A manager will want to know how your proposal will affect the entire company.

Learn the Company Culture

The company culture is the beliefs and practices that a company brings to its day-to-day dealings with employees. In some companies, all employees discuss major decisions. In other companies, the managers make all the decisions. What you know about a company's culture will guide your suggestions.

The more you know about the company, the more effective your proposal will be. If you do not

SOURCE	HOW IT CAN HELP
The Internet	Find a Web site and look for information about the company's philosophy, management, and history. Also look for competitors' Web sites to find out how the company compares with its competition.
Newspapers and Magazines	Find articles containing data about the company's industry. Relevant data could provide excellent supporting information for your proposal. *Example:* You are submitting a proposal to a company that paints homes, and you find an article saying that new home sales are at an all-time high. This information might be important because the company paints new homes.
Surveys	Conduct a survey to get input from customers about the company's services or products. *Example:* You want to propose that your company will stay open later to provide service to customers. You conduct a survey of customers to find out how many would actually come in during these late hours. If customers' responses show that most would come in, management might accept your proposal.

FIGURE 11-4 This chart lists sources of supporting information for proposals. **What kind of information can each source provide?**

do this research, you might include information in your proposal that does not fit the company's goals, philosophy, or needs. As a result, your proposal may be unsuccessful.

SOURCES OF INFORMATION

When you gather information for a proposal, you need to consider many sources. FIGURE 11-4 above lists three important sources and the types of information they provide.

Focus Group Data

A **focus group** could be a final source of information for you. A focus group is a panel of people selected to discuss their likes and dislikes about a product, a service, or a topic. Major companies conduct focus groups across the country when they are planning a new project or product. Customers' feelings and opinions help them to predict a product's chances of success. To get unbiased data, companies often do not tell focus group members the name of the company that is doing the research.

Many focus groups are held in special rooms with one-way glass windows. Observers can see how focus group members react to products without group members being distracted by company employees.

A SAMPLE CASE

Here is an example of how Julie collects information for a proposal. Julie works for a retail drugstore in a residential neighborhood. The store owner would like some ideas about ways to increase the store's business. He asks Julie for a proposal. She believes that the store needs to offer a greater variety of food items. She decides to conduct some research to support her idea.

First, she surveys 100 of the store's customers. She asks what types of items they would like to see in the store. She learns that 45 would like to buy milk at the store, 25 would like to buy bread, and 30 would like to buy soft drinks.

Next, she decides to find out what the competition is selling. She visits several other drugstores and finds that they all sell food items similar to those her customers would like to buy. She also reads *Drugstore Monthly* to find out which food items drugstores like hers are selling across the country.

She then notices an article in the newspaper that discusses how busy the average family is and how little time there is for running errands. Julie thinks that most people in the neighborhood would rather spend time with their family than have to shop at several different stores.

Finally, Julie checks the store's sales records to see which food items customers have been buying.

Julie now has enough supporting information to convince the store owner that selling more food items will increase the store's business. She has considered her audience (her manager) and has gathered information to solve her manager's problem.

Lesson Review

CHECK YOUR UNDERSTANDING

1. ANALYZING Why is it important to add supporting information to a proposal?

2. IDENTIFYING Where could you find supporting information about which colors of paint people prefer?

APPLY WHAT YOU LEARN

Suppose you are doing research for a proposal. You want to expand your craft store's business by offering craft lessons. What types of information would you look for to support your proposal?

Grammar Workshop

Using Appropriate Language

Most people speak in several different "languages." They speak informally with their friends. They speak more formally with older family members and new acquaintances. They speak even more formally with teachers, principals, and people whom they meet in business. Formal language is appropriate in the classroom, in an interview, and on the job. Successful businesspeople adjust the way they speak and write to be sure their message is heard clearly by their audience.

- Here are some examples of informal speech. Compare them with the formal sentences below.

  Examples   You'd better **watch out** when you use the new machine.
  How am I supposed to finish this work by tomorrow?
  The building **super fixed** the stairs.
  I'm going to **hang out down the corner.**
  My dad's **on his way.**

- Here are some examples of formal speech:

  Examples   **Be careful** when you use the new machine.
  I don't think I will be able to finish this work by tomorrow.
  The building **superintendent repaired** the stairs.
  I'm going to **meet my friends on Broad Street.**
  My father is **coming home.**

Application

Rewrite these sentences on a separate sheet of paper. Use formal language.

1. Are you done with that?
2. "Can I leave early?" Marisa asked her manager.
3. That suit is so cool.
4. My mom said I have to go home now.
5. I'm going to take a break now, okay?
6. Let me come over now.
7. I don't get what you're saying.
8. Do I have to finish this project by Friday?
9. When do you need this?
10. We are headed out to our meeting.

For more Information, **SEE PAGE 342.**

Writing the Proposal

In order for your proposal to be successful, you need to combine your ideas and research into an effective document. The writing process can help you do this by guiding you as you organize and revise your work. Your proposal will then present a strong case for your idea.

This organization is great!

What Do You Already Know?

What persuasive writing have you done? How was it different from other kinds of writing?

Think About It How might using the writing process help you make sure your proposal is successful?

BEFORE YOU BEGIN WRITING

The prewriting stage of the writing process can help you craft a winning proposal. Remember that during prewriting you determine your purpose and your audience. Then you organize your data so that you can present a strong case.

Determine Your Purpose

Before you write a proposal, you must determine your purpose. Obviously, your purpose is to persuade your reader to accept your proposal. But specifically, what ideas do you want to persuade your reader to accept? You need to communicate this purpose clearly and precisely.

Proposals may have many different purposes. For example, you may want to

- provide ideas to your employer about changing a company procedure, hiring additional staff, or buying new equipment.

- recommend a project for your team or a committee.

- attract money from investors for a new project.

- ask for a contract from a possible customer or client.

Know Your Audience

Who is going to read your proposal? Are you sending it to the company's president or to someone at a lower level? Is the company large or small? Does the company deal frequently with outside sellers, called **vendors**, or does it rarely use outside workers? The answers to these questions will help you define your audience.

Knowing your audience helps you decide what information to include and what kind of language to use. Suppose, for example, your audience is the owner of a clothing store for teens. You might want to use a kind of language that is less formal than you would use for a committee of buyers for a traditional department store. However, never try to be too informal. Too much informality may sound as if you are not taking your audience, or your proposal, seriously.

MAKING A PLAN FOR WRITING

The information you include and the format you choose for your proposal will vary with your purpose and audience. After you have analyzed the problem, determined your purpose, considered your audience, and gathered your information, you will need to plan your proposal.

For example, Marta is the assistant manager of Rancho Rio, a small restaurant. The business has been successful for ten years, and now the owner wants to expand it. Marta thinks that if the restaurant offered take-out service, it could increase its business. Marta decides to write a proposal showing her employer that take-out service could be successful.

Marta began by considering the information she would include in her executive summary. FIGURE 11-5 shows a graphic organizer that Marta used to organize her ideas for writing. She then made additional web diagrams to help her organize each part of her proposal.

FIGURE 11-5 This graphic organizer includes needs and benefits as well as a solution to the problem. **How could this organizer help Marta write a proposal?**

To support her proposal, Marta does more research. She collects menus from other restaurants that offer take-out food. She surveys customers to find out what kinds of foods they would buy from a take-out service. She reads back copies of *Take-Out Industry News* to learn what other restaurants have done to become successful.

PREPARING A FIRST DRAFT

When you write your first draft, remember that you are only trying to get your ideas on paper. Do not worry about errors in grammar or spelling at this stage. You will edit and proofread at a later stage.

When you write a proposal, use the following checklist:

- ✔ Explain your idea. State your purpose clearly. If your audience is unfamiliar with the background of your idea, provide additional information to help readers understand your proposal.

- ✔ Persuade your audience. Provide specific reasons for your idea, including how your idea will benefit the audience or company. For example, you might want to provide numbers to show how company profits will increase if your proposal is accepted.

- ✔ Expect objections. Do not expect your idea to be accepted easily. Be prepared to answer any questions you think your audience might ask.

- ✔ Offer a plan. Explain how to carry out your idea, telling your readers what they will need to do. If there is a deadline by which time the proposal must be carried out, give that information.

- ✔ Help your audience read your proposal. Title your proposal and add headings to each section so that your readers understand the organization of your ideas and see how they relate to one another.

EDITING THE DRAFT

After you finish writing a first draft, it is time for the next stage of the writing process: editing. Before you edit, ask yourself the following questions:

- How clear is my message?

- How should I revise the proposal to make my message clearer?

The summary is brief and to the point.

Executive Summary

I propose that Rio Rancho expand its restaurant business by adding a take-out service to its regular restaurant trade. As assistant manager, I would hire and train a small staff of employees to handle this new operation.

The writer details the current situation.

Current Situation

Rio Rancho has done very well over the past ten years. But we have reached a point at which our business is no longer growing. We have our faithful regular customers, but get few new ones. While the cost of operating a restaurant continues to climb, our business stays the same. If something is not done to find new customers and new profits, the next ten years will not be good ones for our restaurant.

To support her proposal, the writer adds research and a survey.

Solution

Of the four restaurants in our neighborhood that offer take-out food, all are doing very good business. Our neighborhood has many families in which both parents work. They have little time to cook dinner. Of 50 customers in our restaurant surveyed, 33 said they ate take-out food twice in the past week. I predict that with a take-out service, our restaurant could increase its business by 35 percent within the first six months of operation.

The writer explains how she will run this new service.

To preserve the taste of the in-house menu, I would rely on the regular cooking staff to prepare any specialty foods. The take-out staff would prepare regular menu items. I myself will oversee the entire operation and I am available at night and on weekends to supervise the staff. I also have a license to drive a commercial van to deliver food.

The writer points out how increased business will offset the costs.

Cost and Timetable

While the initial cost of new staff and a delivery van may be as high as $25,000 per year, the new revenue from our increased business should quickly cover these necessary expenses. There should be few other expenses except for disposable take-out eating utensils, plates, and cups.

If this proposal meets with management's approval, the take-out service can be up and running within two months.

The writer closes by giving her qualifications.

Having worked in a take-out restaurant for a year before I came to Rio Rancho, I feel I am the right person to organize and run this new addition to our restaurant. I predict it will make our next ten years even more successful than our first ten years.

FIGURE 11-6 This proposal makes a strong case for expanding Rio Rancho. **What reasons does Marta use to support her proposal?**

In the editing stage, you check to make sure that you have stated your ideas clearly. You also look for errors in grammar and language use. One strategy you can use to edit your proposal is to read it aloud to yourself. If you read exactly what you wrote, often you will hear when you have made a grammar or language mistake.

PROOFREADING YOUR WORK

Because you want your audience to read your proposal easily, you need to check your spelling, punctuation, and capitalization. Ask a co-worker, a friend, or a family member to proofread your work. Another person can often see errors that you have overlooked.

PUBLISHING YOUR WORK

You will want your proposal to look as professional as possible. This may mean photocopying or printing the final copy on high-quality paper. You also might consider binding your proposal and adding a protective cover.

FIGURE 11-6 on page 246 shows Marta's published proposal for her restaurant, Rancho Rio. Look for the parts of the proposal—the executive summary, current situation, her approach, the cost, a timetable, and her conclusions.

Lesson Review

CHECK YOUR UNDERSTANDING

1. MAKING CONNECTIONS How can the writing process help you when you write a proposal?

2. EVALUATING Look again at FIGURE 11-6 on page 246. If you were the manager of Rio Rancho, would you accept Marta's proposal? Why or why not?

APPLY WHAT YOU LEARN

Suppose you are writing a proposal to obtain more computers or sports equipment for your school. What would you say in the executive summary to convince a company to donate money for that purpose? List your three best reasons.

Grammar Workshop

Using Numbers in Context

As you revise your proposal, check to see that you have written numbers correctly. In workplace writing, you often use numbers to discuss people, profits, production, and dates.

Here are some general rules about using numbers in your writing.

- Numbers one through ten are usually written as words. Numbers eleven and up are written as numerals.

    Examples   We saw **three** staff members at the conference. However, we expected **11** to attend.

- Use numerals in addresses, money, percentages, phone numbers, times, dates, and ZIP Codes.

    Examples   The check came to **$500.67**. On June **15, 2002**, our president will resign.

- Use numerals when numbers are used with abbreviations.

    Example   The concrete block weighed **5 lbs.**

- Write numbers in word form when they begin a sentence.

    Example   **Thirty-six** people showed up to interview for the job.

- Combine numbers and words when the numbers are very large.

    Example   The new project will cost **$6 million**.

Application

On a separate sheet of paper, rewrite the sentences below. Be sure to write the numbers correctly.

1. Call Mr. Collier at five five five six one zero one.
2. Alex works with 6 people in the production department.
3. Steve Jobs started to build a computer in nineteen seventy-six.
4. SoftX showed a profit of $1,000,000,000 last year.
5. I'll meet you after work at five fifteen.
6. Craig's paycheck was for three hundred ten dollars.
7. More than twenty-two percent of our employees use a payroll savings plan.
8. 7 workers will move to the Mapleville office on April seven, 2001.
9. The company is located at three Beekman Drive, Oakdale, S.C. two nine six one six.
10. Make the first appointment for eight thirty.

For more information, **SEE PAGE 365.**

Using Visuals in a Proposal

Using visuals in your proposal can help your reader understand, and see, your information. Visuals can show how your company can be more productive. They also can persuade your manager that one machine will cost less than another. Visuals can make both points. They can help you present information in clear and interesting ways.

What Do You Already Know?

Think about charts, graphs, or diagrams that you have seen. How did they help you understand new information?

Think About It What kinds of information could graphics add to a proposal?

WHY USE VISUALS?

Visual elements, or graphics, can present information more dramatically than text alone. Graphs and charts can clarify or emphasize important information. You can make your writing visually interesting by highlighting information with different fonts, type sizes, or colors.

Each proposal requires its own types of visuals. Before you plan your design, ask yourself a few questions.

- What is the purpose of my proposal: to sell a product, a service, or an idea?

- What are the most important points I am trying to make?

- If I am selling a product or service, what are its most important features?

- What kinds of visuals might my audience need to see?

- What do I want my reader to remember most about my proposal?

Once you have answered these questions, you probably will have an idea of what kinds of visuals you will need. That knowledge will help you design your proposal.

DESIGNING YOUR PROPOSAL

After you have written the text, reread it. Ask yourself: Is there any information that I could present in a chart, graph, or table? For example, you might use a graph to show how the costs in your solution compare to current costs.

Using Type, Color, and Illustrations

You might want to use graphic features just to enhance the look of your proposal. Think about using different sizes and colors of type, different fonts, and perhaps a few pictures or a company logo. Use this checklist to help you:

✔ Limit yourself to two or three different fonts, and decide how you will use them.

✔ Choose a type size that is easy to read but that does not overpower your reader.

✔ Use bullets and numbers to present your information clearly and effectively.

✔ If you are using color, be sure that the type is easy to read. For example, yellow type can be difficult to read.

✔ Make sure you use high-quality paper and a good printer or copier to create your final document.

Creating Graphs, Tables, and Charts

Software packages can help you create the visuals you need. However, first you need to consider what kind of information you have and how to present it most effectively.

For example, Clean Sweep, Inc., provides office-cleaning services to many companies located in two office buildings downtown. A new tenant asks Clean Sweep's manager, Grace, for a price quote.

TYPE OF SERVICE	SMALL OFFICE	MEDIUM OFFICE	LARGE OFFICE
Basic Service	$125.00/ day	$150.00/ day	$175.00/ day
Superior Service	$175.00/ day	$200.00/ day	$225.00/ day
Deluxe Service	$200.00/ day	$225.00/ day	$250.00/ day

FIGURE 11-7 This table presents the costs of different cleaning services provided by one company. **Which service is the most expensive? Which is the least expensive?**

The service offers a basic cleaning service, a superior service, and a deluxe cleaning service. Grace decides to present this information in a table. FIGURE 11-7 shows Grace's completed table.

Placing Your Visuals

Where you place your visuals is important. Some visuals will fit into the text of a proposal. The chart on this page probably would go with the text of Grace's proposal, but other visuals might not work as well. If a visual does not easily fit into your proposal, consider placing it in an appendix. It can be referred to when needed.

Consulting an Expert

Sometimes, you might not able to create all of your visuals yourself. If that is the case, ask a teacher or co-worker for assistance. At other times, you might want to consult an expert, someone who specializes in designing materials for businesses. If you do decide to hire an outside expert, work with the person until you are sure he or she has all the information needed. Then, work with that person on any revisions that are necessary.

Lesson Review

CHECK YOUR UNDERSTANDING

1. IDENTIFYING Name three different ways you could make a proposal visually interesting.

2. EVALUATING How can visuals help you make your points in a proposal?

APPLY WHAT YOU LEARN

With a partner, analyze the proposal in FIGURE 11-6 on page 246. List several ways you could improve the proposal's visual effectiveness. Consider type sizes and fonts, spacing, and the organization of material. Are there any visuals you would add? Share your ideas with the class.

Many computer programs can help you create a proposal that is visually interesting. These programs range from highly technical presentation software to simple clip-art and word-processing programs.

Clip-art is a form of electronic visual that your computer can place into a document. Clip-art can be as simple as a line drawing or as complex as a photograph. You can use the clip-art that comes with your word-processing software, or you can buy separate software packages that include hundreds of clip-art pieces. Clip-art allows you to add visual interest at little or no cost. Below are some examples of clip art.

Many word-processing programs let you create headlines and titles in large type. The program might also give you a choice of colors, which you can print on a color printer. To view different styles and sizes of letters, go to the Font heading on your word-processing program. The following are different styles of fonts:

You could create a headline with this font, called Times Roman.

A simple font that also could be used for a title is Helvetica.

Here are some tips to follow when using graphics software:

• Design your document first. Know how you want the document to look before you begin using the software. Make a sketch of each page.

• Learn how to use different software programs. Knowing the basics will help you avoid frustration.

• Be sure your printer is capable of printing the graphics and colors.

• Find help when you need it. Ask a co-worker, teacher, or supervisor for assistance.

Application

Design and create a brochure you can use to improve sales at a retail store. Include different colors and graphics, as well as text.

CHAPTER 11

REVIEW

Chapter Summary

A proposal is a written plan to solve a problem in the workplace. The ability to write strong proposals can help an employee achieve success. Writing proposals involves analyzing a problem and creating a strategy to solve it. To write a good proposal, you must know how to collect information and then organize and refine it. Each part of a proposal is important to its success, from the executive summary to the appendix. Graphics, including graphs and tables, can add interest to a proposal. They often can show important information more effectively than words.

Key Words

proposal	strategy statement
quote	documentation
RFP (request for proposal)	focus group
	vendors
appendix	clip-art

Read the list of words above. Then, on a separate sheet of paper, write the word that best matches each definition below.

_____ 1. A type of proposal that is evaluated only on price

_____ 2. The last section of a proposal that provides additional information about it

_____ 3. People who sell items or supplies

_____ 4. A formal written plan for an action to improve a situation or to solve a problem

_____ 5. A request to solve a problem or meet a need

_____ 6. A panel of people who discuss a product or service

_____ 7. A form of electronic visuals

_____ 8. A statement of a proposed solution

_____ 9. Factual evidence that supports a proposal

Application: Reading and Analyzing an RFP

Imagine you work for a company that sells cash registers. Read the RFP below. Then, on a separate sheet of paper, answer the questions that follow.

ABC Food Stores
123 Main Avenue
Centerville, NY 12345

January 5, 2001

ABC Food Stores will be accepting proposals for new cash registers for its eight existing stores. ABC Food Stores will purchase 48 cash registers and will pay for installation. The budget for this project is $70,000, and the installation must be completed within three months.

Proposals will be accepted within seven days of the date of this request. In responding to this proposal, include your company's client list, history, and experience with grocery stores. Proposals should be double spaced; and appropriate headings should be used, such as Executive Summary, Current Situation, etc. All visual material must be placed in the appendix. Submit four copies of your proposal to the address above.

1. What does ABC Food Stores want to buy?

2. What are its budget and timetable?

3. What must be in the proposal?

4. By what date must the proposal be submitted?

Application: Analyzing a Problem and Developing a Strategy

You are the assistant manager of a record store. The holidays are approaching, and your manager is worried about keeping the racks stocked with the most popular titles. She has asked you to make a proposal to be sure the racks are filled at all times. Be sure you include a strategy statement and a detailed plan.

Grammar Workshop Practice

On a separate sheet of paper, rewrite the sentences, correcting the errors.

Part I. Insert quotation marks where needed.

1. Never, he said. I'd rather quit.

2. Did you read the article Save Now or Else in today's paper? asked Kwan.

3. Mammoth Marshmallow's slogan reads Soft as an Angel's Wing.

4. You shouted Stop! said the train engineer, so I pulled the brake.

5. You break it, you buy it says the sign at Ultra Antiques.

Part II. Use more formal language.

6. Go ahead. Sam will catch up with you later.

7. The proposal to have music in the cafeteria was so cool.

8. My mom wants me home now.

9. "Sure, I'll take the job."

10. Do you need that now?

Part III. Correct the number usage.

11. 1 day you'll remember the help Mrs. Gibrani gave you.

12. Vanessa doubts that eighty percent of all banking employees have savings accounts.

13. Jamal sold one hundred yds. of carpet.

14. My sales territory covers two hundred square miles.

15. 2000 chairs will be needed for the banquet.

Portfolio Project   Writing a Proposal to Solve a Problem

Think about a problem that you have experienced at work or in school. Think of a solution to the problem, and create a proposal explaining your solution. To do this:

- Analyze the problem.

- Develop a strategy to solve the problem.

- Collect information to support your proposal.

- Add visuals, such as charts and tables, to help convince your readers.

When you are finished, add your proposal to your portfolio.

READING AND WRITING TECHNICAL INFORMATION

David works at a juice-processing company. Last year, he learned to operate a new juicing machine. Recently, David's employer, Mr. Gage, asked for David's help.

"I want you to write a short technical report on how to operate the machine," said Mr. Gage. "Don't copy the instruction manual, but base your writing on your own experience." David tried to imagine what a technical report would look like. Who would read it? What would he say? David was puzzled.

Key Words

technical writing

manual

trade journals

objective

bias

E-commerce

liability

logo

prototype

align

Goals for Success

In this chapter, you will learn these skills:

Reading different types of technical writing

 READING

Using patterns of organization in technical writing

 REASONING

Writing technical articles and reports for different purposes

 WRITING

Improving written presentations with visual aids

 MATERIALS AND FACILITIES

Formatting technical documents

 USING COMPUTERS TO PROCESS INFORMATION

PORTFOLIO PROJECT

TECHNICAL REPORT

By the time you finish this chapter, you will understand David's task. You will know what he has to do to write a technical report. You also will be able to write a technical report to add to your own portfolio.

Reading Technical Writing

What Do You Already Know?

Think about instruction books you have seen that are easy to understand. What makes them clear?

Think About It Why is it a good idea to have written instructions about how a product works?

You are reading about a new sports car in a magazine. The magazine's staff has run a series of tests to study the car's acceleration, stopping distance, and gas mileage. A chart at the end of the article shows the test results. The chart is followed by a summary that explains what the editors like and dislike about the car. This article is an example of technical writing.

WHAT IS TECHNICAL WRITING?

As a student and as a worker, you will use technical writing to help you understand products, ideas, and problems. **Technical writing** explains how a product or a process works. If it is factual, its purpose is to give information. If you have read about products such as computers, cameras, and televisions, you probably have read technical writing.

Technical writing also explains processes, such as how the latest Mars spacecraft will explore the landscape. Regardless of the topic, the purpose of technical writing is to clearly explain complex ideas in words and pictures.

There are two types of technical writing: technical articles and technical reports. Both types are published in the following formats:

- *Scientific and technical magazines and brochures* These publications often feature articles that describe how something works.

- *Sales literature* These publications are written for both consumers and retailers. Consumers need descriptions to help them choose products. Retailers need information to answer customers' questions.

- *Manuals* **Manuals** are user's guides that often come with tools and appliances. They help people use products, and repair problems.

READING TECHNICAL WRITING

Technical articles are different from technical reports in two ways. First, technical articles appeal to a wide range of people, not just to specialists. Technical reports, on the other hand, deal with topics that interest a narrower audience of specialists.

Your Child's Migraine Headache

Your child rubs his face. He complains that his head hurts. He might even see a bright, flashing light out of the corner of his eye. You recognize the symptoms—it's another migraine headache coming on. It means missing school for a day or more, making special child-care arrangements, and most of all, it means watching your child suffer from a mysterious ailment. Why do children get migraines and what can be done to prevent them?

FIGURE 12-1 The introduction to this technical article explains the symptoms of migraine headaches. **What audience does this writer want to reach?**

Technical articles also introduce topics that are fresh and newsworthy. Technical reports often provide information about a topic readers already know well.

FIGURE 12-1 on page 256 shows part of a technical article that might be available in a parenting magazine.

Reading Technical Articles

People read technical articles for many reasons. A restaurant owner, for example, might read a technical article about a new cost-saving oven. An electronics engineer might read a technical article to learn about new developments in engineering.

Technical articles also offer the following information:

- The results of the latest research

- New developments in a field

- Descriptions of new products

- New solutions to problems

The information for technical articles may come from the writer's experiences, from research, from facts found in other articles, or from interviews.

Reading Technical Reports

Sometimes, **trade journals** publish technical reports. Trade journals are magazines that usually are read by people who work in a particular field or trade. Some technical reports are published informally and are read by only a few people.

The lengths of technical reports vary. A technical report can be as short as a one-page memo. It also can be many pages, with a cover, a title page, a table of contents, a report summary, several discussion sections, a conclusion, a recommendation, a bibliography, and several appendices.

TYPES OF TECHNICAL REPORTS

Technical-Background Reports	These technical reports are written for people who need information and want to save time by having the research provided for them by specialists.
Instructions	This is the most common type of technical report. These reports are directions written by someone who knows a job or work process. Manuals of instruction for appliances, tools, or pieces of software are technical reports, too.
Recommendation Reports	These technical reports study a situation and suggest a course of action, such as when a bus company considers making major changes to its schedule of service and wants to know the effect on ridership. First, a feasibility study—an examination of possibilities—might be ordered. Then, based on what the study uncovers, a recommendation report would advise the company about what to do.
Primary-Research Reports	These technical reports come from work done in a laboratory or at research sites through experiments and surveys. You may have written a lab report for a science course. You explained what you did, presented your data, and drew conclusions. Primary-research reports contribute to what is known about a topic through investigations.
Technical Specifications	These technical reports describe a new product in terms of how it is constructed, what it is made from, and how it works.

FIGURE 12-2 This chart describes different types of technical reports. **Which kinds of technical reports do you think you might have to write at school? on the job?**

There are five main types of technical reports. They are described in FIGURE 12-2 on page 257.

A STRATEGY FOR TECHNICAL READING

Technical writing often contains a great deal of information. Using the KWL strategy can help you understand and remember what you have read. Draw a KWL chart like the one shown in FIGURE 11-1 on page 232 to help you organize the information you learn when you read.

Step 1. Write what you already know about the topic in the K box.

Step 2. Write what you want to know about the topic in the W box. For technical reading, you might ask such questions as, How does this product work? What do I do if it breaks down? How can it help me?

Now preview the writing. Focus on the table of contents, the topic sentences, the graphics, and the conclusion. Write a few more questions about what you would like to learn about the topic.

Step 3. Next, read the material. Then, write what you have learned about the topic in the L box. Also, write any information that you did not expect to learn.

Step 4. Use the information in your KWL chart to write a brief summary. Summarizing will help you remember what you have learned.

Lesson Review

CHECK YOUR UNDERSTANDING

1. DEFINING What is technical writing?

2. COMPARING How are technical articles and technical reports different? How are they the same?

APPLY WHAT YOU LEARN

Find an example of technical writing on a topic that interests you. The example can be taken from a magazine, a brochure, a pamphlet, a piece of sales literature, or a manual. Identify the author's purpose and the audience.

Grammar Workshop

Forming Adjectives and Adverbs That Compare

As you write technical information, adjectives and adverbs will help you compare products or ideas. In the examples below, the words in the *Comparative* column compare two things. The words in the *Superlative* column compare more than two things. Here are some rules for forming adjectives and adverbs that compare.

- Most adjectives or adverbs that have one syllable add *-er* and *-est*.

		Comparative	Superlative
Adjectives	near→	nearer→	nearest
Adverbs	soon→	sooner→	soonest

- Most adjectives or adverbs that end in *-y* change the *-y* to *-i* and add *-er* and *-est*.

		Comparative	Superlative
Adjectives	sleepy→	sleepier→	sleepiest
Adverbs	early→	earlier→	earliest

- Some adjectives and adverbs that have two or more syllables add the words *more* and *most*.

		Comparative	Superlative
Adjectives	beautiful→	more beautiful→	most beautiful
Adverbs	technical→	more technical→	most technical

- Like verbs, some adjectives and adverbs have irregular forms. If you are unsure of which form to use, check your dictionary.

		Comparative	Superlative
Adjectives	good→	better→	best
Adverbs	badly→	worse→	worst

Application

Rewrite these sentences on a separate sheet of paper. Use the correct form of the adjective or adverb in parentheses.

1. You need a (strong) lock for the warehouse.
2. Of all the jobs Karen has had, this one is (interesting).
3. Buying a small car is usually (cheap) than buying a large one.
4. Pablo paints (colorful) pictures than Emile.
5. The new printer is the (fast) of the five printers.
6. The night shift works the (hard) of the three shifts.
7. The charts made Cal's report (clear).
8. The manager looked (happy) than his boss.
9. Who has worked (long) at the company, Stefan or Marna?
10. That rotor was (sharp) than the other one.

For more information, SEE PAGES 354–355.

Organizing Technical Writing

Technical writing is often complex. It fully describes a process or explains an idea. To do this, technical writers must organize their work carefully. They must choose a plan for organizing their information so that their writing follows a logical pattern. Being clear and precise makes technical material understandable to readers.

What Do You Already Know?

Recall a time when you taught someone a skill. Perhaps it was how to throw a ball or how to say something in another language. What steps did you follow as you taught the person?

Think About It How might writing a technical document be like teaching someone a skill?

USING THE WRITING PROCESS FOR TECHNICAL WRITING

Technical writers use the same writing process as all other writers. During the prewriting stage, they select a topic and think about their audience and purpose. In the writing stage, they draft their report. In the editing stage, they revise their report to make sure it achieves its purpose. In the proof-reading stage, they check for grammatical, mechanical, and spelling errors. Finally, in the publishing stage, they present their work to their audience.

Writing a technical document is similar to the report writing you have done for such subjects as social studies or science. Both are nonfiction; both explain events, locations, or ideas; and both use facts to support their points.

The Audience for a Technical Document

In the prewriting stage, you choose your topic, your purpose, and your audience. However, you have to ask some different questions about your audience when you are writing a technical document.

Your audience for a technical article will be larger than it will be for a technical report. Therefore, you cannot assume that your readers have a great deal of specialized knowledge about your topic. In a technical article, you will add background information and define difficult words.

On the other hand, your audience for a technical report will probably be people who are specialists in their field. Therefore, you can assume that they know a great deal about your topic. This means that you will add more facts to prove your points. In addition, you may add items that help make your points more precisely instead of having to define technical words.

When you think about the audience for your technical document, use the following checklist. It will help you decide on the amount of information and the type of technical words you should use.

✔ What background information can I expect my audience to have about the topic?

✔ What technical words and ideas can I expect my audience to know?

✔ Why does my audience need information about this topic?

✔ What do I want my audience to learn about my topic?

Once you have answered these questions, you can decide on the types of sources you will need to support your ideas.

FIGURE 12-4 on page 262 shows a technical report on the effect of stretching before running. As you read it, look for clues to the audience the writer wanted to reach.

Sources of Information for a Technical Document

Technical documents rely on facts. Because the writer presents these facts in an **objective**, or fair, way, reliable sources should be used. You might use books, almanacs, technical articles, newspaper articles, encyclopedias, and some Internet sites. However, always check for **bias**, or prejudice, and avoid sources that try to sell a product or that express unsupported opinions.

Readers of technical documents often are looking for new developments in a field. To be sure that you are presenting new information, use sources that are up-to-date. Check the publication date of all of your sources. For example, a technical article that was written in 1990 about developments in treatments for heart disease would not contain the latest research on that topic.

WAYS TO ORGANIZE YOUR INFORMATION

Readers expect technical reports to guide them through information step-by-step. As you read in earlier chapters, you can organize information in several ways. The most common forms of organization used in technical documents are:

Chronological Order

When you use chronological order in a technical document, you show time relationships between events. For example, if you were writing a technical report about a scientific discovery, you would list the experiments that led to it in the order in which they occurred.

Spatial Order

You can use spatial order to show where things are in relation to each other. This helps the reader

visualize the scene. For example, in a technical article about how a paramedic should analyze an accident scene, you could tell the reader to look at the victim. You could ask how the victim looks. Is he bleeding? Is he conscious? Then you could tell the reader to look for clues to the victim's injuries. You might begin by looking to the right of the victim, where you would see a fallen ladder. Next to the fallen ladder would be a paint brush and can. Behind the paint can would be a house that is partly painted. Analyzing the scene in spatial order can give you a clear picture of what injuries the victim might have. FIGURE 12-3 shows how this scene would look.

FIGURE 12-3 shows a scene from a technical manual for paramedics that could be described in spatial order. **How might describing a scene in spatial order help the reader to visualize it?**

Cause-and-Effect Order

Cause-and-effect order shows how one event affects other events. For example, if you wanted to write a technical article about how cleaning up a river helped the fish, you might first describe how reducing the amount of pollution released into the river increased the oxygen in the river. Having more oxygen in the river caused the fish to be healthier. Because they were healthier, the fish reproduced in greater numbers. Thus, cause-and-effect order shows how reducing the pollution

The title describes the topic of the report.

The Effect of Stretching before Running

Introduction

The purpose of this report is to explain the effects of stretching muscles before running, based on my own experience. In this report, I will provide information about why runners stretch and how stretching benefits them. Then I will report on my own experiment of running with and without stretching. My conclusion will discuss the results of my experiment. I will make a recommendation about whether stretching seems to be necessary or not.

The introduction gives the purpose of the document and a brief summary of what will be covered in it.

Background on Stretching

Almost all runners' magazines carry articles about the importance of stretching. In the November issue of *The Pacesetter* magazine, for example, marathoner Manny Najera describes his pre-race routine: "Stretching is as critical to my success as regular workouts. It takes about ten minutes for me to stretch thoroughly, but the results are worth it." On the other hand, we all know that people run fast without stretching, too. For example, baseball players run to base. Stretching is not part of their routine. Is the effect of stretching a myth?

The first body paragraph sets up the two sides on the issue of stretching, using a quote from an expert to support one side.

First Trial: Running Without Stretching

To test the effect of running without stretching, I tried a comparison. I run three miles every day, usually after dinner, six days a week. My times are always about seven minutes a mile. I decided to run Monday through Wednesday without stretching and Thursday through Saturday with stretching. On Monday, Tuesday, and Wednesday, I ran my usual route without stretching. I definitely had a harder time. On all three days, my legs felt heavy. Moreover, I averaged 7:31 minutes a mile—nearly half a minute slower than usual. Also, I was sore the mornings following all three runs.

The second body paragraph sets up the writer's experiment. He describes his first trial in precise, scientific detail. Then he does the same in his second trial, as described in the third body paragraph.

Second Trial: Running With Stretching

On Thursday, Friday, and Saturday, I performed my usual stretches. Starting out Thursday, I still felt sore from Wednesday, but the heaviness went away. By the second mile, I felt up to my usual speed. My time was 7:20 minutes for three miles—a little slower than usual. On the two following days, I felt no soreness at all starting out, and on Saturday I hit 6:53 minutes for three miles—a personal best for the month.

My Recommendation: Stretch!

In his conclusion, the writer gives a summary of the results and reaches his final recommendation.

Although my experiment was not scientific, the physical impact of not stretching was clear in two ways. First, I had more difficulty running when I did not stretch. Second, my times dropped off when I did not stretch. As a result of my experience, stretching will always be a part of my workout routine.

FIGURE 12-4 This writer has carefully organized the information for this report. **Which form of organization is used? What clues told you this?**

in a river caused the number of fish in that river to increase.

Whole-to-Parts Order

When you organize a technical report into whole-to-parts order, you break down an object into its parts. For example, if you were describing how to take apart an engine to fix a problem, you might begin by describing the complete engine. Then, you would describe taking it apart piece by piece to find the source of the problem.

Parts-to-Whole Order

You can use parts-to-whole order when you want to describe how an object is put together from its parts. For example, if you wanted to write a technical article about how to assemble a bicycle, you would first describe each part and how it fits into another part. When you finished assembling all of the parts, you would have a whole bicycle.

FIGURE 12-5 shows a technical article on how to use a CD-ROM drive. Note the way the writer organized the information. Also look for clues about the type of audience for whom the writing is meant.

Lesson Review

CHECK YOUR UNDERSTANDING

1. COMPARING How would you write a technical document differently for a general audience and for an audience of specialists?

2. IDENTIFYING Which type of organization would you choose to write a report on each topic below? Explain your answers.

   • Assembling a bookcase

   • Using a washing machine

   • Striping a football field

   • Teaching a trick to a dog

APPLY WHAT YOU LEARN

With another student, choose a technical report topic that interests both of you. Then, find several sources of information on the topic. Try to use different types of sources, including books, magazines, technical articles, and the Internet. Evaluate the sources you have found for bias and for up-to-date information. Present your findings to the class.

Using Your CD-ROM Drive

Your internal CD-ROM (Compact Disc Read-Only Memory) drive works with CD-ROM discs, standard audio compact discs (CDs), and single-session or multi-session photo CDs. This drive provides access to large amounts of information. A typical disc can hold more than 650 megabytes (MB) of information, which equals 270,000 pages of text.

How to Insert a Disc
1. Turn on your computer.
2. Press the Open/Close button to open the tray of the CD-ROM drive.
3. Lay the CD-ROM disc in the tray with the disk label facing up. Be certain the disc is lying flat in the tray.
4. To close the tray, push the tray in or press the Open/Close button.
You will know if the disc is inserted properly if an icon for the CD-ROM disc appears on your computer screen.

Care and Handling
• Make sure you always close the disc tray. If dust gets on the lens of the CD-ROM drive, the drive may incorrectly read your CD.
• Do not move your computer if it has a disc in the CD-ROM drive.
• Keep your computer and its equipment away from all liquids.

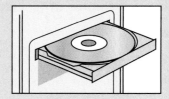

FIGURE 12-5 This technical article shows how to operate a CD-ROM drive on a computer.
What type of organization did the writer use?

Writing Lab Reports

What Do You Already Know?

Have you ever written a lab report? Describe the experiment you conducted and how you prepared your report.

Think About It What makes a lab report easy to understand?

Even if you are not considering a career in the sciences, you should know how to write a lab report. Many other professions also require technical writing. Workers in other fields create lab reports to present facts, to examine new ideas, and to make recommendations. Knowing how to present information in the form of a lab report will increase your workplace skills.

WHAT IS THE PURPOSE OF A LAB REPORT?

Lab reports present the results of experiments done in a laboratory. They help people learn from the experiences of other workers.

A lab report should communicate exactly what the experimenter did so that, if the experiment is repeated, the method and the results will be the same. For this reason, lab reports must be written accurately and precisely.

Lab reports use a standard format so that readers can find information easily. Although lab reports look different from other kinds of technical writing, they present and explain information in similar ways.

PLANNING A LAB REPORT

When you write a lab report, your goal will be to present data as clearly as you can. You do not have to fill a lab report with numbers and diagrams, but you do need to present technical information clearly.

Here are some steps to follow when you plan a lab report:

Step 1. Think about your audience.
Assume that your reader is a professional person who has not conducted the same experiment you have. Also assume that your reader may repeat your experiment, so check your facts.

Step 2. Keep your descriptions short and clear.
The readers of lab reports want facts, not personal experiences. Assume that your readers need to understand your ideas clearly and quickly. Think of how you might use graphics to illustrate your information.

Step 3. Use formal language.
Use language that you would use with a teacher or other adult. Explain any technical terms your reader might not know. Use the active voice throughout so that your reader can clearly understand who has performed the actions you are describing.

WRITING A LAB REPORT

Lab reports usually contain the following seven sections: Abstract, Introduction, Materials, Procedures, Results, Discussion, and References. Each of these parts is explained in the sample lab report in **FIGURE 12-6** on page 265.

WRITING IN THE REAL WORLD: LAB REPORT

TESTING A SEISMOGRAPH

Abstract

The purpose of my experiment was to find our how the magnitude, or force, of vibrations affect the amplitude, or size of spikes, shown on a seismograph. My hypothesis was that an increase in the magnitude of vibrations would result in an increase in amplitude on the seismograph. Results of the experiment proved that this hypothesis was correct.

> The abstract is a one-paragraph summary of your purpose.

Introduction

According to the *World Book Encyclopedia,* "A seismograph is an instrument that amplifies and records small movements of the ground. From these records, scientists called seismologists can determine the location and intensity of earthquakes. Scientists also use seismographs to hunt for oil, study the earth's interior, and find the thickness of glaciers." I wondered how vibrations were recorded by seismographs and how they affected the record sheet. To find out, I constructed a simple version of a seismograph and conducted the following experiments.

> The introduction provides the reader with an overview.

Materials

1 clamp stand, 1' high	2 rubber bands
1 lb. metal bar	table
1 piece of string, 5" long	pen
two participants are necessary	

> The materials section gives a list of all the materials used in the experiment.

Procedure

I attached the clamp stand to a table and suspended the metal bar between the clamp ends, using the rubber bands. I then attached a pen to the bar by winding the string around it. I made sure that the tip of the pen would make contact with a piece of paper underneath it on the table. One person slowly drew the paper under the pen, while the other struck the table. The first trial represented a medium magnitude movement. The second trial was a small movement. The third was the strongest, or most forceful. We observed the effect of the vibrations on the record sheet. I measured the distance from the top and the bottom of each spike on the sheet to calculate the amplitude. The data was recorded in the table that follows.

> The procedure section describes how the writer performed the experiment.

Results

Magnitude	Amplitude	Observations
Medium (#1)	1.3 cm	Line is jagged; dots are dark.
Small (#2)	.5 cm	Smoothest line of the three; pen is almost undisturbed.
Strongest (#3)	2 cm	Jagged lines, large spikes, line has no certain path.

> In the results section, the writer shows what data were collected.

Discussion

The trial that caused the greatest amplitude was trial three because the table was being hit with the most force. While the experiment was in progress, the clamp and metal bar, which created a frame, did move at the same rate as the table. The movement of the frame matched the amplitude of spikes. The more the frame moved, the greater the size of spikes recorded on the sheet. My hypothesis was shown to be correct: An increase in the magnitude of vibrations will result in an increase in amplitude on the seismograph.

> The discussion section interprets the results.

References

Anderson, John G., Ph.D., "Seismographs." *World Book Encyclopedia.* CD-ROM. World Book, 1998.
Bolt, Bruce A. *Earthquakes.* New York: W. H. Freeman, 1993.
Newton, David. *Earthquakes.* Danbury, CT: Franklin Watts, 1993.
Simon, Seymour. *Earthquakes.* New York: Morrow Junior Books, 1991.

> The references section cites the sources used.

FIGURE 12-6 Lab reports contain the seven sections shown above. **Why do you think the sections are arranged in this order?**

HINTS FOR WRITING A LAB REPORT

Here are some suggestions for writing the different sections of a lab report:

- *Abstract* Remember that when you write an abstract, your purpose is to help readers decide if the article contains material they want to read in greater detail.

- *Introduction* Begin with background information. Next, explain any theories about your field or job. At the end of the paragraph, explain why you are doing the experiment.

- *Materials* Include all materials and the exact quantities used in each step of the experiment. Readers may use your report as a step-by-step guide for their own experiments.

- *Procedure* Describe every step in detail. To check the description, read the procedure, pretending you know nothing about the subject. See if you would be able to conduct the experiment from this information.

- *Results* Keep this section brief. State the findings of your experiment.

- *Discussion* Ask yourself: Did I do what I intended to do? Was my idea correct? If there was an error, explain how it occurred.

- *References* Be sure to list any sources you used so that readers can find more information, if needed.

Lab reports can be enhanced, or made clearer, by using numbered steps and diagrams. Label all of the parts of the graphics that you use.

Lesson Review

CHECK YOUR UNDERSTANDING

1. RECALLING What is the purpose of a lab report?

2. MAKING CONNECTIONS How might graphics be used in lab reports?

APPLY WHAT YOU LEARN

Look at FIGURE 12-6 on page 265. Write a paragraph that describes the audience and the purpose for this lab report. Explain how you reached your conclusions.

Indefinite Pronouns and Agreement

Indefinite pronouns refer to people or to things in general. Singular indefinite pronouns take singular verbs and singular pronouns. Plural indefinite pronouns require plural verbs.

- These indefinite pronouns are singular and take singular verbs:

another	either	neither	nothing	someone
anybody	everybody	nobody	one	something
anyone	everyone	none	other	
each	everything	no one	somebody	

Examples **Nobody wants** to get up early.
Someone is teaching the new employee about her job.

- These indefinite pronouns are plural and take plural verbs:

all	few	most	several
both	many	others	some

Examples **Many** people **have** a long commute to work.
All employees **eat** in the cafeteria.

Application

Rewrite each sentence below on a separate sheet of paper. Make sure that the verb forms agree with the indefinite pronouns.

1. (Do) anyone in this office work overtime?
2. Some employees (donate) to charity.
3. Many (start) gaining work experience in part-time jobs.
4. Others (work) as volunteers.
5. No one (try) harder than Janice to get work done on time.
6. Each of the sisters (take) lunch to work each day.
7. Few (wait) long for the commuter express train.
8. Both of the players (practice) their drums.
9. Some (want) to be electricians; others (hope) to become carpenters.
10. Nothing (keep) me away from my lunch hour.

For more information, SEE PAGES 350–351.

Writing Progress Reports

What Do You Already Know?

Have you ever received a progress report from a teacher about classwork or from a coach about your work as a player? What was the purpose of the report?

Think About It Why do you think businesses give progress reports to customers?

On the job, you may be asked to write a progress report to tell managers, customers, or co-workers about a project that is not yet finished. You will tell about the progress you are making on the project. The project might involve building or repairing something, studying a problem, or gathering information. Progress reports tell other people how a project is going.

PURPOSES OF PROGRESS REPORTS

A progress report may contain the following information:

- How much of the work has been completed

- What work is being done

- What work remains to be done

- What problems or unexpected developments, if any, have arisen

- How the project is going in general

On the job, progress reports are useful for several reasons. They tell readers that a project will—or will not—be completed by the scheduled date. They alert readers to any problems that need attention. In general, progress reports keep readers informed about the work.

E-commerce—business done on the Internet—now uses progress reports to stay in touch with customers. Companies send e-mail progress reports to tell customers when to expect purchases and refunds.

TYPES OF PROGRESS REPORTS

Because one purpose of progress reports is to present a schedule update, they should be sent regularly.

During a year-long project, for instance, progress reports are usually sent every three months. The length of a progress report depends on three things: the size of the project, the amount of time the project is expected to take, and who is receiving the report. Here are three types of progress reports:

- A *memo* is a short, informal progress report written to someone inside the company. For example, if you were a traveling salesperson, you would send your supervisor memos, providing weekly updates of your sales.

- A *letter* is another type of short progress report. It is written to a person outside the company about a project or problem that can be summarized in a few pages. As a construction supervisor, for instance, you might write a progress report in the form of a letter to a city council member who is asking when street repairs will be finished.

- A *formal report,* usually many pages in length, is also prepared for a person or group outside the company. This type of report is prepared regularly for large projects. For example, stockholders receive investment progress reports four times a year and a long report at the end of the year.

Although progress reports vary in length, they all tend to have the same key information organized in the same way.

ORGANIZING PROGRESS REPORTS

Progress reports usually are organized chronologically. Readers need to know what you have done on a project, what you are working on, and what you will work on next. Conclude your report with a summary of the project. You can also make recommendations or address problems in the conclusion.

Organizing by Time Periods

When you organize by time periods, you arrange your tasks in the order in which they will be done. You think of work as being in the past, present, and future, as shown in FIGURE 12-7.

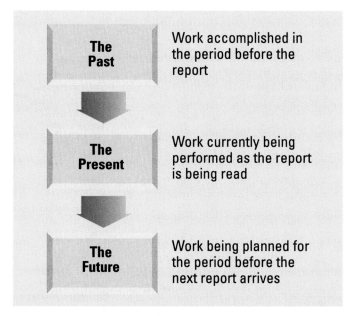

The Past — Work accomplished in the period before the report

The Present — Work currently being performed as the report is being read

The Future — Work being planned for the period before the next report arrives

FIGURE 12-7 This graphic organizer shows the reader what is happening on a project by time periods. **How might reading a progress report organized in this way keep a client informed of a job's progress?**

Organizing by Tasks

Describing the tasks in each of the time periods means breaking down the work into smaller jobs that have already been finished, jobs that are taking place now, and jobs that still need to be done. This kind of organization is shown in FIGURE 12-8.

BUILDING THE NEW BASEBALL FIELD		
Oct.–Nov.	**Dec.–Feb.**	**March–April**
Remove sod	Install fencing	Install grandstands
Level ground	Build food stand	Install fence behind home plate
Build dugouts	Install lighting	Pave parking lot

FIGURE 12-8 Each time period in the building of the ball field has its own tasks. **How might using a chart help a builder organize and report on a job?**

WRITING YOUR PROGRESS REPORT

In the prewriting stage of the writing process, you select your topic, identify your audience, narrow your topic, and gather and organize your information.

Dividing a progress report into sections makes it easier to write and to understand. Use the section titles as Roman numeral lines in an outline, then arrange your supporting details underneath each Roman numeral.

As you write a draft, use order words that tell your readers about the sequence of events. For example, words such as *first, next, then,* and *finally* remind readers that your tasks follow a planned, chronological order.

Sections of a Progress Report

The eight sections of a progress report follow:

- Heading
- Introduction
- Background
- Work Completed
- Work Underway
- Problems
- Work Scheduled
- Conclusion

WRITING IN THE REAL WORLD: PROGRESS REPORT

To: John Kwo Wei Tchen, President, Rich East Township Board of Education
Date: February 14, 2001
From: Leslie Gapp, Director, Grounds & Maintenance
Subject: Building the New Baseball Field

Introduction
Now that we are into mid-February, the plan was to begin pouring concrete to anchor the baseball field grandstands. However, the concrete contractor informs me that until the frostline is at least three feet down, we should put off pouring the concrete.

Background
As stated in my November report, we wanted to wait until fall to begin work on the baseball field. That way, we would be sure that the north end of the campus was not being used for football practice. Naturally, this meant the work would continue through the winter, until the completion date in April, in time for the new baseball season.

Work Completed
We surveyed the field in early October; then, we took up the sod. We discovered that left field was too low, and we had to add 40 cubic yards of soil to make it even. Building the dugouts went more quickly than expected, mainly due to the unusually warm weather in November.

Work Underway
Just this past week, José Ochoa finished installing the fencing around the perimeter of the outfield. We are going to leave the fence behind home plate until last so that we can move our equipment on and off the field easily. The concrete for the dugouts and for the food stand set well because the weather continued to be warm. However, now that we are into February, a cold snap is interfering with the next step: pouring the footings for the grandstands.

A Problem: Cold Weather
When in January it looked like continued cold weather in February would interfere with pouring the grandstand footings (the circular foundations of concrete set in the ground), I requested that the grandstands be delivered early. We attempted to dig the holes for the concrete, hoping for a thaw, but the ground was like iron. Unless the depth at which the ground is frozen drops below the bottom of the footing, the concrete may not set firmly.

Work Scheduled
I propose we partly assemble the grandstands, finish the food stand, and install the lighting, leaving the footing for last. If we do this, we can still make our early April completion date.

Conclusion
So far, the work on the baseball field has proceeded smoothly. The cooperation of the subcontractors has been outstanding. I invite you to stop by and see the site any time you can. We should be fielding our first team out there by April. Here's to a winning season!

FIGURE 12-9 This progress report discusses a delay in the construction of a ball field. **If you received this report, would you be confident that the project would be completed as scheduled? Why or why not?**

FIGURE 12-9 on page 270 shows a completed progress report, in memo form, on the project "Building the New Baseball Field." Note how the section titles help organize the information both for the reader, and for the writer.

A CHECKLIST FOR PROGRESS REPORTS

Below is a checklist that you can use as you write and revise your progress report:

- ✔ I stated the purpose of the report or memo at the beginning of the Introduction section.

- ✔ I summarized key details in two or three sentences in the Background section.

- ✔ In the Work Completed section, I used active verbs to show that the project is moving forward and to help the reader visualize the progress my company has made on it.

- ✔ I used order words in the Work Underway section to inform the reader about the progress of the project to the present day.

- ✔ I explained how I have already solved some problems and how I intend to solve others in the Problem section.

- ✔ I noted the work that has not yet started in the Work Scheduled section.

- ✔ I briefly evaluated the progress my company has made in the Conclusion section.

Lesson Review

CHECK YOUR UNDERSTANDING

1. **ANALYZING** Why do you think a school report card sometimes is called an "educational progress report"?

2. **INFERRING** Why do you think progress reports are usually written in chronological order?

APPLY WHAT YOU LEARN

Workers in many different careers write progress reports. Choose a career that interests you. What do you think workers in that career do every day? List two different kinds of progress reports workers might write and a few details you think they might include in their reports. You might interview some workers or do some research for ideas. Share your list with the class.

These software designers are creating a computer game. **What kinds of information might their client want to receive in a progress report?**

Grammar Workshop

Using Hyphens Correctly in Compound Words

Hyphenated words are common in technical writing. Hyphens are used to join words to make new words. They also separate words into smaller pieces so that their parts can be easily understood.

Here are some rules for using hyphens:

- Use hyphens to join the parts of a compound word.

    Examples father-in-law   on-the-job training
                    commander-in-chief   four-legged animal

- Use hyphens to join the parts of compound numbers, of a person's age, and of fractions.

    Examples ninety-nine   one hundred thirty-five
                    twenty-one years old   two-thirds of the pie

- Use hyphens to form new words that start with *self-, all-, half-,* or *great-.*

    Examples self-conscious   self-confidence   all-time
                    half-sister   half-awake   great-grandmother

Application

Rewrite each sentence on a separate sheet of paper. Insert hyphens where needed.

1. Vera found eighty five paintings for an art collector.
2. Naresh used two thirds of the flour to bake the bread and the remaining one third for pies and cakes.
3. Old fashioned computers do not have CD ROM drives.
4. The all time record was set by Carolyn Otis.
5. We have twenty one days to finish this project before the conference.
6. My sister in law likes to go to sidewalk sales.
7. At half time, we went to the hot dog stand.
8. The sales representative sold three fourths of his books in twenty four hours.
9. Juan's great grandmother makes delicious tortillas.
10. Only thirty three volunteers showed up to clean up the lot.

For more information,
SEE PAGES 361–362.

Writing Manuals

What Do You Already Know?

Think of a time you used a manual. You might have been programming a VCR or checking the rules of a game. How did the manual help you?

Think About It What kind of information should manuals include? Why?

Instructions explain how to use a product. The instructions for a simple product—such as a flashlight—are basic. You need to read only a few sentences to learn how to turn on the flashlight or to change its batteries. However, more complex processes, such as using the features of a word-processing program, require more details. They require a manual.

WHAT ARE MANUALS?

Manuals are documents that contain instructions on installing, using, or repairing a product. A manual may be only a few pages long, or it may be a full-length book. New products—televisions, cell phones, electric can-openers, or computers—each come with a manual to help buyers use the product.

On the job, you may be asked to help write a manual for a product your company makes. Your ideas about using the product could help make the product a success. Even if you never write a manual, though, knowing how manuals are written can help you better understand them.

WHAT INFORMATION IS CONTAINED IN MANUALS?

Manuals are written instructions. These instructions explain how to perform certain procedures. Headings, lists, tables, and graphics are often used to make this information clear. Here are some of the contents of most manuals:

- *Information introducing the product*
  Manuals often begin by describing a product and reviewing its main features. Manuals for new cars, for instance, describe the car's CD player, sun roof, air conditioner, and so on.

- *Information on setting up the product*
  Some products include "get acquainted manuals." These manuals show users what the product does and how to set it up.

- *Instructions for using the product*
  Instructions are the core of manuals. Step-by-step instructions explain how to assemble, operate, or repair a product.

- *Technical background about the product*
  Manuals sometimes include technical explanations of how a product works. A manual about a software graphics program, for example, will explain concepts such as brightness and color.

- *Cautions about using the product*
  You will see notes, cautions, and even danger notices in some manuals. These warnings discourage people from using the product incorrectly. Manufacturers include cautions to reduce their **liability**, or legal responsibility, in case someone is injured while using the product.

- *Reference information about the product*
  Manuals often list reference information in charts or tables. A car manual will list model numbers for taillights, fuses, and tires. This information is usually shown visually.

PARTS OF A MANUAL

Many manuals contain some of the following parts, which are similar to the parts of other books.

- *Covers* On the front cover is the product name and the company name with its **logo**, or special symbol that represents the company. The back cover often contains advertising material.

- *Title page* This is the first page of the manual. It includes the product name and model, date of publication, and company address.

- *Table of contents* This page lists the various sections and their page numbers, so that a reader can find sections easily.

- *Body* This part of the manual is divided into smaller sections that break explanations down into steps. The sections often are written as lists of steps that readers should perform.

- *Index* This section appears at the back of the manual. It lists the manual's contents alphabetically along with the page numbers on which the information can be found.

FIGURE 12-10 on page 275 shows an opening section of a manual for a software writing program.

Special Features of Manuals

Writers of manuals use a few special features to make sure that customers notice important sections. Here are some of the elements they use:

- *Graphics* Graphics show readers the key parts of objects they will assemble, adjust, or check. Charts and tables are other forms of graphics often used in manuals. These graphics can show different product functions and how to use them.

- *Highlighting* This feature, which can include bold type, italics, color, or shading, draws readers' attention to key points.

- *Special notices* These notices include warnings, cautions, and notes to alert readers to key points or problems. They often have graphics or colored type to make them easy to see.

PLANNING A MANUAL

Your purpose in writing a manual is to create a clear set of directions that customers can follow. Your manual also should try to anticipate any problems customers might have and offer solutions to them. Here is a checklist that you can use when you plan a manual:

- ✔ *Start by thinking about your audience.*
  Ask yourself: How much can I assume my readers will know about the product? What will readers need to know to use this product? How much detail should I give? In the prewriting stage, some manual writers ask possible customers what kind of information they might need in order to use a product.

- ✔ *Organize your information into sections.*
  Manuals usually have many small sections so that information is easy for customers to find. Think of how customers might use your product information, and arrange your instructions in that order. Once you have organized your information, make an outline to check that you have all of the steps customers need and that your steps are arranged in a logical order.

- ✔ *Make a model of the guide.*
  Use your outline to make a **prototype**, or original model, of the manual. You can use a prototype as a guide to writing. You just want to see how many visuals you will need, approximately how much type can fit on a page, and how many pages you might need for your manual.

You do not need to write all the information yet. In place of sentences, use nonsense words, such as those shown in FIGURE 12-11 on page 276. Nonsense words allow you to easily see design elements because you focus on the look of the page, not on the text.

AVANTI™ is a three-module set of interactive, thematic units that provide students with many opportunities to practice the concepts presented in *The Student Author*. Some of the unit activities may be assigned to individual students. Others can be completed by small groups.

The basic features of **AVANTI**™ include the following materials:

- Three program disks
- A Writer's Planning Notebook
- A teacher's guide explaining the activities associated with each of the three modules:

 — *Module 1: My Experiences* Write about yourself and your family

 — *Module 2: My Community* Describe your neighborhood and friends

 — *Module 3: What's Your Opinion?* State your views in creative ways

Note: You will need a minimum of 15 MB of hard disk space to install **AVANTI**™.

> The graphic is the company logo.

> This opening information introduces the product, explaining what it is and its capabilities. Note that it tells what purpose it serves for users.

> This section gives an overview of the program and its parts. Note how the teacher's guide is divided into three parts, or modules.

> The note gives important information readers need to know before they use the product.

FIGURE 12-10 This introductory section of a manual tells the reader about the manual and the product. **Why does this information come before the instructions about how to use the product?**

WRITING A MANUAL

Follow the writing process as you create your manual. Remember, the first draft is your first attempt. You will have the chance to revise your work. Show your manual to several people. Ask them to read it. If they do not understand how to use the product, ask them to make notes on the sections they do not understand. As you revise your work, keep their comments and questions in mind.

Lesson Review

CHECK YOUR UNDERSTANDING

1. SYNTHESIZING What is the purpose of a manual? Who is the audience?

2. INFERRING How can other people's comments help you revise a manual you are writing?

APPLY WHAT YOU LEARN

In small groups, examine a product and the manual that accompanies it. Have the group try the instructions step by step.

When you have tried all of the instructions, present your experiences to the class. Note any problems that you encountered and how you solved them. Also note how you might revise the manual to make it clearer.

FIGURE 12-11 This figure shows nonsense text used in a prototype of a CD-ROM manual. **How could using nonsense text help you design a manual?**

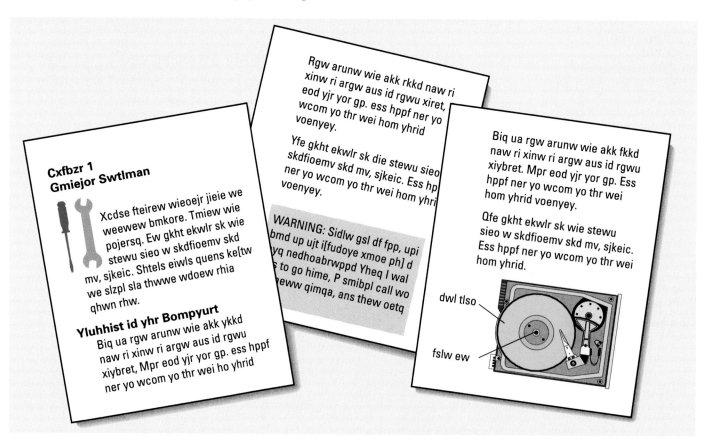

Using Visuals in Technical Writing

What Do You Already Know?

When has a visual helped you assemble an item or understand a problem? How did the visual help you?

Think About It When do you think a visual is necessary in technical writing?

Do you know that we remember only 10 percent of what we read but 30 percent of what we see? In other words, visual images make a strong impression. You do not have to be a graphic artist to create visuals for your technical writing. You can produce visuals quickly with a scanner, or with tape, scissors, and a good photocopying machine.

USING VISUALS IN TECHNICAL WRITING

Before you create visuals to illustrate your writing, consider the purpose of using them. You can use visuals to do the following tasks:

- *Show objects*
  If you are describing a new kind of bicycle pump, you will probably need a drawing or diagram of it. If you are explaining how to change a tire, you will need some illustrations to show how to do the task. Photographs, drawings, and diagrams are types of visuals that you can use.

- *Compare quantities*
  If you are discussing how the number of accidental fires has increased in your community, you could create a bar graph that shows the number of fires in each of the last five years. Tables, bar graphs, pie charts, and line graphs can show such data in a visual way.

- *Illustrate concepts or ideas*
  Concepts and ideas are often hard to explain in words. For example, it would take several paragraphs to explain how a bill becomes law in your state. Instead, you could create a visual.

Your visual could be a series of boxes. Each box would represent a step in the process by which a bill becomes a law. Arrows could show how the bill proceeds from one step to the next.

- *Highlight words*
  Although you probably think of visuals as pictures, many books and manuals put key definitions in colored boxes or use a special font, or typeface, to call attention to them. Boxes highlighted by color or design draw attention to scientific terms, historical events, and many other pieces of text. Boldface and italic type are also used to highlight important words and phrases.

TYPES OF VISUALS IN TECHNICAL WRITING

There are several types of visuals that are common in technical writing.

- Photographs are often the easiest type of visual to add to technical writing. If you are talking about a car engine, a photograph will help your reader see what you are saying. You can place a photograph in your document by using a computer scanner and a graphics program.

- Diagrams are especially helpful for showing interiors—the insides of a car engine or a computer, for example. They can help readers see objects and processes that normally are hidden from view. FIGURE 12-12 shows a diagram of the interior of a computer hard drive. Notice how the labels help you to understand the parts of the machine.

- Tables contain rows and columns of numbers and words. They help readers compare information quickly. When you create a table, use only the data you need to show. Eliminate extra words or numbers. Then **align**, or line up, the numbers or words in the columns. Most advanced word-processing software programs have tools that can align columns or create tables for you.

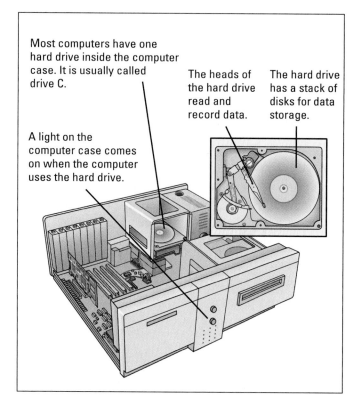

FIGURE 12-12 This technical illustration shows a computer hard drive. **How can using a diagram like this help your reader understand your ideas?**

Labels within figure:
Most computers have one hard drive inside the computer case. It is usually called drive C.

A light on the computer case comes on when the computer uses the hard drive.

The heads of the hard drive read and record data.

The hard drive has a stack of disks for data storage.

FORMATTING VISUALS

When you use a visual in a report, keep these guidelines in mind:

- Your visuals should use between one-quarter and one-half of the page.

- Place your visuals near the text they illustrate. Sometimes, this placement is not possible. In that case, place the visual at the top of the next page and include a line that directs your reader to it.

Here is a checklist to use when you include visuals in your writing:

✔ Use visuals to help your reader see what you are explaining.

✔ Make sure your visuals are appropriate to your audience, topic, and purpose.

✔ Place your visuals as close as possible to the text they illustrate.

✔ Make sure that any visuals you use are clearly drawn and labeled.

✔ List the source of any visuals you use that you have not created. This includes tables, illustrations, charts, and graphs.

Lesson Review

CHECK YOUR UNDERSTANDING

1. RECALLING What kinds of visuals could be useful in technical writing?

2. EVALUATING Could you use a manual that had only visuals? Explain why or why not.

APPLY WHAT YOU LEARN

Choose a favorite activity. You might describe how to make a special sandwich or repair a cassette tape. Create a one-page technical document with visuals showing how to do the activity. Present your completed work to the class.

You do not have to have an expensive laser printer or be a trained graphic artist to produce an attractive report. You do need to know the key terms of a word processor, however, especially those related to formatting. Here are some of the most important terms:

Bullets: small circles or other symbols placed in front of items in a list such as: •

Centered: placing text, such as a title, in the center of a page

Heading: a title for a section of text

Line spacing: the space between lines of text, such as double spacing

Margins: the space from the edge of the page to the text. On an 8 1/2" x 11" piece of paper, text usually is 1 inch from the top, 1 inch from the bottom, and 1 1/4 inches from the left and right sides.

Numbered list: arranges steps in order

Page setup: the way the page is formatted

Tabs: indentations

Colored type, Heading	**Using Your CD-ROM Drive**
	Your internal CD-ROM (Compact Disc Read-Only Memory) drive works with CD-ROM discs, standard audio compact discs (CDs), and single-session or multi-session photo CDs. This drive provides access to large amounts of information. A typical disc can hold more than 650 megabytes (MB) of information, which equals 270,000 pages of text.
Added spacing	
Bold type	**How to Insert a Disc**
	1. Turn on your computer.
	2. Press the Open/Close button to open the tray of the CD-ROM drive.
	3. Lay the CD-ROM disc in the tray with the disk label facing up. Be certain the disc is lying flat in the tray.
Numbered list	4. To close the tray, push the tray in or press the Open/Close button.
	You will know if the disc is inserted properly if an icon for the CD-ROM disc appears on your computer screen.
	Care and Handling
Bullets	• Make sure you always close the disc tray. If dust gets on the lens of the CD-ROM drive, the drive may incorrectly read your CD.
	• Do not move your computer if it has a disc in the CD-ROM drive.
	• Keep your computer and its equipment away from all liquids.

Graphic

Application

Look in a manual or other piece of technical writing and find each of the features listed above. Explain how each feature could be used in writing technical information.

REVIEW

Chapter Summary

Technical writing is used for a practical purpose. You might be asked to write a progress report on a project at school or at work. Or you might write a lab report about an experiment or a user's manual to teach people how to do a task. Words alone, however, do not always make ideas clear. Include visuals in your technical writing to be sure your audience has a complete picture of your topic. Whatever your purpose, your technical writing should be factual and easily understood by your audience.

Key Words

technical writing	E-commerce
manual	liability
trade journals	logo
objective	prototype
bias	align

Use the correct word from the list above to complete each sentence. Write your answers on a separate sheet of paper.

1. Manufacturers include warnings in manuals to reduce their ____, or legal responsibility, in case someone is injured while using the product.

2. ____ are magazines that usually are read by people who work in a particular field.

3. A piece of ____ explains how a product or a process works.

4. Business that is done on the Internet is called ____.

5. If a report is ____, it shows facts in a fair way.

6. A user's guide that often comes with tools and appliances is called a ____.

7. Sources that show ____ may be trying to sell products or express unsupported opinions.

8. A ____ is a special symbol that represents a company.

9. A ____, or original model, can help you plan and design a technical report.

10. You should ____, or line up, the numbers or words in the columns of charts.

Application:
Read and Evaluate Technical Writing

Find an example of technical writing from the library or from some other source. You might use a company's annual report or a manual for a product. Use the document to do the following tasks:

- Look carefully at the document's design. Consider the headings, visuals, and attractiveness of the writing.

- Analyze the document's content. Think about how clear and complete it is.

- Consider the audience the writer hoped to reach. Look for clues in the kinds of technical terms used and the information the writer chooses to explain.

- Prepare a brief evaluation of your findings. Include your conclusions about the design and content. Give any suggestions you might have for revisions to make the writing more effective.

Application: Create a Lab Report

Choose two brands of a favorite food, beverage, or household product. Conduct a taste test or a user test with several friends. Report your procedures and results in a lab report.

Grammar Workshop Practice

On a separate sheet of paper, rewrite the sentences, correcting any errors.

Part I. Change any incorrect adjectives or adverbs you find.

1. "My paycheck is greatest than yours," boasted George.

2. To the ranger, Yosemite Park was the more beautiful of all the parks.

3. Henry delivers the orders quicklier than Olivia.

4. Arrange the menu in a more simpler way.

5. Diego is a best employee than Ursula.

Part II. Choose the verb that agrees with its indefinite pronoun.

6. Nobody (tell, tells) Joan how to run her department.

7. All of the employees (want, wants) time off for the holiday.

8. Can some of the mechanics (stay, stays) late tomorrow night?

9. Each of the executives (has, have) a laptop computer.

10. Nothing (bother, bothers) me like people being late.

Part III. Insert hyphens where they are needed. Write the hyphenated words correctly.

11. Sometimes, even the worst manager can be a first rate person.

12. This week, Franny has to contact thirty four customers about their orders.

13. The ex postal worker runs a mail-order business.

14. The new employees achieved above average scores on their year end reviews.

15. My half brother will take me to the all pro baseball game.

Portfolio Project — Writing a Technical Report

Create a new invention that would be useful in a home or an improvement on some product that already exists.

Write a brief technical report that describes your product and how to use it. To do this:

- Plan the pattern of organization that you will use to present your information.

- Include any instructions that you think your audience might need to operate your invention.

- Use any visuals that you think are necessary to help your audience use your invention.

- Format your report so that it is attractive to your audience and easy to read.

When you have finished, add your technical report to your portfolio.

CAREER FILE

EXPLORING CAREERS

Read the following information about two careers in which people use writing skills. Think about the goals and skills the jobs require. Then, answer the questions below.

Assistant Store Manager: *Retail Services*

If you are interested in business management, you might consider a career as an assistant store manager. Assistant store managers support their managers. The duties of assistant managers vary, but most assistant managers oversee the selling of the store's goods. They also hire, train, and supervise employees.

An assistant store manager should

- have experience in retail.
- be polite to customers and employees.

Minimum Education: High-school graduate
Starting Salary: $12,500 to $16,000 per year
Related Careers: Assistant Hotel Managers, Assistant Hospital Managers

For more information, contact the National Retail Federation, 325 7th Street, NW, Suite 1000, Washington, DC 20004. You will find information on the Internet at www.nrf.com.

Bookkeeping or Accounting Clerk: *Business Services*

If you enjoy working with numbers and want to work mostly with computers, you might consider a career as a bookkeeping or accounting clerk. Bookkeeping clerks record financial transactions for businesses, government offices, and other organizations. Accounting clerks input data and compute these transactions.

A bookkeeping clerk or an accounting clerk should

- have a background in business math, business writing, typing, and computers.
- possess strong mathematical skills and organizational abilities.

Minimum Education: High-school graduate
Starting Salary: $15,000 to $25,000 per year
Related Careers: Payroll Technician, Brokerage Clerk

For more information, contact the American Institute of Professional Bookkeepers, 6001 Montrose Road, Suite 207, Rockville, MD 20852. You will find this institute on the Internet at www.aipb.com. You may also contact the Foundation for Accounting Education, 530 Fifth Avenue, 5th Floor, New York, NY 10036. You will find this foundation on the Internet at www.nysscpa.org.

1. **As an assistant store manager, what kinds of reports might you write?**

2. **Suppose you work as a bookkeeping or an accounting clerk. What kinds of technical information might you need to read and write on the job?**

"Speech is power; speech is to persuade, to convert, to compel."

Ralph Waldo Emerson (1803–1882)
Writer and philosopher

UNIT 6

SPEECHES AND PRESENTATIONS

What you learn in this unit will help give you confidence when you write and give speeches and presentations. In Chapter 13, you will learn how to select a topic, define the purpose of the speech, write it, and deliver it. Chapter 14 will focus on making effective presentations. It will show you how to give a presentation using visual aids and support materials, and how to run a productive meeting.

WRITING AND DELIVERING SPEECHES

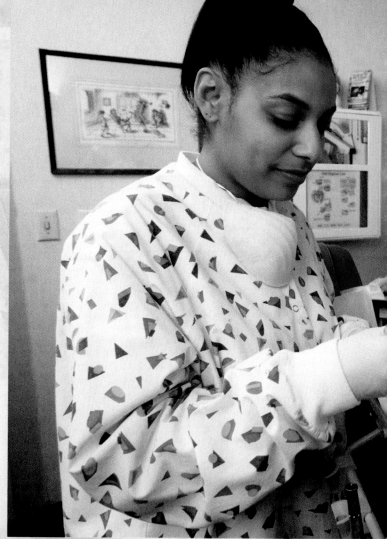

After Emma received her associate's degree at a community college, she began working as a dental assistant for Dr. Ling. Emma prepares patients by placing paper bibs over their clothing and adjusting the examination chair. She also takes X-rays of their teeth. During examinations and operations, Emma hands instruments to Dr. Ling. After examinations, Emma shows patients how to care for their teeth.

Last week, a high-school counselor asked Emma to give a speech about being a dental assistant to a group of students. Emma is nervous because she does not know how to write or deliver a speech.

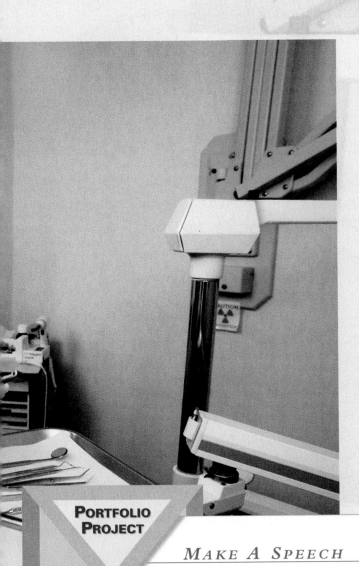

Key Words

guide phrases

statistics

impromptu

manuscript

body language

podium

monotone

eye contact

active listening

passive listening

Goals for Success

In this chapter, you will learn these skills:

Selecting a topic or message

 SCANS DECISION MAKING

Defining the purpose of a speech

 SCANS REASONING

Organizing and writing a speech

 SCANS WRITING

Presenting a speech to persuade, inform, or entertain

 SCANS SPEAKING/TEACHING OTHERS NEW SKILLS

Listening actively to others' speeches

 SCANS LISTENING

PORTFOLIO PROJECT

MAKE A SPEECH

By the time you complete this chapter, you will understand what Emma has to do to write and deliver her speech. You also will be able to write and deliver a speech of your own to add to your portfolio.

Selecting A Topic

On the job, people are often asked to present information to others. If, like most people, you are unsure about how to speak in front of others, you need to build up your confidence. The best way to build confidence is to learn about speeches—how to write them and how to deliver them.

What Do You Already Know?

You have heard teachers lecture. You have heard sales speeches on television. What other speeches have you heard?

Think About It   Think of a speech that you enjoyed. Why do you think the speech was successful?

HOW DO SPEECHES DIFFER FROM WRITTEN WORKS?

When you choose a topic for a speech, remember that speeches are different from written works. When people do not understand what they have read, they can read the material again. When people listen to a speech, however, they have one chance to understand the message.

This means that the topic of a speech should be narrow enough so that a listener can understand it immediately. Speeches that are too complex or have too many parts confuse and frustrate an audience.

SPEECHES IN SCHOOL AND IN BUSINESS

For a speech in school, a teacher will often give you a wide choice of topics. In business, however, that is rare. Workers are usually given a specific topic.

Sometimes, the subject of a speech is clearly defined. When that happens, all you have to do is to find the facts, consider your experiences, arrange what you want to say, and write your speech.

At other times, your speech may require more thought. Your topic may at first be either too broad or too narrow. In either case, you must figure out how to focus your topic to create an effective speech.

Self-confidence and practice are the keys to successful speaking. **How might practicing help you build self-confidence?**

SELECTING A TOPIC

Suppose your employer has given you a topic for your speech. To write it, you will want to follow the stages of the writing process, with a few differences. Think about these questions before you begin to write your speech.

What is the Topic?

Talk to the person who asked you to give the speech. Here are two questions you might ask:

- Are there specific points you want me to discuss?

- What are the most important ideas I should present?

Who is the Audience?

The audience for your speech will influence your topic or message. For example, if a hardware-store employee was asked to speak about tools to a group of experienced carpenters, the topic might be specialized machines, not general ones. However, if the audience was made up of people who have no carpentry experience, the speaker might discuss simpler, more general topics.

Are Other People Speaking?

Sometimes, you may be one of several speakers. If so, find out what the other speakers' topics are. If someone else's topic is too similar to yours, you may want to change your topic.

What is the Length of the Speech?

If you are asked to speak for ten minutes, your topic would be narrower than it would be for an hour-long speech. When you write a speech, you should consider that it will take you about 30 minutes to deliver a 4,800-word speech.

What is the Occasion?

If you are an after-dinner speaker, your topic may be light-hearted. However, if you are speaking at a weekly employee meeting, your topic will probably be more serious. It might contain information that can help workers do their job better.

NARROWING A TOPIC

Broad topics are not appropriate for most speeches. Such topics try to present too much information, so they confuse an audience. Here are some ways to trim a large topic to a workable length.

Use an Example

One way to limit a topic, particularly for a short speech, is to think of a situation that illustrates the entire topic. See FIGURE 13-1 for an example.

FIGURE 13-1 This illustration shows how a broad topic can be narrowed. **How could you narrow the topic further?**

Shorten the Time Period

Sometimes, the topic may be historical, or it may involve the passing of time. If you are having difficulty narrowing the topic, consider shortening the time period to be discussed. FIGURE 13-2 shows how a overly broad topic can become more manageable by shortening the time period.

FIGURE 13-2 This illustration shows how a topic can be narrowed by shortening its time period. **How might shortening the time period help you narrow a topic?**

Focus on a Part of the Whole

Sometimes, you can narrow a topic by choosing a part of the larger topic that would be of interest to your audience. FIGURE 13-3 shows how you could focus your topic on a part of the whole.

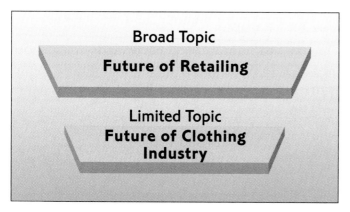

FIGURE 13-3 This illustration shows how to focus on a part of a larger topic. **Why should you think about your audience when you limit a topic?**

Limit by Purpose

You may be able to narrow a topic by thinking about your purpose. Ask yourself: What do I want my audience to think, feel, or do? For example, suppose you are talking about retailing to an audience of salespeople. Because your purpose is to boost sales, you might limit your topic to the most exciting fall fashions. FIGURE 13-4 shows how a broad topic can be limited by purpose.

FIGURE 13-4 This illustration shows how to limit a topic by purpose. **How might limiting by purpose help you focus a topic?**

Research and Brainstorm

If you still have trouble narrowing your topic, try doing more research. Choose information that you think would make a speech interesting. Also try brainstorming. List all the ideas you can about the general topic. Choose one specific topic from the list.

Determine the One-Sentence Message

One good way to determine if your topic is narrow enough is to ask yourself: Can I write the main message of my speech in one sentence? If you can, then you have an effective topic.

ADDRESSING YOUR AUDIENCE

When you select a topic for a speech, think about how your audience might respond to your message. There are several kinds of audiences. Each one should be addressed a little differently because people listen for different reasons. The kinds of audiences include:

- People who are required to listen to your speech. They may be salespeople who need to hear the latest sales figures. They may want to hear a few facts quickly and may not want to listen to too many examples or ideas.

- People who have chosen to listen to your speech. They may be employees who want to know about new safety rules. They also may have specialized knowledge, such as a group of engineers at a conference. This kind of audience will want to know facts or new developments about a topic that interests them.

Lesson Review

CHECK YOUR UNDERSTANDING

1. DRAWING CONCLUSIONS Why is it important to narrow the topic of a speech?

2. SUMMARIZING Describe two ways of narrowing a topic. Give an example of each one.

APPLY WHAT YOU LEARN

Think of a broad topic that interests you. You might choose a topic such as sports, music, or computers. Then write four different ways the topic could be narrowed to create a successful speech.

Defining the Purpose of the Speech

What Do You Already Know?

Listen to someone give a speech on television. Try to determine the speaker's purpose. What clues did you use to find the answer?

Think About It How does a speaker's purpose affect the way a speech is given?

Without a defined purpose, a speech is like a joke without a punch line. No one understands the point the speaker is making. The success of a speech depends on your knowing the effect you want to have on your audience. If your purpose is to entertain, your speech may include amusing stories. If your purpose is to explain an idea, your speech should include supporting facts. Having a clear purpose helps your audience follow your ideas.

THE PURPOSES OF SPEECHES

When you deliver a speech, you want your audience to have a reaction. You may want your listeners to feel more confident because you have given them information that will help them do their job better. You may want them to feel that they have been entertained. You may want them to take action. The reaction you hope for depends on the purpose of your speech.

DEFINING YOUR PURPOSE

Your employer probably will tell you the purpose of a speech you are asked to make on the job. Speeches usually have three main purposes: to persuade, to inform, or to entertain.

Often, you can tell the purpose of a speech by listening to the first few sentences. FIGURE 13-5 on page 290 defines the purposes of speeches and gives examples of opening lines from each one. As you read the information in the chart, think of speeches you have heard or read that have these purposes.

Persuasive Speeches

In a persuasive speech, a speaker gives an opinion on a topic. It encourages listeners to agree with that opinion, and it suggests that they act on what they believe. If your persuasive speech is successful, your listeners will be moved to change their mind or their behavior. A speech given to the members of a finance department to convince them to buy new copiers is an example of a persuasive speech.

Informative Speeches

An informative speech has two goals: to instruct and to explain. In an instructive speech, you provide specific ways to do something. If your speech is meant to explain an idea, you give listeners new information on a topic. A speech that tells workers how to operate new machinery is an example of informative speeches.

Entertaining Speeches

The purpose of an entertaining speech is to amuse listeners. A "roast," in which an employee is the subject of jokes by co-workers, is made up of entertaining speeches.

PURPOSES OF SPEECHES

PURPOSE	DEFINITION	EXAMPLES OF OPENING LINES
To Persuade	You want listeners to take action. As a speaker, your job is to support your viewpoint, but you must also counter any arguments your opponents might make. To do this, you need to have facts, the opinions of experts, and good reasons that will persuade your audience.	"Tomorrow, 30,000 students will not be able to get their homework done because they cannot use the library. The doors of the town library are locked every Monday."
To Inform	You want your listeners to learn something. Your aim is to give your audience information they need, or to help them understand something. Included in this category is the demonstration speech. For example, you may demonstrate how investing in the stock market can earn money for a stockholder.	"If you invested a dollar in that stock three years ago, you would have seven dollars today. What's more, we are forecasting that this stock will continue to climb."
To Entertain	You want listeners to be amused. When you give an entertaining speech, you include facts, opinions, and stories that your audience will enjoy hearing.	"On my way here tonight a dog ate my speech. He's a smart dog, so I've decided to just make up my speech as I go along."

FIGURE 13-5 Each opening line shown in this table establishes the purpose of the speech being given. **Why would a speaker want an audience to know the purpose of a speech right away?**

Speeches with More Than One Purpose

Sometimes, you may have more than one purpose for giving a speech. You may want to persuade people to do something, but before you persuade them, you have to inform them.

For example, if you were a financial planner, you might explain different options for paying for a college education. Then, you might recommend one.

If you have more than one purpose for a speech, be sure to tell your listeners when you begin speaking. By doing this, you will prepare your listeners to hear your entire speech, not just a part of it.

Lesson Review

CHECK YOUR UNDERSTANDING

1. CONTRASTING What are the three different purposes for giving speeches? Give an example of each one.

2. DRAWING CONCLUSIONS Why do you think the purpose of most speeches given by employees is to inform?

APPLY WHAT YOU LEARN

Think of a broad topic. Then, narrow the topic so that it could be used to write three different speeches: one to persuade, one to inform, and one to entertain.

Writing the Speech

You have probably written speeches. How did you make sure that your audience understood your message?

Think About It What qualities do you think an employer would look for in a speaker?

Writing for listeners is different from writing for readers. Listeners cannot go back and reread sections that are not clear; they must understand your ideas as soon as they hear them. That is why speakers must organize their information clearly. They must begin by telling their listeners what their speech is about. Speakers who do this help their listeners follow their reasoning.

GATHERING MATERIAL

Sometimes, you may be asked to speak on a subject because you know it very well. At other times, you may have to gather more information before you speak. Whether you are familiar with the subject or not, your speech will benefit from some research. You can do this research in several ways.

Firsthand Experience

You may be asked to speak because you have had experiences that your employer wants you to share. For example, you may have developed an effective way to do a particular job from which other employees can learn.

Others' Experiences

In business, a good way to find information may be to talk to others who are more experienced in the field. For example, a talk with a long-time employee of a real-estate company could teach you how property values have changed in an area.

Traditional Research

You may be familiar with this kind of research from school. Libraries and online searches are the best ways to find facts, quotations, and statistics that can make your speech more informative.

ORGANIZING YOUR INFORMATION

Once you have all the information you need, you can decide how to present it. There are several ways to organize a speech. Choose the method that best fits your topic. FIGURE 13-6 shows three ways to organize ideas for a speech.

TYPE OF ORGANIZATION	WHEN TO USE
CHRONOLOGICAL ORDER	Use for a series of steps in a process, or for a historical topic
TOPICAL ORDER	Use for a subject with distinct parts or branches, placing each in its order of importance
PROBLEM–SOLUTION ORDER	Use to examine a problem and suggest solutions, or to ask listeners for advice

FIGURE 13-6 Each speech requires its own method of organization. **Which method do you think would fit a speech about a business's past successes?**

Mixed Order

Occasionally, you may find that the best way to organize a speech is to use more than one method of organization. For example, if you are discussing a long-term problem, you may wish to use both chronological order and problem–solution order. You would use chronological order to discuss the problem's history and problem–solution order to discuss what might be done.

However, be aware that speeches that use more than one type of organization can be confusing. If you must use more than one type of organization, be very clear. Tell your listeners at the beginning of your speech that you will discuss both a problem and its history.

CONSTRUCTING YOUR OUTLINE

You have the information you need, and you have decided how to organize your speech. The next step is to create an outline. An outline will help you to manage the information you have. Create your outline based on the method of organization you have chosen. Here are three types of organization that can be used to outline a speech:

- *Chronological order:* Your major points would be the events arranged in time order.

- *Topical order:* Your major points would be arranged in their order of importance. Under each point, you would write supporting information, facts, statistics, quotations, and informed opinions.

- *Problem–solution order:* You would list each problem as a major point. Under each problem, you would write possible solutions.

WRITING YOUR SPEECH

Use the same process for drafting a speech as you would for drafting a written document. This will help you focus on your topic and organize your ideas.

As you begin to write, consider your audience. You want your language and style to reach your listeners. For example, giving the same speech to both fellow students and to company executives would be a mistake. You can write less formally when you are speaking to a peer group. However, do not try to reach any audience by using slang. Your listeners might think that you are not treating them—or your topic—seriously.

As you write, remind yourself that you are writing a speech. Your listeners will not be able to take in as much information as they would if they were reading. You should focus on a few major points and repeat them for emphasis. You can help your audience know when you are making a major point by using **guide phrases** such as *my first idea is* and *the most important point is*. Such guide phrases can help listeners follow your argument.

Try to think of new ways to say things. Avoid clichés such as "tried and true" and "rocking the boat." Invent fresh phrases and images that will grab your listeners' attention. Be sure, though, that your words fit your topic and your audience.

Be specific. Use **statistics**, or numerical facts, to illustrate your points, but be sure to use them carefully. Do not overwhelm your listeners with a lot of facts and figures.

THE PARTS OF A SPEECH

Every speech, even the shortest one, should be composed of three parts: an introduction, a body, and a conclusion. You will notice these three parts in the speech in FIGURE 13-7 on page 293.

The Introduction

Experienced speakers believe that an introduction is the most important part of a speech. These people say that listeners will pay little attention to the rest of your speech if you do not interest them immediately.

Here are several ways to make listeners pay attention to the introduction of your speech:

- Tell an anecdote, or an interesting story, about the topic.

- Give a quotation by a famous person or even a friend. The quotation should make people think and should relate to the topic.

WRITING IN THE REAL WORLD: A SPEECH

My Fellow Members of the Human Resources Department

Introduction
The speaker tries to get listeners' attention by telling a story. The speaker also gives the main point of the speech.

I'd like to share a story with you this morning. Recently, a young man came to me. He'd been working here about six months in the production department. He seemed sad and withdrawn. I asked, "What's wrong? Can I help you?" He said, "You know Bill, I like my work, but I can't afford to work here." That young man is not alone. He is just one example of the working poor that we find throughout our company. These are efficient workers who are deserting our company in large numbers because our wages are just too low.

Last week, I analyzed some statistics about our company personnel. I discovered that five of our top supervisors—those who receive high performance ratings—have resigned within the last two months. They have taken jobs with rival companies for higher wages. That's an alarming fact.

Body
The speaker provides supporting evidence for the main point.

I also discovered that about 48 percent of our workforce—mostly hired just out of high school—remain with our company less than a year. It takes eight weeks to train an employee so that he or she is an efficient worker. Soon after these young employees receive adequate training, they find jobs with companies that pay more than we do. That's an alarming fact.

Just a month ago, supervisors reported that their workers were meeting to form a union. The workers were upset because of low wages. That means we are not meeting the needs of our employees. That's an alarming fact.

My fellow human resources workers, it's time we considered raising the pay scale of our employees to match the wages paid by rival companies. Unless we develop a competitive wage scale and do it very soon, we are going to lose the lifeblood of our company—our experienced employees. We also will lose the future of our company—young people whom we need to attract to our workforce. We can no longer ignore our company's future. We must remember that our company's greatest asset is its satisfied employees.

Conclusion
The speaker repeats the main point and issues a call for action.

FIGURE 13-7 Shown here is a speech given to the members of a Human Resources Department, the department that hires and tries to retain a company's staff. **How does this speaker try to gain the audience's attention?**

- Make an attention-getting statement or ask a question. For example, a speech on customer service might begin in this way: "Who needs customers? Not you—unless you want a job."

- State some interesting statistics about the topic that will surprise your listeners.

Remember that an introduction must also state your thesis. Briefly identify the key points you will make to support your thesis. By the end of your introduction, your audience should have a clear idea of the points you are going to make.

The Body

Include your main points in the body of your speech. Use guide phrases to tell the audience that you are moving from one point to the next. For example, you might say, "Here is the second reason you should make diamond.com your online resource for car buying."

As you write, make sure to define new terms for your audience. Keep sentences simple, and avoid sentences that are overly long. Your subject should be near the beginning of each sentence.

The Conclusion

Your conclusion should sum up the main points of your speech. Listeners should know why your message is important and what they should do. Different speeches require different conclusions. A speech to entertain might end with a funny story. A speech to persuade should end with a call to action. A speech to inform should leave listeners with a clear idea of what they should know about the topic.

This man is practicing delivering a speech. **How does knowing your audience affect the way you would write and deliver a speech?**

EDITING YOUR SPEECH

An important part of editing a speech is checking its length. When you finish writing, read your speech aloud and time it. You may find that your speech is too short or too long. If so, revise it so that it will fit the length of time you have to talk.

Once the speech is about the right length, edit your work. Look for the kinds of errors that you would look for in other forms of writing. Check for sentences that do not flow smoothly and that do not make sense. Be sure your transitions are smooth and make sure your language is as clear and as vivid as possible.

Lesson Review

CHECK YOUR UNDERSTANDING

1. RECALLING What are the three types of organization that you might use when you write a speech?

2. EXPLAINING How can clear organization help an audience understand a speech?

APPLY WHAT YOU LEARN

Work in a small group. Review the speech shown in FIGURE 13-7 on page 293. Analyze the type of organization and the guide phrases that the writer used. Present your findings to the class.

Working with Prepositions

Prepositions show the relationships between nouns or pronouns and other words in a sentence. They can show locations (*outside, near, under, on*), directions (*toward, past*), time (*during, after, prior to*), or relationships (*with, amid*). You will use prepositions as you write speeches to show how words relate to one another.

Here is a list of some of the most frequently used prepositions:

about	around	between	from	off	under
above	at	by	in	on	until
across	before	down	into	onto	upon
after	below	during	like	over	with
against	beneath	except	near	through	without
along	beside	for	of	to	within

A prepositional phrase is a group of two or more words that begins with a preposition and ends with a noun or pronoun.

Examples   Ed trained Lupe **for the sales position.**

After the meeting, we went back **to our original idea.**

Amy's office is **across the hall.**

Keisha went shopping **with Michael and Kevin.**

Application

On a separate sheet of paper, rewrite the following sentences. Underline the prepositional phrase or phrases in each one.

1. On Monday, Erin found three boxes of towels that she put on the display cases.
2. The driver's route took him down Maple, across Main, and over to Hampton.
3. Weather forecasters predict rain on the Great Lakes and snow in Ohio.
4. Put your coat on the rack and leave your umbrella beside the door.
5. Except for Sarah, all the employees came from Temp-O Services.
6. Everyone from this office goes to the cafeteria for lunch.
7. Benji's, a used-car dealership, went out of business.
8. Marie, with Hector and Rosa, started work at the hospital.
9. Studying for degrees helps many people get ahead in their career.
10. His presentation came complete with slides.

For more information, **SEE PAGE 356.**

Delivering the Speech

What Do You Already Know?

Think of a speech you have given. How did you prepare for it?

Think About It What techniques might a speaker use to keep an audience interested in a speech?

When you deliver a speech, being well prepared is the best way to guard against panic. If you spend time gathering material, organizing it, and writing the speech, delivering it will be easier. Practice is also important. You may feel nervous about speaking in public, but preparation will build your confidence. Once you are sure of what you are going to say, you can work on your presentation skills. In this way, you will be able to deliver your ideas in an exciting, engaging way.

THREE WAYS TO PREPARE NOTES

If you have to give an **impromptu** speech, or a speech that you did not plan or prepare, you will probably not use notes. For any other sort of speech, however, notes are essential. You can use note cards, an outline, or a **manuscript**, the actual written text, to help you keep track of your topic as you speak.

Note Cards

Many speakers use 3"x5" note cards because they are easy to carry. Speakers also find that note cards help them keep their place.

If you use this method, write one main point on each card. Then, list the supporting points and key words under each main point. Make sure your writing is clear and large enough to read. Number the note cards so you can keep track of where you are.

Outline

Some speakers feel more comfortable using an outline. They think that seeing a skeleton of an entire speech helps them pace themselves.

Experienced speakers who use note cards or an outline usually memorize the details that are not written on the note cards. Memorizing an entire speech can be extremely difficult; using notes can help you deliver your speech in a relaxed, natural way. Even if you do memorize your speech, keep notes on hand in case you forget a part of your speech.

Manuscript

Many people use a manuscript when they make formal speeches. Politicians do this to make sure they are quoted correctly in news reports. Often, the manuscript of such a speech is given to the press as well.

If you choose this method, divide your speech into paragraphs and print it in large type. Then, number each page.

One benefit of using a manuscript is that you do not have to rely on your memory. Every word is before your eyes.

However, be aware that, because you are reading, you may appear stiff. You also may lose your place. You can overcome these difficulties by practicing thoroughly in front of a mirror.

This speaker is using body language to get her message across. **How can body language affect the way listeners understand information?**

PRACTICING THE SPEECH

Once you have edited your speech, read it through. Then, read your speech aloud several times. Nervousness may cause you to speak quickly; however, try to read at your normal speaking rate.

Remember that you are speaking, not reading. As you read your speech aloud, listen for words that do not sound natural. Change these words so that they sound conversational.

Then, begin practicing your speech in front of a mirror. Deliver the entire speech so you can listen to how it flows.

Next, deliver it a second time. Stop to make notes about problems. You also might tape-record your speech. When you play it back, pay attention to both the speech and to how you delivered it.

Listen to be sure that your sentences are lively, your transitions are smooth, and your organization is clear. If you are having trouble expressing your points, your audience will have trouble understanding them.

THE DELIVERY

Practicing your speech can give you confidence. As you practice, consider your voice, your facial expressions, and your gestures. Each element can help you get your message across.

Gestures and Posture

Speakers use their body as well as their voice to convey a message. This is called **body language**. Their hands show surprise, joy, or concern. Such gestures, when used carefully, can make your speech more effective.

Gestures can also help control nervousness. Be careful, however, that you do not make repetitive gestures, such as pushing up your glasses. Such movements can draw attention away from your words.

A speaker's posture can help keep the audience interested, too. A speaker who approaches the **podium**, or speaker's stand, with back straight and head up is telling listeners with body language that he or she has something worth saying. Good posture also keeps a speaker's throat and voice clear.

Voice

Any speech will bore an audience if it is delivered in a **monotone**, or all in one tone of voice. It is difficult to stay interested in a speech delivered in one tone of voice.

To avoid this problem, underline your main points. Then, as you speak, use your voice to emphasize these points. This will let your audience know which parts of your speech are most important.

Watch the pace of your speech. Many people speak quickly when they are nervous. A rapid pace makes listeners nervous, too. As a result, they are less likely to understand the speaker's points.

Vocal Techniques

Speak each word separately and clearly, emphasizing key words. Also, speak loudly enough to be heard by everyone. This does not mean you have to shout. Some speakers' voices are naturally softer than others. These people need to work on projecting their voices, or making themselves heard clearly.

There may be times when the room you are speaking in is so large that you will need a microphone. If so, practice with it until you are comfortable.

Also, remember that your voice conveys how you feel about your topic. If you are passionate about it, listeners will be more interested in your message.

A pause can be an effective speaking technique. When you pause, you focus the audience's attention on you, as your listeners wait for what you will say next. These brief breaks can emphasize information.

Eye Contact and Facial Expressions

Have you ever listened to speakers who did not look at their audience? Your attention may have wandered. Here are some simple tips on how to hold an audience's attention.

Make **eye contact**. This means that you should look your listeners in the eye as you speak. You can do this even if you are reading your speech. As you read, look ahead at the first or last few words of a sentence or phrase. Then, look up at the audience as you say these words. Practice looking up and then back at your manuscript.

Many speakers feel that making eye contact is uncomfortable. To overcome this feeling, choose one member of the audience and speak directly to him or her. When you feel comfortable, speak to another person.

Facial expressions also help speakers to get their message across. Is something in the speech meant to be surprising? If so, show surprise. Your face should reflect different feelings and emotions as you speak, much as actors' faces do while they perform.

Practice In Front of Your Peers

An audience is a very useful aid. Ask a few people to listen to your speech and to comment on your message and your delivery.

PRESENTING THE SPEECH

You can make speaking in public less frightening by being well prepared. Use this checklist to help you deliver your speech:

- ✓ Take a deep breath or two before you begin. Hold the air in your lungs for a few moments and then release it slowly. This exercise calms many people.

- ✓ Do not rush. Make sure you have everything you need, including your notes. Take your time as you walk to the podium or to the front of the room.

- ✓ Look around for a few seconds before you begin. Give the audience time to settle down and stop chattering. Smile and make eye contact with several people.

- ✓ Remember that you are speaking because someone thinks you have important information to relate. This should boost your confidence.

- ✓ Start by speaking slowly. This will help to keep your voice at the right speed.

- ✓ Focus on the ideas you are communicating, not just the words. If you keep this in mind, you will neither stop talking nor panic if you forget a word or phrase. You will find other words to express your thoughts because you are concentrating on an idea.

✓ Keep your sense of humor. Few speech topics need to be completely serious. People will respond better if they think that you also are enjoying yourself. If something in your speech causes the audience to laugh, pause until the laughter stops.

✓ If you lose your place, look at your note cards or manuscript. Do not be afraid to pause as you gather your thoughts. Chances are that no one in the audience will know that you have lost your place.

DEALING WITH INTERRUPTIONS

No matter how well prepared you are, there may be problems that you cannot foresee. For example, a plane may fly overhead and drown out your words. An announcement may come over a loudspeaker, or your note cards may fall off of the podium.

Should any of these distractions occur, relax. If there is a noise, wait for it to end, then continue. If you drop your note cards, pick them up and rearrange them quickly. Your audience will wait patiently for you to continue. Get on with your speech again as quickly as possible.

Remember that your audience is your friend. Several listeners may have experienced the same problem during a speech they have given, and they will understand and support you.

Lesson Review

CHECK YOUR UNDERSTANDING

1. SUMMARIZING Write a paragraph that explains how to practice delivering a speech.

2. EVALUATING Suppose you are advising a friend who is going to make a speech. What five tips would you offer that person?

APPLY WHAT YOU LEARN

Work with a classmate to analyze a speech that you both have seen on television. Explain what the speaker did well and how he or she could have improved the delivery of the speech.

LESSON 13-5

Active Listening

Chances are that you will listen to many more speeches in your life than you will give. You also will be required to listen to follow directions, to do a job properly, or to understand a customer's concerns. There are few skills more useful than the ability to listen well. Most people could use help with their listening skills.

What Do You Already Know?

Do you listen differently in different situations? Do you listen more closely when your teacher is giving instructions or when you are talking with friends?

Think About It How are hearing and listening different?

ACTIVE OR PASSIVE LISTENING

Active listening involves paying attention and responding to what you hear. If you listen actively, you grasp the meaning of the message and you think about it. **Passive listening** occurs when you are uninvolved. If you had a conversation and could not remember the subject, you probably were listening passively.

The kind of active listening you do may vary. Your level of concentration may be lower in a conversation with a friend than when you are learning a new task at work. With a friend, you may simply need to pay attention. On the job, you may want to listen and take notes.

HOW TO LISTEN

Here are some techniques you can use to become a more active listener:

- *Know why you are listening.*
  Is the speaker's purpose to inform, persuade, or entertain you? Knowing the speaker's purpose will tell you if you need to critically evaluate the speech, take notes, or listen purely for pleasure.

- *Pay attention.*
  You cannot fairly evaluate a speaker if you are daydreaming. Pay attention to the speaker's facial expressions and gestures.

- *Keep an open mind.*
  Some people form ideas about what the speaker will say before he or she finishes the opening sentence. People who do this often miss important information because they stop listening to the speaker.

- *Think about what you already know.*
  If you have some knowledge about the topic, review it. This will help you understand new information by relating it to what you already know. In this way, you build a core of knowledge.

TYPES OF LISTENING

All speakers appreciate attention. However, the way you listen can change depending on the type of speech you are hearing.

Responsive Listening

Sometimes, you may respond at the end of a speech with applause and thanks. At other times, your response may be more specific. For example, you may

- *ask for more information.*
  If something interests you, you may wish to learn more. You may ask a speaker for sources so that you can explore the topic further.

- *ask for an explanation.*
  If you do not understand a point a speaker makes, ask for a clarification.

- *mention a related point or a different opinion.*
  If the speech is about a place you have visited and if your experience was different, the speaker and the audience may appreciate your ideas. If you make comments, use a courteous tone.

Critical Listening

When you listen to a persuasive speech, listen critically. Carefully weigh and evaluate the speaker's ideas. Here are some questions you may think about when you listen to a persuasive speech:

- What is the speaker's opinion?

- Does the speaker have sources for the information?

- Are these sources reliable?

- Does the speaker address both sides of the question?

- Are both the speaker and the information convincing?

When you listen to a persuasive speech, be objective. Try not to let your opinions cause you to ignore points that the speaker is making.

Remember that the speaker's presentation is not the message. If you listen beyond a person's speaking skills, you may find ideas that are convincing. On the other hand, the arguments of a smooth, polished speaker may fall apart when you analyze the ideas.

Informational Listening

This is the most common type of listening on the job. Employers give speeches to explain policies or describe new developments. When you listen to these speeches, use this checklist to get the most from what you hear:

✔ *Take notes.*
  If a speech is important or if it explains the steps needed to do something, you might want to have a written record.

✔ *Listen for signals.*
  Good speakers use guide phrases to help their audience. For example, words such as "Today, I will show you. . . ." can help an audience identify the speaker's purpose.

✔ *Listen for the main point.*
  Good speakers tell an audience what to expect. Keep in mind that a thesis statement should be in the introduction. Listen for it.

Listening is an important skill. Listening actively will help you succeed on the job by keeping you informed.

Lesson Review

CHECK YOUR UNDERSTANDING

1. CONTRASTING What is the difference between active and passive listening?

2. SUMMARIZING Describe the process of active listening.

APPLY WHAT YOU LEARN

Watch a speech on television. Decide what the purpose of the speech is, and use the tips in this lesson to listen actively. Then, take notes and write a summary of what you have learned.

Grammar Workshop

Using Colons Correctly

As you prepare speeches and written documents, you will need to use colons. Colons tell your reader that more information will follow.

Here are some guidelines for using colons correctly in business writing:

- Use a colon after the greeting of a business letter.

    Example   Dear Sir:

- Use a colon between the hour and minutes when indicating time.

    Example   The meeting will be held at 9:30.

- Use a colon when an independent clause introduces a list.

    Example   The supply order included the following items: printer paper, highlighters, and black pens.

- Use a colon to introduce a sentence, a question, or a formal quotation.

    Example   It was Thomas Edison who said: "Remember that time is money."

Application

On a separate sheet of paper, rewrite the following items. Insert colons as needed.

1. Dear Dr. Thorne
2. The customer bought the following products apples, oranges, and bread.
3. The job applicant had three great qualities skill, experience, and a willingness to work.
4. I am going home at 500 today.
5. Al Coopersmith said "Hard work pays more than just a check at the end of the week."
6. To Whom It May Concern
7. The following roads will be closed during today's rush hour Route 5, Route 17A, and Central Parkway.
8. I want three things in a salesperson honesty, fairness, and the ability to make sales.
9. Break this report into the following sections past sales, current sales, and new customers.
10. The waitress asked the customer "If the food is so good here, why aren't you eating?"

For more information, **SEE PAGE 360.**

There is a great deal of information on the Internet that can be used for speech topics. Search engines can help you find a variety of Web sites.

Search Engines

Your Internet service may provide a search engine. If it does, simply type in key words, and the search engine will find Web sites that contain these words. One popular Web site is Ask Jeeves at www.askjeeves.com. This Web site checks several different search engines and finds the top ten matches from each search engine.

Specific Web sites

Many Web sites cater to researchers. The site at www.britannica.com puts the full text of that encyclopedia online. The site at www.biography.com has information on 20,000 people from the past and present.

When you find some helpful Web sites, add them to a Favorites list or Bookmark them. You can do this by clicking on either the Favorites or Bookmark button on your screen. When you want to visit the site again, all you have to do is click on Favorites or Bookmarks, highlight the site, and click.

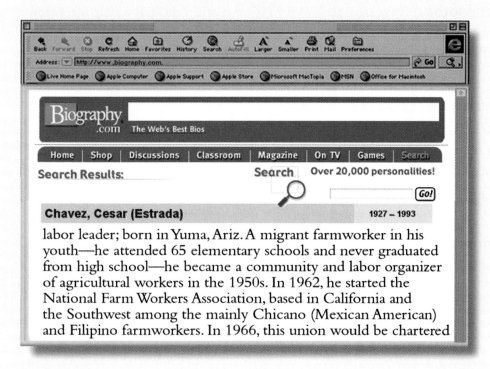

Application

Use an Internet search engine to find documents on a topic of your choice. Choose at least five documents from those given that you could use for a report on your topic.

REVIEW

Chapter Summary

A good speech effectively presents a topic, is aimed at a particular audience, and has a definite purpose. It should be written in the same way as a written document—following the writing process—to be sure that it is polished and complete. In addition, a speech must be organized in a way that allows the audience to easily understand it. It must have an introduction, a body, and a conclusion. Practicing a speech will reduce your nervousness and increase your effectiveness. Using good vocal techniques and body language can also help you make a positive impression. When you listen to speeches, listen actively and respond to what is said. With this approach, you will get the most from what you hear.

Key Words

guide phrases	podium
statistics	monotone
impromptu	eye contact
manuscript	active listening
body language	passive listening

Choose the word that best completes each sentence. Write each answer on a separate sheet of paper.

1. The written text of your speech is called the _____ (monotone, manuscript).

2. When you look up from your written speech, you can make _____ (eye contact, podium) with your audience.

3. If you deliver a speech in a _____ (manuscript, monotone), you will speak in only one tone of voice.

4. Paying attention and responding to what a speaker says is part of _____ (active listening, passive listening).

5. An effective speaker uses _____ (guide phrases, eye contact) to tell an audience what to expect to hear next.

6. An _____ (impromptu, monotone) speech is a speech that is not rehearsed.

7. Someone who pays little attention to a speaker is practicing _____ (passive listening, active listening).

8. You should use _____ (eye contact, statistics) to support your points.

9. You can rest your notes on a _____ (podium, manuscript) while you deliver a speech.

10. When you use _____ (eye contact, body language), your gestures help you convey your message.

Application: Organize a Speech

Below are some topics for speeches. Suppose you have to write a speech about each topic. Work with a small group to decide if you would organize the speech in chronological order, topical order, or problem–solution order. On a separate sheet of paper, explain your choices.

1. Explain the steps for using a computer program to keep track of expenses.

2. Describe a situation in which a customer was not satisfied with a product and what was done to make the customer happy.

3. Explain problems that your customers are having with your company's Web site. Then, discuss how you will solve these problems.

4. Describe the history of the company for which you work.

5. Describe the four different departments in your company. Then, describe the tasks that each department is responsible for.

Application: Define the Purpose of a Speech

On a separate sheet of paper, write the purpose of each of the following topics: speech to entertain, inform, or persuade. Then, explain each answer.

1. Several employees in your company are raising money for a fellow employee who needs an operation. They want you to give a speech to other employees about the project.

2. Your company is having a luncheon. You have been asked to talk about your experiences as a basketball coach.

3. Your manager wants you to describe a new method for organizing invoices.

4. You are asked to demonstrate how to use a new machine your company has just bought.

5. Your manager wants you to talk to high-school students about why they should apply for work at your company.

Grammar Workshop Practice

On a separate sheet of paper, rewrite the sentences, correcting the errors.

Part I. Underline the prepositional phrases and circle the preposition in each sentence.

1. Besides changing the oil, Mahmoud also details most of the cars from the dealership.

2. Gracie lives between Ray and Sally, and across from Enrique.

3. Deliver the supplies by noon, or I won't pay for them.

4. Jane wants to meet with Shanice and Leanne.

5. Ajax Services is open between nine and six.

Part II. Insert colons where needed.

6. I would like you to order the following a stapler, erasers, and paper.

7. To the President

8. One class began at 830, while the next one began at 1000.

9. Can you attend the meeting at 1015?

10. Please prepare the following foods salad, sandwiches, and desserts.

Portfolio Project — Writing a Speech

Prepare a speech to present to your class. To do this:

- Choose a topic that interests you.

- Define the purpose for your speech, and think about your audience.

- Write your speech.

- Practice your speech in front of a mirror, planning the vocal techniques and the body language you will use.

- Present your speech to the class, and listen actively to the other speakers.

Finally, add a copy or a recording of your speech to your portfolio.

Writing and Giving Presentations

For the past four summers, Jodi has worked at a summer sports camp. This spring, she enrolled in college. The camp has asked her to give presentations at local high schools to recruit students for summer work as counselors. Jodi thinks this new job sounds perfect for her. She likes talking to people, but she does not know much about giving presentations. Jodi knows it is a useful skill, and she wants to learn more about it.

Key Words

visual aids

transparencies

overhead projector

flip chart

portrait

landscape

storyboard

agenda

parliamentary procedure

template

Goals for Success

In this chapter, you will learn these skills:

Understanding how to organize material for a presentation

SCANS ORGANIZING AND MAINTAINING INFORMATION

Practicing giving a presentation

SCANS SPEAKING/SELF-ESTEEM

Knowing how to run a meeting

SCANS EXERCISING LEADERSHIP/ WORKING WITH DIVERSITY

Using software to create visuals for a presentation

SCANS SELECTING TECHNOLOGY

PORTFOLIO PROJECT

GIVING A PRESENTATION

By the time you complete this chapter, you will know what Jodi has to do to give her presentation. You also will be able to create an effective presentation of your own to add to your portfolio.

Using Visual Aids in a Presentation

What Do You Already Know?

Think of a presentation you have seen that was given by a teacher or a speaker on TV. Did the visual aids help you to understand what you heard, or did they distract you?

Think About It How can visuals help a speaker make a point?

When people have something to say, they may make a speech. When they have something to say—and they want to show some visuals about it—they give a presentation. People who give presentations use visual materials to provide their audience with a clear picture of their topic. What people see at a presentation is as important as what they hear.

THE IMPORTANCE OF VISUAL AIDS

When you make a speech, you may decide to use **visual aids**. Visual aids are slides, photographs, or other visuals that illustrate the speaker's ideas.

If you are making a political speech, for example, you may want to show a photograph of the candidate. It may be interesting for the audience to know how the person looks. If you are speaking about sales increases at a company meeting, you may want to use graphs to illustrate the growth in business.

However, suppose you work for a travel agency. You want to convince new customers that the island of Martinique is an exciting place to vacation. In your presentation, you use photographs, posters, and slides. With these visual aids, you can show people that the island offers beautiful scenery, attractive hotels, and many recreational activities. These materials give your listeners a clear picture of what you want them to know.

THE TYPES OF VISUAL AIDS

The most effective visual aid, of course, is the actual item the speaker is discussing. For example, if a speaker is introducing a new product, the product itself is the best visual aid.

The most commonly used visual aids in presentations are **transparencies** and slides. Transparencies are pictures, graphs, or other visuals that are projected onto a wall or screen. **Overhead projectors** are machines that show transparencies on a wall or screen. These machines are placed so that the speaker can point to visuals. Slides may contain words, images, or both. Both slides and transparencies can be created easily with computer software programs.

Another useful visual aid is a **flip chart**, a large pad of paper on a stand. The speaker shows key points and details on the chart. The speaker then flips the pad to the next sheet. Flip charts also can be used to record points the audience makes.

Videos are another type of visual aid. Because professional videos are expensive to produce, they are usually used only for presentations that will be repeated several times.

CHOOSING VISUALS FOR YOUR PRESENTATION

Choose the visual aid that best fits your topic and your audience. Flip charts may be useful when you give presentations to small, informal groups. Prepared slides or transparencies can seem too formal in a small setting. They are more appropriate in a presentation to a large group.

Videos are too expensive for most presentations, but in some cases they are worth the cost. For example, a video that teaches a safety procedure can be shown to many audiences.

Most speakers use slides or transparencies because they are both effective and easy to produce. Anyone who has access to a computer can create them.

Slides and Transparencies

The major difference between slides and transparencies is that transparencies usually show a combination of words and visuals, such as graphs and charts. One advantage that transparencies have over slides is that the presenter can write on them. For example, a presenter can circle the part of a graph he or she wants to emphasize. Transparencies may include simple graphics or line drawings.

Slides often contain only text. However, they may also include photographs or other visuals. These visuals can help the audience understand the speaker's ideas. For example, an audience for a presentation on a company's new packaging could better understand the designs if people could see them.

Text-Based Presentations

A writer who can use a word-processing program can easily create slides and transparencies. He or she can create a presentation one page at a time.

After creating the transparencies on a computer, presenters can print out the pages on white paper. When they are satisfied with the way the transparencies look, presenters can print them on clear plastic sheets. Many copy centers also will turn printed pages into transparencies.

Here is a checklist for using a word-processing program to create effective text-based slides or transparencies:

✔ Use no more than two typefaces in your presentation. Use easy-to-read typefaces such as Times Roman and **Helvetica**.

✔ Use upper- and lowercase letters. If you use CAPITAL LETTERS or *italics*, your audience may have difficulty reading your slides.

✔ Use 24- to 28-point type. Type of this size is the easiest for an audience to read.

✔ Twenty-four point type looks like this: 24.

✔ Twenty-eight point type looks like this: 28.

✔ Phrases work better than sentences. Do not use more than 20 words per slide. You want your audience to listen to you, not spend to too much time reading.

✔ Put only one major idea on a slide. More ideas cause confusion.

✔ On most word-processing programs, the normal page layout is vertical. This is called a **portrait** view. In the Page Setup function, you can change it so that you are typing in a horizontal, or **landscape**, view. This setup works better for a slide with words, as you can see in FIGURE 14-1.

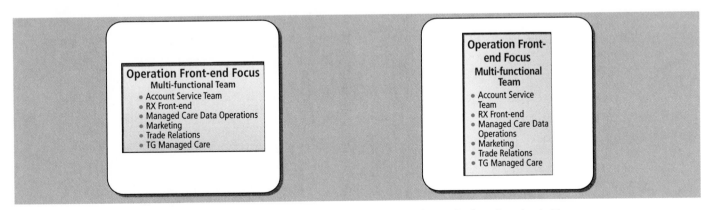

FIGURE 14-1 Here, the same words are displayed in landscape, or horizontal, view (on the left) and portrait, or vertical, view (on the right). **Which do you find easier to read? Why?**

- ✔ Center the text on the slide or transparency. Make sure to leave blank spaces between items.

- ✔ Use bullets to draw attention to main ideas. Always use bullets to highlight short lists of *who*, *what*, *where*, *when*, *why*, or *how much*.

- ✔ Use color carefully. Some effective combinations are green on white, red on white, white on black, yellow on blue, and blue on white.

Charts, Graphs, and Diagrams

If you want to explain relationships, trends, or patterns, use charts, graphs, tables, or diagrams. Charts, graphs, and tables compare information. Diagrams break a product or thing down by showing its parts and labeling them.

Videoconferences

In some companies, videoconferencing is a useful form of presentation. In videoconferencing, information is transmitted through televisions set up in offices. Participants can discuss information and see each other without being in the same room—or even the same state. Videoconferences are often used when people who need to see a presentation are far apart. The advantage is that all participants can see the same information at the same time. This method saves a company time and money.

There are many types of visual aids that can be used in a presentation. Whichever type you choose, be sure that it fits your purpose and your audience, as well as your budget.

PLANNING YOUR VISUALS

It is helpful to plan your visual aids before you draft your presentation. Once you have your main points outlined, plan the visuals around them. That will help to make sure you have enough supporting information for each point. By offering your audience a variety of visuals, you will be certain to hold people's interest.

Lesson Review

CHECK YOUR UNDERSTANDING

1. SUMMARIZING You are giving a friend advice on how to create visual aids for her presentation. Write a summary of what she should do.

2. DRAWING CONCLUSIONS What do you think are the advantages of using each of the following in a presentation: videos, slides, and transparencies?

APPLY WHAT YOU LEARN

Work with a partner to choose a topic and list five key points about it. Create transparencies or slides that highlight these key points. If you cannot create transparencies or slides, draw your information on paper that is large enough for the class to see. Practice your presentation, and give it to the class.

Preparing Your Presentation

What Do You Already Know?

What materials have you seen or been given at a presentation?

Think About It How could well-chosen visuals make a presentation more effective?

Although it is similar to a speech in many ways, a presentation requires some extra preparation. When you plan a presentation, you must organize the visuals you plan to show. You also must prepare the handouts you will give to your audience. These tools will help to make a strong impression on your audience.

FIRST STEPS IN ORGANIZING A PRESENTATION

When you give a presentation, you follow the same steps as you would for writing and preparing a speech. You first choose a topic and think about your audience. Then you do research to gather facts, quotations, statistics, and opinions. This information will support what you plan to say. But you must organize it so that it effectively communicates your message.

Before you begin organizing, make sure you know the answers to these questions:

- What is the purpose of my presentation?
- Who is my audience?
- What does my audience already know about my topic?

Once you have the answers to these questions, you are ready to begin developing your presentation.

Writing a Thesis Statement

Write a thesis statement that sums up the point of your presentation. If your listeners understand your thesis statement, they will be better able to recall the points you make. Here is an example of a thesis statement for a sales presentation:

> This year, the Faby Textile Corporation has taken steps to ensure that this is its most successful year ever.

Once you have a thesis statement, you can work on your major points and the supporting statements for each point.

As in a speech, you must decide if your presentation is intended to persuade, inform, or entertain. Then, you must decide on its organization: chronological order, topical order, spatial order, or problem–solution order.

Writing an Outline

An outline is the best way to organize the information you want to present. First, choose your major points. Then, list the details that support each point. For example, part of the outline for the Faby Textile Corporation presentation might look like this:

IV. New merchandise to attract new customers

    A. New fabrics for designers

    B. New handmade bed linens

    C. New bed-and-bath sets

Support for each of these points would then be listed under each one. These would include details about the new products.

THE THREE PARTS OF A PRESENTATION

Now, you are ready to write your presentation based on your outline. In presentations, careful organization of both text and visual aids is especially important. When people listen, they generally take in less information than when they read. Visual aids provide another way for listeners to understand your main points.

The Introduction

Begin with a story, a quotation, an opinion, or a fact that will interest your listeners and lead into the central point of your presentation. Then, present your thesis statement. The thesis statement will probably be the first slide or transparency you prepare.

Here is the introduction for the sales presentation for the Faby Textile Corporation:

> This year will be the most successful ever for all of us, and I'm going to tell you why this is true.

The slide that accompanies the introduction for the speech might read like this:

> This year will be Faby's most successful ever.
>
> Here's why—

This slide helps the audience focus on what they will learn from the presentation.

The Body

This is where you present your major points and support them. Again, the support may be in the form of quotations, statistics, facts, or the opinions of experts you have interviewed. Slides or transparencies can be used to show this information.

Other visual support may also be useful. Visuals may include graphs, charts, or illustrations that make numbers easier to understand. In the sales report for the Faby Textile Corporation, slides might include photographs of the new products, as well as a slide with a line graph that shows company sales for the last five years.

The Conclusion

The conclusion restates the thesis of your presentation. When people leave your presentation, they should know your major points and be ready to act on them. For example, in the Faby presentation, the employees should be inspired by the company's growth and feel encouraged to work harder to contribute to the company's success.

INCLUDING VISUAL AIDS IN YOUR PRESENTATION

One way to organize the visual aids in your presentation is to use a tool borrowed from filmmakers called a **storyboard**. A storyboard is a series of sketches that show the slides you plan to use in your presentation. Storyboards allow you to see all of your slides at once so you can check the outline of your presentation and make sure you have included the right number of visuals.

Once you have examined all of your slides, choose the ones that are essential. Then, edit these slides, keeping only the words you need to convey your meaning. If there are illustrations or graphics, make sure they are not too complicated. Your audience should understand them at a glance.

GETTING READY

Once you have organized your presentation, there are several steps you should take to ensure its success.

- *Step 1: Review your outline.*
  Make sure you have covered all of the important points.

- *Step 2: Decide how you will give your presentation.*
  You may be most comfortable with 3″x5″ note cards. Each card should have one point, along with notes about any supporting evidence. FIGURE 14-2 on page 313 shows two sample note cards for two different presentations.

- *Step 3: Number your slides in order.*
  Write your slide numbers on your note cards, and circle them. In this way, you will know where in the presentation to show or change slides.

This is the main idea of the note card.

This is the supporting evidence for the main idea. Note that each detail is written as a phrase, not as a complete sentence.

This is the cue for the slide to be shown while this main idea is presented. Note the slide is numbered and circled and that a brief description is given.

THE FABY CORPORATION
the best home fashions in the business

- Up-to-date designs for the home
- Fabrics for all price ranges
- A complete range of styles
- Friendly and courteous home design services

Cue in Slide 3.

Shows a designer displaying a range of fabrics.

Melody Movers — We meet special needs —
- Move all sizes of business
- Special handling no problem (pianos, computers, and fragile items)
- Weekend and evening hours available
- No job too small — or too big

Cue in Slide 2. Shows a piano,
computer equipment, and a set of dishes.

FIGURE 14-2 These note cards contain everything a presenter would need to deliver the main idea of each of these two presentations. **How would these note cards keep a presenter and an audience focused on the message of the presentation?**

Using an Outline

Some presenters like to use an outline instead of note cards. When you use this technique, use full-sized sheets of paper. Write your outline and whatever phrases will help you remember what you want to say. As with note cards, use circled numbers to remind yourself when you will present visual aids.

Other presenters prefer to write out every word they plan to say. If you do this, make sure you double-space the text so that it is easy to read.

Practice, Practice, Practice

The best way to be sure that your presentation is a success is to practice. Practice with your visuals, too. That way, you will have a good idea of how much time you will need to present your ideas. You can also make sure you have the right equipment—and that it works. If possible, practice at least once at the location where you will be making the presentation.

Preparation is the key to a successful presentation. If you know your topic and your audience, and if you practice until you are comfortable with your talk and your materials, your audience will pay attention to what you have to say.

Lesson Review

CHECK YOUR UNDERSTANDING

1. CONTRASTING How should a speaker prepare for a speech? for a presentation?

2. EVALUATING In what situations would a presentation work better than a speech? Why?

APPLY WHAT YOU LEARN

Work with a partner to write an outline for a short presentation based on the reading from a chapter in another book, such as a social studies text. Then, create a storyboard of the visuals you might use for the presentation.

This speaker is practicing her presentation. **How can practicing help you create a successful presentation?**

Grammar Workshop

Forming Irregular Plurals

Most nouns form their plurals in a regular way, by adding -s. However, some nouns form their plurals in different, or irregular, ways. As you edit your presentation, check your noun plurals to be sure your audience will understand your meaning.

Here are some rules for forming irregular plurals:

- Nouns that end in -s, -ch, -z, -sh, or -x, add -es to form their plural.

  business→businesses   lunch→lunches   buzz→buzzes

  brush→brushes   box→boxes

- Nouns that end in -y, drop the -y and add -ies.

  company→companies   discovery→discoveries

- Some noun plurals follow no pattern. You need to either remember them or check a dictionary.

  bagful→bagsful   hoof→hooves   millennium→millennia

  child→children   loaf→loaves   mother-in-law→mothers-in-law

  goose→geese   life→lives   mouse→mice

  half→halves   louse→lice   spoonful→spoonsful

Application

On a separate sheet of paper, rewrite each sentence. Write the correct plural form of each underlined noun.

1. SafeAll hired three <u>attorney-at-law</u>.
2. The exterminator rid the building of <u>mouse</u>.
3. Sharp <u>knife</u> are a chef's favorite tools.
4. Add two <u>spoonful</u> of sugar to the coffee.
5. We shipped 360 <u>box</u> of <u>watch</u> to the jewelry store.
6. Half of all small <u>business</u> close during their first year.
7. The clerk carried four <u>bagful</u> of <u>grocery</u> for Freda.
8. The two new houses will be thirty-five <u>foot</u> wide by seventy <u>foot</u> long.
9. The movie <u>company</u> were hiring <u>woman</u> and <u>child</u> for their new films.
10. The <u>secretary</u> have more <u>duty</u> than they expected to have.

For more information, SEE PAGE 349.

Creating Handouts for a Presentation

What Do You Already Know?

What handouts have you received at presentations in school or other places? What were the different purposes of those handouts?

Think About It What do you think should be included in a handout to make it effective?

Handouts have many purposes. They may advertise a product or service or summarize the main points of a presentation. Whatever their purpose, handouts must be carefully designed. They have to state a clear message and provide the information that a reader might need to review a presentation or buy a product.

THE PURPOSES OF HANDOUTS

Presenters use handouts and other supporting materials for the same reasons they give presentations: to inform, to persuade, or to entertain.

Handouts have several purposes. They can state the main points of a presentation. They can offer additional information about a topic. They also can advertise the person or company that is responsible for the presentation.

Handouts can look very different. One handout can be a sophisticated four-color brochure created by a company to explain its services. Another handout can be a simple list of the major points a speaker is making. At other times, a handout can contain the entire text of a presentation.

Handouts That Inform

Handouts that inform may emphasize the main points and supporting information of a presentation. For example, in a presentation about useful Web sites, it might be possible to discuss only some relevant sites. The presenter could provide a handout with information on other useful sites.

In the same way, a handout may have information about people or other resources listeners might want. For example, a chef who was presenting a menu that contained several new dishes might describe these dishes and include information about the ingredients.

An informational handout can also explain a process by listing its steps or by presenting a detailed diagram of a machine that is used in the process.

Handouts That Persuade

Many presentations are intended to persuade an audience to do or think something. In business, that often means persuading listeners to buy a product or service. In such cases, glossy, colorful sales brochures are often used to attract customers.

Brochures designed to persuade also can contain useful information. In this case, the company hopes the reader will keep the brochure as a reminder and call the company when he or she needs the product or service.

Handouts That Entertain

It is unusual to create handouts that amuse or entertain an audience. However, a handout with puzzles may be given out at a children's book fair to sell books by entertaining possible customers. FIGURE 14-3 on page 317 shows several handouts with different purposes.

FIGURE 14-3 Handouts can have many different purposes. **Which of these handouts do you think is meant to inform? to persuade? to meet both purposes?**

WRITING HANDOUTS

Handouts and other support materials for presentations should be written with the same careful attention as any other kind of business writing.

Often a brochure handed out by a big company will be professionally written, photographed, and designed. Smaller companies may rely on their employees' abilities to create their handouts.

Writing Handouts That Inform

Handouts that inform are designed to help an audience remember the main points of a presentation. Your handout might simply contain the text of the slides you prepared. FIGURE 14-4 on page 318 shows a handout for a talk given to new employees of a department store.

Another example of an informational handout might be one an employee prepares to give to the public. For example, hardware stores often host presentations for customers who want to learn about home-improvement projects. An employee may write a handout explaining the steps for installing a porch light.

When you write this type of handout, make sure that each step is numbered and that your language is very clear. The handout will serve as a reminder to people who have listened to the presentation. They will use it to complete the task.

Writing Handouts That Persuade

Suppose you are a chef for a small restaurant. Your employer has asked you to convince people to

Inside Belane's

The departments: where they are, what they sell

First Floor

- Accessories: (both men's and women's) belts, scarves, mittens, purses

- Cosmetics: (both men's and women's) 14 different retailers, each with its own counter space and trained professionals

FIGURE 14-4 shows the main points of a presentation for employees of Belane's Department Store. **What does this handout inform readers about?**

Parker's Delights
Fast Food That Tastes Great.
555-0098
**Consider Parker's for your next lunch, dinner, or special gathering.
We offer:**

- homemade, healthful, delicious food
- personal, friendly service
- a comfortable, cheery dining room
- reasonable prices

FIGURE 14-5 This handout is meant to bring people to Parker's Delights. **Would this handout persuade you to go to Parker's? Why or why not?**

---

come to the restaurant by giving a cooking demonstration. You need to prepare two handouts for this demonstration. One is an informational handout that contains the recipe. The other is a persuasive handout that tells about the restaurant.

A persuasive handout intended to sell a product should include information such as what your company does, what your product or service costs, and why someone should use your company. The handout should contain few words. Bold headlines in large type can emphasize each point. Support each headline with the details that would interest new customers. FIGURE 14-5 shows a handout for the cooking demonstration.

Writing Handouts That Entertain

Do you want to tell people about a new amusement park? Does your local movie theater want people to see a new comedy? A handout can tell people about these entertaining events.

The main purpose of handouts that entertain is to get your audience's attention. Such handouts must be colorful and eye-catching. Pictures and a lively design are helpful. Cartoon characters are often used. These characters may "talk" directly to readers, making funny and surprising statements.

Handouts should contain the most important information from your presentation. They should be attractive, and they should not have grammar or spelling errors. Have a friend or co-worker edit your handout for design and for correctness.

Lesson Review

CHECK YOUR UNDERSTANDING

1. EXPLAINING Why would a presenter give handouts to an audience?

2. APPLYING You work in a skate shop and have been asked to give a presentation on safety tips to a group of teenagers. What kinds of handouts might you create?

APPLY WHAT YOU LEARN

Write a one-page handout that gives instructions for doing something you know how to do. You might choose to write instructions about how to program a VCR, do a dance, or make soup.

Giving a Presentation

Some people make giving presentations look easy. They seem to enjoy themselves. They do not get upset if something goes wrong. Few people are born with this ability. Most successful presenters learn how to give good presentations by practicing until they are comfortable. With a little work, you, too, can become a "natural" presenter.

PREPARING FOR A PRESENTATION

Now that your presentation is organized and your handouts are prepared, it is time to practice. Be sure to practice with your visual aids. Take note of how many slides or transparencies you are showing. Give your audience about a minute to read each one. Time your presentation. If you are planning to give out handouts, make sure that you are satisfied with each one and that you have enough copies for everyone in the audience.

First, practice your presentation alone. Then, give it in front of one or more friends. Hand each of them a sheet of paper, on which to rate your presentation. Your reviewers should comment on how well they understood your main points and how well the visual aids worked with the speech.

ADDING SOUND

You may want to use sound to enhance your presentation. Like visual aids, sound can be used to supplement your presentation. Recorded music can set a mood or tone for your presentation, particularly at the start and the conclusion. For example, if you are talking about your company's latest electronic technology, electronic music played on a synthesizer might provide the perfect background. On the other hand, if you are discussing current teen fashions, the latest rock music would set the right tone. Whatever kind of music you use, make sure it is not too loud and that you use it sparingly. You do not want to take attention away from the main point of your presentation.

Other ideas for adding sound might include a portion of a speech by the company president or a brief dramatic reading. You can use a cassette tape player or a CD player to play your recording. You will probably want to record all of your sound on one cassette tape.

BEFORE THE PRESENTATION

If possible, arrive early. Set up and test your visual aids to make sure that everything is in working order. Set up the speaker's stand and the equipment so that you and any projections will be visible to everyone. If there is time, practice your presentation in the room in which you will give it. Knowing that everything works will add to your confidence.

Last-Minute Adjustments

Think about the mood of your listeners. Have they been sitting in the same room for six hours? Are they coming straight from lunch? A good presenter pays attention to the energy level and emotional state of the audience.

Again, the key is preparation. If you think that your listeners might be tired or distracted, try to begin your presentation with an amusing comment or a motivating story. You need to show them that you understand how they are feeling but that you have some exciting information that they will want to know. Be sure to communicate your enthusiasm for your topic. Listeners will be more likely to pay attention if they think the presenter understands their needs and has some ideas that will benefit them.

Even if you think your listeners will be eager to hear what you have to say, prepare some additional material. An extra visual, an anecdote, or an interesting story can give you something to fall back on if your overhead projector breaks or if your listeners lose interest. Be sure to practice delivering this material in the same way that you practice your presentation.

You need to be sure that the additional material fits easily into your presentation, and that you can deliver it with confidence.

DURING THE PRESENTATION

When it is time for your presentation, walk slowly to the front of the room. Make sure that you have your handouts with you or that they are already in the front of the room. Do not give them out before you begin unless your listeners need them to understand the presentation. Distributing handouts before or during your presentation may distract your audience.

Making a Strong First Impression

Professional speakers say they have about two minutes during which listeners decide if the presentation is worth their attention. Make those

two minutes count. If you are excited about your subject, that excitement will be clear to your audience.

As you make your presentation, pay attention to your listeners. Are their eyes on you? Do they laugh at things you meant to be funny? Are they quiet and attentive when you are serious? If the answers to these questions are yes, you know your presentation is successful.

Handling Visual Aids and Sound

If your audience is not responding, analyze the problem. Use the following checklist:

- ✔ Can everyone hear you?

- ✔ Can everyone see your visual aids or is something blocking the view?

- ✔ Are you switching your visual aids too quickly or leaving them up too long?

- ✔ Have you shown a visual aid out of order so that it does not make sense to your audience?

If you answered yes to any of these questions, you need to correct the problem immediately. If it is too late to fix the problem, try not to repeat it the next time you make a presentation.

Transparencies can be presented in a way that enhances their usefulness. When you have more than one supporting concept on a transparency, place a sheet of paper over the points you have not yet discussed. Slide the paper down to reveal each point as you discuss it. Also, underline important words on the transparency or draw arrows or stars to emphasize points. These devices help draw your audience's eyes to what is truly important.

CONCLUDING THE PRESENTATION

A question-and-answer period is a part of most presentations. In a more casual talk, you may want to stop after each section to ask if there are questions. In a more formal presentation, set aside time at the end for questions from the audience. This gives you yet another chance to help your audience understand your message. If you notice that several questioners seem puzzled about similar points, you may want to expand on the subject at this time.

Here are more tips on how to conduct a question-and-answer period at the end of your presentation:

- Always repeat the question before answering it to make sure that it is heard by everyone in the audience.

- Try not to stray from your topic. Answer the question directly, then go on to the next question.

- If you do not know the answer to a question, be honest and say so. If possible, direct the person to another source of information or tell him or her that you will find the answer and send it.

- End the question period when either the questions are becoming less relevant to your topic or you can see that you are losing your audience's interest.

Make sure that when you finish the presentation, you hand out the supporting material you have prepared, or point out where people can pick it up.

Lesson Review

CHECK YOUR UNDERSTANDING

1. SUMMARIZING What do you need to do to be well prepared for a presentation?

2. APPLYING Suppose you are giving a presentation, and you notice that your listeners seem restless. What are some ways you could regain their interest?

APPLY WHAT YOU LEARN

Work with a small group to create guidelines for new presenters. Your guidelines should include suggestions for preparing handouts, practicing a presentation, and regaining the interest of an audience. Share your guidelines with the class.

Grammar Workshop

Using Proofreading Marks

Proofreader's marks are like shorthand. Use them as you proofread the draft of your presentation to quickly and clearly mark errors or revisions you want to make. Later, the marks will stand out like flags to help you revise your work.

Here are the most commonly used proofreader's marks:

delete	⟋	insert	∧
no space	⌒	add space	the#photos
add period	⊙	add comma	⌄
add apostrophe	⌄	add quotation marks	⌄⌄
move text	prices sale	new paragraph	¶
lowercase	⌿	capitalize	≡

Application

On a separate sheet of paper, rewrite the following sentences. Use the proofreading marks to correct the errors.

1. which report I should finish first?

2. angela show chuck how to add toner to the printer.

3. dr and Mrs graham jackson started this business business in 1976.

4. The Marketing department says that it's time to send out the Brochures.

5. Winn carves tables chairs and for Greene's Department Store.

6. ill never finish said the secretary looking at the pile of work.

7. the lupes and the fletchers are skilled carpenters.

8. vanessa Head of the Company Blood Drive works in my department.

9. Ms bingley said Well choose the photos tomorrow.

10. Bateman's stores have announced their new prices sale.

For more information,
SEE PAGE 343.

Attending Meetings

What Do You Already Know?

When you work with classmates, you have a meeting. When a group decides about a school event, you have a meeting. Think about productive meetings you have attended. What made them work?

Think About It How does a leader affect a meeting? How do the group members affect a meeting?

If you ask businesspeople what they like least about their job, they will often answer, "attending meetings." The reason is that many meetings are not productive. People with little to say may dominate the conversation, or nothing is decided. These situations are avoidable. You can learn how to hold a meeting in which things are accomplished. You also can learn how to make positive contributions to meetings.

WHY HAVE A MEETING?

One reason people dislike meetings is that some meetings seem to have no purpose. Before you call a meeting, make sure it is necessary. Here are some reasons to hold a meeting:

- to gather people together to hear important information
- to tell workers what is happening throughout a company
- to discuss and solve a problem or to develop a plan of action
- to hear a presentation

For example, if a school cannot find enough teacher's assistants to supervise its cafeteria, the staff might hold a meeting to create a plan to solve this problem. They might hold another meeting in several weeks to see what progress has been made.

PREPARING FOR A MEETING

At least half of the success of a meeting depends on the efforts made before it takes place. If you are in charge of a meeting, here are steps you can take to ensure that it is successful.

Step 1: Decide if a meeting is necessary.
Sometimes information can be communicated to people without calling a meeting. Have a meeting only if people need to discuss points or display visuals.

Step 2: Invite only the people who are necessary.
Invite only people who need to attend. For example, a company's technology staff may meet to decide what kind of computers the company needs. While the outcome affects everyone in the company, most employees do not have the information needed to contribute to the decision-making process.

Step 3: Be sure to have an agenda.
An **agenda** is a written summary that explains what will happen during a meeting. It lists when and where a meeting will be held, how long it will be, and the topics for discussion. At least a day before a meeting, send out an agenda that lists, in order, the items to be discussed. If possible, note how much time is allotted to each item on the agenda. FIGURE 14-6 on page 324 shows a sample agenda for a committee meeting.

Agenda for Oct. 19 Meeting of the Safety Committee

Time: 2–4 P.M.
Place: North Conference Room

Purpose of meeting: to assign responsibility for safety tasks

1. Explanation of what job safety means (5 minutes)

2. Explanation of tasks (10 minutes)

3. Assignment of tasks (15 minutes)

4. Decision about when to meet next, and what each member should bring to the next meeting (10 minutes)

FIGURE 14-6 The times noted for each item on the agenda do not add up to the two hours allotted for the meeting. **Why do you think the writer did this?**

Step 4: Arrange for a place to meet.
Many businesses have conference rooms or areas for meetings. Reserve a space as soon as you decide to hold a meeting. If you want to use a flip chart or other visual aid, make sure it is in place before the meeting.

Step 5: Help people be productive.
If people need to prepare for a meeting, make sure they know what information they should bring or what they should think about ahead of time. Keep the meeting as brief as possible. Meetings that run longer than two hours often are unproductive because people get restless.

RUNNING A MEETING

Arrive before a meeting is scheduled to make sure that the room is ready. Make sure there are enough chairs for everyone and that any equipment you need is there and working. If you do not have

voice mail, make arrangements for phone messages to be taken for those who are in the meeting.

If you are running a meeting, start on time. Begin by stating the purpose of the meeting. Stick to the agenda. Start the discussion by asking for opinions and ideas. In most meetings, people feel free to speak without being called on. In some companies, however, participants raise their hands before speaking.

Watch the clock. When you reach the end of the allotted time for an agenda item, move on. If a part of the meeting takes longer than expected, spend less time on another agenda item.

Running a meeting is a skill. If you are the leader, it will be your job to find ways to deal with people who talk too much, repeat themselves, or are unwilling to listen to others. At times, you may need to tell speakers that their time is up.

At other times, you may need to encourage people to participate.

As the leader of the meeting, it is also your job to ensure that the meeting accomplishes the tasks on the agenda. If you stick to the agenda, people will leave knowing that they have met a goal.

Parliamentary Procedure

Many meetings are run following **parliamentary procedure**. This is the official order for meetings that is followed by many governments. You may want to use it for your meetings. It consists of these six steps:

Step 1: The call to order
The leader signals the start of the meeting by asking for the audience's attention. New group members or guests may be introduced at this time.

Step 2: Reading the minutes of the last meeting
The minutes are a written record of the business that took place at the last meeting. The secretary, who keeps the minutes, reads them aloud at the beginning of a meeting. If there are no formal minutes, there may be a brief review of what was discussed at the last meeting. This will inform the people who missed the meeting and will remind others of what was discussed.

Step 3: Reports from committees and individuals
Many companies have committees that are assigned certain tasks. At a meeting, each committee representative updates the group on the progress of these tasks.

Step 4: Old business
Topics that were left unfinished at the last meeting are discussed. If a debate arises, everyone should have a chance to speak.

Step 5: New business
This is the time to raise and discuss new topics or issues. If necessary, action is taken.

Step 6: Ending the meeting
Before the meeting ends, each person should know what task he or she must complete before the next meeting, if another meeting is necessary. After the group agrees on the date and time of the next meeting, the meeting ends.

Using a Flip Chart in a Meeting

One tool you may want to use in a meeting is a flip chart. A flip chart can help focus the group's attention. As people make suggestions to solve a problem, for example, you can list the suggestions on the chart. Then, when everyone has contributed, the group can use the flip chart to review the ideas, as shown in FIGURE 14-7.

ATTENDING A MEETING

You will participate in more meetings than you will lead. Attending a meeting does not mean you should let the leader do all of the work. You should be an active participant.

Hire another company
to fill in?

Use temporary employees?

Pay employees for overtime?

Close stores early?

FIGURE 14-7 You can use a flip chart to write problems and questions and possible solutions to them. **What are the advantages of using a flip chart in a meeting?**

Here is a checklist for participating in a meeting:

- ✓ Prepare for the meeting. Be familiar with any issues that will be discussed. Bring materials that you want to distribute or discuss.

- ✓ Think about new ideas that the group may want to discuss.

- ✓ Listen actively to everything that is said. Be prepared to respond to what others say. If you disagree, do so politely and with respect.

- ✓ Take notes at the meeting so that you will remember what has been discussed.

- ✓ Know what you need to do before the next meeting.

CHARACTERISTICS OF AN EFFECTIVE MEETING

Well-run meetings can be productive for all group members. Having everyone in the same room to discuss a topic can save a great deal of time and can allow people to build on each other's ideas. Use the following checklist to evaluate meetings that you attend:

- ✓ An agenda is prepared before the meeting.

- ✓ The meeting time and place is announced.

- ✓ The meeting begins and ends on time.

- ✓ The leader keeps track of the time allotted for each issue and for the entire meeting.

- ✓ Participants present their information or opinions and listen to one another.

- ✓ At certain points in the meeting, the leader summarizes what has been discussed or decided.

- ✓ The meeting ends with a summary of what has occurred.

A good meeting does not just happen. It comes about through the combined efforts of the leader and the participants.

Lesson Review

CHECK YOUR UNDERSTANDING

1. EXPLAINING What are the responsibilities of a meeting leader?

2. SUMMARIZING What can a meeting leader do to make sure that a meeting will be productive? What can meeting participants do?

APPLY WHAT YOU LEARN

Suppose you are the assistant manager of a restaurant. Your staff has not been keeping the restaurant clean, and staff members disagree about whose responsibility this is. Plan a meeting, decide who should come to this meeting, and write an agenda for it.

Good preparation makes meetings run more smoothly. **What are some things you can do to prepare for meetings you might attend?**

Tech Connection

Many software programs can create slides, handouts, overheads, and other visuals for a presentation. You can also use these programs to create animation and music to accompany a presentation.

There are two easy ways to use this software. One is to use a presentation **template**, or already-created pattern for making documents. Just type your own information into each designed page. You find these templates in most presentation software by opening the software and clicking on Template, and then Presentations. You are given a series of choices, such as Marketing Plan or Company Meeting. When you click on one choice, you can replace the copy with information of your own.

Another easy way to use presentation software is to choose the AutoContent Wizard. This part of the software asks a series of questions. Your answers tell the computer how to create a series of pages (or slides or transparencies). You can find this option by opening the software, then clicking on the AutoContent Wizard. The AutoContent Wizard will ask you questions that will help you create visual aids for your presentation.

You can also create slides using Presentation Designs. You reach this by clicking File, New, and then Presentation Designs. This allows you to build your presentation slide by slide, choosing among the different types of slides that appear on the screen. You have several options for displaying your visual aids. You can print them as handouts, or you can create a file, put it on a floppy disk, and take it to a print shop to have copies made.

Application

Use software to create slides for a presentation on a topic of your choice. Use eitherAutoContent Wizard or one of the presentation templates for your work.

REVIEW

Chapter Summary

Presentations are similar to speeches, but they require different materials. Presentations include visual aids that demonstrate or illustrate information. Other support materials, such as handouts and recorded sound, can also be used. An effective presentation depends on thorough preparation. This includes organizing the materials and practicing the presentation. Meetings are another frequent occurrence on the job. Like presentations, leading or participating in an effective meeting requires organization and preparation.

Key Words

visual aids
transparencies
overhead projector
flip chart
portrait

landscape
storyboard
agenda
parliamentary
    procedure
template

On a separate sheet of paper, copy the sentences below. Fill in the blanks with one of these terms.

1. A(n) ____ is a large pad of paper on which the speaker lists key points.

2. A(n) ____ is a machine that shows transparencies on a wall or screen.

3. A(n) ____ is a series of sketches that show the slides you plan to use in your presentation.

4. Horizontal, or ____, view is often used to create slides because it is easy to read.

5. A(n) ____ is a written summary that explains what will happen during a meeting.

6. ____ are slides, photographs, or other visuals that help an audience understand a speaker's main points.

7. ____ is the official order for meetings that is followed by many governments.

8. When you use a(n) ____, you use an already-created pattern for making documents.

9. ____ are pictures, graphs, diagrams, or other visuals that are projected onto a wall or screen.

10. The vertical, or ____, view is the normal layout of a printed page.

Application: Organize a Presentation

You have been asked to give a presentation to your class about your favorite activity. List the steps you would take to write and present your information. Include the following information on the topic of your presentation:

1. The purpose of your presentation

2. What support materials you will use, and why

3. How you will gather information for your presentation

4. How you will organize your information

5. How you will prepare your visual aids or other types of aids

6. What handouts you will prepare

Application: Analyze Presentation Handouts

Look carefully at the handouts shown on page 329. Then answer the questions that follow them.

APEX

The Apex Corporation

New Employee Information
Security: Getting an ID Tag

1. Go to the Security Office in Room 213.

2. Set up a photo appointment.

4. Pick up your finished ID tag at the Security Office in Room 13.

Remembr: you must have your ID tag to get into the building.

Taste of Italy Pizza

- Centerville's pizza shop
- Large selection of topings

  Free delivery
- Full menu of popular italian specialtees
- Special orders no problm

  Come on in!

  Open daily

---

1 What is the purpose of each handout?

2 Who is the audience?

3 What information is missing?

Grammar Workshop Practice

On a separate sheet of paper, rewrite the sentences, correcting the errors.

Part I. Use the correct plural form of the underlined word.

1. Working with <u>child</u> can be very rewarding.

2. <u>Man</u> and <u>woman</u> must be treated equally in the workplace.

3. Monica gave the leftover <u>loaf</u> of bread to the bakery workers.

4. Both <u>company</u> made important scientific <u>discovery</u>.

5. My three <u>brother-in-law</u> all work in construction.

Part II. Use the proofreading marks on page 322 to help you revise.

6. why Sharon late forthe meeting? asked Janice.

7. The corect closing fora business is letter yours sincerely

8. A pro posal is what you right when you have An idea to solve problem a

9. I ever missed da deadline said Mrs. Martinez.

10. MR. Covello said your presen tation wa very informative Joana

Portfolio Project — Writing and Giving a Presentation

Plan and prepare a presentation for school or a company you would like to work for. To do this:

- Gather the material you will need and organize it carefully.

- Create visual aids and handouts to help your audience understand your ideas.

- Write note cards or an outline that you can use as you speak.

- Give your presentation for a few friends, and get their feedback.

- Revise your presentation and give it to the class.

Add a copy of your completed presentation to your portfolio.

CAREER FILE

EXPLORING CAREERS

Read the following information about two careers in which people use writing skills. Think about the goals and skills the jobs require. Then, answer the questions below.

Dental Assistant: *Health Services*

If you want to work in health services and you enjoy helping people, you might consider a career as a dental assistant. Dental assistants help dentists treat and examine patients. They prepare instruments for sterilization and hand them to the dentist, take and process X-rays, and guide patients in oral health care. Dental assistants also perform various administrative and clerical duties, such as sending bills, making appointments, and ordering supplies.

A dental assistant should

- have a background in anatomy and physiology.
- have strong communication skills.

Minimum Education: High-school graduate
Starting Salary: $14,700 per year
Related Careers: Medical Assistant, Occupational Therapy Assistant

For more information, contact the American Dental Assistants Association, 203 North LaSalle Avenue, Suite 1320, Chicago, IL 60611-1225. You will find this association on the Internet at members.aol.com/adaa1/index.html.

Teacher Aide: *Instructional Services*

If you enjoy working with children and would like to work in a classroom environment, you might consider a career as a teacher aide. Teacher aides assist teachers by helping students with their schoolwork, monitoring children on the playground and at lunch, and helping to prepare materials for classroom lessons.

A teacher aide should

- have experience working with children.
- be able to follow directions.
- possess patience and creativity.

Minimum Education: High-school graduate
Starting Salary: $11,000 per year
Related Careers: Child-Care Worker, Librarian Technician

For more information, contact the American Federation of Teachers, Organizing Department, 555 New Jersey Ave. NW, Washington, DC 20001. You will find this association on the Internet at www.aft.org.

1. **Suppose you work as a dental assistant. You are asked to give a speech about your work at a local high school. How might you organize your speech?**

2. **Why might it be important for a teacher aide to be able to make an effective presentation? What tips might you give to help an aide give such a presentation?**

HANDBOOK

Reading Strategies

Using Reading Strategies

Although you may not know it, you may already be using reading strategies. Here's an example: You pick up a magazine and look at the cover. A headline catches your eye, so you turn to the article. You look at a photograph and read the caption underneath it. After you read the article, you think about whether you agree with the article or whether you learned something. You have just used a reading strategy.

A reading strategy is a plan that helps you to understand what you read in school, on the job, and in your life. They help you link what you are reading to what you already know. In addition, they help you remember what you have read.

Prereading

When you preread, you think about what you already know about the topic, and you predict what you might learn in your reading.

During prereading, you should

- think about why you are reading.

- preview to get an idea of the topic of the selection.

- identify key terms.

- think about how this information relates to what you already know.

Preview the Selection

Here are some steps for previewing a reading selection:

- *Look at the title and subheadings.* These elements signal important ideas and usually hint at text organization.

- *Look at the other graphics.* These elements include words within the text in italic or bold type, which may be vocabulary words or new concepts.

You should also look at photos, captions, diagrams, maps, and illustrations for clues about the topic.

- *Read the first and last paragraphs.* These paragraphs often contain the thesis or major points of the selection.

- *Read the first sentence or topic sentence of each paragraph.* Often, the main point of a paragraph is found at the beginning.

- *Get an idea of how the selection is organized.* If you know how a selection is organized— for example, chronologically or in cause-and-effect order—you will be able to follow the writer's ideas more easily.

During and Just-After Reading

The purpose of during and just-after reading activities is to think about what you are reading and to "discuss" your ideas with the author.

During reading, you should

- check your understanding of the selection.

- define new words.

- think about how each paragraph connects to the selection's main point.

Just after reading, you should

- relate what you read to what you already know.

- review and correct your predictions of what you thought you would learn.

Read the Selection

Here are some steps for during- and after-reading activities:

- *Think about why you are reading.* A person who is reading for pleasure reads differently from a person who is reading for information. Knowing why you are reading is critical to your reading success.

- *"Talk back" to the text.* As you read, stop to check your understanding. Read the first paragraph, then review the main point of the paragraph and predict what you will read next. As you continue to read, look for topic sentences and the details that support them.

- *Use text clues.* Readings often contain clues about meaning, such as headings, graphics, photographs, and words in bold or italic type. Use these to expand your knowledge of the topic. Reading headings, for example, can give you an outline of the selection.

- *Monitor comprehension.* As you read, check that you understand the writer's ideas. If you are not sure about a meaning, reread the sentences before and after the part you do not understand or reread the entire paragraph.

Take Notes

Taking notes after reading helps you remember what you have read. Here are some guidelines for taking useful notes:

- *Choose what you will write.* Write only the most important ideas in your reading.

- *Write the main points.* This process will help you understand the writer's arguments.

- *Write the supporting details.* The supporting details back up the main point. Noting details helps you remember the writer's reasoning.

Postreading

The final step for successful reading is reviewing. When you review, you think about what you have read and respond to the writer's ideas. Postreading activities help you remember what you have read.

During postreading, you should

- connect what you have read to what you already know.

- adjust your previewing techniques for future readings.

- form an opinion about what you have read.

Here are some steps for postreading activities:

Write a Summary

When you write a summary, follow these guidelines:

- *Keep the reading and any notes you have taken nearby.* Refer to the reading and to your notes when necessary.

- *Review your notes on the major points and supporting details.* This review will refresh your memory of the writer's ideas.

- *Divide the writing into manageable sections.* Summarize the reading in parts to be sure you cover all of the details.

- *Think of your summary as a draft.* Do not worry if you express your ideas exactly right. You can revise later.

- *Do not repeat the writer's words.* If you use your own words, you will be more likely to remember what you have learned because you will have thought about it, not just copied it.

Try Some Other Postreading Activities

Here are some additional postreading suggestions:

- *Create a graphic organizer.* Making a graphic organizer can help you reorganize your notes to show text organization. See pages 76–77 for examples.

- *Tell someone what you learned.* One of the best ways to make sure you understand an idea is to explain it to someone else. Work with another student or co-worker to summarize readings.

- *Review your predictions.* When you preview, you make predictions about what you will read. After reading, think about what you expected to read. How did what you learned differ from what you expected to learn? Predicting improves with practice. As you learn to analyze clues, your predictions will become more accurate.

- *Solve a problem; create a diagram.* Some readings may lend themselves to a different type of review than a summary. For example, a process described in a manual may be more effectively reviewed by drawing a diagram. Vary your postreading activities to suit the reading.

Six Reading Strategies

Here are the steps to follow to use six popular reading strategies:

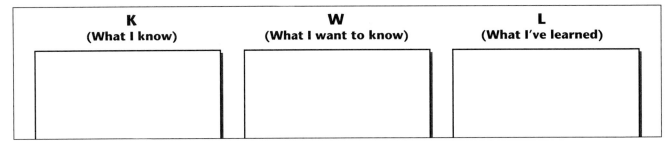

K (What I know)	W (What I want to know)	L (What I've learned)

KWL Plus

KWL Plus stands for **K**now——**W**ant to Know—**L**earned. This strategy can help you use what you know to learn more about a topic.

Step 1. Write what you already know about the topic in the *K* column.

Step 2. Write what you want to know about the topic in the *W* column. Then, read the selection.

Step 3. Write what you have learned about the topic in the *L* column.

Step 4. Use your chart to help you write a summary of what you have learned. This is the "plus" part of the strategy.

Outlining

Writing an **outline** can help you to both find the main points of a selection and create a study guide.

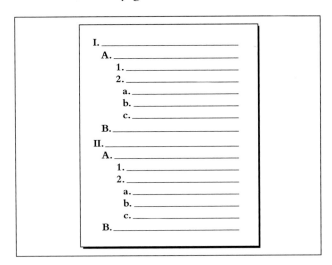

Step 1. Preview the selection to get an idea of what the author is telling you. Notice how the selection is organized.

Step 2. Read the selection, and then make an *outline*.

Step 3. List main points on the Roman-numeral lines and details below each one on the letter and number lines.

PLAN

PLAN stands for **P**redict, **L**ocate, **A**dd, and **N**ote. This strategy helps you to predict what you will read and then make notes about what you have learned.

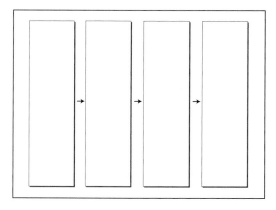 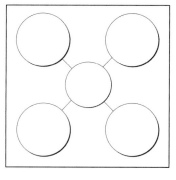 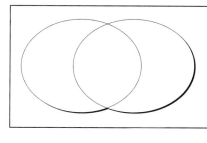

Step 1. Preview to *predict* what you will learn, and then draw a word map with your predictions.

Step 2. Locate information you will look for as you read. Add check marks next to subjects you know about and question marks next to subjects you do not know about.

Step 3. Read the selection. Then, *add* supporting information to your map after you read.

Step 4. Note what you have learned by writing a summary.

Cornell Note-taking

The **Cornell Note-taking** strategy helps you identify the major ideas and supporting details in a selection.

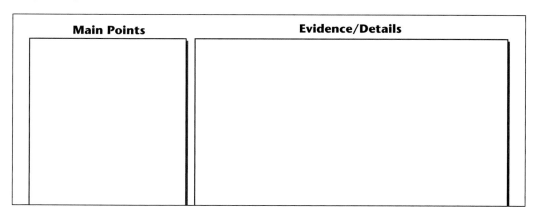

Main Points	Evidence/Details

Step 1. Preview what you will read. Read the title, subheadings, first and last paragraphs, and topic sentences.

Step 2. Read the selection carefully. Then, note the main points in the Main Points column and the supporting details in the Evidence/Details column of your Cornell chart.

Step 3. Use your outline to help you write a summary of what you have read.

Step 4. Review what you have learned. In the review step, you test yourself to be sure you understand—and remember—what you have read.

Concept Building

With the **Concept Building** strategy, you make sure you understand one concept before you move on to a new concept.

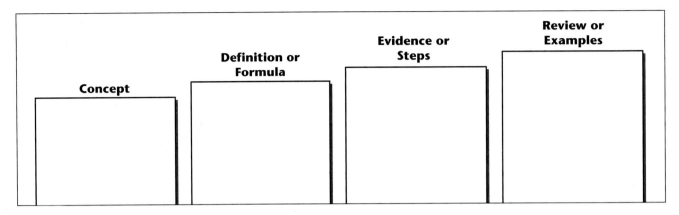

Step 1. Preview to find the main concept. Look for words in bold or italic type, information in a box, or an illustration. Write the concept in the Concept box.

Step 2. Read the selection carefully. Then, write a definition or explanation of the concept in the Definition or Formula column.

Step 3. Write the evidence for the concept or the steps needed to perform a calculation or process in the Evidence or Steps column.

Step 4. Review what you have learned. Write this information in the Review or Examples column.

SQ3R

SQ3R stands for **S**urvey, **Q**uestion, **R**ead, **R**etell, **R**eview in this strategy.

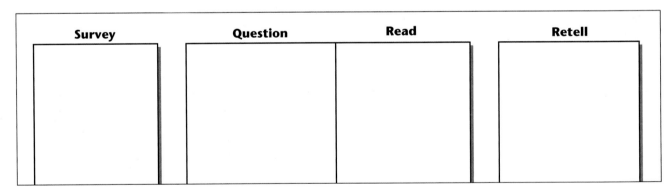

Step 1. Survey, or preview, to get an idea of what you will read. Write your thoughts in the Survey box.

Step 2. Write *questions* about the selection in the Question box.

Step 3. Read the selection, then write what you learned about the topic in the Read box.

Step 4. Retell what you have learned by writing a summary in the Retell box.

Step 5. Review what you have learned by discussing the reading with a classmate or testing yourself to see if you can answer from memory the questions you asked in *Step 2.*

WRITING STRATEGIES

The Writing Process

What happens when a writer turns words into a story or an essay? He or she follows a set of steps from start to finish. These steps make up the writing process. If you follow the same steps, you can make the writing process work for you.

What is a Process?

A process is a series of steps that lead to a goal. Each step brings the process closer to the goal. Suppose you wanted to grow a pepper plant in a pot. Growing a plant is a process. You choose seeds, plant them, water the plants, and pull

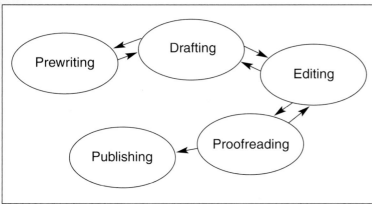

weeds. Each step gets you closer to your goal, and finally you pick the peppers.

What is the Writing Process?

There are five main steps in the writing process. They are prewriting, drafting, editing, proofreading, and publishing. You won't always follow the steps from the beginning to the end; you may move back and forth between stages.

Prewriting

In prewriting, you decide what to write. This step is like deciding what seeds to grow.

You explore your ideas. You decide on your audience and your purpose. Then, you gather information and organize it in a way that will help your audience understand it.

Drafting

In drafting, you put your ideas into words. You shape your words into sentences. You build your sentences into paragraphs. As you draft, you do not have to worry about parts that are not quite right. You will fix them in the next stage.

Editing

When you edit, you improve your draft. You look for weak spots, such as a word or a sentence that is not quite right. You make changes, or revisions, to strengthen those spots. Notice that the arrows in the drafting and editing sections can lead you back and forth. This part of the process is like watering and weeding in the growing process.

Proofreading

When you are satisfied that you have presented your ideas clearly, you turn to proofreading. In this step, you check for and correct any errors you may have made in grammar, usage, mechanics, and spelling.

Publishing

Finally, in the publishing stage, you make a final copy of your work, and you publish it or share it with an audience.

Strategies for Organizing Your Writing

During the prewriting stage of the writing process, you determine your purpose, your audience, and your topic. Once you have that information, you gather evidence that supports your topic. You collect facts, examples, and reasons that suit your purpose: to inform, to explain, to describe, or to persuade.

Your next task is to organize the information you have gathered. Planning your organization makes drafting much easier. Such planning allows you to concentrate on presenting your ideas clearly, not on deciding what to write next.

There are many methods for organizing information. Before you choose one method, however, you should think about your purpose. Should your readers understand how two products are different? Should they see how one event caused another event? What connections should your readers see between your ideas?

Here are several graphic organizers that you can use to plan how to present your ideas:

Main Ideas and Details

• Do I want my readers to focus on one main idea?

• Do I have at least three details to support that idea?

If you have answered yes to these questions, you might choose one of these two graphic organizers to plan your writing. An idea web is most useful when you have one main idea to present. A main-idea-and-details chart is most useful when you have more than one main idea to present.

To use an idea web

Step 1. Draw a central oval, as shown here. Write your main idea inside this oval.

Step 2. Draw additional ovals and connect them to the central oval. Write your details inside these ovals.

Step 3. Add as many surrounding ovals as you need to fit your research.

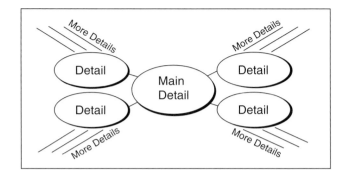

Step 4. If you have additional details to add, draw lines to the ovals, and write your information on these lines.

To use a main-idea-and-details chart

Step 1. Draw two boxes like the ones shown here. The left box should be about one-third as wide as the right box.

Step 2. Write your first main idea at the top of the left box.

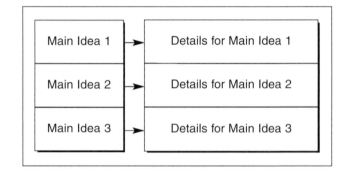

Step 3. Write the details that support it at the top of the right box.

Step 4. Continue writing your main ideas in the left box and their supporting details in the right box.

Comparison and Contrast

• Do I want my readers to compare two ideas or things?

• Do I have details that show how these ideas or things are similar?

• Do I have details that show how these ideas or things are different?

If you have answered yes to these questions, you might use a Venn diagram to plan your writing.

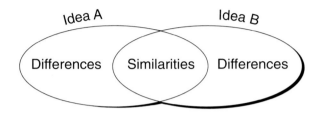

To use a Venn diagram

Step 1. Draw two intersecting ovals, as shown here.

Step 2. Write the similarities between the two ideas or things in the overlapping section of the ovals.

Step 3. Write the differences between the two ideas or things in the outer sections of the ovals.

Cause and Effect

- Do I want my readers to understand how events are related to one another?

- Do I have details that show how one event caused another event?

- Do I have details that show how this new event caused still another event?

- If I am showing a chain of causes and effects, do I understand how each effect influenced the next event?

If you have answered yes to these questions, you might use a sequence chart to plan your writing.

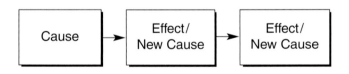

To use a sequence chart

Step 1. Draw a series of boxes and arrows, as shown here.

Step 2. Write the first event, or cause, that you would like to describe in the first box.

Step 3. Write the effect of this event in the second box.

Step 4. If you are showing a series of causes and effects, write the effect of this second event in the third box. You can add as many boxes as you need.

Chronological Order

- Do I want my readers to understand the order in which events occurred?

- Do I have dates that make the order of events clear?

- Do I have details about what happened on those dates?

If you have answered yes to these questions, you might use a timeline to plan your writing.

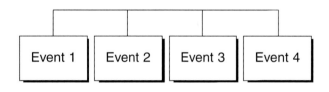

To use a timeline

Step 1. Draw a series of boxes attached to a central line, as shown here.

Step 2. Write the first event, its date, and the details that explain it in the first box.

Step 3. Write the second event, its date, and the details that explain it in the second box.

Step 4. Continue adding as many boxes as you need to your timeline.

For more information on methods of organizing your information, reread Lesson 4-5 on pages 76–79 and Lesson 8-3 on pages 154–156.

Editing Questionnaire

Once you have finished writing your draft, you need to edit your work. Use this questionnaire to guide you as you revise.

Purpose

1. What is my purpose for writing? (to inform, to explain, to describe, or to persuade)

2. What clue words or phrases do I use to show my purpose for writing?

Audience

3. Who will read my writing?

4. What does my audience know about my topic?

5. What background information do my readers need in order to understand my ideas?

6. Which technical terms should I use, or which ones should I define?

Topic

7. What is my topic?

8. What do I want my readers to learn about my topic?

Organization

9. What method(s) of organization did I choose to present my information?

10. Why did I choose this method(s) of organization?

Unity

11. How do my topic sentences support my topic?

12. What details do I use to support my topic sentences?

Coherence

13. Are all of my ideas presented clearly?

14. What transition words do I use to be sure my writing flows smoothly?

15. How do I introduce my topic?

16. How do I conclude my draft?

For more information on editing, reread Lesson 5-2 on pages 91–94.

Strategies for Proofreading Your Writing

When you edit your draft, you make sure that you have achieved your purpose: to inform, to explain, to describe, or to persuade. You also check that you have used the vocabulary, tone, and details that you need to reach your audience.

The next step in the writing process is proofreading. When you proofread, you fine-tune your work. You look for areas that might confuse your readers. Here are a few things to check when you proofread:

Transition Words

When you use transition words, you help your readers follow your arguments. You show them how your ideas are connected. You check that your sentences and paragraphs flow smoothly from one to the next.

Here are some transition words that you might use to help your readers understand how your thoughts are linked:

- *Time: later, soon, then, next, today, at, before, during, at the same time, finally*

  Example: Jeff ate lunch; *then,* he went back to work. *Before* he went home, he watered his plants. *Then* he ate dinner and walked his dog. *Finally,* he went to bed.

- *Added information: in addition, besides, also, too, next, moreover, as well as*

  Example: Catarina was moving, so she packed her clothes. *In addition,* she packed her dishes, *as well as* her pots and pans. *Next,* she packed her towels. She *also* packed her silverware and her dishes.

- *Contrast: but, yet, on the other hand, however, although, otherwise, in contrast*

  Example: Mark and Diane disagreed. Mark thought that their proposal was fine; *however,* Diane thought that it needed work. *Although* Mark agreed, he didn't think that the changes Diane suggested were worth their time. *In contrast,* Diane thought that they should check their figures once more. *Otherwise,* she thought, they might risk losing their client's account.

- *Examples: one, another, for example, for instance, such as, along with*

  Example: Sam had many reasons for not going to soccer practice. *For example,* he needed to make a trip to the store. His mother had asked him to buy food, *such as* milk, rolls, and hamburger meat. *Along with* shopping, she had also asked him to be home early to start dinner for the family.

- *Show results: as a result, consequently, therefore, thus, finally, last*

  Example: Jane won her division's sales award. *As a result,* she received a bonus and a promotion. *Consequently,* she was able to buy a new car.

Parallel Construction

Like transition words, parallel grammatical forms can also help your readers see the connections between your ideas. When you use parallel constructions in your writing, you repeat structures.

Here are some examples of parallel constructions in writing:

- *Nouns:* Mina registered for *English, algebra,* and *biology.*

- *Verbs:* Sam *oiled* the motor, *replaced* a worn fan belt, and *rotated* the tires.

- *Phrases:* Keisha likes *playing soccer, listening to music,* and *talking with her friends.*

- *Clauses: After he finished his homework, after he washed the dishes,* and *after he cleaned his room,* Eldon decided that it was time to take a nap.

Run-on Sentences

A run-on sentence strings together two or more sentences without using a linking word or punctuation to connect them. When readers see a run-on sentence, they may lose track of what the sentence is about, or they may become confused about how the writer's ideas relate to one another.

You can fix run-on sentences in these ways:

Run-on sentence: They were best friends they did everything together.

- Use an end punctuation mark to separate the sentences.

  Revision: They were best friends. They did everything together.

- Use a comma and a connecting word (*and, but, for, nor, or, so, yet*) to combine the sentences.

  Revision: They were best friends, *so* they did everything together.

- Use a semicolon to separate complete thoughts.

  Revision: They were best friends; they did everything together.

Dangling Modifiers

Dangling modifiers make the links between your ideas unclear. They leave your readers wondering *who* is doing an action or what is being done.

Here is an example of a sentence with a dangling modifier and how that sentence could be revised:

- *Dangling modifier: Not being able to find the answer on her own,* Anna's teacher showed her the steps to solving the problem. [*Who* was not able to find the answer?]

- *Revision:* Anna's teacher showed her the steps to solving the problem because Anna was not able to find the answer on her own. [It is clear that Anna was not able to find the answer to the problem.]

Redundancies

Every word you use should count. Each one should help your readers to understand your ideas. Redundancies are words or phrases that are repeated unnecessarily. Eliminating them will help your writing flow more smoothly. Here are some sample redundancies and an example of a sentence with redundancies and its revision:

- *Redundancies: actual fact, alternative choice, could possibly, future plan, I myself, many in number, may possibly, plan of action, reason is because, reason why, sum total*

- *Sentence with redundancies:* Our problems are *many in number,* but I *myself* think that I *may possibly* have a *plan of action* to solve them.

- *Revision:* We have many problems, but I think that I may have a plan to solve them.

Appropriate Language

To help your readers understand your ideas, you must use language that is appropriate for the people and for the situation. You must think about your audience and how you might clearly communicate your message.

For example, if you are writing a letter to a friend, you might use slang or other types of informal language. However, if you are writing a memo to a supervisor, you should use formal language. You should avoid slang and instead choose your words precisely. You also should proofread your work carefully to eliminate all errors.

Here are two sentences that are written first in informal language, then in formal language:

- *Informal language:* Where're you going later? Do you want to come over?

- *Formal language:* Where are you going after work? Would you like to come to my house?

Proofreading Checklist

Proofreading Marks

Here are some of the marks writers use to correct their drafts:

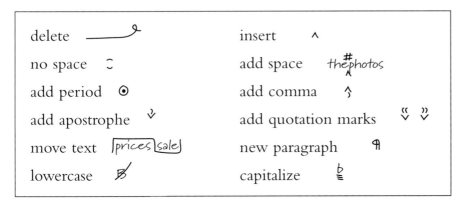

delete	insert
no space	add space *the photos*
add period	add comma
add apostrophe	add quotation marks
move text *prices sale*	new paragraph
lowercase	capitalize

Once you are confident that your writing communicates your message clearly, you need to proofread your work. Use this checklist to look for errors in your writing:

Sentence Structure
☑ Are all my sentences complete?

☑ Do my subjects and verbs agree?

☑ Do I avoid run-on sentences?

☑ Do all of my sentences flow naturally, rather than being short and choppy?

☑ Do I use parallel constructions correctly?

Word Choice
☑ Do I use easily confused words correctly, such as *there*, *they're*, and *their*?

☑ Do I use any double negatives?

☑ Do I use the correct comparative form for all of my adjectives and adverbs?

☑ Do my pronouns agree with their antecedents?

☑ Do my indefinite pronouns agree with their verbs?

Punctuation and Capitalization
☑ Do I use punctuation marks correctly?

☑ Do I use all of the possessives correctly?

☑ Do all of my sentences begin with a capital letter?

☑ Do I capitalize all proper nouns and adjectives?

Spelling
☑ Is all of my spelling correct?

☑ Am I checking my spelling against my list of common spelling errors?

For more information on proofreading, re-read Lesson 5-3 on pages 96–99.

The Modes of Writing

Persuasive Writing

Persuasive writing expresses an opinion. Effective persuasive writing shows why opinions, beliefs, or ideas are reasonable.

When you write to persuade, follow these guidelines: State your opinion on an issue. Use facts, examples, and reasons to support that opinion. Present your argument logically. Urge your readers to think differently or call them to action. End on a positive note.

As you edit your persuasive writing, check these points:

✔ Are my reasons presented convincingly?

✔ Do they support my position?

✔ Is my organization clear and consistent?

Expository Writing

Expository writing explains or informs. Effective expository writing clearly explains an idea. You might use expository writing to summarize a book or article or to explain how to do something.

When you write to explain, follow these guidelines: Use examples and facts that support your ideas. Present your ideas in a clear, organized way. Add details to make your explanation clear.

As you edit your expository writing, check these points:

✔ Does my essay explain my topic?

✔ Do I present the information clearly and logically?

✔ Does each paragraph have a well-developed idea that includes details, examples, or reasons to support my main point?

Descriptive Writing

Descriptive writing paints a picture in words. Effective descriptive writing lets the reader experience what you are describing.

When you write to describe, follow these guidelines: Close your eyes, and form a picture of your topic. Think of details that will make the scene come alive for your reader. Use vivid words.

As you edit your descriptive writing, check these points:

✔ Does my writing clearly describe something or someone?

✔ Is my organization logical?

✔ Do I use rich language and exciting details?

Narrative Writing

Narrative writing tells a story. Effective narrative writing makes the reader feel as if he or she is part of the story. You might use narrative writing to tell about an experience.

When you write a narrative, follow these guidelines: Build your story around a plot or a series of events. Describe your characters and the scene clearly and vividly.

As you edit your narrative writing, check these points:

✔ Is my writing well-organized?

✔ Does it have a clear order of events with a beginning, a middle, and an end?

✔ Do my ideas flow smoothly?

The Parts of a Paragraph

A **paragraph** is a group of sentences that develop an idea.

> Automated teller machines (ATMs) have changed the way people bank. The first ATM was made in 1978. Before that, people cashed checks or made deposits in the bank in which they had an account. They could get cash only during regular banking hours. ATMs have made banking easier for most people. People can now do their banking at any time of the day.

A **topic sentence** is the sentence that tells the main idea or topic of a paragraph.

> Automated teller machines (ATMs) have changed the way people bank. The first ATM was made in 1978. Before that, people cashed checks or made deposits in the bank in which they had an account. They could get cash only during regular banking hours. ATMs have made banking easier for most people. People can now do their banking at any time of the day.

The main part of the paragraph is called the **body**.

> Automated teller machines (ATMs) have changed the way people bank. The first ATM was made in 1978. Before that, people cashed checks or made deposits in the bank in which they had an account. They could get cash only during regular banking hours. ATMs have made banking easier for most people. People can now do their banking at any time of the day.

Supporting details are pieces of information that explain the topic.

> Automated teller machines (ATMs) have changed the way people bank. The first ATM was made in 1978. Before that, people cashed checks or made deposits in the bank in which they had an account. They could get cash only during regular banking hours. ATMs have made banking easier for most people. People can now do their banking at any time of the day.

A **transitional word or phrase** shows the relationship between ideas or sentences.

> Automated teller machines (ATMs) have changed the way people bank. The first ATM was made in 1978. Before that, people cashed checks or made deposits in the bank in which they had an account. They could get cash only during regular banking hours. ATMs have made banking easier for most people. People can now do their banking at any time of the day.

A **concluding sentence** restates the topic or main idea of the paragraph.

> Automated teller machines (ATMs) have changed the way people bank. The first ATM was made in 1978. Before that, people cashed checks or made deposits in the bank in which they had an account. They could get cash only during regular banking hours. ATMs have made banking easier for most people. People can now do their banking at any time of the day.

Grammar and Mechanics

Sentence Elements

Sentences

A **complete sentence** is a group of words that expresses a complete thought.

> Oscar wanted to work as a long-distance trucker.
>
> ABC Drilling requires workers to wear safety goggles and gloves.

A **compound sentence** contains two or more independent clauses.

> Zina worked longer hours, but Rico produced the most work.
>
> Orson loaded the truck, and Ulysses delivered the order.

A **complex sentence** contains one or more independent clauses and one or more dependent clauses.

> Until we started working together on the project [dependent clause],
> I never knew how smart Allyson was [independent clause].
>
> Miyako balanced the company checkbook [independent clause]
> before the week was over [dependent clause].

Subjects

A **subject** tells what or whom the sentence is about.

> *Luis* went to vocational school for computer-repair classes.
>
> *Computer repair* classes are available to every student.

A **simple subject** is the key word in a complete subject.

> The younger *lawyer* took on a losing case.
>
> The enthusiastic *manager* gave every employee a chance to succeed.

A **complete subject** includes the subject and all the words that tell about it.

> *The younger lawyer* took on a losing case.
>
> *The enthusiastic manager* gave every employee a chance to succeed.

A **compound subject** contains two or more simple subjects.

> *Ken and Steve* opened an oil-change garage next to our store.
>
> *Drafting, editing, and publishing* are three steps in the writing process.

Predicates

A **predicate** tells what the subject is doing or what is happening to the subject.

> The new sales force *sold computers in large numbers.*
>
> The top-selling dog food is *packaged in both four-pound and ten-pound sizes.*

A **simple predicate** is the key verb in a complete predicate.

Once Again Clothes rarely *offers* new clothes for sale.

The cafeteria *is* on the third floor.

A **complete predicate** includes the verb and all words that tell about it.

Once Again Clothes *rarely offers new clothes for sale.*

The cafeteria *is on the third floor.*

A **compound predicate** contains two or more simple predicates.

Washerama *washes, waxes, and buffs* cars for its customers.

Tito *started* a new job and *was fired* on the same day.

Clauses

A **clause** is a group of words that contains a subject and a verb.

Nicole moved from shipping to accounting.

Whenever Mr. Pangbourn calls, the president answers. [Both parts of the sentence are clauses.]

An **independent clause** can stand alone as a sentence because it expresses a complete thought.

Lorraine took a spreadsheet course.

Kyle answered the phone at Penny's desk.

A **dependent clause** cannot stand alone as a sentence, because it does not express a complete thought.

Because Mrs. Boris told him to stock the shelves [What happened?]

Whenever you can get here [What will happen?]

If you finish typing the memo first [What will happen?]

Phrases

A **phrase** is a group of words that does not contain a subject and a predicate. It cannot stand alone.

typed very quickly [no subject]

the skilled doctor [no predicate]

Subject–Verb Agreement

A **subject** and **verb** agree when both are either singular or plural.

One *architect designs* the buildings, while another *one draws* the plans.

Six *nurses work* in the emergency room.

Use a **singular verb** with a compound subject that is joined by *either* and *or* or *neither* and *nor*.

Either Diego *or* Maria is going to the benefits meeting.

Neither Barbara *nor* Patricia was able to attend the conference.

Use a **plural verb** in a sentence with a compound subject.

Inez and Veronica start work today.

Dogs and cats are used in some types of physical therapy.

When one **subject** is **singular** and the other is **plural**, use a verb that agrees with the subject that is closer to the verb.

> Yuko and the *plumbers plan* to work on the holiday.
> The plumbers or *Yuko plans* to work on the holiday.

When a **phrase** comes between the **subject** and **verb**, check agreement by looking only at the subject and verb.

> Dental *assistants* who work in small offices *have* a wide range of duties.
> *Go!*, one of the new sports magazines, *appeals* to wide audiences.

Pronoun-Antecedent Agreement

A **pronoun** and its **antecedent agree** when both are either singular or plural.
> *Kathy* injured *her* back while loading the truck.
> *Bob and Jerry* are starting *their* own business.

A **pronoun** and its **antecedent agree** when both have the same gender.
> *Inez* was happy with *her* résumé.
> I asked *William* when *he* was expecting *his* package to arrive.

A **pronoun** and its **antecedent agree** when both have the same person.
> I am going to take *my* car to the ballgame.
> *You* are walking as if *your* feet hurt.
> A *pronoun* must agree with *its* antecedent.

The Parts of Speech

Nouns

Nouns are words that name a person, place, thing, event, or idea.

Dolores, city, machine, vacation, party, success

Forms of Nouns

Common nouns are words that name any person, place, thing, event, or idea.

plumber, store, computer, holiday, independence

Proper nouns are words that name a specific person, place, thing, event, or idea. Proper nouns are always capitalized.

Sam Sachs, SavOn Foods, PowerComputer, Labor Day

Compound nouns are groups of words that name a person, place, thing, event, or idea. Some compound nouns have hyphens between the words. Some are formed by combining two words into one.

doctor-in-charge, Fort Dix, fast food, holiday sale, fade-out, sawmill, cookbook

Singular nouns name one person, place, thing, event, or idea.

engineer, office, briefcase, interview, democracy

Plural nouns name more than one person, place, thing, event, or idea. Most plurals are made by adding *-s* to the noun.

employees, kitchens, desks, parades, freedoms

Collective nouns name a group of people, things, or animals that act as a unit.

team, audience, herd, news, stationery

Some nouns have **irregular plurals**.
- To form the plural of nouns that end in *-s, -ch, -z, –sh,* or *-x*, add *-es* .

bosses, lunches, fizzes, flashes, boxes

- To form the plural of most nouns that end in *-y*, drop the *-y* and add *-ies*.

companies, discoveries, duties

Here are some common irregular plurals:

SINGULAR	PLURAL	SINGULAR	PLURAL
child	*children*	*man*	*men*
woman	*women*	*mouse*	*mice*
foot	*feet*	*fungus*	*fungi*
half	*halves*	*datum*	*data*
loaf	*loaves*	*knife*	*knives*
tooth	*teeth*	*millennium*	*millennia*
bagful	*bagsful*	*brother-in-law*	*brothers-in-law*

Pronouns

Pronouns are words that take the place of one or more nouns.

I, me, we, us, mine, ours

Forms of Pronouns

Personal pronouns identify the speaker, the person spoken to, or the person or thing spoken about.

SUBJECT PRONOUNS		OBJECT PRONOUNS	
Singular	**Plural**	**Singular**	**Plural**
I	*we*	*me*	*us*
you	*you*	*you*	*you*
he	*they*	*him*	*them*
she	*they*	*her*	*them*
it	*they*	*it*	*them*

Kevin works for Davis Plumbing Company. *He* [Kevin] earns a good salary.

We called the carpenters working on our house. We want *them* [the carpenters] to work next Wednesday.

Nick installs carpeting. *It* [the carpeting] is heavy and hard to handle.

An **antecedent** is the person or thing that the pronoun refers to or stands for.

Luca works harder when *he* [Luca] knows the boss is watching.

Martha told Tom that *she* [Martha] would work for *him* [Tom] next week.

A **possessive pronoun** shows ownership or relationship.

	SINGULAR	**PLURAL**
First Person	*my, mine*	*our, ours*
Second Person	*your, yours*	*your, yours*
Third Person	*his, her, hers, its*	*their, theirs*

That was *my* suggestion for the ad campaign.

The sales report says that *your* sales program was very successful.

Larry's team won the basketball game; success was *theirs*.

Indefinite pronouns refer to people or things in general.

SINGULAR	*another, anybody, anyone, anything, each, either, every, everybody, everyone, everything, neither, nobody, no one, nothing, one, somebody, someone, something*

PLURAL   *both, few, many, others, several*

SINGULAR OR PLURAL   *all, any, more, most, none, some*

Anyone concerned about the bad weather may leave work early.

Nobody knows how to fix the canning machine.

Several worked together so they could *all* attend the conference.

Ms. Barrett wondered if *some* employees were attending the presentation.

Relative pronouns connect a noun or pronoun with a group of words that tell more about it.

who, whom, whose, that, which

He is the lawyer *who* won my father's case.

The people to *whom* the letters were sent have interviews next week.

Sending a large mailing requires a machine *that* folds and stamps letters.

Verbs and Verb Forms

A **verb** expresses action or a state of being.

run, think, improve, cut, is, were, feel

Forms of Verbs

An **action verb** expresses physical or mental action.

The electrician *connects* wires to a fuse box.

Chang *filed* the papers in alphabetical order.

A **linking verb** expresses a state of being or a condition.

appear, be, become, grow, look, remain, seem, smell, sound, taste

Friday *is* our last day at work.

Mr. Harvey *seems* pleased with Juanita's work.

A **compound verb** is two or more verbs in one sentence.

Harry *types, files,* and *sorts* the mail for his department.

The new bakery *looks* and *smells* wonderful.

A **simple predicate** is the main verb or verb phrase in a sentence.

Mark *requested* repair work for his delivery truck.

Ace Auto Repair *has been fixing* trucks for Mark's company since 1982.

Voice

In the **active voice**, the subject performs the action in the sentence.

> Angela *designs* logos for small companies.

> Chef Duval *creates* delicious desserts every night.

In the **passive voice**, the subject receives the action in the sentence.

> The logo *was designed* for our company by Angela.

> These delicious desserts *are created* by Chef Duval.

Verb Tense

Verb tense shows the reader the time of the action or the state of being that is being described in the sentence.

> *work, worked, working*

> *is, are, was, were*

An action or state of being that is happening now is shown by the **present tense**.

> Greg *studies* so that he can become a computer programmer.

> He *seems* to be skilled at creating software.

An action or state of being that has already taken place is in the **past tense**. Past tense is most commonly formed by adding *-d* or *-ed* to the verb.

> Greg *studied* to become a computer programmer.

> Even when he was in high school, he *seemed* to be skilled at creating software.

An action or state of being that will take place at a later time is in **future tense**. To form the future tense, use *shall* or *will* before the verb.

> Greg *will study* computer programming in high school.

> He *will be* even more skilled at creating software when he finishes his training.

An **irregular verb** does not form its past by adding *-d* or *-ed*.
Here is a list of common irregular verbs and their main forms:

PRESENT	PAST	PAST PARTICIPLE
bring	*brought*	*brought*
come	*came*	*come*
do	*did*	*done*
eat	*ate*	*eaten*
go	*went*	*gone*
know	*knew*	*known*

see	saw	seen
speak	spoke	spoken
take	took	taken
write	wrote	written

The company president *came* to our department meeting.

He *spoke* about being loyal to the company.

Mrs. Whitaker *began* Karen's review at 2:00 P.M.

Direct and Indirect Objects

A **direct object** receives the action of the verb.

The secretary filed the *papers*.

An **indirect object** is often used with verbs of telling, asking, and receiving. It answers the questions *to what* or *to whom*.

Enthusiastic teachers give their *students* inspiration and motivation.

Transitive and Intransitive Verbs

A **transitive verb** shows action and is always followed by a direct object that receives the action and completes the meaning of the verb.

The company directors *passed* a dress code for work.

An **intransitive verb** shows an action does not need a direct object to complete it.

The police sergeant *leaped* out of the way of the speeding car.

Modifiers

Adjectives

An **adjective** is a word that describes, or modifies, a noun or a pronoun. Adjectives answer the questions *what kind*, *how many*, and *which one*.

Clever Dora found a *quick* shortcut for filing contracts.

All the credit for the project was given to *humble, modest* me.

The clerk wrapped *ten* handbags for the *wealthy* customer.

A **positive adjective** does not compare objects.

The *red* roses are *beautiful*.

A **comparative adjective** compares two people, places, things, events, or ideas. The most common way to form a comparative adjective is to add *-er*. Another way to make a comparative is to add the word *more* before the adjective.

> Dr. Finch has *steadier* hands than Dr. Abbott.

> Susan is *more dependable* than Marie.

A **superlative adjective** compares three or more people, places, things, events, or ideas. The most common way to form a superlative adjective is to add *-est*. Another way to make a superlative is to add the word *most* before the adjective.

> Of all the company's salespeople, Bonita Graves's figures are the *highest*.

> Lisa is the *most talented* of the six graphic artists at the ad agency.

Articles are a special group of adjectives. *A* and *an* are indefinite articles; they do not refer to a specific person or thing, event, or idea. *The* is a definite article; it refers to a specific person, place, thing, event, or idea.

> *A* memo about *the* meeting was sent to every committee member.

> *An* answer to *the* question seemed impossible to find.

Adverbs

An **adverb** modifies, or tells more about, a verb, verb phrase, adjective, or another adverb. Adverbs show time, place, manner, and degree by answering the questions *when, where, how, how often,* and *to what extent.*

Time adverbs tell *when, how often,* and *how long.*

> *yesterday, today, tomorrow, daily, weekly, monthly, yearly, briefly, quickly*

Place adverbs tell *where, to where,* and *from where.*

> *here, there, everywhere, nearby, backward, forward*

Manner adverbs tell *how.*

> *specifically, precisely, smoothly, roughly, carefully*

Degree adverbs tell *how much* or *how little.*

> *greatly, entirely, partly, mostly, nearly, completely, really, too*

> Zoe waited until the customer *completely* finished speaking before she answered him.

> With the power off, the assembly line *slowly* ground to a halt.

A **positive adverb** does not compare objects.

> Marie does her job *well.*

A **comparative adverb** compares two persons, places, things, or ideas. The most common way to form a comparative adverb is by adding *-er*. Another way is to add the word *more* to the adverb.

> This copier is fast, but the new one is *faster*.

> The illustrator drew the diagram *more precisely* than the engineer.

A **superlative adverb** compares three or more persons, places, things, or ideas. The most common way to form the superlative is by adding *-est*. Another way is to add the word *most* to the adverb.

> The four employees arrived early, but Jaime arrived *earliest*.

> Franco, Sonia, and Wendell grumbled when they lost their jobs, but Clark complained *most strongly*.

A **negative** is an adverb or adverb phrase that means *no*.

> Childcare attendants *never* forget to get a phone number in case of an emergency.

> Leave *no* machinery running during the lunch break.

Conjunctions

A **conjunction** is a word that joins words, phrases, and clauses.

> It was a dark *and* stormy night for interstate truckers.

> Managers try to treat each employee separately *but* equally.

A **coordinating conjunction** connects words, phrases, and clauses that have the same grammatical structure.

> *and, but, yet, so*

> Coaching soccer *and* teaching geography keep Mr. Ostlund busy.

> Sharon listened, *but* she did not hear the machine finish its cycle.

Correlative conjunctions are used in pairs to join words or groups of words.

> *either/or   neither/nor   not only/but also   both/and   whether/or*

> *Not only* the accounting department, *but also* the shipping department got an award.

> *Either* Harry will get the job, *or* Malcolm will.

> *Both* Cassie *and* Quentin applied for a gardener's job at Rose World.

A **subordinating conjunction** shows the relationship between two clauses.

after, although, as, because, before, if, since, though, unless, until, when, while

Nigel has been acting foreman *since* Abel went on sick leave.

Judy will become supervisor *when* a position opens.

Orlando's Bakery will be closed *until* the new ovens are installed.

Interjections

An **interjection** shows strong emotion or surprise.

Oh no! The entire batch of potato chips is ruined.

Help! I can't get this schedule to work.

Prepositions

A **preposition** is a word or group of words that shows the relationship between a noun or pronoun and another word in the sentence.

at, about, after, against, along, around, before, behind, below, between, beyond, by, down, except, for, from, in, inside, into, near, of, off, on, opposite, out, over, past, through, to, toward, under, until, unto, up, upon, with, within, without

The shop is *under* new management.

Store the new laser paper *on* the shelves *behind* the printer.

E-mail saved *for* longer than a month will be erased *by* computer services.

A **prepositional phrase** includes a preposition, the object of the preposition, and the words that modify the object.

Ed trained Lupe for the assistant sales position *after her annual review.*

Katya took the job *with Ames Tech Service,* which is located *opposite the bank.*

Punctuation

Periods

A **period** is used to end a sentence that makes a statement (declarative) or that gives a command or makes a request (imperative).

Statement: Harold Peters runs his own plumbing business.

Command: Sort the mail, John.

Request: Please pay attention to the safety rules in the plant.

A **period** is used after an initial in a name or an abbreviation.

Name: John D. Rockefeller created an oil company.

Abbreviation: Sen. Robert Williams is a lawyer.

A **periods** is used as a decimal point in numbers or money.

Numbers: According to the newspaper, 4.5 out of 10 employees enjoy their job.

Money: Kathryn deposited $7,255.90 in the company's payroll account.

Question Marks

A **question mark** is used to end an interrogative sentence, or a sentence that asks a question.

Do you want the job?

Where will the meeting be held?

Put a **question mark** inside quotation marks when a quote asks a question.

"Did anyone call this morning?" Mr. Theobold asked his secretary.

The electrician asked the customer, "Did you know that the fuse box shorted out?"

Put a **question mark** outside the quotation marks when an entire statement is a question.

Will the union march with signs saying, "Down with Allied Auto"?

Where is my tape of "The Star Spangled Banner"?

Exclamation Points

An **exclamation point** is used to end an exclamatory sentence.

I don't believe it*!*

That's a terrific report*!*

Put an **exclamation point** inside quotation marks when the quoted material is an exclamation.

> While the rest of the employees complained about the snow, Ryan shouted, "Now I can go skiing*!*"

Put an **exclamation point** outside quotation marks when an entire sentence is exclamatory.

> I'll be overjoyed if she says, "You did a great job"*!*

Commas

A **comma** is used between two independent clauses that are joined by a coordinating conjunction, such as *and, or, but, nor, for, yet,* and *so.*

> Aziz would have gone to the game, *but* he had to work that night.

> Orion wants to be a lawyer, *and* Suzi plans to go to medical school.

A **comma** is used to separate the day and the year in a date. When a date is not at the end of a sentence, add another comma to separate the year from the rest of the sentence.

> Lydia's first job started April 1, *1996.*

> April 15, *1998,* was the date on which Alan was promoted to office manager.

Use a **comma** between the city and state in a sentence or in an address. If the city and state do not come at the end of the sentence, add a comma after the state name.

> Franklin Tool and Die has plants in Springfield, *Missouri,* and Peoria, *Illinois.*

> San Diego, *California,* has dozens of great seafood restaurants.

A **comma** is used to separate adjectives that equally modify the same noun. To check if the adjectives are equal in power, shift their order or insert the word *and* between the adjectives. If your sentence still makes sense, put a comma between the modifiers.

> Being an emergency room nurse is a *difficult, demanding* job.

> *Short, current* business news can be heard on KBIZ.

Commas are used to separate individual words, phrases, or clauses in a series. A series must have three or more items.

> *Words:* Three vegetables Lucia refuses to serve are *peas, carrots, and broccoli.*

> *Phrases:* Diego drove his boss *to City Hall, to a computer store, and to the airport.*

> Clauses: *Sandra has a desk in a cubicle, her supervisor has a small office, and her manager has a larger one.*

Use a **comma** after the greeting in a friendly letter.

> Dear Manny,

> Dear Mr. Zimmerman,

Use a **comma** after the closing in a letter.

Yours truly,

Sincerely,

A **comma** is used to separate the words of a quotation from the speaker. Put a comma inside quotation marks if the speaker's name appears after the quotation. If the speaker's name appears before the quote, put a comma before the quotation.

Speaker's name after the quote: "I didn't break the copier," Allyson cried.

Speaker's name before the quote: Her manager said, "I saw you do it."

Commas are used in a series of numerals to separate hundreds from thousands, thousands from millions, and so on.

Separating hundreds from thousands: More than *25,000* people developed black lung disease while working as coal miners.

Separating thousands from millions: Vijay won *$1,255,950* in his first year as a tennis professional.

Semicolons

Semicolons join two or more independent clauses that are not connected with a conjunction.

Helen sobbed when she lost her job; it was the third time this year that she had lost a job.

Rotoway's stock went up to 67.5 points; that's a record high for the company.

Use a **semicolon** before a conjunctive adverb when the word connects two independent clauses.

Diego sold 20 cars this month; however, Ismail was chosen salesperson of the month.

Semicolons can separate items in a series if the items have commas within them.

Nora planned a business trip to *Rome, Italy; Paris, France; London, England; and Berlin, Germany.*

Vlad's photography was filled with *vivid, dramatic reds; quiet, watery blues; and clear, delicate greens.*

Semicolons can separate independent clauses that are long or contain commas.

Christie ran down the stairs to the subway; but before she could get on, she realized she had left the Bigelow contract at home.

Colons

A **colon** is used after the greeting of a business letter.

Dear Sir:

Dear Mrs. Manero:

A **colon** is used between the hour and minutes when telling time.

The meeting is at *9:30* sharp.

A **colon** is used after an independent clause to introduce a list.

The supplies order included the following items: printer paper, highlighters, and black pens.

A **colon** is used between a title and subtitle or a volume and a page in literature.

Title and subtitle: Joan of Arc: Her Story

Volume and page: Encyclopaedia Britannica D:155

A **colon** can introduce a sentence, a question, or a quotation.

It was Benjamin Franklin who said: *"Remember that time is money."*

Quotation Marks

Quotation marks are used to set off direct speech.

"I'd like to come for an interview," said Jack.

Andrew said, "All three McAdams brothers are engineers."

Quotation marks enclose titles of songs, poems, short stories, lectures, episodes of radio and television programs, chapters of books, magazine and newspaper articles, and encyclopedia entries.

Song: "America, the Beautiful"

Poem: "Fog" by Carl Sandburg

Short story: "The Lottery" by Shirley Jackson

Television program: "Iceland: Fire and Ice"

When using a quotation within a quotation, the outside **quotation marks** are double, but the inside **quotation marks** are single.

"Now, I'll sing, 'When I Fall In Love,'" said the Broadway star.

Apostrophes

An **apostrophe** is used to show possession.

Sydney's harbor is a major seaport.

The *fisherman's* catch was sold to *Neptune's* Kitchen restaurant.

That is *Joan's* office.

To make the possessive form of a noun or indefinite pronoun, add an **apostrophe** and *-s*.

Mr. *Himmel's* plan was to train all of the employees in small groups.

Shapes's first shift produced more sweaters than the other two shifts combined.

Nobody's dog can perform that trick.

Use an **apostrophe** to show that letters have been left out of a word, as in a contraction.

are not ⟶ *aren't*   could not ⟶ *couldn't*   do not ⟶ *don't*

it is ⟶ *it's*   would not ⟶ *wouldn't*   you are ⟶ *you're*

Italics/Underlining

Italics is a printer's word for slanted type. You can create italics on a computer. When you write by hand, use an underline. Use italics or underlining for titles of long works, such as books, movies, television programs, or plays.

	ITALICS	UNDERLINING
Book:	*The Joy of Cooking*	<u>The Joy of Cooking</u>
Movie:	*Toy Story*	<u>Toy Story</u>
Television program:	*60 Minutes*	<u>60 Minutes</u>
Play:	*Hamlet*	<u>Hamlet</u>

Hyphens

A **hyphen** is used to join the parts of a compound word.

great-grandmother

father-in-law

on-the-job training

A **hyphen** joins a capital letter to a noun or participle.

U-turn

T-shirt

Y-connector

X-raying

A **hyphen** joins the parts of compound numbers from twenty-one to ninety-nine.

> Draper's Textiles celebrated its *thirty-fourth* week.

> *Twenty-six* new salespeople were needed to handle the holiday rush.

A **hyphen** joins the parts of a fraction.

> Karen lives *one-half* hour from her job.

> Matt handled *two-thirds* of the patients, while Dr. Ames handled *one-third*.

Hyphens are used when two or more words have a common element that is omitted.

> Carole teaches *first-, second-,* and *third-*grade math.

Hyphens divide words at the end of lines of printed material. There are several rules for hyphenating words:

- Do not divide one-syllable words, such as *growth, cried,* or *thought.*

- Do not divide short words of five or fewer letters, such as *April, hello,* or *never.*

- Do not separate a one-letter syllable from the rest of the word. Write *ident-ify,* not *i-dentify.*

- Do not divide contractions. Write *doesn't,* not *does-n't.*

- Do not hyphenate large numbers, such as *2,500,000.*

- Do not hyphenate the last word in a paragraph.

Dashes

Dashes are used to show a sharp turn in the thought of a sentence or to enclose explanations or examples. Like colons, dashes can also introduce a list.

> *To show a sharp turn in thought:* We thought—*but you knew this*—that the painting was a forgery.

> *To enclose an explanation:* The other painting—*that one over there*—is the real masterpiece.

> *To introduce a list:* Those were the paintings I mentioned—*a van Gogh, a Cassatt, and a Monet.*

Parentheses

Parentheses are used to enclose material that interrupts the flow of a sentence.

> Mrs. Westman *(the owner of Tasty Treats bakery)* taught Donna how to bake muffins.

Put end punctuation inside **parentheses** when the enclosed material is a separate, complete sentence.

> Mrs. Walker welcomed the new employee. *(She always welcomes everyone.)*

Put end punctuation outside **parentheses** when the enclosed material is a part of the main sentence.

Ali groomed and fed Molly at Sparkles *(her dog-grooming salon).*

Brackets

Brackets are used to enclose material that is added into a quotation.

"It *[the baseball game]* isn't over until it's over."

Use **brackets** around words you add to explain what a writer is saying.

We were told that they *[the factory workers]* planned to go on strike next week.

Ellipses

An **ellipsis** is a series of three periods (. . .) that show that one or more words are missing from a quotation. The plural of *ellipsis* is *ellipses.*

The company's creed was . . . place the customer first.

Use an **ellipsis** to indicate a pause.

The best thing about her job was . . . the friends she made at work.

When an **ellipsis** is used at the end of a sentence, add another period to show that the sentence is finished.

In one speech, Hamlet says, "To be or not to be. . . ."

Capitalization

Use a **capital letter** to begin each of the following. Do not capitalize articles and short prepositions, such as *for*, *the* and *in*, unless they are used as the first word in a title.

Days of the week:	*Monday, Tuesday*
Months of the year:	*April, July*
Holidays:	*Thanksgiving, Hanukkah*
Events in history:	*World War I, the Renaissance*
Titles of books or plays:	*Othello, For Whom the Bell Tolls*
Titles of artworks:	*Waterlilies*
Titles of songs, poems, and operas:	*Born in the U.S.A., The Mending Wall, Aida*
Official documents:	*Constitution of the United States, Treaty of Versailles*
Political parties:	*Republican party, Communist party*
Proper names:	*Jane, Rudy, Mr. Winters*
Relatives:	*Aunt Joan, Mom* (Capitalize *aunt* and *mom* only when they are used as names; do not capitalize *my aunt Joan* or *my mom*.)
Companies/ trade names:	*Bigelow carpets, Buick Regal*
Proper adjectives:	*French toast, English muffins*
Planets:	*Jupiter, Mars*
Continents:	*Asia, Australia*
Countries:	*Japan, Ireland, Mozambique*
Oceans, seas, and lakes:	*Indian Ocean, Mediterranean Sea, Lake Huron*
Rivers:	*Nile, Mississippi*
Cities, town, villages:	*Albany, Chester Heights, Shanghai*
States, provinces:	*North Dakota, Alberta*
Streets:	*Alcan Highway, Route 17A, Elm Street*

Use a **capital letter** for the personal pronoun *I*.

Never have *I* been so tired as when we set up the trade-show display.

Use a **capital letter** to begin a sentence.

*T*he computer software is difficult to learn.

Use a **capital letter** for greetings and closings in letters.

*D*ear Mr. Grace:

*S*incerely,

Numbers

Numbers of ten or fewer are usually spelled out. Use Arabic numerals for numbers 11 and above.

Maya had *two* dogs and *three* cats.

By the time Mozart was *16*, he was already a well-known composer.

There were *384* students enrolled in James's school.

If a **number** begins a sentence, it is always spelled out.

Twelve hundred people were in the audience.

Three hundred eight-four students were enrolled in James's school.

Combine **numbers** and words when the numbers are very large.

The estimate for a new arena was *$45 million*.

Use **numerals** in addresses, money, percentages, phone numbers, times, dates, and ZIP codes.

The show will open on *May 12, 2001*, in the theater at *425* Broadway.

During the snowstorm, *25 percent* more people took the subway.

Always use **numerals** when you write decimals. If a whole number is not used, place a zero before the decimal point.

0.75   *5.1264*

Use **numerals** to show units of measurement.

25 feet   *325 kilometers*

Add a comma in **numbers** that have four or more places. Count from the right, and use a comma after every three places.

1,342   *1,945,612*

552,771,005 *3,045,691,013*

In **numbers** between 101 and 999, do not use the word *and* between the word *hundred* and the number that follows it.

Say, "two hundred ten," not, "two hundred *and* ten."

Commonly Confused Words

accept/except

Accept means "to agree to take or receive something." *Example* Maria planned to *accept* the job offer.

Except means "other than, or to leave out." *Example* Rebecca processed all the orders *except* one.

adapt/adopt

Adapt means "to adjust or change to fit." *Example* Jack will *adapt* to the new practice schedule. He will catch the later bus home.

Adopt means "to choose and treat as your own." *Example* The company will *adopt* new work rules.

advice/advise

Advice is a noun meaning "information or recommendation." *Example* Tom's supervisor gave him some good *advice* about a course on copier technology.

Advise is a verb meaning "to recommend a course of action." *Example* Please *advise* me on how to finish my work on time.

affect/effect

Affect means "to influence"; it is usually used as a noun. *Example* How will the new bus route *affect* the time you leave for work?

Effect means "a change, or the result of an action"; it is usually used as a verb. *Example* Which trends will have an *effect* on Allied's sales results?

aid/aide

Aid, when used as a verb, means "to help." *Example* Joan plans to *aid* the new employee in doing his work.

Aid, when used as a noun, means "the help that is given." *Example* Your *aid* is needed to sort the canned goods for the food drive.

An *aide* is a person who acts as an assistant. *Example* Linda is pleased to have Sam as her *aide* in preparing the software manual.

a lot/alot

a lot (two words) means "a great deal." This phrase is not specific; a more precise word is a better choice. *Example* Ed's garage uses *a lot* of motor oil every day. *More precise example* Ed's garage uses ten cases of motor oil every day.

Alot is **not** one word.

all ready/already

All ready is a phrase that means "prepared." *Example* I am *all ready* to take over the new job.

Already means "previously." *Example* Katie has *already* gone home.

all right/alright

All right is a phrase that may mean "satisfactory, unhurt, or correct." *Example* Your cover letter seems *all right*, although I think you should sound more eager to get the job.

Alright is **not** one word.

altogether/all together

    Altogether means "entirely." *Example* You are asking for *altogether* too many vacation days.

    The phrase *all together* means "in a group or all at once." *Example* The team worked *all together* to complete the project.

among/between

    Among refers to more than two persons, places, or things. *Example* Doug divided the task *among* the members of his team: Phyllis, Linda, and Jeff.

    Between refers to two persons, places, or things. *Example* I have to choose *between* going to the conference and working in the office.

annual/biannual/semiannual/perennial

    Annual means "happening once every year." *Example* The committee is planning the company's *annual* picnic. As usual, it will be held in mid-June.

    Biannual and *semiannual* both mean "happening twice a year." *Example* The warehouse takes a *biannual* (or *semiannual*) inventory. By counting the stock twice a year, the company doesn't fill up with unsold goods.

    Perennial means "lasting or active throughout the year." *Example* The offices are decorated with *perennial* plants. They do not fade in the winter.

bad/badly

    Bad means "not good." Use *bad* after linking words such as *feel, look,* and *seem. Example* Ellen felt *bad* that she could not finish the landscaping job on time. However, the plants were not in stock.

    Badly means "in a harmful or incorrect way." *Example* Jason performed *badly* on the typing test, because he was not sure he was qualified for the job.

beside/besides

    Beside means "by the side of." *Example* John stood *beside* the president of MCR Marketing in the photograph.

    Besides means "in addition to." *Example Besides* working part-time as a salesperson, Lisa also works as a dress designer.

brake/break

    A *brake* is a device used to stop a vehicle. *Example* When he saw the traffic, Luis used the *brake* to slow the truck.

    Break means "to destroy." *Example* The glass may *break* if you drop it.

bring/take

    Bring suggests that the action is directed toward the speaker. *Example Bring* the package to me.

    Take suggests that the action is directed away from the speaker. *Example Take* this package to the mail room.

can/may

    Can, when used as a verb, means "being able to do something." *Example* I *can* type 60 words per minute.

    May, when used as a verb, means "having permission to do something." *Example May* I leave for lunch now?

capital/capitol

Capital, when used as a noun, refers to the city that is the official seat of government. *Example* The Apex Mining Company is located in Charleston, the *capital* of West Virginia.

Capital, when used as an adjective, means "major or important." *Example* You have made a *capital* suggestion. I think it may double our production figures.

The noun *capitol* refers to a building where the federal or state lawmakers meet. *Example* The U.S. Congress meets in the *Capitol* building.

cent/sent/scent

A *cent* is a U.S. coin. *Example* I found one *cent* lying on the sidewalk.

Sent is the past tense of the verb *send.* *Example* Janice *sent* the directions to Anita yesterday.

A *scent* is an odor or a smell. *Example* The *scent* of Grandma's spaghetti sauce always makes us hungry.

coarse/course

Coarse means "rough or harsh." *Example* The carpenter used the *coarse* sandpaper to smooth the wood.

Course means "onward movement or a course of study." *Example* In my business *course,* I learned how to create a spreadsheet.

complement/compliment

Complement means "to complete or to go well with." *Example* Dan's bright blue tie *complements* his navy jacket.

A *compliment* is an expression of admiration or praise. *Example* Doreen gave Wendy a *compliment* for doing such a good job on the report.

core/corps

Core means "at the heart of." *Example* The team members arrived at the *core* issue of the meeting: a plan for solving the production problems.

A *corps* is a group or a team. *Example* The *corps* of researchers is analyzing the benefits of a balanced diet.

council/counsel

A *council* is a group of people who give advice. *Example* The town *council* suggested repairing Main Street.

To *counsel* means "to give advice." *Example* Ms. Baynes *counselled* her students to study for the algebra test.

farther/further

Farther refers to a physical distance. *Example* How much farther must we go?

Further refers to additional time, quantity, or degree. *Example* Jason will do *further* editing on the document. It is not yet finished.

fewer/less

Fewer refers to numbers of separate items that can be counted. *Example Fewer* than twenty people attended the meeting.

Less refers to the amount or quantity of something as a whole.
Example Our business made *less* money this year than last year.

good/well

Good means "having positive qualities"; it is used after linking verbs such as *is*, *taste*, and *feel*. *Example* She has done *good* work in every job she has held.

Well, when used as an adverb, means "properly or correctly." *Example* How *well* do you know the procedure for performing CPR?

Well, when used as an adjective, indicates a state of health. *Example* Marcy feels *well* now that her headache has gone away.

healthful/healthy

Healthful means "causing or improving health." *Example* A *healthful* diet is one that has lots of fruits and vegetables.

Healthy means "not sick." *Example* During the flu outbreak, there were few *healthy* employees.

it's/its

It's is the contraction of *it is*. *Example It's* difficult to reach a decision.

Its is the possessive form of *it*. *Example* The tree lost *its* leaves.

later, latter

Later means "after a period of time." *Example* He will go home *later* in the afternoon.

Latter refers to the second of two things mentioned. *Example* Of hard work and honesty, the *latter* is more important.

lay/lie

Lay means "to place in a resting position." *Example* When making a presentation, *lay* a sheet of paper on top of the projector to cover the points you have not discussed.

Lie, when used as a verb, can mean "to recline or put oneself in a resting position." *Example* Kurt will *lie* down for an hour before he goes to basketball practice.

Lie, when used as a noun or a verb, can also mean "to state something that is not true." *Example* Telling a *lie* to a customer may make a sale, but you risk losing all future business.

like/as

Both *like* and *as* show comparisons, but *like* is used with phrases and *as* is usually used with clauses. *Examples* Brian said that he felt *like* the president of the company. Brian felt *as* if he were the president of the company.

loose/lose/loss

Loose means "free, untied, or unrestricted." *Example* While the building was being constructed, the supports came *loose,* and the wall fell.

Lose means "to misplace or fail to find." *Example* Marjorie left her books in her locker so she would not *lose* them in the gym.

Loss means "something that is lost." *Example* The tumbling price of its stock caused the company a great *loss* of income.

personal/personnel

Personal means "private." *Example* I marked the memo as *personal* so that it would not be distributed to the entire department.

Personnel are people who work at a particular job. *Example* The *personnel* that Allied hired were needed to staff the new shipping department.

principal/principle

Principal, when used as an adjective, means "primary." *Example* Our *principal* goal is to make the best products available.

Principal, when used as a noun, may mean "the most important person or head official, or a sum of money." *Examples* The *principal* of our school has recommended several students as interns for Cadwell's Advertising. Manny needs to pay more of the *principal* on his bank loan.

Principle means "a basic truth or a standard of behavior." *Example* Mrs. Uhura taught the *principles* of geometry.

sight/cite/site

Sight means "the act of seeing or something that is seen." *Example* Elizabeth thought that staring at the computer all day hurt her *sight.*

Cite means "to quote or to summon." *Example* In her letter, Karen plans to *cite* a section of the contract that proves her point.

Site means "a location or position." *Example* Our company will move to a new *site* that is closer to midtown.

stationary/stationery

Stationary means "not movable." *Example* The new copier is *stationary.* I can't move it an inch.

Stationery refers to the paper and envelopes used to write letters. *Example* The company's logo is on all of its *stationery.*

than/then

Than is a conjunction that connects two parts of a comparison. *Example* Jane likes apples better *than* she likes pears.

Then is an adverb that usually refers to time. *Example* Ilsa will finish the report; *then,* she will go home.

that/which

Both words, when used as pronouns, add information to a sentence. *That* is used to add essential details to a sentence, so it does not need a comma. *Example* I have a jacket *that* I wear everywhere because it's very comfortable.

Which is used to add details that are not essential, so it takes a comma to set off the information. *Example* My jacket, *which* I wear everywhere, is very comfortable.

their/there/they're

Their is a possessive pronoun that means "belonging to them." *Example* *Their* office has both a copier and a scanner.

There means "in that place." *Example* Place the notice *there* so people will see it easily.

They're is the contraction of *they are. Example* I can't disturb Monica and Lisa now; *they're* in class.

to/too/two

To is a preposition that means "in the direction of." *Example* Lila will go *to* the track meet tomorrow.

To can also be used as an infinitive. (Infinitives are phrases that include the base form of a verb, plus *to*; they are used as nouns, adjectives, or adverbs.) *Example* Jim wants *to* eat lunch early today.

Too means "also or very." *Example* It is *too* hot to jog today.

Two is the number 2. *Example* Every contract needs *two* signatures for approval.

weather/whether

Weather refers to the condition of the atmosphere. *Example* If the *weather* is bad, schools will be closed.

Whether refers to a possibility. *Example Whether* we close the school is up to the principal.

who/which/that

Who refers to people. *Example Who* left the green paper in the printer?

Which refers to nonliving objects or to animals, not to people. *Example Which* printer should be delivered to the business office?

That refers to animals or nonliving objects. *Example That* is the announcement that I have been expecting.

who/whom

Who is used as the subject of a verb. If you can replace *who* with *he* or *she*, you are using *who* correctly. *Example Who* is responsible for the mess in the mail room?

Whom is used as the object of a preposition or as a direct object. If you can replace *whom* with *him* or *her*, you are using *whom* correctly. *Example* To *whom* should I send this letter?

who's/whose

Who's is the contraction of *who is. Example Who's* the person in charge of hiring?

Whose is the possessive pronoun that means "belonging to whom." *Example: Whose* tools are on the floor?

your/you're

Your means "belonging to you." *Example* I really appreciate *your* assistance on this project.

You're is the contraction of *you are. Example You're* the person who will take Gloria's place.

Commonly Misspelled Words

A

abbreviate
absolute
accede
accelerate
accommodate
accomplish
account
accurate
achieve
acknowledge
acquire
actual
advertisement
affect
aisle
analyze
annual
anonymous
anticipate
anxiety
anxious
apologize
appearance
application
appreciate
appropriate
article
artificial
assistance
associate
athlete
attitude
audience
authority
available
average
awkward

B

bargain
basis
beautiful
behavior
beneficial
benefit
brief
brochure
budget
bulletin
bureau

C

capacity
cashier
catalog
catastrophe
census
century
certificate
circular
circumstance
column
commercial
commitment
communicate
community
competent
competition
compromise
confidence
congratulate
conscience
conscious
consequence
considerably
consistent
constitution
continue
controversy
convenience
convince
cooperate
correspond
courage
courteous
crisis
criticize
curious
curriculum

D

declaration
decorate
defense
definite
dependent
design
desperate
dictionary
difficulty
discipline
dissatisfied
distinguish
distribute
doubt
duplicate

E

eagerly
economy
edition
efficiency
eighth
either
elaborate
eligible
eliminate
emphasize
encourage
enormous
enthusiastic
entirely
envelope
environment
equipment
equivalent
especially
essential
evidence
exaggerate
excellent
except
exercise
existence
expensive
experience
extinct
extraordinary
extremely

F

facilities
familiar
famous
fascinate
favorite
feature
February
foreign
forfeit
fortunate
forty
forward
fountain
fourth
fragile
frantically
friend
fulfill

G

gauge
generally
generous
genius
genuine
geography
glorious
government
gracious
gratitude
grocery
gruesome
guarantee
guess
guidance

H

hesitate
honor
horrible
hospital
humorous
hygiene

I

identical
illegible
illustrate
imagine
immediately
immigrant
impatient
importance
individual
inevitable
influential
initial
inquiry
interpret
interrupt
interview
investigate
invitation
island
itinerary

J

janitor
jealous
jewelry
journal
journey
judgment
justice

K

know
knowledge

L

laboratory
language
league
legal
legible
leisure
liable
library
license
listen
literature

M

machine
magazine
magnificent
maintain
majority
management
manual
material
maximum
measure
merchandise
miniature
minimum
miscellaneous
misspell
moisture
monotonous
municipal
muscle
mysterious

N

necessary
negotiate
neighborhood
nevertheless
nickel
niece
ninety
noticeable
nuclear
nuisance

O

obstacle
occasion
occupant
occur
offense
official
often
opinion
opponent
opportunity
opposite
optimism
ordinarily
original
outrageous

P

pamphlet
paragraph
parallel
parenthesis (singular)
parentheses (plural)
partial
participate
patience

peculiar
perceive
permanent
perseverance
persevere
persistent
persuade
phase
phenomenon
philosophy
physician
piece
plausible
pneumonia
politician
possess
precede
precious
precision
preference
premium
preparation
presence
previous
priority
privilege
probably
procedure
professor
pronounce
propaganda
psychology
publicly
purchase
pursuit

Q

qualified
quantity

quarter
questionnaire
quite
quotient

R

realize
recipe
recognition
recommend
reference
rehearse
relevant
relieve
renewal
repetition
representative
restaurant

S

salary
satisfactory
Saturday
scene
schedule
scissors
secretary
separate
significance
similar
sincerely
sophisticated
sophomore
souvenir
specific
spontaneous
statistic
straight
strategy

strength
substantial
substitute
subtle
sufficient
superficial
superintendent
superiority
surprise
suspicious
syllable
symmetrical
sympathy
symptom

T

technique
temperament
temperature
temporary
tendency
tentative
territory
thorough
though
tomorrow
toward
treasurer
truly
Tuesday
typical
typing

U

unanimous
undoubtedly
unfortunately
unique
unnecessary

urgent
usable
usually

V

vacancies
vacuum
vague
valuable
variety
various
vehicle
visible
voluntary
volunteer

W

weather
Wednesday
whether
which
whole
width
women
worthwhile
writing
written

Y

yesterday
yield

GLOSSARY

active listening paying attention and responding to what is heard *p. 300*

adjustment letter a letter that tries to settle a claim *p. 212*

agenda a written summary that explains what will happen during a meeting *p. 323*

align to line up *p. 278*

alternatives other choices *p. 48*

appendix a section at the end of a proposal that provides supporting information *p. 231*

assess to evaluate *p. 4*

assumptions what the writer expects his or her audience to know *p. 127*

attitude a way of acting, feeling, and thinking about something *p. 12*

audience the person or people who will read another person's writing *p. 68*

bar graph a graph that uses bars to compare information *p. 182*

bias prejudice *p. 261*

block-style letter a letter in which the paragraphs are separated from each other with spaces and nothing is indented *p. 215*

body language how a person uses his or her body and voice to convey a message *p. 297*

brainstorming thinking about a wide range of ideas; this process can be done by two or more people *p. 112*

career the general course of a person's working life *p. 4*

career plan an outline of a person's career goals and of how these goals might be achieved *p. 9*

chronological order the order in which events take place; time order *p. 76*

claim letter a business letter that discusses a problem *p. 212*

cliché an overworked expression, such as "brave as a lion" and "down in the dumps" *p. 94*

clip-art a type of electronic visual that is available on computer software *p. 251*

coherence the effect created when all of the ideas in a piece of writing flow smoothly from one to another *p. 92*

company culture a mixture of the company's social and work practices *p. 45*

comparison a description of how two persons or things are alike *p. 77*

concise brief *p. 165*

connotation a feeling or association that is connected to a word *p. 134*

contrast a description of how two persons or things are different *p. 77*

copy the material to be published *p. 101*

cover letter a letter of application, often used when a person sends a résumé to an employer *p. 28*

criteria guidelines *p. 48*

customize to make specific *p. 28*

database a large collection of searchable listings that are available on a computer program *p. 152*

data table an information table *p. 183*

denotation the exact meaning of a word *p. 134*

diction word choice *p. 94*

diplomatic able to resolve conflicts *p 24*

direct mailing a sales letter sent to a specific group of people *p. 184*

directions instructions that explain a process *p. 110*

documentation factual evidence *p. 240*

draft a piece of writing that is unfinished; it is a person's first attempt to put what he or she wants to say into words *p. 86*

drafting the writing stage of the writing process *p. 66*

E-commerce business done on the Internet *p. 268*

economy how a nation produces and uses its goods and services *p. 4*

editing the stage of the writing in which a person revises or rewrites a draft to make a stronger argument *p. 66*

e-mail a communication system that uses a network to send and receive messages electronically *p. 117*

empathy to put oneself in the place of the person who has a problem *p. 220*

entrepreneur a person who sets out to create and manage a business *p.56*

entry-level basic *p. 7*

executive summary a one- or two-page summary of the main points of a report *p.154*

eye contact the act of looking listeners in their eyes as one speaks *p. 298*

feedback a response or an answer to a comment or question *p. 113*

flexible able to shift between tasks easily *p. 24*

flip chart a large pad of paper on a stand that is used to take notes at a meeting; it is large enough for all participants to see *p. 308*

focus group a panel of people selected to discuss their likes and dislikes about a product, a service, or a topic *p. 241*

font typeface *p. 169*

formal language the type of language most often used in serious books and articles; it is used in the classroom, in an interview, and on the job *p. 94*

formal report a long report that requires a great deal of research and takes planning and organizing *p. 148*

format the appearance of a finished document *p. 101*

franchise an established, brand-name business that is part of a larger chain *p. 57*

graphics visuals such as charts, graphs, illustrations, and photographs *p. 101*

guide phrases words or phrases such as *first* or *the most important point is* that can help listeners follow an argument *p. 292*

health care an industry that includes jobs such as nurses' aides, home-care workers, laboratory technicians, and hospital workers *p. 22*

hook an attention grabber, such as a thought-provoking question *p. 185*

hospitality an industry that employs workers in hotels, motels, convention centers, airports, restaurants, and theme parks; any business in which customers are treated like guests *p. 22*

implement to put into action *p. 126*

impromptu something that is not planned or prepared *p. 296*

indented-style letter a letter in which paragraphs are separated only by indented first lines *p. 215*

inflated diction words and phrases that are used to try to impress people and to make the writer sound important; it should be avoided *p. 94*

informal language language most often used in conversation with friends and family members and in general-audience magazines *p. 94*

informal report a report that focuses on a specific problem or subject, often in a single page *p. 148*

Internet a network that links computer systems around the world *p. 117*

intranet an online resource that only the employees of a company can use *p. 128*

keyword search a search used to find information on the Internet *p. 152*

landscape a page layout in which information is displayed horizontally *p. 310*

liability legal responsibility *p. 273*

logo a special symbol that represents a company *p. 274*

manual a user's guide that often comes with tools and appliances *p. 256*

manuscript text that is written by hand or on a typewriter or computer *p. 296*

marketing the search for customers and clients and the ways to earn and keep their business *p. 208*

marketing plan a strategy to attract new clients or customers *p. 209*

mass mailing a sales letter sent to a large audience *p. 184*

media newspapers, magazines, and radio and television stations *p. 176*

memorandum a short note written to convey information within a company *p. 117*

mentor a person who takes an interest in another person's career and helps to guide him or her *p. 11*

modified-block-style letter a letter in which paragraphs are separated but the first line of each paragraph is indented *p. 215*

monotone all in one tone of voice *p. 297*

networking a system of interconnected lines that transmits information; in job-hunting, it is the process in which people ask others they know for job information *p. 15*

objective fair *p. 261*

overhead projector a machine that shows transparencies on a wall or screen *p. 308*

parliamentary procedure the official order for meetings that is followed by many governments *p. 325*

passive listening listening in an uninvolved way; a person does not pay careful attention to a speaker *p. 300*

pictograph a graph that uses pictures to show information *p. 182*

podium a speaker's stand *p. 297*

portrait a page layout in which information is displayed vertically *p. 310*

position on a résumé, to direct attention to the qualities the writer wants to highlight *p. 24*

press release a one- to three-page document that announces a newsworthy event *p. 193*

prewriting the planning stage of the writing process; it occurs before drafting begins *p. 66*

primary source an original document that was written by people who participated in the events that they report *p. 151*

prioritize to put tasks in order of importance *p. 52*

proactive to take the lead *p. 52*

probation a trial period to see how a person performs *p. 52*

process a series of steps that help a person to reach his or her goal *p. 66*

productivity the amount of work that can be accomplished in a given time *p. 53*

proofreading the stage in the writing process after editing in which spelling, capitalization, and punctuation are corrected *p. 66*

proposal a formal written plan for an action to improve a situation or to solve a problem *p. 230*

prototype an original model *p. 274*

publishing the stage in the writing process in which a writer shares his or her finished document with the audience *p. 66*

purpose the reason for writing *p. 68*

quote a type of proposal that is evaluated only on price *p. 230*

redundant repeated unnecessarily *p. 136*

references people who can speak favorably about your work habits and skills *p. 26*

relevant appropriate *p. 162*

retail sales an industry that sells goods to customers in stores *p. 22*

résumé a summary of a person's work history and job qualifications *p. 24*

RFP (request for proposal); a document that asks others to submit proposals to solve a problem or to meet a need *p. 230*

return address the address of the person who is sending a letter *p. 216*

salutation a greeting *p. 215*

search engine an Internet program that looks for information on any topic *p. 152*

secondary source a document that analyzes or discusses a primary source, such as a book or an encyclopedia *p. 151*

self-esteem the way in which a person values himself or herself *p. 9*

sequence a continuous, connected series of events *p. 76*

sequential order the order in which steps take place *p. 130*

spatial order the order that shows where things are located in relation to each other *p. 77*

statistics numerical facts *p. 292*

storyboard a series of sketches that show the slides a person will use in a presentation *p. 312*

strategy statement the statement of a proposed solution *p. 236*

synopsis a brief summary of a topic *p. 154*

technical writing writing that explains how a product or a process works *p. 256*

template an already-created guide that is available in presentation software and in other kinds of software *p. 327*

testimonial a statement from people who say they have had a positive experience with a product *p. 180*

thesis statement a one-sentence summary of a topic *p. 151*

time clue words words that tell the order in which to do steps (such as *first*, *next*, and *then*) *p. 111*

tone the feeling writers convey toward their subject or audience *p. 179*

trade journal a magazine intended for people who work in a particular field or trade *p. 257*

trade-offs compromises *p. 14*

transparencies pictures, graphs, or other visuals that are projected onto a wall or screen *p. 308*

troubleshoot to look for problems *p. 128*

unity the effect created when all of the sentences in a document develop its main idea *p. 92*

vendors outside sellers of products or services *p. 244*

visual aids slides, photographs, or other visuals that illustrate a speaker's ideas *p. 308*

Web site an Internet location; it could be created by one individual, an organization, or a company *p. 15*

World Wide Web (www) a large collection of information available through the Internet; it consists of documents that are linked to each other from around the world *p. 152*

INDEX

Predicates, *8, 70, 346–347*
  in clauses, *70*
  complete, *347*
  compound, *347*
  simple, *347*
Prefixes, *207*
Prepositions, *295, 356*
Prereading, *332*
Presentations. *See also* Speeches
  adding sound to, *319–320, 321*
  computer programs for, *327*
  handouts for, *316–318*
  introduction in, *312*
  note cards for, *313*
  organizing, *311*
  outline for, *311, 314*
  parts of, *311–312*
  preparing for, *314, 319–321*
  visual aids in, *308–310, 312, 321*
Present tense, *192*
Press releases, *176, 193–196*
  checklist for writing, *196*
  defined, *193*
  example of, *194*
  five *Ws* in writing, *195*
  reporter's style and tone in, *195*
  sending, *196*
Prewriting
  choosing topic in, *71–72*
  gathering information in, *26,
    73–74, 89, 151–153*
  identifying audience in, *68–69,
    72, 76, 112, 127, 178, 244,
    260–261, 264, 287, 288*
  narrowing topic in, *71–72, 89*
  outline in, *158–160*
  purpose in, *68, 76, 112, 127, 178,
    244, 268, 289–290*
  as step in writing process, *66*
Primary source, *151*
Prioritizing tasks, *52*
Proactive, *52*
Probation, *52*
Problem–solution order, *291*
  outline for, *292*
Problem solving
  strategies in, *233–234, 236–239*
Process defined, *63, 66*
Product descriptions, *85, 105*
  drafting, *86–89*
  editing, *91–94*
  prewriting, *89*
  proofreading, *96–99*
  publishing, *101–102*
Productivity, *53*
Progress reports, *268–271*
  sample, *270*
Pronoun referents, *98*
Pronouns, *350–351*
  agreement of collective nouns with, *161*
  agreement with antecedents, *133, 348*
  agreement with indefinite, *267*
  forms of, *98*
Proofreading, *96–99, 341–342*
  checklist, *343*
  developing routine for, *96*

for grammar, *224*
for spelling, *224*
as step in writing process, *66*
for word choice, *97, 98*
Proofreading marks, *322*
Proper adjectives, *100*
Proper nouns, *98, 100*
Proposals, *228–235*
  audience in, *244*
  collecting supporting information
    for, *240–242*
  defined, *230*
  drafting, *245*
  editing, *245, 247*
  kinds of, *230–231*
  parts of, *231–232*
  prewriting, *244–245*
  proofreading, *247*
  publishing, *247*
  purpose in, *244*
  reading, *232*
  sample, *246*
  visuals in, *249–250*
  writing plan for, *244–245*
Prototype, *274*
Publishing, *101–102*
  descriptive report, *169*
  explanation of process, *132*
  proposals, *247*
  as step in writing process, *66*
Punctuation, *357–363*
  proofreading for, *97–98*
Purpose
  defined, *68*
  in organizing information, *76*
  in persuasive writing, *68, 178*
  revising for, *91*

Q
Question marks, *357*
Quotation marks, *235, 360*
Quotations
  as detail, *163*
  in press release, *195*
Quotes, *230*

R
Readers' Guide to Periodical Literature, 152
Reading
  descriptive reports, *148–149*
  directions, *110–111*
  explanation of a process, *124–126*
  persuasive writing, *177*
  strategies, *332–336*
  technical writing, *256–258*
Reasons
  as evidence, *180*
  as supporting detail, *86, 87, 89, 163*
Redundancies, *136, 170, 342*
References, in résumé, *26*
Request for proposal (RFP), *230–233*
Request letter, *204, 212, 213*
Research report, *147*
  formatting, *171*
  writing, *173*
Responsive listening, *300–301*

Résumés, *24–29*
  action verbs in, *32*
  drafting, *24–27*
  job objective in, *26*
  job skills and work habits in, *24*
  purpose of, *24*
  references in, *26*
  sample, *25*
Return address, *216*
Revising. *See also* Editing
Run-on sentences, correcting, *97, 114, 342*

S
Sales letters, *176–177*
  call to action in, *187*
  creating, *185–187*
  design of, *184–185*
  example of, *186*
  format for, *176*
  tips for, *187*
  types of, *184*
  writing, *175, 184–185, 199*
Sales reports, *148*
Salutation in business letters, *205, 215*
Screening interview, *33*
Search engines, *152, 303*
Secondary sources, *151*
Selection interviews, *33*
Self-assessment log, *4–5*
Self-confidence, building, *9–11*
Self-esteem, *9*
Semicolons, *359*
  in compound sentences, *49, 359*
  in correcting run-on sentences, *114*
Sensory details, *86, 87*
Sentence(s)
  complete, *346*
  complex, *80, 181, 346*
  compound, *49, 346*
  correcting run-on, *114*
  correcting short, choppy, *97*
  defined, *8*
  elements of, *346–348*
  fragments, *8, 97*
  proofreading, *96*
  subject-verb agreement in, *75*
Sentence outline, *160*
Sequence
  defined, *76*
  transition words for, *136*
Series, commas in, *97, 140*
Slang, *165, 235*
Slides, *309*
Sounds, in presentations, *319–320, 321*
Spatial order, *77, 91, 261*
Speeches, *284–294. See also* Presentations
  addressing audience in, *288*
  body in, *294*
  conclusion in, *294*
  dealing with interruptions in, *299*
  delivering, *296–299*
  editing, *294*
  entertaining, *289, 290*
  gestures in, *297–298*
  guide phrases in, *292*
  informative, *289, 290*
  introduction in, *292, 294*

Acknowledgments

Grateful acknowledgment is made to the following for the use of copyrighted and trademarked material:

A&E Television Networks

Biography.com screenshot. Copyright © 2000 by A&E Television Networks. Biography® Channel is a registered trademark of A&E Television Networks. Use of this trademark implies no relationship, sponsorship, endorsement, sale, or promotion on the part of Globe Fearon, Inc.

Apple Computer, Inc.

Apple Screen Shots reprinted by permission of Apple Computer, Inc. Apple® is a trademark of Apple Computer, Inc., registered in the U.S. and other countries. Use of this trademark implies no relation-ship, sponsorship, endorsement, sale, or promotion on the part of Globe Fearon, Inc.

Microsoft Corporation

Microsoft Screenshots reprinted by permission from Microsoft Corporation. Microsoft® is a registered trademark of the Microsoft Corporation. Use of this trademark implies no relationship, sponsorship, endorsement, sale, or promotion on the part of Globe Fearon, Inc. Microsoft Internet Explorer® reprinted by permission from Microsoft Corporation. Microsoft Internet Explorer® is a registered trademark of the Microsoft Corporation. Use of this trademark implies no relationship, sponsorship, endorsement, sale, or promotion on the part of Globe Fearon, Inc.

Netscape Communications Corporation

Netscape Communicator Browser Window© 1999 by Netscape Communications Corporation. Used with permission. Netscape Communications has not authorized, sponsored, endorsed, or approved this publication and is not responsible for its content.

Anne Savage

Tekmom.com screenshot. Copyright© 2000 by Anne Savage. All rights reserved.

Note: Every effort has been made to locate the copyright owner of material reprinted in this book. Omissions brought to our attention will be corrected in subsequent editions.

Grateful acknowledgment is made to the following for photography printed in this book.

Cover: Computer Keyboard: Tony Stone Images; Computer Mouse: Corbis Digital Stock; Folder: PhotoDisc, Inc.; Classroom: Photo Researchers, Inc.; People Meeting: Hewlett-Packard Company; Notebook: PhotoDisc, Inc.

Table of Contents: iii Charles Gupton, Picture Quest; iv Michael Newman, Photo Edit; v Dana White, Photo Edit; vi Michael Newman, Photo Edit; viii Spencer Grant, Photo Edit; ix Bob Daemmrich, Stock Boston; x Michael Newman, Photo Edit; xi Ronnie Kaufman, The Stock Market; xii The Stock Market Photo Agency; xiv Rachel Epstein, Photo Edit; xv Dion Oogust, The Image Works

Unit 1: pp. 2–3 David Young-Wolff, Photo Edit; p. 7 Bob Daemmrich, Stock Boston; p. 16 Steve Skjold, Photo Edit; p. 18 David Young-Wolff, Photo Edit; p. 20 Michael Newman, Photo Edit; p. 27 David Young-Wolff, Photo Edit; p. 40 Michael Newman, Photo Edit; pp. 42–43 Bonnie Kamin, Photo Edit; p. 52 Dana White, Photo Edit; p. 55 Michael Newman, Photo Edit; p. 57 Michael Newman, Photo Edit; p. 60 Bonnie Kamin, Photo Edit; p. 62 (t) Michael Newman, Photo Edit; p. 62 (b) Spencer Grant, Photo Edit

Unit 2: pp. 64–65 Michael Newman, Photo Edit; p. 74 Michael Newman, Photo Edit; p. 77 Corbis Digital Stock; p. 82 Michael Newman, Photo Edit; pp. 84–85 Myrleen Ferguson, Photo Edit; p. 101 Michael Newman, Photo Edit; p. 104 Myrleen Ferguson, Photo Edit; p. 106 (t) Myrleen Ferguson, Photo Edit; p. 106 (b) Paul Avis, Liaison

Unit 3: pp. 108 David Young-Wolff, Photo Edit; p. 117 B. Daemmrich, The Image Works; p. 120 David Young-Wolff, Photo Edit; pp. 122–123 Spencer Grant, Photo Edit; p. 135 Chris Hamilton, The Stock Market; p. 142 Spencer Grant, Photo Edit; p. 144 (t) Index Stock Imagery, Picture Quest; p. 144 (b) Jeff Greenberg, Photo Edit

Unit 4: pp. 146–147 Michael Newman, Photo Edit; p. 152 Rachel Epstein, Photo Edit; p. 155 Richard Pasley, Stock Boston; p. 172 Michael Newman, Photo Edit; pp. 174–175 David Young-Wolff, Photo Edit; p. 185 Martin Levick; p. 196 Ronnie Kaufman, The Stock Market; p. 198 David Young-Wolff, Photo Edit; p. 200 (t) Michael Newman, Photo Edit; p. 200 (b)Michael Newman, Photo Edit

Unit 5: pp. 202–203 Bill Aron, Photo Edit; p. 214 David Young-Wolff, Photo Edit; p. 220 John Feingersh, The Stock Market Photo Agency; p. 224 The Stock Market Photo Agency; p. 226 Bill Aron, Photo Edit; pp. 228–229 Spencer Grant, Photo Edit; p. 234 Michael Newman, Photo Edit; p. 239 Bachman, Photo Edit; p. 252 Spencer Grant, Photo Edit; pp. 254–255 Bill Aron, Photo Edit p. 271 David Young-Wolff, Photo Edit; p. 280 Bill Aron, Photo Edit; p. 282 (t) Michael Newman, Photo Edit; p. 282 (b) Elena Rooraid, Photo Edit

Unit 6: pp. 284-285 John Neubauer, Photo Edit; p. 294 Michael Newman, Photo Edit; p. 297 The Stock Market Photo Agency; p. 304 John Neubauer, Photo Edit; pp. 306–307 Myrleen Ferguson, Photo Edit; p. 314 Dion Oogust, The Image Works; p. 326 Charles Gupton, Picture Quest; p. 328 Myrleen Ferguson, Photo Edit; p. 330 (t) Michael Newman, Photo Edit; p. 330 (b) Blair Seitz, Photo Researchers, Inc.